Implementing Microsoft Dynamics NAV

Third Edition

Explore the capabilities of Dynamics NAV 2016 and discover all you need to implement it

Alex Chow

Laura Nicolàs Lorente

Cristina Nicolàs Lorente

Vjekoslav Babić

David Roys

BIRMINGHAM - MUMBAI

Implementing Microsoft Dynamics NAV
Third Edition

First Edition: January 2009

Second Edition: February 2013

Third Published: April 2016

Production reference: 1050416

Published by Packt Publishing Ltd.
Livery Place
35 Livery Street
Birmingham B3 2PB, UK.

ISBN 978-1-78439-755-5

www.packtpub.com

Credits

Authors
Alex Chow
Laura Nicolàs Lorente
Cristina Nicolàs Lorente
Vjekoslav Babić
David Roys

Reviewers
Stefano Demiliani
Tony Hemy

Acquisition Editor
Manish Nainani

Content Development Editor
Abhishek Jadhav

Technical Editors
Ryan Kochery
Menza Mathew
Deepti Tuscano

Copy Editors
Kausambhi Majumdar
Vikrant Phadke
Alpha Singh

Project Coordinator
Judie Jose

Proofreader
Safis Editing

Indexer
Monica Ajmera Mehta

Graphics
Disha Haria

Production Coordinator
Conidon Miranda

Cover Work
Conidon Miranda

About the Authors

Alex Chow has been working with Microsoft Dynamics NAV, formerly Navision, since 1999. Over the years, he has conducted hundreds of implementations across multiple industries. His customers range from $2-million-a-year small enterprises to $500-million-a-year multinational corporations.

Over the course of his Dynamics NAV career, he has often been designated as the primary person responsible for the success and failure of Dynamics NAV implementations. The fact that Alex is still in the Dynamics NAV business means that he's been pretty lucky so far. His extensive career in the Dynamics NAV business is evidence of his success rate and expertise.

With a background in implementing all functions and modules inside and outside of Microsoft Dynamics NAV, Alex has encountered and resolved the most practical to the most complex requirements and business rules. Through these experiences, he has learned that sometimes you have to be a little crazy to have a competitive edge.

Believing that sharing these experiences and knowledge would benefit the Dynamics NAV community, Alex writes about his journey at www.dynamicsnavconsultant. com. He founded AP Commerce (www.apcommerce.com) in 2005. It is a full-service Dynamics NAV service center. In addition, Alex has written a book about Dynamics NAV titled *Getting Started with Dynamics NAV 2013 Application Development* by Packt Publishing.

He lives in southern California with his beautiful wife and two lovely daughters. He considers himself the luckiest man in the world.

Laura Nicolàs Lorente started working with Dynamics NAV back in 2005, first in the support department, mostly solving functional issues and doubts. She soon jumped to full deployment: consulting, analysis, development, implementation, migration, training, and support. Right from the beginning, she realized that it was very important for a Dynamics NAV consultant to have deep knowledge of business workflows. Technical skills are just not enough. So, she started to train herself in accounting, taxation, supply chains, logistics, and so on.

Laura discovered a whole new world and she found it very interesting. After having enough consultancy experience, she got a chance to manage the first project on her own. And then she realized that even tech and business knowledge are not enough—she also needed management skills. That is why, after reading different management books and trying different approaches on the projects she worked on, she decided to deepen her knowledge by taking a master's degree in project management. Laura is now transitioning to agile management and agile development for better project success. She continues her training in the three areas (technology, business workflows, and management) whenever she gets the chance. The Internet is a huge source of inspiration for her: groups, forums, blogs, books, and so on. She also contributes by sharing her knowledge and experience with the Spanish Dynamics NAV community. Laura is also the coauthor of the book *Implementing Microsoft Dynamics NAV 2013, Packt Publishing* which had really good feedback from different Dynamics NAV experts.

Cristina Nicolàs Lorente has been working with Dynamics NAV since 2005. She started in the ERP world as a developer, but soon evolved into a complete Dynamics NAV professional, doing all the tasks involved in Dynamics NAV implementations: consultancy, analysis, development, implementation, training, and support to end users. When Cristina started developing solutions for Dynamics NAV, she had no idea about accounting or any kind of business workflow. They don't teach those kinds of things for a technical university career. Soon, she discovered that it is important to know the set of tools used, but even more important to understand the meaning of whatever you develop. Without knowing the accounting rules, practices, and legal requirements, it is impossible to develop useful accounting functionalities even if you are the best developer of all. Only when you fully understand a company's processes will you be able to do the appropriate developments. Having that in mind, Cristina has taken courses in accounting, warehouse management, and operations management. She is also willing to take courses on any other company-related topics. She thinks that the best way to learn is to teach what you are learning to someone else. She has actually learned almost everything she knows about Dynamics NAV by responding to user questions on Internet forums, by writing a blog about Dynamics NAV, and of course by writing the book you have in your hands. When you have to write about something, you have to experiment, try, investigate, and read. It is definitely the best way to learn. Cristina is also the coauthor of the book *Implementing Microsoft Dynamics NAV 2013, Packt Publishing*.

Vjekoslav Babić is a Microsoft Dynamics NAV expert, consultant, and architect with 18 years of experience in the IT industry and 14 years of experience delivering project success on large-scale, international, and high-risk and implementations of Microsoft Dynamics solutions. He has project experience in various industries, including retail, telecommunications, insurance, food and beverages, manufacturing, distribution, and many more. He has been awarded the Microsoft Most Valuable Professional award since 2010. Vjekoslav is an avid author and has published more than 400 technical articles about software development, database design, and Internet technologies in a number of online and printed magazines, as well as on his blog at `http://vjeko.com/`. He speaks regularly at Microsoft Dynamics NAV conferences worldwide.

Based in Zagreb, Croatia, he runs his own Microsoft Dynamics NAV consultancy business.

You can contact Vjekoslav through his blog at `http://vjeko.com/`.

David Roys has worked in the computer industry since 1992 and currently works as a Dynamics NAV programmer and consultant for Intergen, a leading Microsoft Gold Partner. He is the Dynamics Presidents Club member in New Zealand.

After coauthoring the original *Implementing Microsoft Dynamics NAV* book by Packt Publishing in 2009, David has written two novels.

About the Reviewers

Stefano Demiliani is a Microsoft Certified Solution Developer (MCSD), MCAD, MCTS on Microsoft Dynamics NAV, MCTS on SharePoint, MCTS on SQL Server, and a long-time expert on other Microsoft-related technologies. He has a master's degree in computer engineering from the Politecnico of Turin, Italy.

He works as a senior project manager and solution developer for EID (`http://www.eid.it`), a company of the Navlab group (`http://www.navlab.it`), one of the biggest Microsoft Dynamics groups in Italy (where he's also the chief technical officer). Stefano has a long-time experience of Microsoft Dynamics NAV, since the first versions of the ERP. His main activity is architecting and developing enterprise solutions based on the entire stack of Microsoft technologies (Microsoft Dynamics NAV, Microsoft SharePoint, Azure and .NET applications in general, OLAP, and BI solutions for data analysis), and he's often focused on engineering distributed service-based applications.

He works as a full-time NAV consultant, having spent more than 15 years on international NAV projects, and is available for architecting solutions based on Microsoft's ERP and for NAV database tuning and optimization (performance and locking management). He's the author of different Microsoft-certified NAV add-ons (such as the first cost accounting add-on on NAV).

Stefano has written many articles and blogs on different Microsoft-related topics, and he's frequently involved in consulting and teaching. He has worked with Packt Publishing in the past for many Microsoft Dynamics NAV-related books.

You can get more details and keep in touch with him by going to `http://www.demiliani.com` or via Twitter (`@demiliani`) or LinkedIn.

Tony Hemy has been deeply rooted in Microsoft Dynamics NAV from the age of 16. Over the years, he has architected and customized Microsoft Dynamics NAV solutions for global organizations such as Warner Brothers and Viacom, earning an outstanding reputation and the role of technical reviewer on four books published on Dynamics NAV. Tony also served for more than 5 years as a reserve soldier with the British Army, where he expanded not only his technical skills but also his personal skills, which have contributed to his disciplined work ethic and his determination to always do things right.

His hands-on development experience with Microsoft Dynamics has given him an exceptional ability to help clients define the proper requirements that will enable them to achieve their objectives. He has delivered extended capabilities through every version, every module, and every feature of Dynamics NAV, building thousands of unique configurations along the way. Tony also oversees software development, where he manages and mentors a talented development team and facilitates the best practices and standards that ensure clients receive the highest quality solutions and service. Tony is well-traveled, well-rounded, and well-liked for his personable nature and "no shortcuts" approach, whether he is writing complex code or coaching his team.

www.PacktPub.com

Support files, eBooks, discount offers, and more

Did you know that Packt offers eBook versions of every book published, with PDF and ePub files available? You can upgrade to the eBook version at www.PacktPub.com and as a print book customer, you are entitled to a discount on the eBook copy. Get in touch with us at customercare@packtpub.com for more details.

At www.PacktPub.com, you can also read a collection of free technical articles, sign up for a range of free newsletters and receive exclusive discounts and offers on Packt books and eBooks.

https://www2.packtpub.com/books/subscription/packtlib

Do you need instant solutions to your IT questions? PacktLib is Packt's online digital book library. Here, you can search, access, and read Packt's entire library of books.

Why subscribe?

- Fully searchable across every book published by Packt
- Copy and paste, print, and bookmark content
- On demand and accessible via a web browser

Instant updates on new Packt books

Get notified! Find out when new books are published by following @PacktEnterprise on Twitter or the *Packt Enterprise* Facebook page.

Table of Contents

Preface   **xi**

Chapter 1: Exploring Microsoft Dynamics NAV – An Introduction   **1**

Understanding Microsoft Dynamics NAV   **2**
The functional areas within Dynamics NAV   **3**
History of Dynamics NAV   **5**
Functional areas   **9**
  Financial Management   10
    General Ledger   11
    G/L budgets   11
    Account Schedules   12
    Cash Management   14
    Fixed Assets   14
    VAT reporting and intrastat   15
    Sales tax   15
    Intercompany transactions   17
    Consolidation   18
    Multicurrency   18
  Sales and marketing   19
    Customers   20
    Order processing   21
    Approvals   23
    Pricing   24
    Marketing   24
  Purchase   25
    Vendors   25
    Order processing   25
  Approvals   26
    Pricing   26
    Planning   26

Warehouse	28
Items	28
Locations	30
Transfer orders	30
Assembly	30
Pick and put-away	31
Inventory	31
Manufacturing	33
Product design	34
Capacities	36
Planning	37
Execution	38
Costing	38
Subcontracting	39
Job	39
Job card	40
Phases and tasks	40
Planning	41
Time sheet	43
Invoice jobs	43
Work in process (WIP)	43
Resource planning	44
Resource card	44
Pricing	46
Service	46
Service items	47
Contracts	49
Price management	49
Service orders	51
Service tasks	51
Fault reporting	52
Human resources	52
Employees	53
Absence registration	54
Country localizations	54
Vertical and horizontal solutions	54
Accessing Dynamics NAV	**55**
Windows client	55
Web client	57
Tablet client	58
SharePoint client	59
Web Services	59
Development Environment	60
Summary	**62**

Chapter 2: What's New in NAV 2016?   63

Application changes   63
Improvements for the application users   64
Cues with color indicator   64
Mandatory fields   65
Simplified user interface for small businesses   65
Tablet client   67
New application features   69
Automatic payment and bank reconciliation   69
Signing up for the Bank Data Conversion Service   69
Reconciling payments automatically   71
Reconciling bank statements automatically   71
Social Listening   72
Power Business Intelligence   72
RapidStart services   72
Schedule reports   74
E-mailing documents   76
Document exchange service (OCR Services)   77
Exchange rates update   78
Native integration with Dynamics CRM   78
Universal app   78
Workflow management   78
Posting Preview   79
Deferrals   79

Development changes   79
Document reporting   80
Upgrade automation – an overview   83
Upgrade automation – the application code   83
Upgrade automation – data   83
Enhancement in security and encryption   84
Changes to C/AL functions, data types, properties, and triggers   84
.NET interoperability   90
Enhancements in RoleTailored client control add-ins   90

IT changes   91
Dynamics NAV Server administration   91
Windows PowerShell cmdlets   91

Summary   95

Chapter 3: Dynamics NAV – General Considerations   97

The data model   98
Master data   98
Documents   99
Journals   104

Entries	108
Creating ledger entries	111
Combining all concepts	116
No save button	**117**
The main advantage	118
When is the data verified?	119
The main drawback	120
The posting routines	**120**
Posted data cannot be modified (or deleted)	121
Navigating through your data	**123**
The Navigate functionality	123
Other ways to browse data	125
Sorting on list pages	127
Filtering for the data you need	127
Saving views for the filters you've set	129
Real-time data gathering – the SIFT technology	**131**
Everything leads to accounting	**132**
The Dynamics NAV database	**133**
The TableRelation property	134
Coded data rules	136
Summary	**138**
Chapter 4: The Implementation Process – From the Reseller	**139**
What is an implementation?	**140**
Methodology	**142**
The Waterfall approach	145
The Agile approach	147
Using the best of both	148
Microsoft Dynamics Sure Step	148
Project types based on the Waterfall approach	149
The Agile project type	153
Roles	**155**
Salesperson	156
Project manager	156
Business consultant	156
Key users	157
Analyst	158
Developer	159
Implementer	159
End users	159
Summarizing the roles	160

Phases   **161**
  Presales   161
  Getting the project requirements   162
  Designing the solution   165
    Configuration   165
    Modifying standard Dynamics NAV functionality   168
    New functionalities   168
    Data migration   168
  Development   168
  Deployment   169
    Software and hardware installation   169
    Configuration   170
    Data migration   170
    User-acceptance test   171
    End users' training   171
    Go-live!   171
  Post Implementation Support   172
Summary   **173**

Chapter 5: The Implementation Process on the Customer Side   **175**
Definition of goals   **176**
Measuring goals   **177**
Defining the internal processes   **179**
  Questions to be asked   179
Improve before automating   **183**
Getting the requirements   **183**
Change management   **185**
Get involved in testing the system   **186**
Involve end users   **187**
Summary   **188**

Chapter 6: Migrating Data   **189**
Tools to migrate data   **189**
  RapidStart Services   190
    Creating a new company using PowerShell   191
    Changing the profile to RapidStart Services Implementer 193
    Using the configuration wizard   194
    Creating a data conversion package   195
    Configuration worksheet   200
    Using Excel templates   205
    Configuration templates   208
    Configuration questionnaire   210
    Summarizing RapidStart Services   212

Using XMLports to migrate data   213
  The XMLport structure   214
  Running the XMLport   216
  Writing code inside the XMLport   217
Writing your own tools   223
Converting data from the old system to Dynamics NAV's needs   **223**
  Fields particular to Microsoft Dynamics NAV   224
Master data   **225**
Open entries   **226**
  Customer entries   226
  Vendor entries   231
  Bank entries   231
  Item entries   231
  Fixed-asset entries   233
  General Ledger balances   235
Historical data   **235**
Open documents   **236**
Choosing a go-live date   **239**
  Going live at the beginning of the fiscal year   239
    What cons do we have?   240
  Going live in the middle of a fiscal year   240
Summary   **241**
Chapter 7: Upgrading Microsoft Dynamics NAV   **243**
Upgrading philosophy   **244**
Upgrades prior to Dynamics NAV 2013   **245**
Upgrades from Dynamics NAV 2013 forward   **245**
Upgrading process checklist   **246**
  Upgrading from 2013, 2013 R2, or 2015   247
    Technical upgrade (converting the database) 247
  Upgrading from 2009, 2009 SP1, or 2009 R2   259
    Upgrading the 2009 application code   259
    Upgrading the 2009 data   260
  Upgrading from 5.0 or 5.0 SP1   261
    Upgrading the 5.0 application code   261
    Upgrading the 5.0 data   262
  Upgrading from 4.0, 4.0 SP1, 4.0 SP2, or 4.0 SP3   263
    Upgrading the 4.0 application code   264
    Upgrading the 4.0 data   265
  Upgrading from 3.60 or 3.70   266
    Upgrading the 3.60 or 3.70 application code 267
    Upgrading the 3.60 or 3.70 data   268

Upgrading steps to NAV 2013   **269**

Preparing to upgrade   269
    Migrating to SQL Server   270
    Testing the database   270

Upgrading the application code   271
    Getting object versions   271
    Converting objects to the Dynamics NAV 2013 format   272
    Carrying out customizations to the new version   273
    Transforming forms to pages   273
    Transforming reports   274

Upgrading the data   274

Upgrading tools   **275**

Upgrade toolkit   275

Text format upgrade   276

Form transformation   278

Report transformation   278
    Upgrading hybrid reports   279
    Upgrading classic reports   280

Comparing text tools   280

MergeTool   281
    Downloading MergeTool   281
    Installing MergeTool   281
    Using MergeTool   282

Summary   **292**

Chapter 8: Development Considerations   **293**

Setup versus customization   **293**

Data model principles   **295**

Basic objects   296
    Object elements   299

How tables are structured   302
    Understanding table structures   304
    The final picture   312

The structure of pages   313
    Understanding page structures   314

The posting process   **326**

The codeunit structure for sales posting   326

The codeunit structure for General Journal posting   327

Where to write customized code   **328**

Validating fields   328

Batch jobs   329

Formatting customized code   **330**

Summary   **330**

Chapter 9: Functional Changes on Existing Implementations   331

General guidelines   331
What is a functional change?   332
The Requisition Worksheet   332
Fixed Assets   333
Item Tracking   333
Extending a customized functionality   334
Interactions with other functionalities   334
The Requisition Worksheet   334
Fixed Assets   335
Item Tracking   336
     Creating a new item   338
     Creating and posting a purchase order for the new item   339
     Creating and posting a sales order for the new item   341
     Turning on Item Tracking for the new item   341
Extending a customized functionality   342
Writing a to-do list to implement a change   343
The Requisition Worksheet   343
Fixed Assets   345
Item Tracking   347
Extending a customized functionality   348
Choosing the right time   349
The Requisition Worksheet   350
Fixed Assets   350
Item Tracking   350
Extending a customized functionality   351
Planning the change   351
The Requisition Worksheet   352
Fixed Assets   354
Item Tracking   356
Extending a customized functionality   357
Summary   359

Chapter 10: Data Analysis and Reporting   361

Using filters and FlowFilters   362
Creating views   364
Statistics   366
Charts   368
The Show as Chart option   368
Adding charts to the Role Center page   369
Creating and configuring charts   371

Using reports   **373**
  Finding reports   374
  Running reports   376
  Types of reports   379
    List reports   380
    Test reports   380
    Posting reports   380
    Transaction reports   381
    Document reports   381
    Other reports   382
Account schedules   **383**
Analysis views   **386**
  Understanding dimensions   387
    Setting up new dimensions   388
    Categorizing dimensions   389
    Accessing dimensions   391
  Creating an analysis view   394
  Updating analysis views   397
  Using analysis views   398
    Analysis by dimensions   398
    Analysis views as a source for account schedules   400
Extracting data   **401**
  Sending data to Microsoft Office applications   402
    Sending data to Microsoft Word   403
    Sending data to Microsoft Excel   404
  Extracting data through web services   404
  Other ways to extract Dynamics NAV data   405
Understanding report development   **405**
  Reports anatomy   405
  Defining the dataset   407
  Designing the visual layout   409
Summary   **411**
Chapter 11: Debugging   **413**
  The art of debugging   **413**
  Debugging in Dynamics NAV 2016   **414**
    Break Rules   416
  Placing breakpoints   **417**
    From the Object Designer   417
    In the current statement of the debugger   418
    Conditional breakpoint   420
    Debugger Breakpoint List   420

Line-by-line execution	**421**
The Step Into option	422
The Step Over option	423
The Step Out option	424
The Continue option	425
The Call Stack FactBox	**426**
The Watches FactBox	**427**
Adding variables from the Debugger Variables List window	428
Adding variables from the code viewer	429
Summary	**430**
Chapter 12: Popular Reporting Options with Microsoft Dynamics NAV	**431**
What is a query?	**432**
Query Designer	**433**
Defining our first query	434
Adding additional data to the query	439
Charts	**441**
Web services	**443**
External applications	446
Excel and PowerPivot	446
Power BI	**449**
Jet Reports Express	**452**
Downloading Jet Reports Express	452
Installing Jet Reports Express	453
Report pack for Jet Reports Express	453
Summary	**454**
Index	**455**

Preface

Let me start out by saying congratulations on your decision to work with Dynamics NAV. When I started working with Dynamics NAV (formerly known as Navision) back in 1999, Dynamics NAV was nothing more than an accounting system out of Denmark. After a couple of releases, acquisition by Microsoft, and a couple more releases, Dynamics NAV has become a full ERP (enterprise resource planning) software with rich functionalities. With every release, we see improvements in the technical aspect as well as the functionality aspect. And they're not done yet.

At the time of writing, Dynamics NAV's installation base is 110,000 companies. No other ERP software for the small and medium-sized market comes close to that number.

In addition, Dynamics NAV has a wide range of add-on solutions available. Most of these add-ons are built directly within the Dynamics NAV environment with the same user interface. So, using these add-ons, your company will not need to learn any other new software.

One of the main selling points of Dynamic NAV from the very beginning is the ability to customize it exactly the way you run your business. Because of its flexibility, you can find a lot of tutorials and explanations on how to develop specific tasks, but not a lot of tutorials on how to create a project from scratch.

To take advantage of the flexibility that's built into Dynamics NAV, a deep understanding of the standard application is required. Just because you're able to completely rewrite Dynamics NAV does not mean you should. Without knowing what you have out of the box, you may end up creating a function that's already part of the standard system, wasting your valuable time and resources.

What this book covers

Chapter 1, Exploring Microsoft Dynamics NAV – An Introduction, introduces you to what an ERP is and what you can expect from Dynamics NAV. It introduces all the functional areas found in Dynamics NAV 2016 and the different environments available, such as the Windows client, the web client, the SharePoint framework, or web services. For the nostalgic, we have also included details on the history of Dynamics NAV.

Chapter 2, What's New in NAV 2016?, gives an overview of the changes made within the application. Dynamics NAV 2016 introduces quite a few new features, that is, new functionalities and tools available for the end user, such as the improvements that can be made to the Windows client or the assembly management feature. The chapter also covers development and IT changes.

Chapter 3, Dynamics NAV – General Considerations, is all about the Dynamics NAV structure, its data model, how information flows, how posting routines works, how users can navigate through their data, why everything leads to accounting, and how data integrity is approached.

Knowing the Dynamics NAV philosophy on how things are done is important for everyone. It is important for users because they need to know how to work with Dynamics NAV and also need to be aware of the consequences of what they do; it is also important for consultants, analysts, and developers because they need to use the same structures and the same way to make information flow when developing new functionalities.

Chapter 4, The Implementation Process (from the Reseller), explains the meaning of implementation and covers different methodologies that can be applied while implementing Dynamics NAV. Several people may get involved in an implementation process, each one playing their own role and performing different jobs. This chapter also covers the phases and tasks needed to complete a Dynamics NAV implementation, from presales to deployment.

Chapter 5, The Implementation Process on the Customer Side, explains what is expected from the company's team (users, key users, and project leader), and how to deal with the change that the new ERP will make for everyone in the company. For a really successful implementation of Dynamics NAV, the company that NAV has been implemented for has to actively participate in the project.

Chapter 6, Migrating Data, covers the tools that can be used to import data into Dynamics NAV, such as RapidStart services or XMLports. Companies may be new to Dynamics NAV, but they are usually not new companies. They have been working for a while and they have all kinds of data, such as their customers, vendors, items, and accounting information.

This chapter also explains which kind of data is commonly migrated to Dynamics NAV and the strategies used to migrate it. With a step-by-step example, the chapter enables you to migrate master data, open entries, historical data, and open documents.

Chapter 7, Upgrading Microsoft Dynamics NAV, explains the migration process from Versions 3.xx, 4.xx, 5.xx, 2009, and 2013. Upgrading to a different version of Dynamics NAV is not a "Next-Next-Finish" process. It is a complete project that has to be planned and executed carefully.

We will explain the steps that have to be followed for all the versions and the tools that are out there to help us get through the whole process.

Chapter 8, Development Considerations, covers the main development considerations that should be taken into account when developing for Dynamics NAV. This includes a deep explanation of the data model principles in Dynamics NAV and how the posting processes are designed. It also includes explanations about where and how to write customized code.

Almost every Dynamics NAV implementation implies development. The customized code must fit inside the application's standard code and it should look as if it were part of the standard. This makes it easier for the user to understand how customized modules work and for partners to support them.

Chapter 9, Functional Changes in Existing Implementations, explains how to handle functional changes in existing implementations with a set of four examples. After working with Dynamics NAV for a while, companies may ask for functional changes on their implementations, such as adding some extra developments or starting to use an existing functionality. Some extra things have to be taken into account when dealing with such projects.

Chapter 10, Data Analysis and Reporting, provides an overview of the tools available to analyze Dynamics NAV data, both inside and outside the application, such as the use of filters and FlowFilters, statistics, charts, existing reports, analysis views, account schedules, or how to extract data from Dynamics NAV. Data analysis and reporting is an important part of the management of a company.

This chapter also includes a report development section that is meant to explain the anatomy of reports, to show how to define your dataset, and to show how the visual layout is designed.

Chapter 11, Debugging, covers debugging in Microsoft Dynamics NAV. Conditional breakpoints, debug other user sessions, and debug C/AL code in the RTC client instead of incomprehensible C# code. All these features will convert the debugging experience into a happy experience.

Chapter 12, Popular Reporting Options with Microsoft Dynamics NAV, explains what other popular options you can utilize with Dynamics NAV. There is a standard NAV reporting tool, but with the advances in reporting technology, such as BI, Excel, and so on, there are a lot of other options you can utilize to have your Dynamics NAV data come alive.

What you need for this book

To successfully follow the examples in this book, you will need to install Microsoft Dynamics NAV 2016.

Who this book is for

This book is meant for Dynamics NAV implementation consultants, project managers, and developers who want to get a deeper view of what Dynamics NAV can offer.

It is also meant for Dynamics NAV developers who want to learn more about the whole application.

And finally, this book may be useful to IT managers of all kinds of companies that are considering the implementation of Dynamics NAV in their organizations, to fully understand what to expect and how to accomplish it.

Conventions

In this book, you will find a number of styles of text that distinguish between different kinds of information. Here are some examples of these styles, and an explanation of their meaning.

Code words in text are shown as follows: "The `Customer` table is the master data table for the Sales and Marketing area."

New terms and **important words** are shown in bold. Words that you see on the screen, in menus or dialog boxes for example, appear in the text like this: "Not all items in the **Navigate** tab are secondary master data".

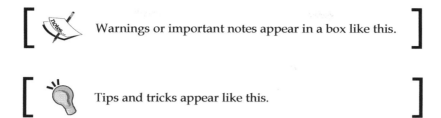

Warnings or important notes appear in a box like this.

Tips and tricks appear like this.

Reader feedback

Feedback from our readers is always welcome. Let us know what you think about this book—what you liked or may have disliked. Reader feedback is important for us to develop titles that you really get the most out of.

To send us general feedback, simply send an e-mail to feedback@packtpub.com, and mention the book title via the subject of your message.

If there is a topic that you have expertise in and you are interested in either writing or contributing to a book, see our author guide on www.packtpub.com/authors.

Customer support

Now that you are the proud owner of a Packt book, we have a number of things to help you to get the most from your purchase.

Downloading the color images of this book

We also provide you with a PDF file that has color images of the screenshots/ diagrams used in this book. The color images will help you better understand the changes in the output. You can download this file from http://www.packtpub.com/ sites/default/files/downloads/Bookname1234OT_ColorImages.pdf.

Errata

Although we have taken every care to ensure the accuracy of our content, mistakes do happen. If you find a mistake in one of our books—maybe a mistake in the text or the code—we would be grateful if you could report this to us. By doing so, you can save other readers from frustration and help us improve subsequent versions of this book. If you find any errata, please report them by visiting `http://www.packtpub.com/submit-errata`, selecting your book, clicking on the **Errata Submission Form** link, and entering the details of your errata. Once your errata are verified, your submission will be accepted and the errata will be uploaded to our website or added to any list of existing errata under the Errata section of that title.

To view the previously submitted errata, go to `https://www.packtpub.com/books/content/support` and enter the name of the book in the search field. The required information will appear under the **Errata** section.

Piracy

Piracy of copyright material on the Internet is an ongoing problem across all media. At Packt, we take the protection of our copyright and licenses very seriously. If you come across any illegal copies of our works, in any form, on the Internet, please provide us with the location address or website name immediately so that we can pursue a remedy.

Please contact us at `copyright@packtpub.com` with a link to the suspected pirated material.

We appreciate your help in protecting our authors and our ability to bring you valuable content.

Questions

If you have a problem with any aspect of this book, you can contact us at `questions@packtpub.com`, and we will do our best to address the problem.

1

Exploring Microsoft Dynamics NAV – An Introduction

Microsoft Dynamics NAV is an **Enterprise Resource Planning (ERP)** system that is specifically made for growing small to mid-sized companies.

 This is, at least, what Microsoft's marketing department says. In reality, Dynamics NAV is being used by large and publically-traded companies as well around the world.

An ERP is a software that integrates the internal and external management information across an entire organization. The purpose of an ERP is to facilitate the flow of information between all business functions inside the boundaries of organizations. An ERP system is meant to handle all the functional areas within an organization on a single software system. This way, the output of an area can be used as the input of another area, without the need to duplicate data.

This chapter will give you an idea of what Dynamics NAV is and what you can expect from it. The topics covered in this chapter are the following:

- What is Microsoft Dynamics NAV?
- The functional areas found in Microsoft Dynamics NAV 2016
- A history of Dynamics NAV
- How to use Dynamics NAV on different environments (Windows client, Web client, SharePoint framework, Web Services, and so on)

Understanding Microsoft Dynamics NAV

Microsoft Dynamics NAV 2016 is a **Role Tailored ERP**. Traditionally, ERP software is built to provide a lot of functionalities where users will need to hunt down the information. This is more of a passive approach to information in which the user will need to go somewhere within the system to retrieve information.

Dynamics NAV works differently. The role-tailored experience is based on individuals within an organization, their roles, and the tasks they perform. When users first enter Dynamics NAV, they see the data needed for the daily tasks they do according to their role. Users belonging to different roles will have a different view of the system; each of them will see the functions they need to properly perform their daily tasks. Instead of the users chasing down information, the information comes to them.

Here's an example of the main screen for an order processor. All the relevant information for a user who is processing sales orders are displayed in a **business intelligent (BI)** format:

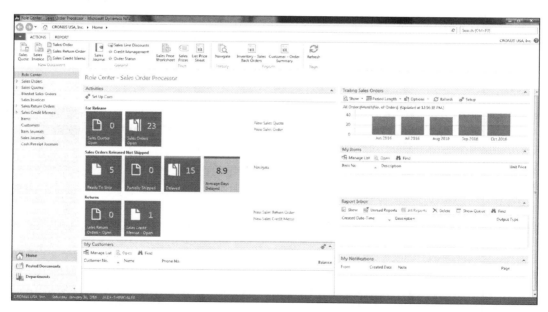

The functional areas within Dynamics NAV

Dynamics NAV covers the following functional areas inside an organization:

- **Financial management**: Most of the functionalities from "off-the-shelf" accounting software can be found in this module. The functionalities include, but are not limited to, G/L budgeting, financial reporting, cash management, receivables and payables, fixed assets, VAT and tax reporting, intercompany transactions, cost accounting, consolidation, multicurrency, intrastate, and so on.

- **Sales and marketing**: This is for the companies that want to track customer orders and determine when the items can be promised to be delivered to the customer. This area covers customers, order processing, expected delivery, order promises, sales returns, pricing, contacts, marketing campaigns, and so on.

- **Purchase**: This module is required when you buy goods and services and you want to keep track of what you have ordered from your vendors and when the goods should be delivered to your door, so you can make the stuff or ship the stuff to your customers. This area includes vendors, order processing, approvals, planning, costing, and so on.

- **Warehouse**: Where are your items in your warehouse? This functional area answers this question for you. Under the warehouse area, you will find inventory, shipping and receiving, locations, warehouse bin contents, picking, put-aways, assembly, and so on.

- **Manufacturing**: The manufacturing area includes product design, bills of materials, routing, capacities, forecast, production planning, production order, costing, subcontracting, and so on.

- **Job**: This module is typically used for companies that deal with long and drawn out projects. Within this job area, you can create projects, phases and tasks, planning, time sheets, work in process, and likewise.

- **Resource planning**: If your company has internal resources for which you keep track of cost and/or revenue, this module is for you. This area includes resources, capacity, and other tools to keep track of cost and revenue for resources.

- **Service**: This functional area is design for a company that sells items to their customers that need to be serviced periodically, with or without warranty. Within this service area, you can manage service items, contract management, order processing, planning and dispatching, service tasks, and so on

- **Human resources**: This involves basic employee tracking. It allows you to manage employees, absences, and so on.

These areas are covered in more detail in the next section of this chapter.

One of the best-selling points about Dynamics NAV is that it can be customized. A brand new functional area can be created from scratch or new features can be added to an existing functional area. All the development is done with the programming language called C/AL.

When someone creates a new functional area, a vertical (a wide range of functions for a specific industry) or horizontal (a wide range of functions that can be applied across an industry), they usually create it as an add-on. An add-on can be registered with Microsoft, with the appropriate fees of course. If some features are added to an existing area, usually it is a customization that will only be used on the database of the customer who asked for the feature.

Making add-ons available greatly enhances the base Dynamics NAV functionalities to fit the needs of every industry in every business.

One thing unique about Dynamics NAV is that the entire code is located on a single layer. Therefore, if you customize an area, you have to do it by modifying the standard code and adding code in the middle of the standard object definition. This made it a little tough to upgrade in the prior versions of Dynamics NAV. However, with the release of Dynamics NAV 2016, code upgrades can be done automatically using Power Shell! We will dive into Power Shell later.

Dynamics NAV uses a three-tier architecture:

- SQL Server is the data tier and is used to store the data in a database.
- Microsoft Dynamics NAV Server is the middle or server tier, managing the entire business logic and communication. It also provides an additional layer of security between clients and the database and an additional layer for user authentication.
- On the client tier, we will find Windows clients and the web client. Dynamics NAV 2016 also supports other kinds of clients including Web Services (both SOAP and OData), mobile tablets, a SharePoint client through the Microsoft Dynamics NAV Portal Framework, and the NAS service.

You can install Dynamics NAV in more complex scenarios, as you can have multiple instances of any of the core components.

History of Dynamics NAV

We are not historians, but we thought that it would be important to know where we come from and where we are going. Some of the current restrictions or features can be better understood if we know a bit of the history of Dynamics NAV. This is why we have added this section.

Dynamics NAV was first developed by a Danish firm and the program was called **Navision A/S**. In 2002, Microsoft bought Navision A/S and included it in the Microsoft Business Solution division. The product has gone through several name changes. The names: Navision Financials, Navision Attain, and Microsoft Business Solutions Navision Edition, have been used to refer to the product that is currently called Microsoft Dynamics NAV. Note that all the previous names included the word Navision. This is why many people keep calling it Navision instead of NAV.

Prior to Dynamics NAV 2009, the development environment was actually the primary end user interface before Microsoft revamped the user interface that we call the **Role Tailored Client (RTC)**.

One of the greatest technological breakthroughs with the original Navision (the name before it was called Dynamics NAV) was that the application programming objects, the user interface, and the database resided together, in one file! Back in the late 1990s and early 2000s, no other software came close to having an efficient design like this. This was the main menu for Navision Financials version 2.0:

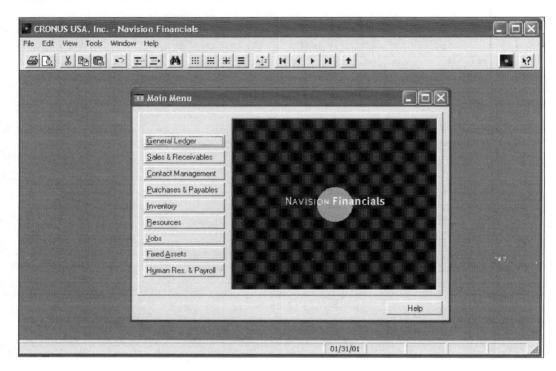

We're now more than a decade away from 2000 and technology has changed quite a bit. Dynamics NAV has been very up to date with the latest technology that has the best impact for businesses. However, most of these improvements and updates are mostly in the backend. This is an important reason why Dynamics NAV has never faded into history. There were a couple of user interface improvements; however, largely, it mainly looks and feels very much the same as before. This is the main menu for Dynamics NAV 5.0:

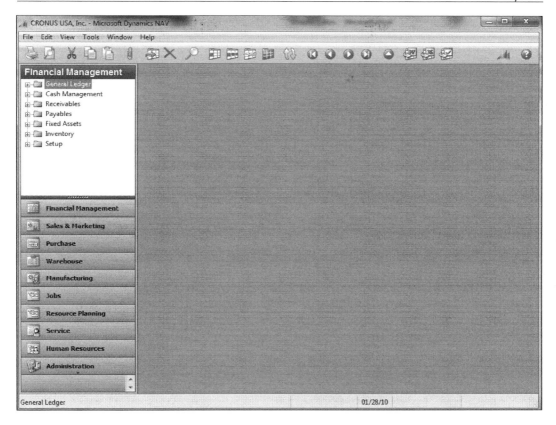

Then something happened. With the rise of a company called Apple, people started paying more attention to the aesthetics and the overall interface of the technology they're using. People demanded not just powerful software with a strong backend, but they also wanted an elegant design with a simple and intuitive user interface.

Because of this shift in user perception, what was once the greatest innovation in accounting software since sliced bread, had become not obsolete, but outdated.

When you put the old interface (called Classic Client) against some of the newer applications, even though the backend was light years ahead, the Classic Client was the ugly one. And we all know somebody who made a terrible decision based only on looks, but not really what's inside.

So when NAV 2009 was introduced, the Role Tailored Client was released, which is the interface you see when you install Dynamics NAV for end users. NAV 2009 was unique in that it allowed both Classic Client and Role Tailored Client to coexist. This is mostly to appease the existing NAV gurus and users who did not want to learn the new interface.

In addition, NAV 2009 replaced the classic reporting with the **report definition language client-side (RDLC)** reporting. RDLC reports brought in a big change because the layout of the report had to be designed in Visual Studio, outside Dynamics NAV, to bring in the advantages of SQL Server Reporting Services technology; while pages changed the way of developing the user interface.

This is what NAV 2009 in the RTC looked like:

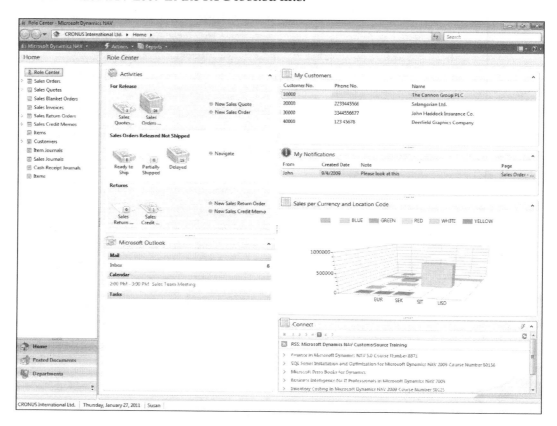

At the first glance, NAV 2009 and NAV 2016 do not look too different. You will have to understand that there were significant user interface and usability changes. We can list out these changes, but if you're not already familiar with Dynamics NAV (or Navision), you'll will find this disinteresting.

That grace period expired when NAV 2013 was released and the Classic Client user interface was completely removed. Microsoft basically renamed the Classic Client as **Development Environment**. For the foreseeable future, it looks like the Development Environment and the Windows Client environment will remain separated.

Now we're at Dynamics NAV 2016, with tons of performance and usability enhancements, which is what this book is about.

Functional areas

The core functionalities of Dynamics NAV have not dramatically changed over the years. New functional areas have appeared and the existing ones still work as they did in the previous versions. In NAV 2009, Microsoft was focused on changing the entire architecture (for good), and NAV 2013 is the consolidation of the new architecture. NAV 2016 enhances what was released with NAV 2013. All these architectural changes were made to bring Dynamics NAV closer to the existing Microsoft technologies, namely, Microsoft Office 365, .NET, SQL Server, Azure, and so on; in the meantime, the core functionality has not undergone a drastic face-lift compared to the architecture.

Microsoft has been adding small functional features and improving the existing functionalities with every new release. As you have seen earlier in this chapter, the base Dynamics NAV 2016 covers the following functional areas:

- Financial Management
- Sales & Marketing
- Purchase
- Warehouse
- Manufacturing
- Job
- Resource Planning
- Service
- Human Resources

In Dynamics NAV, the financial management area is the epicenter of the entire application. The other areas are optional and their usage depends on the organization's needs. The sales and purchase areas are also commonly used within a Dynamics NAV implementation.

Now let's have a closer view of each area.

Financial Management

As we said, financial management is the epicenter of Dynamics NAV. Actually, accounting is the epicenter and general ledger is included inside the financial management area. What else can be found here? The following screenshot shows the main page of the **Financial Management** department:

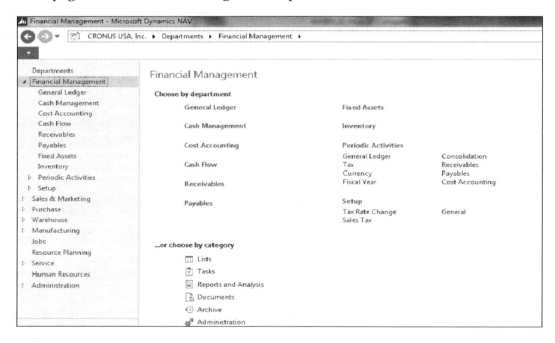

We'll give a few details about each of these areas.

General Ledger

Accountancy is the act of recording, classifying, and summarizing in terms of money and the transactions and events that take place in a company. Accountancy is thousands of years old; the earliest accounting records, dating back to more than 7,000 years, were found in Mesopotamia. The fact that it survived this long must mean that it's important.

Of course, nowadays we don't use the same accounting system, but it is interesting that accounting is useful in every single company, no matter how different it is from any other company. Probably the fact that keeping accounting records is mandatory in almost all countries helps! For one thing, you need it to figure out how much money you made so you can pay your taxes.

Accountancy has its own language: accounts, credit amounts, and debit amounts. This language is managed through strict and clear rules such as **generally accepted accounting principle (GAAP)**. Dynamics NAV has implemented these rules using posting groups so the system can translate everything to an accounting language and post it to the general ledger entries on the fly.

An important difference between Dynamics NAV and the other accounting systems is that you don't need to open an individual account for each customer, each vendor, each bank, or each fixed asset. Dynamics NAV does not keep detailed information about them on the general ledger. Only one or a few accounts are needed for each group. This is something that shocks accountants when they use Dynamics NAV for the first time. Then again, most accountants are easily shocked.

G/L budgets

The **General Ledger** part also contains G/L budgets. This feature allows you to create accounting budgets with different levels of details. You can break down the budget by different periods (day, week, month, quarter, year, or any accounting period), by accounts (on single posting accounts or heading accounts), by business units, or by dimensions.

The budget can be edited inside Dynamics NAV or can be exported to Excel, edited there, and then imported back to Dynamics NAV. You can do multiple imports from Excel and the new entries can be added to the existing ones.

You can also create distinct budgets inside Dynamics NAV and then combine them in a single budget. The following screenshot shows the main **Budget** page:

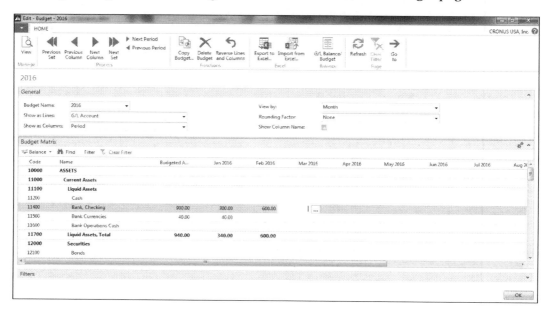

After presenting the budget, you can find different ways of tracking it. Either from the **G/L Balance/Budget** page, or from **Trial Balance/Budget** report, or from the account schedules defined by you.

Account Schedules

Account Schedules are meant for reporting and analysis of financial statements. If it were up to me, I would rename the function to say "Financial Statement Setup", but I'm sure someone higher up believes account schedules makes sense to the majority of the population.

Dynamics NAV includes some standard statements, but the good thing about it is that you can modify the existing ones or you can create new ones in order to meet specific requirements of an organization.

Account schedules can be made of ledger entries, budget entries, or analysis view entries. Analysis view entries are used to summarize ledger entries by a period and a set of dimensions. You can also combine entries from these different sources into a single schedule.

You can also define what kind of information is shown in the rows and columns. Each column can show data from different periods so you can compare amounts over different periods. Account schedules are therefore a powerful tool that end users can use to create their own customized financial reports. The **Acc. Schedule Overview** window has been displayed in the following screenshot:

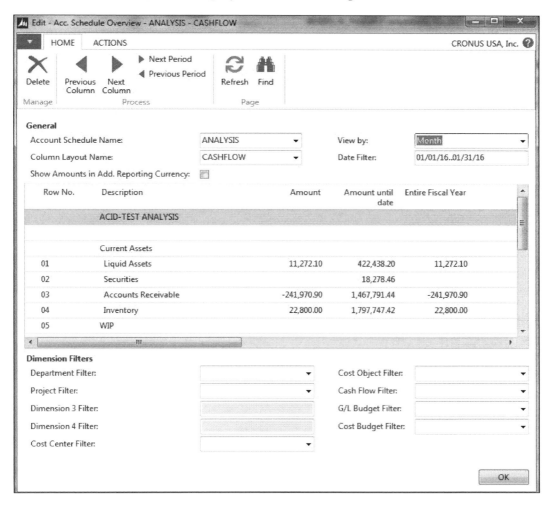

Cash Management

The Cash Management feature is used to manage a company's bank accounts. You can process the payments received from customers, payments to vendors, and bank reconciliation.

You can create a bank account card for each account the company has in banks. Whenever a transaction is made in Dynamics NAV using a bank account, the system will post an entry in the bank account entry, plus a related G/L entry according to the bank posting group. The posting of bank entries is done from the cash receipt journal or from the payment journal. Other journals such as the general journals could also be used.

> It's recommended that you only set up bank accounts for the banks on which you do a full bank reconciliation. For banks that you don't reconcile, such as your money market account or investment accounts, you can just make the transaction on the G/L level.

The payment journal includes a **Suggest Vendor Payments** action to help you decide what is to be paid.

Fixed Assets

The **Fixed Assets** functionality is used to manage a company's assets, their cost and depreciation, and also it's related to maintenance and insurances.

Fixed assets has unlimited depreciation books that track depreciation expenses reliably. All the ordinary methods of depreciation are available, plus the ability to create custom depreciation methods is also available.

Fixed assets includes two different journals: the FA G/L journal and the FA journal. The FA G/L journal is used to post entries on the FA ledger entry and also a corresponding entry on the G/L entry. The FA journal is used only to create entries on the FA ledger entry. This means that depending on your configuration, you may not be posting anything related to FA in the G/L entry. You therefore need to be careful and know exactly when to post on the G/L and when not to, but keep everything synchronized.

VAT reporting and intrastat

Value Added Tax (VAT) doesn't really apply to people doing business in the countries where VAT is not required, such as the United States. It is a transaction that is paid by the end consumer and business. In Dynamics NAV, you can find a table called `VAT Entry` where all VAT transactions are recorded, mainly through purchase and sale invoices. In addition, the corresponding amounts are also posted on the accounts determined by its posting groups.

As in many other areas, all VAT processes are mainly based on their own entries, not on the amounts found in the accounting areas.

A process named `Calculate and Post VAT Settlement` helps you to post the G/L transactions for a VAT settlement. Dynamics NAV also includes VAT statements that are pretty similar to account schedules we discussed before. Therefore, you can define your own VAT statements that will help you to submit them to the tax authorities.

Intrastat is a a required reporting process for all **European Union** (EU) companies that trade with other EU countries/regions. Each company within the EU is responsible for reporting the movement of goods to their statistics authorities every month and delivering the report to the tax authority. In Dynamics NAV, the intrastat journal is used to complete periodic intrastat reports.

The intrastat journal requires item entries to contain information related to tariff numbers, transaction types, and transport methods. The tariff numbers are assigned to each item card, while transaction types and transport methods are assigned to sales and purchase documents.

Sales tax

Sales tax is a tax that is only calculated and paid for the sale of certain goods and purchases. Since the tax is applied during the point of sale, the seller will be the responsible party calculating and collecting this tax. Then either monthly or quarterly, the seller gives the collected sales tax to the government.

There are four major components in sales tax that you will need to set up.

- **Tax Groups**: This is the classification of goods and services that you sell to your customers.

- **Tax Jurisdictions**: These are the different jurisdictions that you need to report sales tax to. In the United States, depending on where you sold the product, there may be up to seven jurisdictions you need to report your sales tax to.

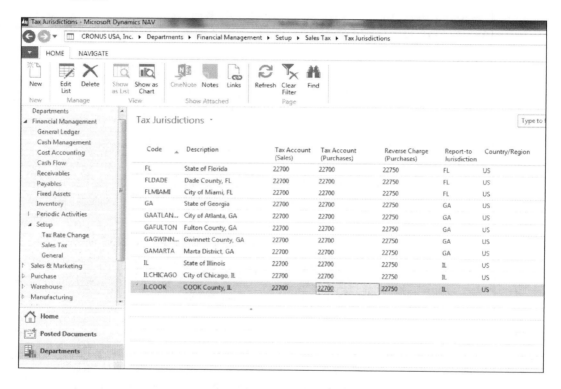

- **Tax Area**: This allows you to group the jurisdictions together so that it's a lumped percentage for all the jurisdictions you report to.

- **Tax Details**: This is where you define to which jurisdiction you sell certain types of products and/or services and whether they are liable for sales tax or not; and at what percentage rate.

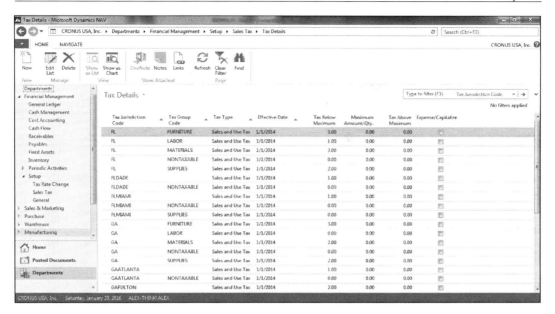

Intercompany transactions

Intercompany postings are used to buy/sell goods and services between companies that are set up in your database. This function eliminates the need to enter purchase and sales orders manually in each of the companies that you buy and sell.

When company A creates a document that needs to be sent to company B, the following flow occurs:

1. Company A creates the document and sends it to their IC outbox.
2. Company A sends all the transactions from their IC outbox.
3. Company B receives the transactions in their IC inbox.
4. Company B converts the IC inbox transactions to a document and processes it.

A transaction can be sent to the partner's inbox directly if both companies coexist on the same database, or you can also send transactions by e-mail or through XML files.

Consolidation

The **consolidation** is the process of adding up general ledger entries of two or more separate companies (subsidiaries) into a new company, called the consolidated company. Each individual company involved in a consolidation is called a business unit.

Note that we have only talked about adding up general ledger entries; no other entries on the system are used for consolidation purposes. In the chart of accounts of each business unit, you can indicate which accounts are to be included in the consolidation.

The consolidation process creates a summarized G/L entry on the consolidated company for the period you have selected while running the process, and for each account and combination of dimensions, if you choose to copy dimensions on the consolidated company. The consolidation functionality contains a process to help you register the consolidation eliminations.

Multicurrency

Multicurrency can be used if you buy or sell in other currencies besides your local currency. You can assign currency codes to bank accounts and also to customers and vendors. You can also use multicurrency to record general ledger transactions in an additional currency (besides your local currency). The additional currency feature is very useful for international companies that need to report in a currency different than the one they use in their daily transactions. You can register exchange rates for each foreign currency and specify from which dates the exchange rates are valid. Each time you post a transaction in a different currency, a conversion is made to translate that currency amount into the local currency amount. All entries in Dynamics NAV keep all the amounts in the transaction currency and the local currency in separate fields.

The adjust exchange rates process will help you to update the amounts of posted transactions to the new assigned rates. The following image shows how the currency exchange rates are defined for the USD currency:

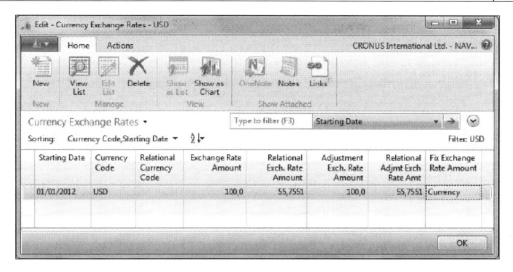

Sales and marketing

The sales area can be used to manage all common sales processes information, such as quotes, orders, and returns. There are also tools to plan and manage different types of customer information and transaction data.

The following screenshot shows the main page of the **Sales & Marketing** area:

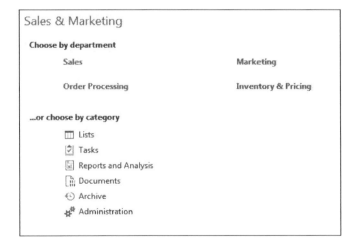

Customers

In the **Sales & Marketing** area, everything revolves around customers. The customer card contains a lot of information, but only a few fields are mandatory in order to be used by the customer on transactions; they are the ones that correspond to the posting groups. All other fields can be filled or not, depending on how you want the sales area to work.

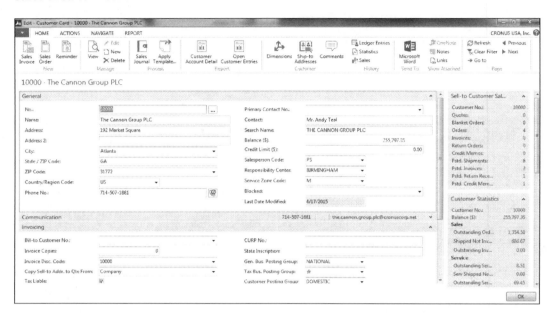

You can define a salesperson for the customer, to track the sales of each salesperson. You can set a credit limit for each customer so that you get a warning when you try to create a new order for the customer and the credit limit is exceeded. You can group your customers by price and discounts groups to help you define prices. You can define different payment terms and methods. You can indicate how you are going to ship the goods to each customer, and you can also indicate a currency and language for the customer. Besides this, you can also create multiple bank accounts and credit cards.

Many times, a company establishes criteria to fill up all of this information. As an example, the company could have a norm that high-value customers will be part of a particular price group, will use specific posting groups, and will have particular payment terms. In this case, you can create as many customer templates as the defined criteria and apply a template each time a new customer is introduced to the system. In the following screenshot, you can see all the fields that can be included in a customer template:

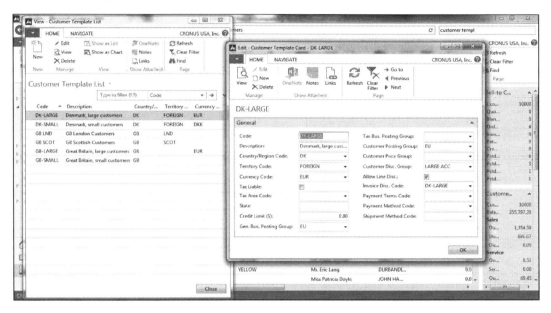

Order processing

The order processing part is all about documents. Dynamics NAV allows you to create quotes, blanket orders, orders, return orders, invoices, and credit memos.

The sales process can start with any of the previously mentioned documents depending on the company's needs. In the following diagram, you can see the information flow through the documents. The documents with a gray background are the ones from where the process can start:

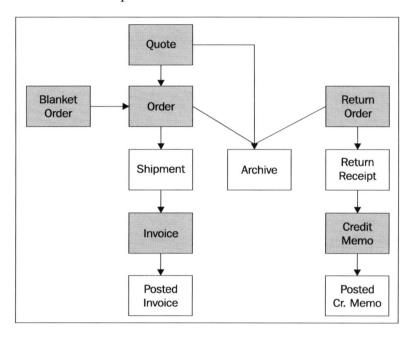

All the data from one document is carried forward to the next document. In addition, you can also create new documents by copying the data from any other sales document on the system.

In the previous diagram, the documents with the gray background are passed to the documents with the white background through a posting process, but posting routines can take a while to process.

Dynamics NAV 2016 has a feature called background posting. If background posting is enabled, then data is put in a queue and posted later in the background. This allows users to keep working while the system posts their documents.

When you select a customer in a document, many fields from the customer card are copied to the document header. This is considered as default data from that customer. You can change most of that data on a particular document.

Approvals

The approval system allows a user to submit a document for approval according to a predefined hierarchy of approval managers with certain approval amount limits. The approval of a document can be initiated by an e-mail notification sent to the user. Similarly, reminders of overdue approvals can be also sent. Pending approvals can also be viewed from the **Order Processing** menu.

The system allows you to create several approval templates where you can choose the document types to be included in an approval process and which approval and limit type to be used for each document. Document amounts are the main criteria to include a document in an approval process. The different limit types that can be used are as follows:

- **No limits**: The document is included in the approval process, no matter how small or big the total amount is. It will then depend on the user setup.

- **Approval limits**: The document is included in the approval process if the total amount is greater than the amount limit.

- **Credit limits**: If a sales document that will put a customer over their credit limit is created, the document is sent for credit limit approvals. After this, amount approvals may also have to approve the document.

The following screenshot shows how the **Approval Templates** page looks like:

Approval Code	Approval Type	Document Type	Limit Type	Additional Approvers	Enabled	Table ID
P-BLANKET OR...		Blanket Order	No Limits	No	☐	38
P-CREDIT MEMO	Sales Pers./Purc...	Credit Memo	No Limits	No	☐	38
P-INVOICE	Sales Pers./Purc...	Invoice	No Limits	No	☐	38
P-ORDER	Sales Pers./Purc...	Order	Approval Limits	No	☐	38
P-ORDER	Approver	Order	Approval Limits	No	☑	38
P-QUOTE	Approver	Quote	Request Limits	No	☐	38
P-RETURN ORDER	Sales Pers./Purc...	Return Order	No Limits	No	☐	38
S-BLANKET ORD...		Blanket Order	No Limits	No	☐	36
S-CREDIT MEMO	Sales Pers./Purc...	Credit Memo	No Limits	No	☐	36
S-I-CREDITLIMIT		Invoice	Credit Limits	No	☐	36
S-INVOICE	Sales Pers./Purc...	Invoice	No Limits	No	☐	36
S-O-CREDITLIMIT		Order	Credit Limits	No	☐	36
S-ORDER	Sales Pers./Purc...	Order	Approval Limits	No	☐	36
S-QUOTE	Sales Pers./Purc...	Quote	No Limits	No	☐	36
S-RETURN ORDER	Sales Pers./Purc...	Return Order	No Limits	No	☐	36

Pricing

The pricing option allows you to specify how you want to set up the sales price agreements. You can specify prices and discounts. Both prices and discounts can be for an individual customer, a group of customers, all the customers, and for a campaign. You need to specify one price for each item. If no price is found, the last sales price of the item will be used. When a price agreement is created, you can specify whether VAT is included in the price or not. Sales prices and sales discounts are introduced in separate tables.

Dynamics NAV always retrieves the best price. The best price is the lowest permissible price with the highest permissible line discount on a particular date.

In addition to specific item prices and discounts, you can also indicate invoice discounts or service charges. This can only be set up for individual customers, not for a group of customers or a campaign.

When you create a sales document, a **Sales Line Details FactBox** indicates how many **Sales Price** and **Sales Line Discounts** can be applied to the document.

You can see the details by clicking on each blue number found on the FactBox. The sales price worksheet will help you change and update your current prices.

Marketing

The marketing functionality revolves around contacts. A contact can be a prospect that is not yet your customer or your existing customer. Your company most likely does business with another company. And you're probably not the only person working at your company; the same can be said about the other company.

Contact is a way for you to keep track of all the people working within a particular company so you know who is working in what department.

You can create a contact and indicate their business relations. A contact can be related to customers, vendors, or bank accounts. You can categorize your contacts based on their industry groups or job responsibilities. Or you can create your own profile criteria, for example, educational level, marital status, or hobbies.

The task management feature allows you to create and organize marketing campaigns. You can create to-do lists and link them to contacts and/or campaigns.

The opportunity management area allows you to keep track of sales opportunities, have an overview of what is in the pipeline, and plan ahead accordingly.

All of the interactions you do with your contacts are kept in the **Interaction Log**. This is where you can see a history of all the interactions you've had with your contacts.

Purchase

The purchase area can be used to manage all the common purchase processes information, such as quotes, orders, and returns. There are also tools to plan your purchases according to your company's needs.

The main page of the **Purchase** area is shown in the following screenshot:

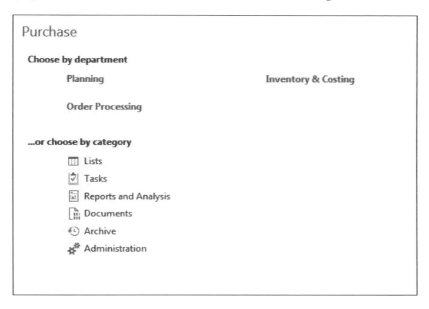

We'll give a few details about each of these areas, although most processes are similar to the ones we have discussed in the *Sales & Marketing* section.

Vendors

In the **Purchase** area, everything revolves around vendors. Vendors' cards are pretty similar to customers' cards. Please refer to the *Customer* section of this chapter to see what you can expect from vendors.

Order processing

The order processing part is all about documents. Dynamics NAV allows you to create quotes, blanket orders, orders, return orders, invoices, and credit memos.

Please refer to the *Order processing* subsection of the *Sales & Marketing* section in this chapter to see what you can expect from order processing.

Approvals

The approval system allows the user to submit a document for approval according to a predefined hierarchy of approval managers with certain approval amount limits. The approval system works as explained in the *Approvals* subsection of the *Sales & Marketing* section of this chapter.

Besides the different limits explained before, the purchase approval system includes a new type of limit:

- **Request limits**: By using the request limit in combination with the request amount approval limit, a purchase request process can be set up for internal purchases in the company.

Pricing

The pricing option allows you to define purchase price agreements. It works similar to the pricing model of the *Sales & Marketing* section of this chapter, with one difference. In the *Sales & Marketing* section, we said that both prices and discounts could be set for an individual customer, a group of customers, for all customers, and for a campaign. In the *Purchase* section, it can only be set for individual vendors.

Planning

If you purchase goods, the requisition worksheet can help to plan your purchases. You can manually enter items on the worksheet and fill in the relevant fields, or you can also run the **Calculate Plan** process. This calculates a replenishment plan for the items that have been set up with the replenishment system of purchase or transfer; for example, the program will automatically suggest an action you should take to replenish the item: it could be increasing the item quantity on an existing order or creating a new order.

You can also use the **Drop Shipment** function to fill in the requisition worksheet lines. This function retrieves the sales orders that you want to designate for a drop shipment. You use **Drop Shipment** when an item is shipped directly from your vendor to your customer. The system may sometimes suggest planning lines that need extra attention by the planner before they can be accepted.

The **Calculate Plan Batch** job investigates the demand and supply situation of the item and calculates the projected available balance. The balance is defined as follows:

Inventory + Scheduled receipts + Planned receipts – Gross Requirements

This also respects the minimum order quantity, the maximum order quantity, and the order multiple of each item.

The following screenshot shows how the **Req. Worksheet** page looks like after you have run the **Calculate Plan Batch** job:

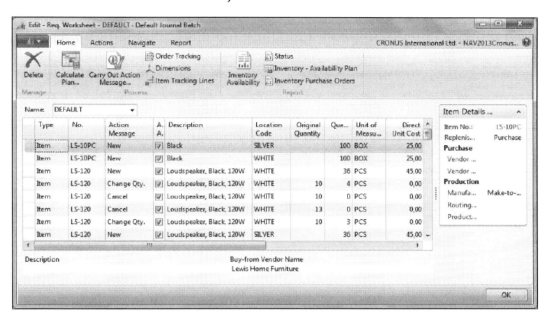

When you have finished reviewing the suggested purchases, you can use the **Carry Out Action Message** option to create new purchase orders and modify or cancel the existing ones.

Warehouse

After the goods have been received and before they are shipped, a series of internal warehouse activities takes place to ensure an effective flow through the warehouse and to organize and maintain company inventories. Typical warehouse activities include putting items away, moving items inside or between warehouses, and picking items for assembly, production, or shipment. The following screenshot shows the main page of the **Warehouse** area:

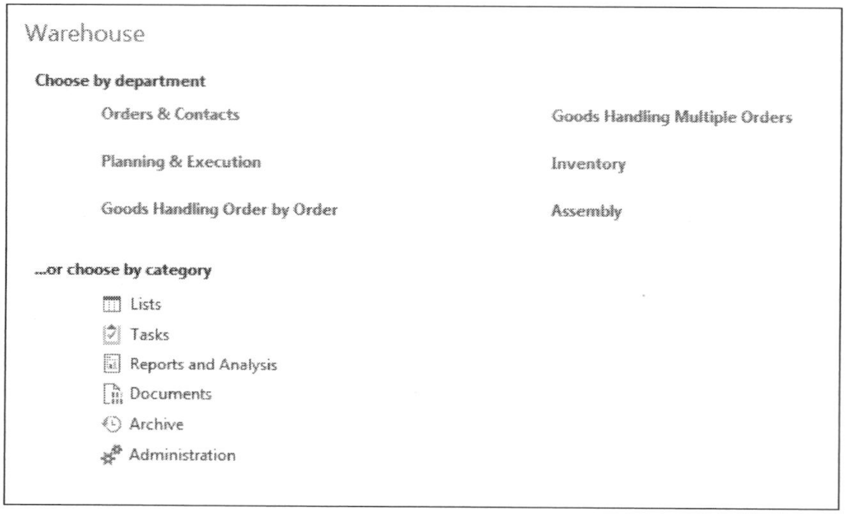

Warehouse

Choose by department

Orders & Contacts   Goods Handling Multiple Orders

Planning & Execution   Inventory

Goods Handling Order by Order   Assembly

...or choose by category

- Lists
- Tasks
- Reports and Analysis
- Documents
- Archive
- Administration

Items

In the **Warehouse** area, everything revolves around items. The item card contains a lot of information, but only a few fields are mandatory in order to be able to use the item on transactions: the base unit of a measure and the fields corresponding to the posting groups.

All the other fields can be filled or unfilled depending on how you want the **Warehouse** area to work.

You can create multiple units of measure. You can categorize your item using the item category code and the product group code. You can indicate a shelf number for the item. You can use different costing methods, namely, FIFO, LIFO, average, standard, and so on. You can indicate how the replenishment of a product is going to be done (we have seen it in the *Purchase* section of this chapter). You can also set up a lot of other information about the item such as cross-references, substitutes, and so on.

One item can have multiple variants. This is useful if you have a large number of almost identical items, for example, the items that vary only in color. Instead of setting up each variant as a separate item, you can set up one item and then specify the various colors as variants of the item.

As part of your warehouse management, you may need to use multiple locations. We will cover locations in the next section. If you use multiple locations, you can create stock-keeping units for your items. Stock-keeping units allow you to differentiate information about an item between different locations. As an example, the replenishment system of an item may be different on different locations. Stock-keeping units also allow you to differentiate information between two variants of the same item. Information on the stock-keeping unit has priority over the item card.

One interesting feature about the item property is item tracking. You can track an item by serial number, lot number, expiration date, or a combination of all of them. You can create different tracking codes and set them up with different tracking policies. The following screenshot shows an **Item Tracking Code Card**:

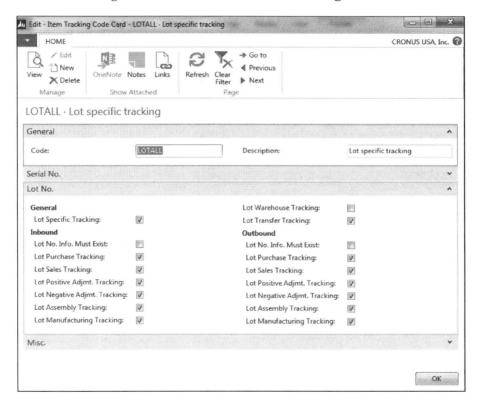

These policies reflect where it is mandatory to track the item; for example, you may only need to track a lot of purchases but not sales.

Locations

You must set up a location in Dynamics NAV for each warehouse location or distribution center. Even if you only have one warehouse or one location, you should still set this up.

You can specify the location elsewhere in the program, for example, on purchase and sales documents. This will then record the transactions for the location when you post, and you will be able to track the item inventory and item value on each location.

You can specify an unlimited number of bins in each location. A bin denotes a physical storage unit. You can then use bins on put-away and pick operations so that you can know where a specific item is stored.

Transfer orders

Transfer orders are used to transfer items between locations. The transfer order is a document similar to a sales order or a purchase order. The transfer order contains information about the source location, the destination location, and the date connected to the shipping and receiving of the order. An in-transit location must be used when working with transfer orders. The posting process of transfer orders is done in two separate steps, shipping and receiving.

Assembly

Assembly is used to create a new item, for example, a kit combining components in simple processes. This can be seen as a small manufacturing functionality, but does not require the complexity of full manufacturing.

To use this feature, you need to define assembly items. An assembly item is an item defined as sellable that contains an assembly **bill of materials (BOM)**. Items can be assembled to order or assembled to stock.

You can create assembly orders that are used to manage the assembly process and to connect the sales requirements with the involved warehouse activities. Assembly orders differ from the other order types because they involve both output and consumption when posting.

Pick and put-away

Inventory can be organized and handled on the locations at the bin level. Multiple variables can be defined per bin as follows:

- Their type
- The type of actions that can be performed on the bin: pick, put-away, ship, and receive
- Their maximum capacity
- Their desired minimum capacity

With all this information, you can create pick and put-away documents that will tell you the following:

- Where to pick your inventory for shipment purposes
- Where to store your inventory when it is received

There are also documents to manage internal inventory movements, move inventory from one bin to another, and calculate the replenishment of pick bins.

Inventory

Each single item card contains a field called **Inventory** that specifies how many units of the item are in an inventory. Units are counted using the base unit of measure indicated on the item card. Dynamics NAV automatically calculates the content of the field using the **Quantity** field in the **Item Ledger Entry** table. This means that every time a new **Item Ledger Entry** record is created, for example, after posting a sales order, the inventory of the item is updated.

You can filter the **Inventory** field so that its contents are calculated only on the basis of one or any combination of global dimension values, locations, variants, lots, or serial numbers.

An inventory is used in combination with other fields to know the availability of an item. Item availability can be shown by an event, a period, a variant, a location, the BOM level, and timeline. The following screenshot shows the **Item Availability by Periods** page:

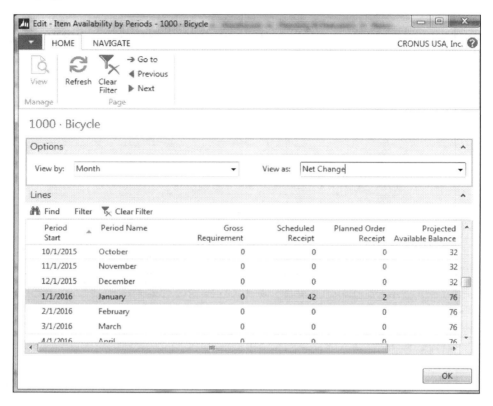

At least once in every fiscal year, you must take a physical inventory to see whether the quantity registered is the same as the physical quantity in stock. The physical inventory journals have been designed to help you during such a task. But an inventory is not only about units, it is also about the value of those units and their cost.

You can indicate different costing methods for an item. The choice determines the way a program calculates the unit cost. You can select any of the following costing methods: FIFO, LIFO, specific, average, and standard.

The system uses value entries to keep track of each item ledger entry's cost. One or more value entries can exist per item ledger entry. Every time you post an order, invoice, credit memo, and so on, the program creates value entries because all of these operations affect the item value. In addition, you can use the revaluation journal to change any item ledger entry cost. Some other concepts, such as freight or handling charges, may also affect the item value. You can use item charges to assign those charges to item ledger entries.

Manufacturing

The **Manufacturing** area is used to manage production. This involves the design and engineering work that will specify how and when items are handled, the components and resources that go into creating an end item, and the routings that define the process requirements of a given produced item.

The **Manufacturing** area also provides tools to schedule production activities, manually or automatically pull production components for consumption, record time consumption, post finished operations that do not qualify as finished output but as scrapped material, and so on.

The following screenshot shows the main page of the **Manufacturing** area:

Manufacturing

Choose by department

    Product Design   Execution

    Capacities   Costing

    Planning

...or choose by category

    Lists

    Tasks

    Reports and Analysis

    Archive

    Administration

Product design

The product design starts on the item card. You need to create one item card for each end item that you want to produce and also one item card for each component that you need to consume to obtain the end product.

For each component you have to specify whether you purchase it, assemble it, or produce it. You also need to specify whether you need the component to stock or you just need it when an order is made. You can specify all of this information on the **Replenishment** tab of the item card as shown in the following screenshot:

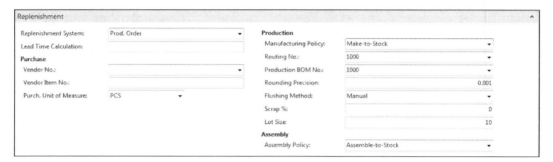

For items that need to be produced, you have to create a BOM. It is a listing of all the sub-assemblies, intermediates, parts, and raw materials that go into a parent item and the quantities needed of each component.

Production BOMs may consist of several levels. You can use up to 50 levels. One production BOM always corresponds to one level. You have the possibility to copy the existing BOMs to create a new BOM.

The following screenshot shows the **Production BOM** for item number **1000, Bicycle**:

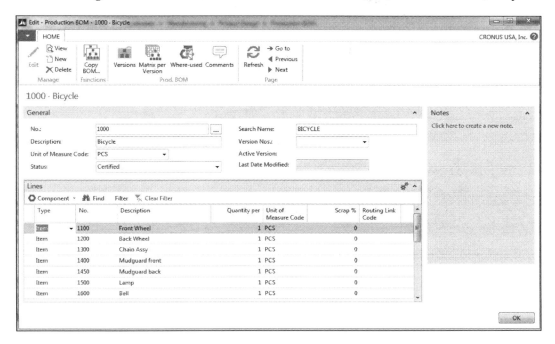

You also need to define routings to show the production process. The routings form the basis for production planning and control. Routings include detailed information about the method of manufacturing of a particular item. It includes the operations to be performed and sequenced. You can also include information about tools, resources, and personnel and quality measures.

Routing is the basis of process scheduling, capacity scheduling, material need scheduling, and the production documents.

The program also supports the production of parts families, that is, the same or similar item can be manufactured with a single routing. A production family is a group of individual items whose relationship is based on the similarity of their manufacturing processes. Forming production families can optimize material consumption.

Capacities

The program distinguishes between three types of capacities:

- Work centers
- Machine centers
- Resources

These are arranged hierarchically and each level contains subordinate levels. You can assign various machine centers to each work center. A machine center may only belong to one work center.

The planned capacity of a work center consists of the availability of the corresponding machine centers and the additional planned availability of the work center.

The planned availability of the work center group is thus the sum of all the corresponding availabilities of the machine centers and work centers. The availability is stored in calendar entries. To work with capacities, you need to create several calendars:

- **Shop calendar**: This calendar defines a standard work week according to the start and end time of each working day and the work-ship relation. It also defines fixed holidays during a year.

- **Work center calendar**: This calendar specifies the working days and hours, shifts, holidays, and absences that determine the work center's gross available capacity measured in time according to its defined efficiency and capacity values.

- **Machine center's availability**: In this calendar, you can define the time periods when machine centers cannot be used. The machine centers are not assigned their own shop calendar; the shop calendar of the work center is used. The calendar for the machine center is calculated from the entries of the assigned shop calendar and the calendar absence entries of the machine center.

- **Resource capacities**: Resources, such as technicians, have their own capacity. You can use work-hour templates that contain the typical working hours in your company; for example, you can create templates for full-time technicians and part-time technicians. You can use work-hour templates when you add capacity to resources.

Planning

The planning system takes all the demand and supply data into account, nets the results, and creates suggestions to balance the supply to meet the demand. Another goal of the planning system is to ensure that the inventory does not grow unnecessarily.

The terms running the planning worksheet or running MRP refer to the calculation of the master production schedule and material requirements based on the actual and forecasted demands. The planning system can calculate either **Master Planning Schedule (MPS)** or **Material Requirements Planning (MRP)** on request, or it can calculate both at the same time.

- **MPS**: It is the calculation of a master production schedule based on the actual demand and the production forecast. The MPS calculation is used for end items that have a forecast or a sales order line. These items are called MPS items and are identified dynamically when the calculation starts.

- **MRP**: It is the calculation of material requirements based on the actual demand for components and the production forecast of the component level. MRP is calculated only for items that are not MPS items. The purpose of MRP is to provide time-phased formal plans, by item, to supply the appropriate item at the appropriate time in the appropriate location and in the appropriate quantity.

Several planning parameters have to be filled in the item, or the stock-keeping unit and the manufacturing setup, in order to tell the system how you want to plan your supply. The planning parameters control when, how much, and how to replenish, based on all the settings. Some of the planning parameters are: dampener period and quantity, quantity reorder policy and reorder point, maximum inventory, and manufacturing policy or combined MPS/MRP calculation.

Planning is affected by many additional factors, such as the planning horizon defined by the order and the ending dates specified when you run MPS/MRP from the **Planning Worksheet** or **Order Planning** page.

The forecasting functionality is used to create anticipated demand; it allows your company to create what-if scenarios to plan for and meet the demand. Accurate forecasting can make a critical difference in the custom levels with regards to promised order dates and on-time delivery.

The sales forecast is the sales department's best guess at what will be sold in the future, and the production forecast is the production planner's projection of how many end items and derived sub-assemblies will be required to produce in specific periods to meet the forecasted sales.

Execution

When materials have been issued, the actual production operations can start and then be executed in the sequence defined by the production order routing.

An important part of executing production is to post the production output to a report progress and to update the inventory with the finished items. Output posting can be done manually, or it can be done automatically with the use of backward flushing. In this case, material consumption is automatically posted along with the output when the production order changes to finished.

You also have to post the scrapped materials and consumed capacities that are not assigned to a production order, such as maintenance work. You can use the output journal and the capacity journal respectively to perform these operations.

Finally, you need to put-away the output of the production. You will perform your put-away task according to how your warehouse is set up as a location. The inbound warehouse request will inform the warehouse that the production order is ready for put-away.

In basic warehousing, where your warehouse location requires put-away processing, but does not receive processing, you use the inventory put-away document to organize and record the put-away of the output. In advanced warehousing, where your location requires both put-away and receive processing, you create either an internal put-away document or a movement document to put away the output.

Costing

Many manufacturing companies select a valuation base of standard cost. This also applies to companies that perform light manufacturing, such as assembly and kitting. A standard cost system determines an inventory unit cost based on some reasonable historical or expected cost. Studies of the past and estimated future cost data can then provide the basis for standard costs. These costs are frozen until a decision is made to change them. The actual cost to produce a product may differ from the estimated standard costs.

Standard costs of the manufactured item can consist of direct material cost, labor cost, subcontractor cost, and overhead cost. A batch job can be run to create suggestions to change item costs as well as the standard cost on a work center, machine center, or resource cards. After revising the suggested changes, another batch job will help you to implement them.

Subcontracting

When a vendor performs one or more operational steps in production, subcontracting is a standard operational step in many manufacturing companies. Subcontracting can be a rare occurrence or can be an integral part of all production processes. Dynamics NAV provides several tools to manage subcontract work:

- **Subcontract work center**: This is a work center with an assigned vendor (subcontractor). The subcontract work center can be used on a routing operation, which allows you to process the subcontracted activity. In addition, the cost of the operation can be designated at the routing or the work center level.

- **Work center cost based on units or time**: This feature enables you to specify whether costs associated with the work center are based on the production time or a flat charge per unit. Although subcontractors commonly use a flat charge per unit to charge for their services, the program can handle both the options: production time and flat charge per unit.

- **Subcontracting worksheet**: This feature allows you to find the production orders with the material ready to be sent to a subcontractor and also allows you to automatically create purchase orders for subcontract operations from the production order routings. Then the program automatically posts the purchase order charges to the production order during the posting of the purchase order. Only production orders with a released status can be accessed and used from a subcontracting worksheet.

Job

The **Job** area supports common project management tasks, such as configuring a job and scheduling a resource, as well as providing the information needed to manage budgets and monitor progress. The jobs feature is meant to manage long-term projects that involve the use of man hours, machine hours, inventory items, and other types of usage that you need to keep track of.

Job card

The **Job Card** page shows information about the job, such as the job number, job name, and information about job posting. There is one card for each job. The following screenshot shows a **Job Card** page:

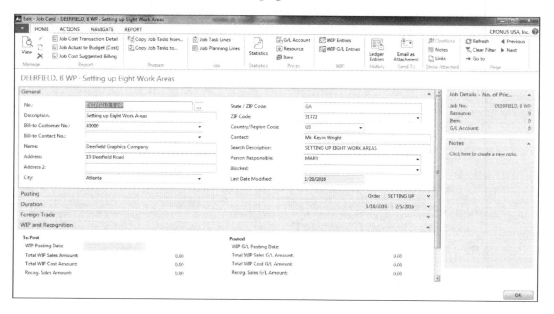

Phases and tasks

A key part of setting up a new job is to specify the various tasks involved in the job. Every job must have a minimum of one task. You create tasks by adding **Job Task Lines**, as shown in the following screenshot:

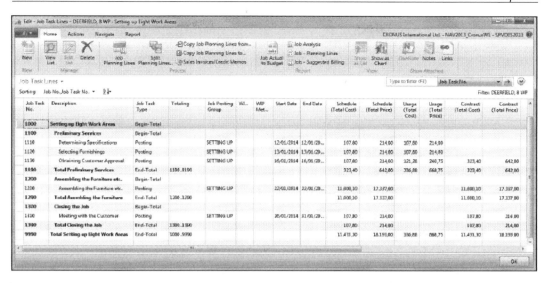

You have additional tools that help to you copy task lines from one job task to another. You can copy from a job task in the job you are working with, or from a job task linked to a different job.

Planning

You can define each task that you have created for a job into planning lines. A planning line can be used to capture any information that you want to track for a job. You can use planning lines to add information such as which resources are required or to capture which items are needed to fulfill the job.

For example, you may create a task to obtain customer approval. You can associate that task with planning lines for items such as meeting with the customer and creating a services contract.

For each planning line, you must define a line type, which can be schedule, contract, or both. This is explained as follows:

- **Schedule**: This line type provides the estimated usage and costs for the job, typically in a time and materials type contract. Planning lines of this type cannot be invoiced.

- **Contract**: This line type provides an estimated invoicing to the customer, typically in a fixed price contract.

- **Both schedule and contract**: This line type provides a scheduled usage equal to what you want to invoice.

In addition, you can specify an account type and fill in information such as quantity. As you add information, cost information is automatically filled in; for example, when you enter a new line, the cost, price, and discount for resources and items are initially based on the information that is defined on the resource and item cards.

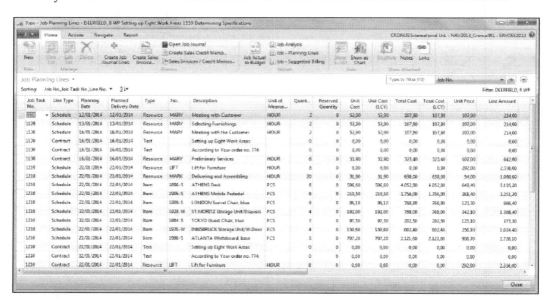

Time sheet

You can track machine and employee hours on the project using time sheets. Using the jobs functionality will provide a good overview, not only of individual jobs, but also of the allocation of employees, machinery, and other resources being used in all projects. You can also use this functionality for many types of services and consultancy tasks.

Time sheets in Microsoft Dynamics NAV handle time registration in weekly increments of seven days. You use them to track the time used on a job, service orders, and assembly orders. In addition, you can use them to record simple resource time registration and employee absences. Time sheets can be set up, so an approval is required before you can post them to the relevant job journal.

Invoice jobs

During a job's development, job costs such as resource usage, materials, and job-related purchases can accumulate. As the job progresses, these transactions get posted to the job journal. It is important that all costs get recorded in the job journal before you invoice the customer.

You can invoice the whole job or only invoice the selected contract lines. Invoicing can be done after the job is finished or at certain intervals during the job's progress, based on an invoicing schedule.

Work in process (WIP)

If a job runs over a long period, you may want to transfer these costs to a **Work in Process (WIP)** account on the balance sheet while the job is being completed. You can then recognize the costs and sales in your income statement accounts when it is appropriate.

Dynamics NAV allows you to calculate the value of the WIP of your jobs. The calculation is based on the WIP method selected on the individual jobs.

The WIP process creates WIP entries in connection with the jobs. This function only calculates WIP; it does not post it to the general ledger. To do so, another batch job must be run, the job posts WIP to G/L. There are several WIP methods that you can use on your jobs:

- **Cost value**: It starts by calculating the value of what has been provided by taking a proportion of the estimated total costs, based on the percentage of completion. Invoiced costs are subtracted by taking a proportion of the estimated total costs, based on the invoiced percentage.

- **Cost of sales**: It begins by calculating the recognized costs. Costs are recognized proportionally based on the scheduled total costs.

- **Sales value**: It recognizes revenue proportionally based on the usage total costs and the expected cost recovery ratio.

- **Percentage of completion**: It recognizes revenue proportionally based on the percentage of completion, that is, the usage total costs against schedule costs.

- **Completed contract**: Completed contract does not recognize revenue and costs until the job is completed. You may want to do this when there is high uncertainty about the estimates of costs and revenue for the job.

The system also allows you to create your own job WIP method that reflects the needs of your organization.

Resource planning

Many companies use resource management to track the time and effort that is involved in performing and providing services, for example, an employee may visit a site to talk with a customer about a project. This time and effort can be charged to the customer on a sales order.

Resource planning is integrated with jobs, services, and assembly orders. When resources are used or sold in a job, for example, the prices and costs associated with them are retrieved from the information set up in the resource planning area.

But before you can start selling services and jobs or assigning resources to assembly projects, you must set up information about policy and pricing, which can be used in resource transactions. All pricing information is adjustable.

Resource card

The resource card is used to specify resources, which can be employees, machinery, or other company resources.

 A lot of companies use the **Resource Card** to capture the sale of non-stock items and services. This will allow the data entry clerk to select from a list of predefined resources when they are entering a sales document; instead of going to and selecting from the **Chart of Accounts**.

For most companies, an optimal assignment of resources is an important part of the planning and production process. The following screenshot shows the **Resource Card** page:

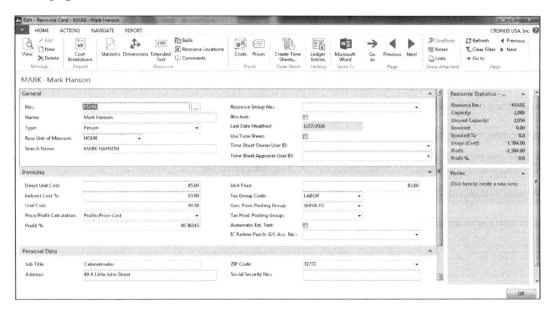

You can base production and project planning on the availability and capacity of resources. Resources can also be included in bills of materials, job planning, and job costing. Resources can be integrated with the general ledger. Resources can also be posted using the documents in sales and receivables. Global dimensions can be used with resources.

You can invoice customers for sales that are composed of various resources. Resource costs can be calculated. You can use general ledger integration to post costs and revenues that are related to the sale of resources.

You can set up alternative costs for resources; for example, if you pay an employee a higher hourly rate for overtime, you can set up a resource cost for the overtime rate. The alternative cost that you set up for the resource will override the cost on the resource card when you use the resource in the resource journal.

Pricing

You can specify the default amount per hour when the resource is created. For example, if you use a specific machine on a job for 5 hours, the job would be calculated based on the amount per hour.

To correctly manage resource activities, you must set up your resources and the related costs and prices. The job related prices, discounts, and cost factor rules are set up on the job card. You can specify the costs and prices for individual resources, resource groups, or all the available resources of the company. For services, you can adjust pricing in the **Service Item** worksheet.

A few batch jobs allow you to get resource price suggestions based on standard prices or based on alternative prices. You can then implement the price changes.

Service

Providing ongoing service to customers is an important part of any business and this can be a source of customer satisfaction and loyalty, in addition to revenue. Managing and tracking a service is not always easy, but Microsoft Dynamics NAV provides a set of tools to help. These tools are designed to support repair shop and field service operations and can be used in business scenarios such as complex customer service distribution systems, industrial service environments with bills of materials, and high volume dispatching of service technicians with requirements for spare parts management. With these tools, you can accomplish the following tasks:

- Schedule service calls and set up service orders
- Track repair parts and supplies
- Assign service personnel based on skill and availability
- Provide service estimates and service invoices

In addition, you can standardize coding, set up contracts, implement a discounting policy, and create route maps for service employees.

In general, there are two aspects of service management: configuring and setting up your system and using it for pricing, contracts, orders, service personnel dispatch, and job scheduling. The following screenshot shows the main page of the **Service** area:

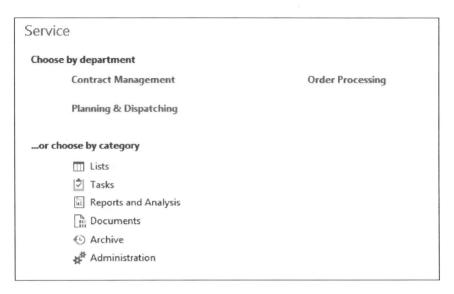

Service items

A service item is an item that has been sold to a customer and has been registered for a service. A service item has a unique identification number and can be linked to an item. You can assign a warranty to service items and specify the response time for their service. Service items can consist of many components.

Service items can be created automatically when you ship sold items, or you can create them manually. The following screenshot shows the **Service Item Card** page:

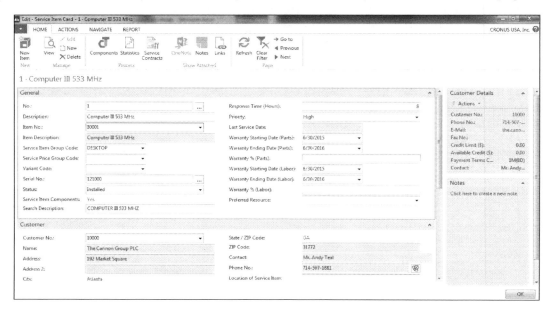

When you have set up service items, you can register them in service orders and service contracts.

Servicing some service items may require specific skills. If this is the case, you can assign skill codes to the items to which these service items are linked, or directly to these service items. This way, when a service is scheduled for the item, you will be able to assign the proper resource to do the job.

Sometimes, you cannot repair a service item, but you can choose to replace it instead. Dynamics NAV offers you a chance to replace it either temporarily or permanently.

Contracts

One way to set up a service management business is to have standard contractual agreements between you and your customers that describe the level of service and the service expectations. You can set up contract templates, which you can then use to create standardized contracts for your business. In addition, you can set up a system to create quotes for services and to turn these quotes into contracts.

After you have set up the template, you can customize the resulting contract to keep track of service hours, or other items that may vary from customer to customer.

Contracts specify general information, which includes information about the serviced customer, the starting date of the contract, the service period, the response time, the bill-to customer, the invoice period, the annual amount, the prepaid and income accounts, price update specifications, and so on. A contract can include more than one service item.

You can also set up a system to keep track of contract status and view how gain and loss information about your contracts is being posted.

Price management

The price management feature allows you to apply the best price to service orders and set up personalized service price agreements for customers. You can set up different service price groups, so you can consider the service item or service item group, in addition to the type of fault that the service task involves. You can set up these groups for a limited period of time, or for a specific customer or currency. You can use price calculation structures as templates to assign a specific price to a specific service task.

For instance, this makes it possible to assign specific items included in the service price in addition to the type of work included. This also makes it possible to use different VAT and discount amounts for different service price groups. To make sure that the correct prices are applied, you can assign fixed, minimum, or maximum prices depending on the agreements that you have with your customers.

Before adjusting the price of a service item on a service order, you are provided with an overview of what the results of the price adjustment will be. You can approve these results, or you can make additional changes if you want to have a different result. The entire adjustment is performed line by line, which means that there are no additional lines created.

The service price adjustment groups are also used to set up the different types of price adjustments. For example, you can set up a service price adjustment group that adjusts prices for spare parts, one that adjust prices for labor, another that adjusts prices for costs, and so on. You can also specify whether the service price adjustment should be applied to just one specific item or resource, or to all items or resources.

Each service price adjustment group holds the information about the adjustments that you want to make on the service lines, as you can see in the following screenshot:

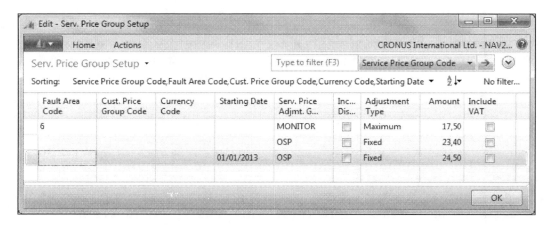

The service price adjustment function does not apply to service items that belong to service contracts. You can only adjust the service prices of items that are part of a service order. You cannot adjust the price of a service item if it has a warranty. You cannot adjust the price of a service item on a service order if the service line linked to it has been posted as an invoice, either completely or in part.

Service orders

Service orders are the documents in the Dynamics NAV Service Management application area in which you can enter information about services (repair and maintenance) on service items. Service orders are created in the following instances:

- When a customer requests a service.
- Automatically by the program at the time intervals defined in service contracts.
- When you convert a service quote to a service order. A service quote can be used as a preliminary draft for a service order.

Service orders and service quotes are composed of the following instances:

- **Service header**: It contains general information about the service, such as the customer, the contract related to the order, the service order status, or the start and finish dates.
- **Service item lines**: They contain information related to the service item such as the service item number, its description, the serial number, or the response time.
- **Service lines**: They contain information about the service costs, such as spare parts (items) used on the order, resource hours, G/L accounts payments, and general costs.

You can lend customers loaner items to temporarily replace the service items that you have received for servicing.

Service tasks

After you have created a service order or service quote and registered service item lines and allocated resources to the service items in the order or quote, you can start repairing and maintaining the service items.

The **Service Task** page can give you an overview of the service items that need servicing. You can update the information on the service items for each task, such as the repair status, or enter service lines for that service item.

Fault reporting

When a customer brings in a service item for repair, you can assign a fault code to indicate the nature of the fault. The fault code can be used with the resolution code to determine the possible repair method to use. In the following screenshot, you can see an example of **Fault Codes** and **Resolution Codes**:

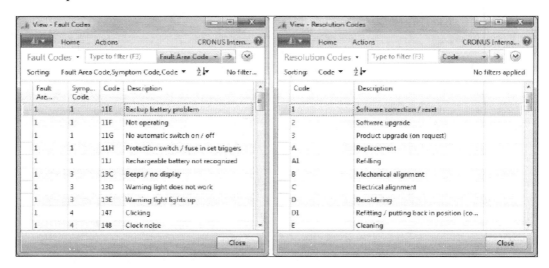

Depending on the level of fault reporting in a company, you might also need to register **Fault Area Codes** and **Symptom Codes**.

Human resources

The human resources feature lets you keep detailed records of your employees. You can register and maintain employee information, such as employment contracts, confidential information, qualifications, and employee contacts. You can also use the human resources feature to register employee absence.

Employees

To use the human resources feature, you need to create employee cards. From the employee card, you can enter basic information about the employee. The following screenshot shows the **Employee Card** page:

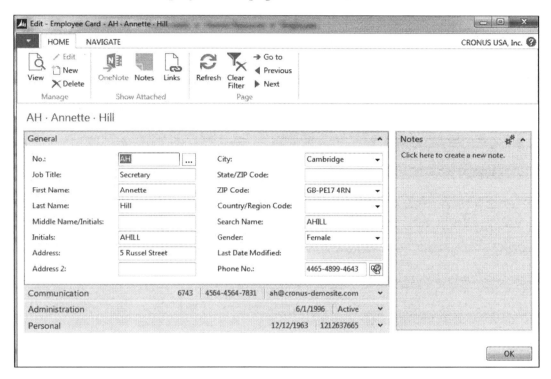

Linked to the employee card, you can set up alternative addresses, relatives, qualifications, and miscellaneous information where you can keep track of any information you want; for example, if the employee uses a company car. You can create as many miscellaneous articles as you need and link them to the employees.

The human resources application area is linked to the resources application area. So when you update certain basic information about the employee (such as name, address, social security number, employment date, and other relevant information related to the employee) in the `Employee` table, the program automatically updates the resource card for the employee.

Absence registration

You can register employee absences and assign different causes of absences. You can then see the information in various ways throughout the program and analyze employee absences. For example, you can compare your company's rate of absenteeism to national or industry-related averages for absenteeism.

A sudden increase in an employee's absences may reflect personal problems on the employee's part. With the **Employee Absence** table, you can take notice of these problems at an early stage.

Country localizations

Dynamics NAV comes with some country/region local functionalities to address specific needs. Most of these local functionalities are related to tax registering and tax reporting, or are legal requirements for the country.

You will find a complete list of local functionalities on this website: `https://msdn.microsoft.com/en-us/library/hh922908(v=nav.80).aspx`

Vertical and horizontal solutions

As we said earlier in this chapter, a good thing about Dynamics NAV is that it can be customized. A brand new functional area can be created from scratch or new features can be added to an existing area.

Many people and companies have developed new functional areas or have expanded the existing ones, and they have registered their solution as an add-on. This means that the standard functionality of Dynamics NAV is much more extensive than the functional areas we have covered in this chapter.

Actually, you can find almost 2,000 registered add-ons or third-party solutions that cover all kinds of functional areas. To ensure quality of the add-ons released for NAV, Microsoft has introduced the **Certified for Dynamics NAV** logo for all add-on partners who have passed rigorous tests through a third-party testing company.

If a customer asks you for a major modification of their Dynamics NAV, the best solution will probably be to look for an existing add-on that already covers your customer's needs. Implementing this solution usually consists of configuration and some limited custom development. On the other hand, if you choose to develop it all from scratch, you might get a lengthy high-cost and high-risk project.

Accessing Dynamics NAV

In the past, Dynamics NAV had a single client access. But technology has changed and evolved, and so has Dynamics NAV. The release of Dynamics NAV 2009 already brought two new ways of accessing the application: the Role Tailored Client and Web Services. Dynamics NAV 2016 also brings new accessibility options: the Web Client and the tablet client. It has also removed the accessibility option, the Classic Client, although it has been maintained and converted for development purposes.

In this section, we will explain the different environments in which you can access your Microsoft Dynamics NAV 2016 application.

Windows client

The Windows client is also known as the RoleTailored client, or the RTC client. That was its name when the client was first released on Dynamics NAV 2009. But Dynamics NAV 2016 has the Web client, which is also a RoleTailored client. So, we cannot call it as the RoleTailored client anymore.

The Windows client is based on the individuals within an organization, their roles, and the tasks they perform. When users first enter Dynamics NAV, they see the data needed for the daily tasks they do according to their role. Users belonging to different roles will have a different view of the system, each of them seeing only those functions they need to be able to perform their daily tasks.

For those of you who haven't used Dynamics NAV 2009 yet, but had the chance to work with Microsoft Dynamics NAV 4.0 or 5.0, you might remember how difficult it was sometimes to locate a specific feature in the jungle of the navigation pane. Switching back and forth between the specific menus in search of a menu item was a frustrating experience, especially for users performing tasks in several functional areas of the application. Unless you used shortcuts, accessing any feature required three or four clicks, provided you knew exactly where it was. The system also didn't do much to help users focus on what was needed to be done, and after you found the feature you needed, you typically had to spend extra time searching for documents or tasks that needed your attention. With the Role Tailored Client, the feature jungle was gone.

The Windows client allows users to widely customize the data they see on each page. They have the ability to personalize the pages according to their requirements by hiding, moving, and configuring parts contained on the pages and also by saving queries, adding filters, and adding or removing fields. The ribbon can also be customized; you can add, remove, and rename actions, menus, and tabs.

The following screenshot shows what the **Role Center** of the Windows client looks like. **Role Center** is the main page of the client, and it is the first page a user sees when entering Dynamics NAV.

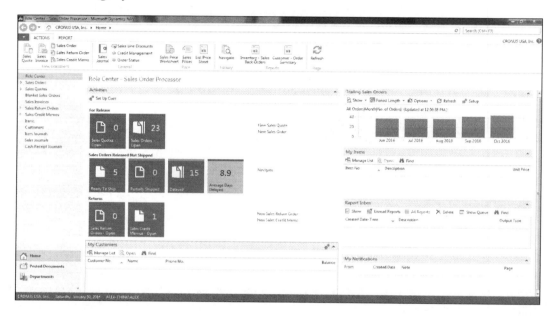

The Windows client supports three methods for authenticating users who try to access the Dynamics NAV Web client:

- **Windows**: This credential type authenticates users using their Windows credentials (Active Directory, local workgroup, or the local computer's users). Because they are authenticated through Windows, Windows users are not prompted for credentials when they start the Windows client.

- **Username**: This setting prompts the user for username/password credentials when starting the client. These credentials are then validated against Windows authentication by the Microsoft Dynamics NAV Server.

- **NavUserPassword**: This setting manages authentication by the Microsoft Dynamics NAV Server but is not based on Windows users or Active Directory. The user is prompted for username/password credentials when they start the client. The credentials are then validated by an external mechanism.

- **AccessControlService**: Using this setting, NAV uses the Microsoft Azure **Access Control service (ACS)** or **Azure Active Directory (Azure AD)** for user authentication services.

Web client

The Microsoft Dynamics NAV Web client gives users access to Microsoft Dynamics NAV data over a network, such as the Internet. From a web browser, users can view and modify data from a user-friendly interface that resembles the Windows client where the starting point is **Role Center**. The **Role Center** page can be customized according to a user's individual needs based on their role, company, and daily tasks. The Web client does not replace the Windows client, but complements it by enabling scenarios that are not possible with the Windows client. The following screenshot shows what the **Role Center** of the Web client looks like:

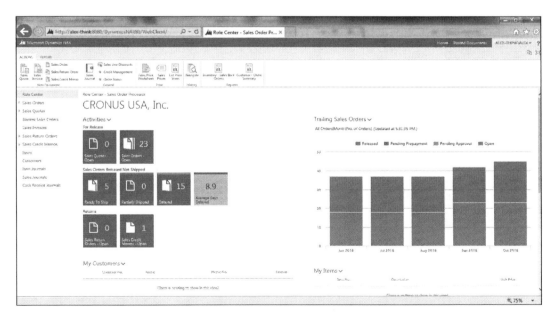

The Microsoft Dynamics NAV Web client supports most of the features that the Microsoft Dynamics NAV Windows client supports; however, there are some exceptions and limitations. The full list of the limitations can be found here:
`https://msdn.microsoft.com/en-us/library/hh168959(v=nav.80).aspx`

Tablet client

With NAV 2016, the tablet client has been introduced. This means that you can download Dynamics NAV on your Apple, Android, and Microsoft tablet devices. The design of the tablet client is focused on how you usually hold the tablet; using both hands holding it like a steering wheel. The design has been done so that you can navigate between screens using your thumb.

The tablet functionalities are based on the web client. So this means that whenever you modify something in a page, it will translate into the web client and the tablet client.

SharePoint client

Microsoft Dynamics NAV SharePoint client enables you to interact with Dynamics NAV data from a Microsoft SharePoint website. The Microsoft Dynamics NAV SharePoint client is built on the Microsoft Dynamics NAV Portal Framework for Microsoft SharePoint 2010, which is a web-based application framework that integrates Microsoft Dynamics NAV with Microsoft SharePoint applications. By integrating with SharePoint, the Microsoft Dynamics NAV SharePoint client can use the business and administration features in Microsoft SharePoint including workflows, business connectivity services, workspaces, SharePoint authentication, and scalability.

With Microsoft Dynamics NAV Portal Framework for Microsoft SharePoint 2010, you can also do the following:

- Display Microsoft Dynamics NAV pages and reports on SharePoint sites using an URL
- Add a page using a Microsoft Dynamics NAV web part and connect the web part to other web parts on a SharePoint page
- Edit data on pages in web applications and update the changes in the Microsoft Dynamics NAV 2013 database using the same metadata and business logic that is rendered in the Microsoft Dynamics NAV Windows client

Working with Microsoft Dynamics NAV pages and reports in the SharePoint client is very similar to working with pages and reports in Microsoft Dynamics NAV Windows client or Microsoft Dynamics NAV Web client. The Microsoft Dynamics NAV SharePoint client is designed for occasional users who typically need an overview of their daily work status and perform relatively simple or light data entry.

Web Services

Microsoft Dynamics NAV provides **Web Services**, which makes it easy for other systems to integrate with Microsoft Dynamics NAV. Web Services allow you to expose the business logic of Dynamics NAV to other environments.

Web Services are a lightweight, industry-standard way to make an application functionality available to a wide range of external systems and users. Microsoft Dynamics NAV 2016 supports creation and publishing of Microsoft Dynamics NAV functionality as Web Services. You can expose pages, codeunits, or queries as Web Services and even enhance a page Web Service with an extension codeunit. When you publish Microsoft Dynamics NAV objects as Web Services, they are immediately available on the network.

Developers can publish two types of Web Services from Microsoft Dynamics NAV objects:

- **SOAP Web Services**: You can publish either Microsoft Dynamics NAV pages or codeunits as SOAP services.

- **OData Web Services**: You can publish either pages or queries as OData services. The OData protocol offers new and flexible opportunities for interacting with Microsoft Dynamics NAV data. For example, you can use OData Web Services to publish a refreshable link to Microsoft Dynamics NAV data that can be displayed in Microsoft Excel with Power Pivot or in SharePoint.

Three different objects can be exposed as Web Services:

- **Page Web Services**: When you expose a page as an OData Web Service, you can query that data to return a service metadata (EDMX) document or an AtomPub document. When you expose a page as a SOAP Web Service, you expose a default set of operations that you can use to manage common operations such as create, read, update, and delete. For SOAP services, you can also use extension codeunits to extend the default set of operations that are available on a page.

- **Codeunit Web Services**: Currently available only for SOAP Web Services, codeunit Web Services provide you with maximum control and flexibility. When a codeunit is exposed as a web service, all the functions defined in the codeunit are exposed as operations.

- **Query Web Services**: When you expose a Microsoft Dynamics NAV query as an OData Web Service, you can query that data to return a service metadata (EDMX) document or an AtomPub document.

Development Environment

You use the Microsoft Dynamics NAV Development Environment to develop Microsoft Dynamics NAV applications. This component, which was also an end user client in the earlier versions of Microsoft Dynamics NAV, was formerly known as the Classic Client.

When you open the development environment, the **Object Designer** opens, which gives you access to Microsoft Dynamics NAV objects. You can use the Object Designer to modify the application or to create new application areas.

You can also use the development environment to create and manage Microsoft Dynamics NAV 2016 databases to create and manage Microsoft Dynamics NAV companies and to upload or change Microsoft Dynamics NAV licenses.

The following screenshot displays how the **Development Environment** looks like:

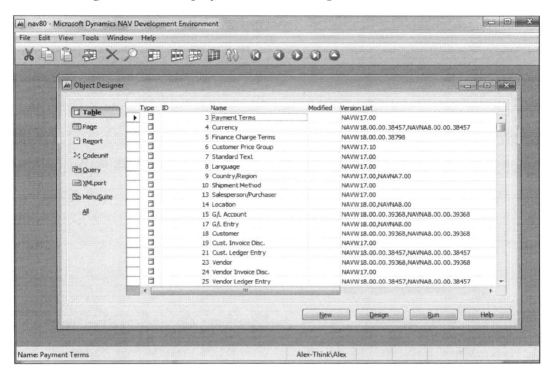

As previously mentioned, whatever you change in the development environment will be reflected in all of the different clients. This significantly reduces the development time to deploy changes to your web client, tablet client, and sharepoint client.

Summary

In this chapter, we have seen that Dynamics NAV is an ERP system targeted at small and medium-sized companies.

Dynamics NAV is focused on roles and their daily tasks and offers solutions in different functional areas including financial management, sales and marketing, purchase, warehouse, manufacturing, job, resource planning, service, human resources, and add-ons created by partners. We have described each functional area so that you know what can be expected.

Dynamics NAV can be used on different environments such as the Windows client, the Web client, tablet client, the SharePoint client, or an external application that connects to Dynamics NAV via Web Services. The development environment is used to develop new features on top of Dynamics NAV.

In the next chapter, we will cover the new features released with Microsoft Dynamics NAV 2016 in detail.

2
What's New in NAV 2016?

There are quite a few new things in Microsoft Dynamics NAV 2016. The previous releases of Dynamics NAV mainly concentrated on application changes or on architectural changes. Dynamics NAV 2013 provides changes for both the aspects at the same time; Dynamics NAV 2016 made drastic improvements on what was built for NAV 2013.

In this chapter, we will have an overview of the new features included in Dynamics NAV 2016. We will first go through the features that end users will appreciate in Dynamics NAV 2016. After this, we will take a look at the features that developers and administrators will appreciate (the IT changes).

The main concepts that we will see are as follows:

- Application changes
- Development changes
- IT changes
- Deprecated features

Application changes

There are many things that have changed in the new release of Microsoft Dynamics NAV. Some features have been removed, some others have changed, and a bunch of new functionalities and improvements have been added.

The first thing that users will see is the new look and feel of Dynamics NAV. Microsoft has implemented a Metro-style design across all of their product lines. Dynamics NAV is no different. The basic design of Metro is essentially focused on the content of the application, and not its graphics.

This new look and feel for the Windows client is not all that different from its predecessors, but you will find subtle differences that give Dynamics NAV 2016 a unique characteristic.

Improvements for the application users

Several improvements have been made to the Windows client to improve user productivity. Let's see them in detail.

Cues with color indicator

On the Windows client page when you log in, the cues will be a bar that changes color based on the data.

The following screenshot shows the cues that are displayed after logging in as an order processor. The color will be based on the setup that's defined by clicking on the **Set Up Cues** button:

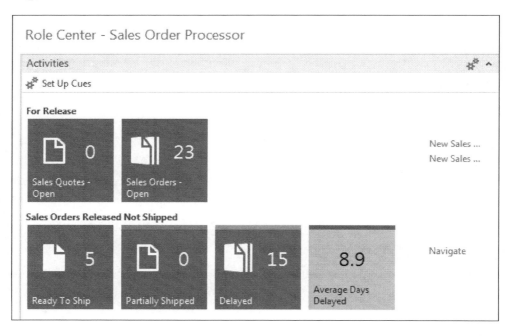

The colors will quickly tell the users which key metric in the cue needs the users' attention. In our case, since we're logged in as an order processor, we've defined that if we have over 20 open orders, it will be flagged as red; this means we have to do something about it.

Mandatory fields

Dynamics NAV 2016 now allows you to specify which fields are important. The important fields are the fields on a record that you have to fill in when creating a new record, for example, a customer card. The important mandatory fields are defined with a red asterisk as shown in the following screenshot:

The asterisk is a warning to the user who enters the data to let them know which fields have been configured as mandatory.

Even though this feature is called **Mandatory Fields**, this will not prevent users from leaving the page or entering a transaction against the record. If these important mandatory fields are not entered, users may get an error message when they work with a record. For example, if certain fields on the customer card are not entered, the user may get an error message when they enter a sales order.

Simplified user interface for small businesses

If you're a small business owner, you're probably doing everything. But what if you want to use the power of Dynamics NAV to facilitate the growth of your business? And you're worried that you may not have the manpower to maintain the data that is going in? With Dynamics NAV 2016, there is a solution for you.

The simplified UX is targeted towards small businesses that mainly want to enter purchase and sales transactions quickly and efficiently. The fields on the simplified UX will not be as elaborate as the interface on the regular pages; however, as the name implies, it'll gets the job done. Note that there's absolutely no reduced functionality when using the simplified UX.

The simplified UX can only be accessible from the small business role center.

In the following screenshot, you can see what a sales invoice looks like using the normal UX.

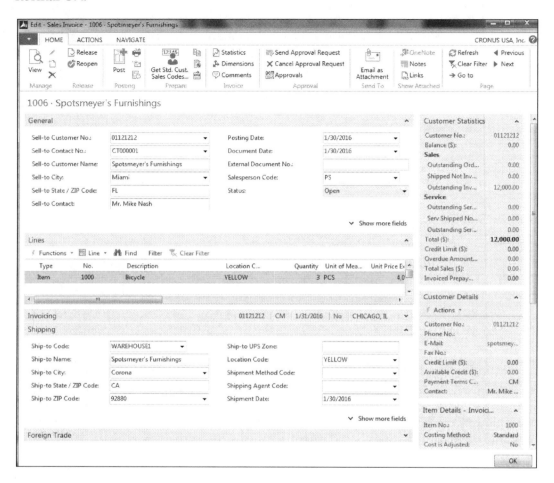

The normal UX shows a lot of fields that the user may need to utilize in order for the sales invoice to have the proper information flow to the relevant parts of Dynamics NAV.

The simplified UX eliminated a lot of non-mandatory fields, so the sales invoice entry is straight to the point. Here's the same sales invoice record using the simplified UX:

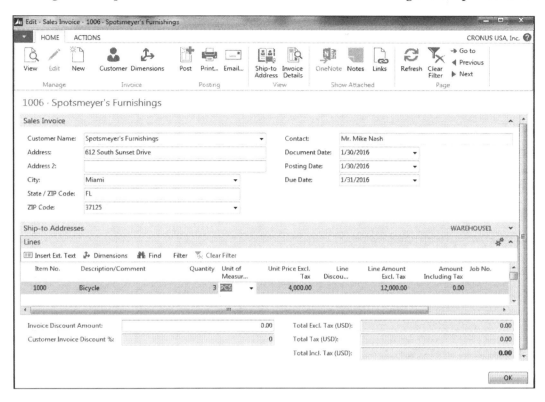

Even though the UX is different, all the data is still stored in the same tables within the same database. This means you can use the regular UX if you choose to.

Tablet client

For years, Microsoft has operated in a closed environment, meaning it does not put its applications on other operating platforms. The changing technology landscape has really forced Microsoft to change its strategy.

With the release of Dynamics NAV 2016, you can now use NAV 2016 on your Apple, Android, and Microsoft tablets. Unfortunately, the mobile phone client is not supported yet.

As mentioned in the previous chapter, the interface for the tablet is designed in a way that you commonly hold a tablet; with two hands holding the tablet like a steering wheel. To browse between the pages, you would just need to move your thumb, as highlighted with the box in the following screenshot:

Similar to the web client, each screen that you see on the tablet is a direct translation of a page in a normal Windows client. Whenever you make a change in the Page Designer, it will be automatically reflected on the web client, tablet client, or any user interface that connects to the NAV service tier.

New application features

Dynamics NAV 2016 has introduced a lot of architectural changes but also some new application functionalities.

Automatic payment and bank reconciliation

If your bank supplies their standard file for your bank statements, you can now import that file directly into NAV and NAV will automatically create, post, and apply the payment to unpaid invoices. In addition, you can use the same import to do bank reconciliation for you!

Each bank will have their own format for the statement file. There are three ways to format the bank statement import for NAV to read the file in:

- Sign up for the **Bank Data Conversion Service**
- Ask your bank whether they can supply the file in the SEPA CAMT format
- Ask a Dynamics NAV developer to create an import process for you

Signing up for the Bank Data Conversion Service

Microsoft has developed a file transfer service for Dynamics NAV called the **Data Exchange Framework**. The purpose of this framework is to let you import/export bank and payroll transactions between the bank and Dynamics NAV.

You can read more about the **Data Exchange Framework** here: https://msdn.microsoft.com/en-us/library/dn495318(v=nav.80).aspx

In order to utilize the **Bank Data Conversion Service**, you must first sign up for the service. To sign up, go to **Bank Data Conv. Service Setup** in Dynamics NAV as shown in the following screenshot:

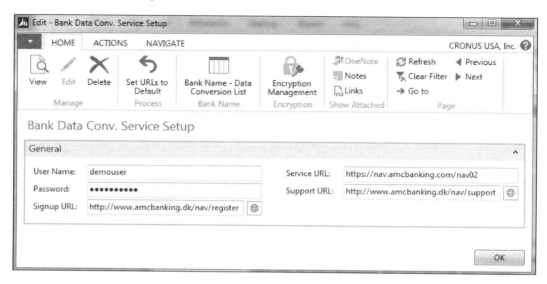

Microsoft has partnered with a company called AMC Banking. This company actually does the conversion for you when you sign up for this service.

Click on the **Signup URL** and create an account. Once you have an account created, change the username and password, and follow the instructions on the website to complete the setup.

Once the signup is complete, click on **Bank Name – Data Conversion List** and it will populate the page with all the supported banks that can be converted.

To finish the setup, go back to the **Bank Account** card and go to the **Transfer Fast** tab. The fields you will need to fill in are the following:

- **Bank Statement Import Format**: This is the format that we will use to import bank statements.

- **Payment Export Format**: This is the format that we will use to export payment data.

The following screenshot shows the fields:

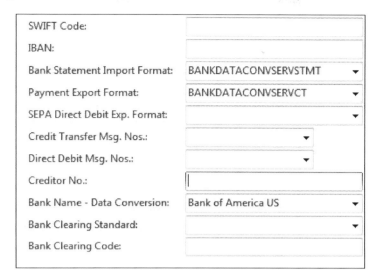

Reconciling payments automatically

Once the bank statement import has been setup, you can now import it into the **Payment Reconciliation Journal**. The step-by-step instructions on how to reconcile automatically can be found on MSDN here:

```
https://msdn.microsoft.com/en-us/library/dn414552(v=nav.80).aspx
```

Reconciling bank statements automatically

Similar to payment reconciliation, you can now do bank reconciliation using the same bank statement import file. The step-by-step instructions on how to do bank reconciliations automatically can be found here:

```
https://msdn.microsoft.com/en-us/library/dn414563(v=nav.80).aspx
```

Social Listening

With NAV 2016, Microsoft introduced the **Social Listening** tool that allows you to gather sentiments from social media and networks about your customers and items. This means that you will get real-time feedback on how your products and customers are doing without having someone to manually do research on the different social media outlets.

Social Listening is a tool within the Dynamics CRM; however, you can sign up for Social Listening as a standalone tool, as well.

 Here's a *How Do I* video that shows you step by step how to set it up:
`https://msdn.microsoft.com/en-us/dynamics/nav/`
`dn903719.aspx`

Power Business Intelligence

With the introduction of Office 365, Microsoft included something called **Power BI (Power Business Intelligence)**. What used to cost a lot of money for a BI solution, Microsoft is now essentially including it as part of the Office 365 package. This means that you can utilize Power BI to have a graphical dashboard for your business using live data from Dynamics NAV.

The best way to send data to Power BI is to utilize a new object type called **Query**. The Query object type was actually introduced in NAV 2013. So, as long as you can publish the query as a web service, Power BI utilized with Excel will suck the data up!

Technically speaking, you do not need NAV 2016 to use Power BI. If you're using at least NAV 2009, you can use Power BI as your business intelligence tool.

RapidStart services

If you're migrating from your legacy system to Dynamics NAV, one of the most important steps is to migrate the data from your legacy system to Dynamics NAV. Using the RapidStart service, you can now map the data from your old legacy software directly to Dynamics NAV.

This will eliminate the need for a NAV developer to write custom import processes that are only used once.

To utilize the RapidStart service, go to **Configuration Packages** as shown in the following screenshot. From there, you will be able to specify the tables you want to import to Dynamics NAV.

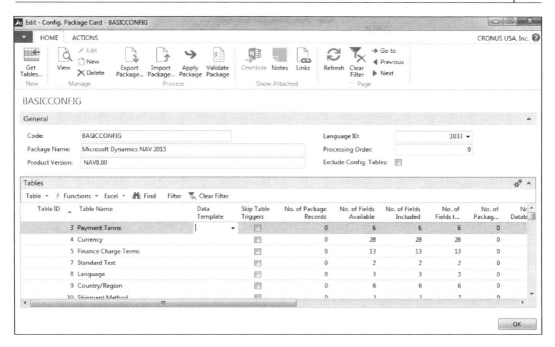

Each line on the Configuration Package represents a table in Dynamics NAV. To specify the fields within a table, click on the line of the table you wish to map the fields for, click on the **Table** toolbar, and click on **Fields**. The **Edit – Config. Package Fields** window appears as shown in the following screenshot:

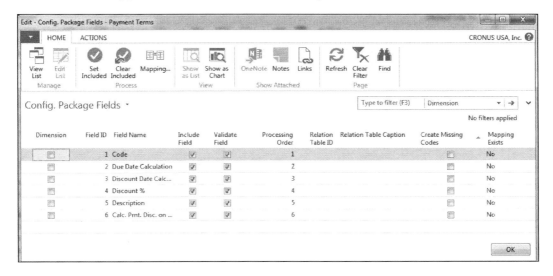

A couple of key functions of the **Configuration Package** to keep in mind are as follows:

- Data can be imported with or without validating against business rules that are built into the tables
- You can create import/export for all the tables within Dynamics NAV
- You can specify fields you want to import/export within each table
- You can export the data format that you have configured in Excel so your legacy system adheres to the format you specify
- After the data is imported, you can manage conflicts and duplicate data in a worksheet

 To learn more about how to import Customer Data in the configuration worksheet, visit: `https://msdn.microsoft.com/en-us/library/dn757271(v=nav.80).aspx`

Schedule reports

One of the major drawbacks of the base Dynamics NAV product is the ability to schedule reports, or the lack thereof. With the release of NAV 2016, you can now schedule any reports in Dynamics NAV to be run on a certain date and at a certain time using **Job Queue**.

Job Queue is a feature in Dynamics NAV that was introduced in version 4.0. It basically allows you to schedule processes to run at a certain time and day. The schedule of report is done using Job Queue. Job Queue should run in the background while using NAS for a report to be scheduled properly.

When you run a report in NAV 2016, you will now see a new option called **Schedule**, as follows:

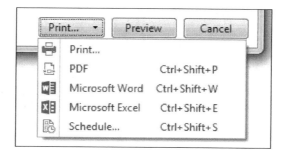

When you click on **Schedule**, it will prompt you for a description, output type, and when to start and end:

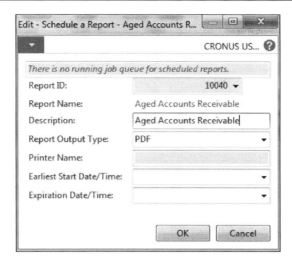

Once you click on **OK**, the report will be sent to Job Queue Entries to be processed with the Job Queue. The following screenshot shows the **Edit – Job Queue Entry Card** report for ID 10040:

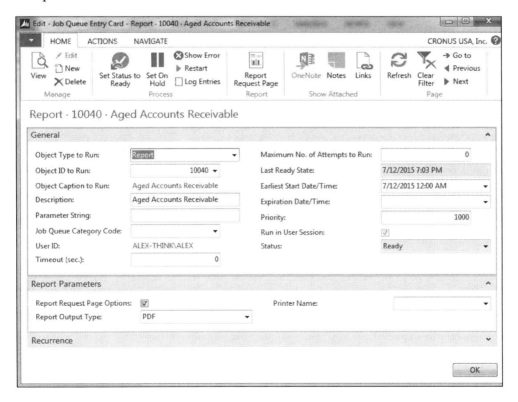

Once the report is run, it will be automatically removed from the **Job Queue** entries and put them into the **Report Inbox**. On your **Role Center**, you will see a new factbox called **Report Inbox**. This will be where all of the scheduled reports will be placed:

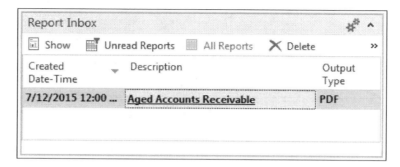

Click on **Show** and it will show the report based on the output type you have defined.

 For more information on schedule reports, visit: `https://msdn.` `microsoft.com/en-us/library/dn757302(v=nav.80).aspx`

E-mailing documents

Automatic e-mail of invoices is probably one of the top requests we get from our clients. With NAV 2016, you're now allowed to, for example, send out invoices as you post them.

On the sales order, you'll see a new icon called **Post and Email**. After the invoice is posted, a prompt will be displayed with the customer's e-mail address defined on the customer card. In addition, you can add custom messages to the e-mail as shown in the following screenshot:

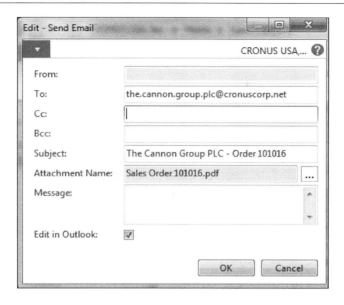

If you want to continue to edit the document in Outlook, check the **Edit in Outlook** checkbox and it will open the message in Outlook with the attachment in PDF.

Document exchange service (OCR Services)

Microsoft has teamed up with a company called Lexmark that allows you to scan incoming documents and automatically create the relevant purchase documents.

> For step-by-step information on setting up the document exchange service, please visit the following site:
>
> https://msdn.microsoft.com/en-us/library/
> dn951538(v=nav.90).aspx

Exchange rates update

This should've been there a while ago, but Microsoft has released an out-of-the-box functionality that will update the exchange rates based on whatever foreign exchange website that provides web service data feed. In the standard NAV demo company, it hooks up to Yahoo.

Native integration with Dynamics CRM

This is really more of an upgrade from the previous integration tools. The previous version of the CRM connector was not really flexible about what data you want to send from and to Dynamics CRM. As a result, partners had to purchase a connector created by a third party.

The latest release of the connector allows you to have flexibility regarding what table and what fields you want to integrate with CRM. In addition, the pages Dynamics NAV allows you to drill down to CRM information.

 For information on setting up the connector for NAV 2016, please visit the following page:
`https://msdn.microsoft.com/en-us/library/`
`mt299426(v=nav.90).aspx`

Universal app

Dynamics NAV is now a universal app; basically, if you have this in a laptop, the application will be displayed in a regular web client. If you turn your device into a tablet, then it will turn the application to tablet mode.

Basically, any device will be able to display Dynamics NAV including your mobile phone!

Workflow management

As organizations grow more complex and the orders that come in become more challenging, having a system-managed workflow is a must. Dynamics NAV 2016 introduced the ability to set up workflow processes when processing orders through an organization.

You're allowed to set up workflow processes when certain conditions are met. It allows you to notify the proper personnel, set up approval requests and approvals, and archive a workflow process for a specific order.

For more information on setting up a workflow for your Dynamics NAV implementation, please visit the following link:

```
https://msdn.microsoft.com/en-us/library/
dn892100(v=nav.90).aspx
```

Posting Preview

Prior to posting a journal, you will be now able to preview the impact of the transaction before you actually commit it to the financial ledgers.

Prior to this feature, users needed to ask IT to create a test database using the latest data. Depending on how large your database is, it may take a long time. In addition, it's a time waste for your IT staff. This process is horribly inefficient.

The Posting Preview function can be found throughout Dynamics NAV.

Deferrals

If you have revenues or expenses that are recognized over a period of time, you can now use deferral posting.

For more information on Deferrals, please visit the following link:

```
https://msdn.microsoft.com/en-us/library/
dn368450(v=nav.90).aspx
```

Development changes

Dynamics NAV 2016 has introduced some development changes. These are the changes regarding the development environment with new ways to develop document type reports and changes in the standard C/AL code, which has been redesigned in some areas.

Document reporting

When Microsoft introduced **Report Definition Language Client-side (RDLC)** as its main report-writing tool, a lot of NAV developers cried foul. Why? Because programming NAV reports using RDLC was like pulling teeth! Add to the complexity of creating an actual report, what you get when you preview a report is often times not what gets printed out on PDF or paper. This is especially true when creating document type reports such as a sales order or sales invoice.

With the horrendous feedback for the development for RDLC reports, Microsoft got to work and released a tool to develop document type reports using Word for layout. This means you can use the pre-made templates for invoices using Word.

There are four pre-made reports with Word document layouts in NAV 2016. They are as follows:

- 1304 - Mini Sales - Quote
- 1305 - Mini Sales - Order Conf.
- 1306 - Mini Sales - Invoice
- 1307 - Mini Sales - Credit Memo

These reports can only be accessed using the SMALL BUSINESS role center.

To see and configure the **Word Layout** designer, let's perform the following steps:

1. First, start the Development Environment for NAV 2016. Find report **1305** and click on **Design**:

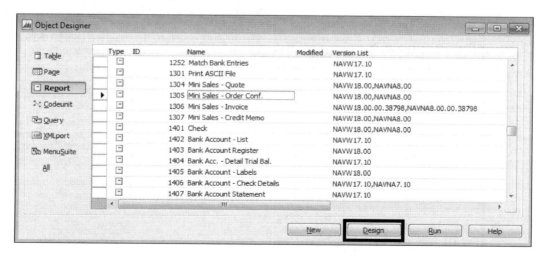

2. Next, navigate to **Tools | Word Layout | Export**.

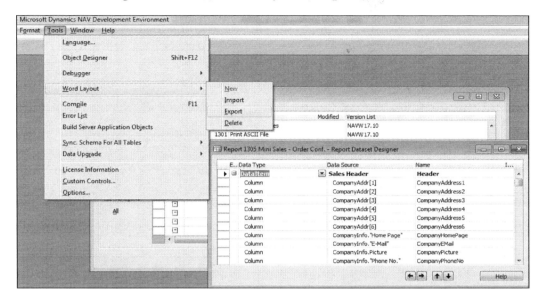

3. Next, navigate to **Tools | Word Layout | Export**. The following screenshot shows the **Edit – Report Layout Selection** window:

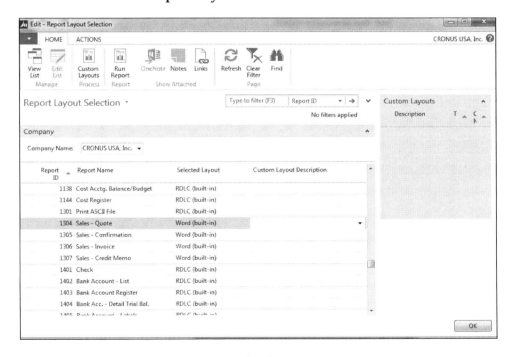

4. From here, NAV will prompt you for a place to save the **Word** layout. Open the Word document and apply any preformatted templates from Word.

5. When you're done with editing the layout, import it back to the NAV 2016 Development Environment, go into the designer mode for report `1305`, then navigate to **Tools** | **Word Layout** | **Import**.

    Please note that you're allowed to keep the RDLC layout or the Word layout. However, you will need to tell Dynamics NAV which layout to use. This can be controlled by going to **Report Layout Selection**.

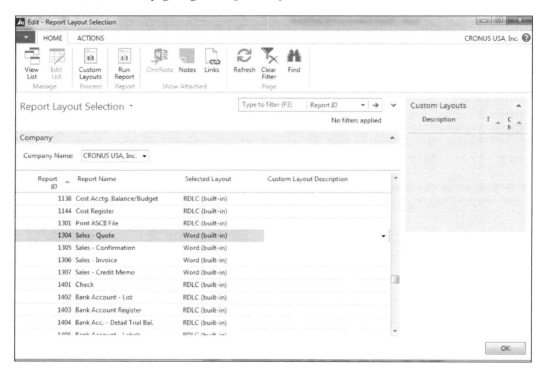

For a step-by-step tutorial on how to edit the Word Layout for NAV 2016, please visit the following link:

https://msdn.microsoft.com/en-us/library/
dn789519(v=nav.90).aspx

Upgrade automation – an overview

Upgrading your Dynamics NAV basically consists of three main parts:

- Convert the database to the new version
- Upgrade the application code to the new version
- Upgrade the data to the new version

Of the three processes, upgrading the application code and the data takes up the most time. This can cause companies to shy away from upgrading to the latest version of Dynamics NAV.

Upgrade automation – the application code

The first problem with upgrade is upgrading the application code. Prior to NAV 2016, to upgrade the application code, you had to export the objects of the previous version and the next version into text files. Then you would use any off-the-shelf software or freeware to merge the modifications done on the older version to the new version.

To remedy this, Microsoft introduced a PowerShell script called `Merge-NAVApplicationObject`. When you run this command using PowerShell, it will automatically merge the code for you. If the process detects a conflict or a problem that it cannot resolve on its own, it will place the conflicts into a separate area for you to resolve it manually.

What used to take hundreds of hours for a version upgrade can now be done in a fraction of the time!

 To learn more about upgrading the application code using PowerShell, please visit: `https://msdn.microsoft.com/en-us/library/dn271652(v=nav.90).aspx`

Upgrade automation – data

The second time-consuming portion of the upgrade is upgrading the data. Initially, after you're done with modifying the application, you had to run an upgrade toolkit that converted the data from the prior version to the new version. Depending on the size of the database file, the processes would take hours, even days per company!

To remedy this problem, Microsoft included four PowerShell commands (called cmdlets) in Dynamics NAV 2016 Administration Shell:

- `Start-NAVDataUpgrade`: This starts the process of the data upgrade.
- `Stop-NAVDataUpgrade`: This stops the upgrade process that's currently running.
- `Resume-NAVDataUpgrade`: This resumes the upgrade process that was stopped.
- `Get-NAVDataUpgrade`: This gets the status of the upgrade that's currently running.

With these new commands and PowerShell, you can complete the upgrade of data in a fraction of the time that it used to take.

To learn more about upgrading data through the Administration Shell, please visit:

`https://msdn.microsoft.com/en-us/library/dn762348(v=nav.90).aspx`

Enhancement in security and encryption

Microsoft's strategy to move from desktop computing to cloud computing is no secret. The release of Office 365 reinforces their cloud- and subscription-based strategy.

Microsoft introduced OAuth Authentication for OData and SOAP endpoints. This allows for more secure connections between custom apps, Dynamics NAV, and Office 365.

Changes to C/AL functions, data types, properties, and triggers

Dynamics NAV 2016 has introduced new functions, properties, and triggers. There are also some data types, functions, properties, and triggers that have changed or have been removed.

The following table provides an overview of all the changed properties and their replacements:

Property	Type of change	Description of the change
AutoFormatType	New	Includes the setting that enables you to create a custom format to add characters before and after a data value
AutoReplace	New	New property in XMLports
AutoSave	New	New property in XMLports
AutoUpdate	New	New property in XMLports
FunctionType Property (Upgrade Codeunits)	New	Used for automated upgrades described previously
PaperSourceDefaultPage	New	New report property
PaperSourceFirstPage	New	New report property
PaperSourceLastPage	New	New report property
DrillDownFormID	Changed	Name changed to DrillDownPageID
CardFormID	Changed	Name changed to CardPageID
LookupFormID	Changed	Name changed to LookupPageID
RunFormLink	Changed	Name changed to RunPageLink
RunFormOnRec	Changed	Name changed to RunPageOnRec
RunFormView	Changed	Name changed to RunPageView
SubFormLink	Changed	Name changed to SubPageLink
SubFormView	Changed	Name changed to SubPageView
UseReqForm	Changed	Name changed to UseRequestPage
TransactionType	Changed	In Microsoft Dynamics NAV 2013, the default transaction isolation level is REPEATABLE READ. In the earlier versions of Microsoft Dynamics NAV, it was SERIALIZABLE. This affects the FIND and NEXT function calls when the transaction type is Update, Snapshot, or UpdateNoLocks.
BottomMargin	Removed	–
PaperSourceOtherPages	Removed	–
SaveTableView	Removed	–

The following table provides an overview of all the changed triggers and their replacements:

Trigger	Type of change	Description of the change
OnAfterModifyRecord	New	New XMLport trigger
OnBeforeModifyRecord	New	New XMLport trigger
OnCreateHyperlink	Removed	–
OnHyperlink	Removed	–
OnPreSection	Removed	–
OnPostSection	Removed	–

The following table provides an overview of all the changed data types and their replacements:

Data type	Type of change	Description of the change
BLOB	Changed	If you call the CALCFIELDS function (Record) on a BLOB field, you will get the value of BLOB, that is, in the database, and not the value that you wrote to BLOB OutStream.
Code	Changed	The Code data type supports Unicode. Limits are not enforced on the length of a Code variable.
Text	Changed	Text supports Unicode in Microsoft Dynamics NAV 2013. Limits are not enforced on the length of a Text variable. You can specify a maximum length in the C/AL Globals or C/AL Locals window when you create a variable, but it is not required.
Binary	Removed	Binary was used to store fixed lengths of binary data in a record. BLOB should now be used for this purpose.

The following table provides an overview of all the changed functions and their replacements:

Function	Type of change	Description of the change
SETAUTOCALCFIELDS(Record)	New	New function to calculate FlowFields at the same time that you retrieve them from the database
CURRENTEXECUTIONMODE	New	New function
STARTSESSION	New	New function
STOPSESSION	New	New function
CALCFIELDS (Record)	Changed	The CALCFIELDS execution is decoupled from the Microsoft Dynamics NAV SIFT index definitions
CALCSUM (FieldRef)	Changed	The CALCFIELDS execution is decoupled from the Microsoft Dynamics NAV SIFT index definitions
CALCSUMS (Record)	Changed	The CALCFIELDS execution is decoupled from the Microsoft Dynamics NAV SIFT index definitions
COUNT (Record)	Changed	The COUNT function does not always ignore security filters. It adheres to the SecurityFiltering property.
COUNT (RecordRef)	Changed	The COUNT function does not always ignore security filters. It adheres to the SecurityFiltering property.
CREATETOTALS	Changed	Redundant in Microsoft Dynamics NAV 2013 reports. We recommend that you use the SUM function in Visual Studio instead.
Debugger functions	Changed	New functions have been introduced
INSERT (Record) and INSERT (RecordRef)	Changed	You cannot call the INSERT function on a record for table 2000000001, the object table, or table 2000000006, the company table
MODIFY (Record) and MODIFY (RecordRef)	Changed	Microsoft Dynamics NAV 2013 does not let you modify the database by using an old copy of a record. You cannot call the MODIFY function on a record for table 2000000001, the object table, or table 2000000006, the company table.

Function	Type of change	Description of the change
DELETE (Record) and DELETE(RecordRef)	Changed	You cannot call the DELETE function on a record for table 2000000001, the object table, or table 2000000006, the company table.
RENAME	Changed	Microsoft Dynamics NAV 2013 does not let you modify the database by using an old copy of a record.
FormHandler	Changed	Name changed to PageHandler
ModalFormHandler	Changed	Name changed to ModalPageHandler
ISSERVICETIER	Changed	Obsolete in Microsoft Dynamics NAV 2013, but still supported. This function always returns true.
RECORDLEVELLOCKING (Record and RecordRef)	Changed	Not used in Microsoft Dynamics NAV 2013. The function is still available and compiles, but always returns true.
READCONSISTENCY (Record and RecordRef)	Changed	Not used in Microsoft Dynamics NAV 2013. The function is still available and compiles. Because Microsoft Dynamics NAV 2013 uses SQL Server's locking mechanisms and does not use snapshots like the earlier versions of Microsoft Dynamics NAV did, the return value is always false.
SETCURRENTKEY (Record)	Changed	In Microsoft Dynamics NAV 2013, you do not have to define keys only for the SIFT indexes. Fewer SIFT indices and fewer Microsoft Dynamics NAV keys can improve performance.
BEEP	Removed	–
COMMANDLINE	Removed	–
COUNTAPPROX	Removed	–
ENVIRON	Removed	–
EXPORT (BLOB)	Removed	–
EXPORTOBJECTS	Removed	Not supported in Microsoft Dynamics NAV 2013. Use the finsql.exe executable with the ExportObjects command instead.
IMPORT (BLOB)	Removed	–

Function	Type of change	Description of the change
IMPORTOBJECTS	Removed	Not supported in Microsoft Dynamics NAV 2013. Use the `finsql.exe` executable with the `ImportObjects` command instead.
LANGUAGE	Removed	–
NEWPAGE	Removed	–
NEWPAGEPERRECORD	Removed	–
OBJECTID	Removed	–
OSVERSION	Removed	–
PAGENO	Removed	–
PAPERSOURCE	Removed	–
SAVEASHTML	Removed	–
SAVEASXML	Removed	–
SETPERMISSIONFILTER (Record)	Removed	Not supported in Microsoft Dynamics NAV 2013. Instead, you change the `SecurityFiltering` property from `Validated` to `Filtered`.
SETPERMISSIONFILTER (RecordRef)	Removed	Not supported in Microsoft Dynamics NAV 2013. Instead, you change the `SecurityFiltering` property from `Validated` to `Filtered`.
SHELL	Removed	–
SHOWOUTPUT	Removed	–
SYNCHRONIZEALLLOGINS	Removed	–
SYNCHRONIZESINGLELOGIN	Removed	–
TOTALSCAUSEDBY	Removed	–
URL	Removed	–
VARIABLEACTIVE	Removed	–
YIELD	Removed	–

The following table provides an overview of all the changed objects and their replacements:

Objects	Type of change	Description of the change
The Query object	New	New object type
Test Pages	New	New objects and functions
Dataports	Removed	–
Forms	Removed	–
The RequestOptionsForm system variable	Removed	–

.NET interoperability

Dynamics NAV can be extended with the .NET Framework assemblies. We can reference assemblies and call types directly from the C/AL code of Dynamics NAV objects, such as pages and codeunits. Dynamics NAV objects can also subscribe to events that are published by the .NET Framework types.

Enhancements in RoleTailored client control add-ins

Control add-ins have been enhanced with the following features:

- **Additional data types are supported with database binding**: Dynamics NAV 2016 now supports data types, such as DateTime, Boolean, Char, Decimal, Int32, Int64, and Guid. Data binding and firing of the OnControlAddIn C/AL trigger is enabled by implementing respective interfaces.

- **Methods and properties can be exposed to C/AL code**: To extend user interface controls on a page, methods and properties can be exposed in a control add-in assembly so that they can be called by the C/AL code on page triggers.

- **Control add-ins can be sized**: We can now specify an area of a page that a control add-in occupies, both with a fixed size or by setting the control add-in to resize as the page window resizes in the Dynamics NAV Windows client.

IT changes

Several changes regarding IT have been introduced with the release of Dynamics NAV, including the following:

- Easier installation and deployment
- Easier administration
- New clients
- New services

Dynamics NAV Server administration

Dynamics NAV 2016 includes a new server administration tool for administering Dynamics NAV Server.

It is a snap-in for the Microsoft Management Console. When installing the server option, the server administration tool is a default feature.

Once the server option is installed, you will find it on your Windows **Start** menu with all the other Dynamics NAV components installed on the same machine.

From the server administration tool, we will have a clear picture of all the Dynamics NAV instances running on the machine, their version, status, and configuration (name, the database to which the instance connects, ports for the different types of services, and so on).

From the server administration tool, we can add or remove instances (we can even add instances running on a different server), edit their settings, start or stop the services, and so on.

Windows PowerShell cmdlets

Dynamics NAV 2016 comes with a set of PowerShell cmdlets that allow us to perform administrative tasks on our Dynamics NAV installation.

You will also find it on your Windows **Start** menu with all the other Dynamics NAV components installed on the same machine.

When you run the cmdlets, a list of all the available `cmdlet` command types for Dynamics NAV will be displayed.

NAV 2016 introduced some new cmdlets. These cmdlets and their descriptions are taken from the Microsoft MSDN website.

The following are the cmdlets for merging Application Objects for an upgrade as described under the *Upgrade automation – an overview* section in this chapter:

Cmdlets	Description
Compare-NAVApplicationObject	Compares text files with Microsoft Dynamics NAV application objects and then calculates the delta between the two versions. The result of the comparison is a number of text files with the calculated delta.
Get-NAVApplicationObjectProperty	Gets Microsoft Dynamics NAV application object properties from the specified application object text files.
Join-NAVApplicationObjectFile	Combines multiple application object files into one text file.
Merge-NAVApplicationObject	Compares the changes that have been made to the application objects between two versions of Microsoft Dynamics NAV, and applies the difference to a third set of application objects. The result of the merge is a number of text files with the merged application objects. Any conflicts that the cmdlet cannot merge are identified in conflict files.
Set-NAVApplicationObjectProperty	Sets Microsoft Dynamics NAV application object properties in the specified application object text files.
Split-NAVApplicationObjectFile	Splits a text file that contains two or more application objects into separate text files for each application object.
Update-NAVApplicationObject	Applies a set of deltas to specified application objects. The files that describe the delta are generated by the Compare-NAVApplicationObject cmdlet.

The following are the cmdlets to upgrade data as described under the *Upgrade automation – an overview* section of this chapter:

Cmdlets	Description
Start-NAVDataUpgrade	Starts the data upgrade process for upgrading data in the business (tenant) database.
Resume-NAVDataUpgrade	Resumes a data upgrade process that has been suspended because of an error.
Stop-NAVDataUpgrade	Stops a data upgrade process.
Get-NAVDataUpgrade	Gets information about the data upgrade process that is currently running or the last completed data upgrade process.

The following are the cmdlets to update captions in Application Object Files. These are very useful when you are trying to put in (or take out) additional languages for your Dynamics NAV software:

Cmdlets	Description
Export-NAVApplicationObjectLanguage	Exports captions from specified text files with Microsoft Dynamics NAV application objects. The captions are exported to text files.
Import-NAVApplicationObjectLanguage	Imports strings in a specified language into text files that contain Microsoft Dynamics NAV application objects.
Join-NAVApplicationObjectLanguageFile	Combines multiple text files with captions for Microsoft Dynamics NAV application objects into one text file.
Remove-NAVApplicationObjectLanguage	Deletes captions in a specified language from Microsoft Dynamics NAV application objects.
Split-NAVApplicationObjectLanguageFile	Splits a text file that contains multilanguage captions for two or more application objects into separate text files for each application object.
Test-NAVApplicationObjectLanguageFile	This cmdlet tests captions in Microsoft Dynamics NAV application objects to test and validate that the strings have been translated for the specified languages.

The following are the cmdlets for the Office 365 Administration setup with Dynamics NAV:

Cmdlets	Description
Set-NavSingleSignOnWithOffice365	Performs configuration changes to support a single sign-on with Office 365 for a Microsoft Dynamics NAV Windows client and a Microsoft Dynamics NAV Web client.
New-NavSelfSignedCertificate	Facilitates the creating of self-signed certificates that are used to protect communication between a NAV service and a Microsoft Dynamics NAV Web client.

Prior to NAV 2013 R2, you were allowed to backup data from a specific company, then restore that data in a completely separate database in a completely separate environment. In NAV 2013 R2, with the introduction of mutli-tenant, backups by company were no longer available.

This made it extremely hard for NAV partners or customers to move data from a specific company to another environment. You had to take the entire SQL database and replace the database in your development environment. Testing based on scenario data became almost impossible. This is especially frustrating when you only want to replace the data, and not the application objects.

A lot of developers were relieved when these cmdlets were introduced in place of the company backups. The following are the cmdlets for importing and exporting NAV data:

Cmdlets	Description
Export-NAVData	Exports data from a Microsoft Dynamics NAV database. You can export company-specific data, and you can choose to include global data, application data, or application objects.
Import-NAVData	Imports data into a Microsoft Dynamics NAV database from a file. You can import the entire data in the file, or you can choose to include specific companies, global data, application data, or application objects. Note that you can only import an application into an empty database.

Cmdlets	Description
Get-NAVDataFile	Gets information from a file that has been exported from a Microsoft Dynamics NAV database. The extracted information includes the types of data that the file contains and company names.

Summary

Dynamics NAV 2016 introduces several changes compared to the previous versions of the application. These changes are applicable to all the application areas; there have been changes to the client in the way it accesses the application, to the functionality, to the way development is done, and also there have been changes related to IT.

In this chapter, we went through most of the relevant changes for an implementation introduced in Dynamics NAV 2016.

In the next chapter, we will see some general considerations about Dynamics NAV, such as the data model used in the application, the way posting routines are developed, and the SIFT technology.

3
Dynamics NAV – General Considerations

Knowing the Dynamics NAV philosophy of how things are done is an important aspect of successfully implementing Dynamics NAV for any organization.

This is also important for users and people working in a company that use or will use Dynamics NAV as their ERP. They have to know how to do their job in Dynamics NAV and be especially aware of the consequences of what they do.

Everyone involved in the implementation needs to fully understand the way NAV works; not only because they are the people responsible for transferring that knowledge to users, but also because they will most likely be designing and developing new functionalities and modifying existing ones. For this, it is important to use the same philosophy Dynamics NAV uses in all its standard functionalities. Breaking away from the core philosophies of Dynamics NAV will confuse your end users.

In this chapter, we will cover the following topics:

- The structure of Microsoft Dynamics NAV 2016
- The way information flows in Microsoft Dynamics NAV 2016
- Other general considerations

The data model

If you have never worked with Microsoft Dynamics NAV and have started playing around with it, there are a few words you will see over and over again including setup, journal, posting group, post, document, entry, dimension, and so on. You may not have a clue about what all these mean or what they are used for. But don't worry, we will explain it all!

Dynamics NAV is structured into different functional areas, namely **Financial Management**, **Sales & Marketing**, **Purchase**, **Warehouse**, **Manufacturing**, **Jobs**, **Resource Planning**, **Service**, and **Human Resources**.

Each of the functional areas has its own setup, where the behavior of each of the areas is defined. A general setup also exists on the **Administration** menu.

Master data

Each of the functional areas has a master data table. The Customer table is the master data table for the Sales & Marketing area. The `G/L Account` table is the master data table for the Financial Management area. There are also other master tables and secondary master tables, which relate to the main master table in a functional area. For instance, the `Customer` table has quite a few secondary master data tables such as **Contacts**, **Bank Accounts**, **Ship-to Addresses**, or **Cross-References**. They are defined in this way because a single customer may have multiple contacts, bank accounts, ship-to addresses, or cross-references.

The secondary master data of a main master data register can be found in the **Navigate** tab (although not all items in the **Navigate** tab are secondary master data):

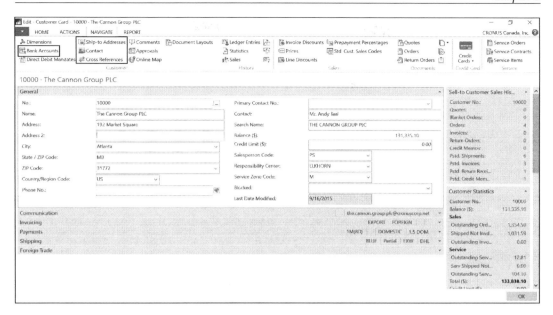

So far we've seen what we could call core master data tables, which hold the basic information in a functional area, and we've seen that these tables may have some secondary master data tables associated with them.

A different kind of master data also exists in Dynamics NAV. We could call it information helper master data tables. A few examples of this kind of information are locations, currencies, payment terms, payment methods, units of measure, item-tracking codes, and so on.

Some helper master data may have its own secondary master data. Locations have zones and bins, and currencies have exchange rates.

Documents

Several documents exist in Dynamics NAV, such as sales documents (quotes, orders, invoices, return orders, and credit memos), purchase documents (quotes, orders, invoices, return orders, and credit memos), warehouse documents (transfer orders, receipts, put-aways, shipments, and picks), and manufacturing documents (production orders).

A document combines information from different master data tables and is one of the entry points to a transaction.

For example, a **Sales Order** document combines information from the `Customer` table (the customer that buys), the `Item` table (the items that are being sold), the `Resources` table (the resources that will provide the services the company offers), and other information related to a sales order.

When the sales order is processed, it will lead to one or more transactions such as `Item` transactions (the stock of the item will be reduced with the quantity being sold) and **General Ledger** transactions (accounting entries will be created when the sales invoice is posted).

A document always has a header-lines structure presented in a single screen. In the header section, we will find general information that applies to the entire document, such as **Sell-to Customer No**. In a `Sales Order` document, we will find the status of the document, or the shipment date. In the lines section, we will find detailed information about the document, such as the list of all the items being sold in a sales order:

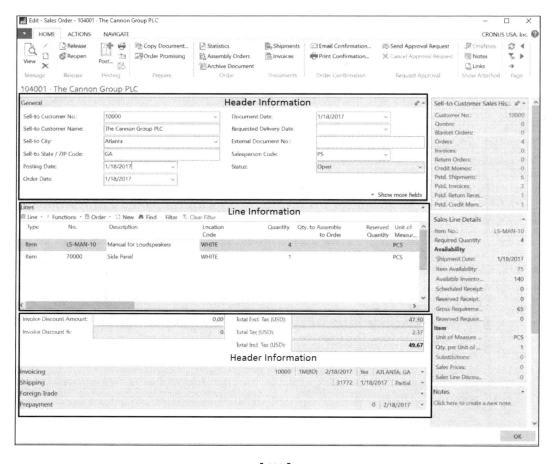

Under the **Actions** tab, you will always find one or more printing options to print the currently selected document. A printed document in Dynamics NAV looks somewhat like the following screenshot:

Printed documents in Dynamics NAV have all the common information that is needed. Most companies that implement Dynamics NAV ask their partners to modify the layout of the printed documents, at least those that are sent (either as a PDF file or as a printed paper copy) to their customers or vendors.

Besides the **Print** option, you will also find the **Post** action in a document, both in the **Home** tab (where the most common posting actions are found) and in the **Actions** tab (where all posting actions can be found):

Posting is the most important action in Dynamics NAV.

Before a document has been posted, it is a document for which the action that is supposed to be done, is still undone. That is, a non-posted Sales Order is an order for which the items that were ordered have not yet been shipped or the services that had been requested by the customer have not been provided. You can see non-posted documents as a work area in which the user can enter the required information and post it when it is ready.

When you post a document, you are telling Dynamics NAV that the actions for the document has been completed (a sales order has been shipped, the items of a production order have been produced, a purchase order has been received, a sales invoice has been accounted for, and so on).

The posting action modifies the original document (to state that it has been posted) and creates new documents, that is, posted documents. For example, when a sales order is posted with the **Ship** option selected, `Posted Sales Shipment` is created, and when a sales invoice is posted, `Posted Sales Invoice` is created.

You will find posted documents from a Dynamics NAV functional area under the **Archive** category of the corresponding area:

Sales & Marketing, Archive

History
Sales Quote Archives
Sales Order Archives
Sales Return Order Archives
Posted Sales Invoices
Posted Sales Shipments
Posted Sales Credit Memos
Posted Return Receipts
G/L Registers
Customer Ledger Entries
Detailed Cust. Ledg. Entries
Value Entries

Marketing

History
Campaign Entries
Opportunity Entries
Interaction Log Entries

Journals

In Dynamics NAV, you will see journals all over the place, in every single functional area. Just to name a few, if you move around the **Departments** menu, you will find a lot of different types of journals such as **General Journal**, **Payment Journal**, **Item Journal**, and so on:

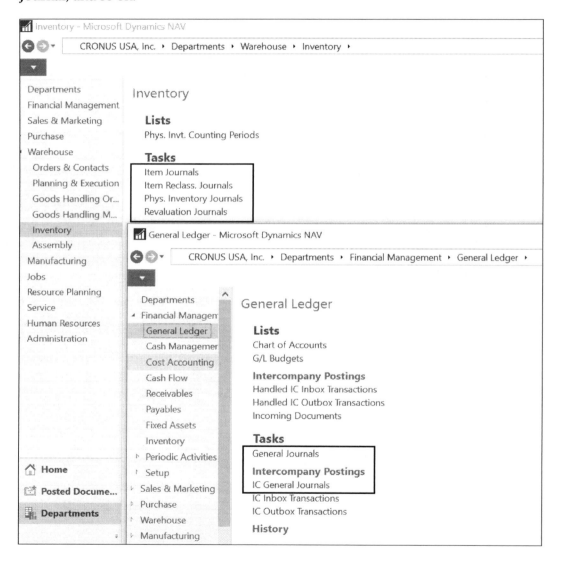

Journals are where all kinds of transactions in Dynamics NAV, such as accounting transactions, sales transactions, item transactions, and so on, take place. When you post a document, such as a sales order, NAV will use the journals internally to post to the appropriate ledger tables.

You can actually write down all the company transactions in journals and post them there (journals also have a posting action) without using any kind of document. In fact, some companies follow this method, although we would not recommend it.

Imagine you want to post a sales invoice in which you have sold an item, a resource, and a fixed asset. Using the appropriate G/L accounts, you have to do the following:

- Post all the transactions by going to **Item Journal** and posting the necessary movements to reduce the stock
- Go to **Resource Journal** and post the necessary services associated with the order
- Go to **FA Journal** and post the reduction of the fixed assets associated with the order
- Go to **General Journal** and post the accounting transaction of the sale and accounts receivable

That's quite a lot of work to just make a sale and would surely make your accounting department angrier and grumpier.

This is one of the benefits of having documents in Dynamics NAV. It goes to the appropriate journals depending on the document and concepts used in the document. This creates necessary journal lines and posts these various journals.

So why are journals important to users if all the important transactions are done using documents? The reason is there are always transactions that do not have a document, so a journal will have to be used.

Among the journals, the one that is the most used in Dynamics NAV is probably **General Journal**. It is mainly used to post accounting transactions. There are many accounting transactions, such as salary payment to employees and many others, that a company has to make, and the company does not have a document to make them (not in Dynamics NAV at least).

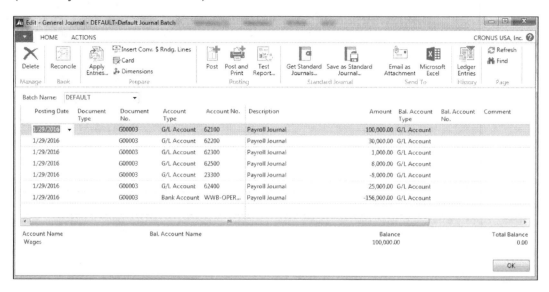

Another journal that is commonly used is **Item Journal**, where stock increases and decreases not associated with a document can be registered. What happens if an item is broken and thrown away? There is no document in Dynamics NAV to enter such a transaction. Well, the place to actually do this is **Item Journal**, where the user can post a stock decrease for the item that is broke.

Many journals that we've seen on the Dynamics NAV menu are actually the same journals, but they show and let the user enter different information and have preselected options and built-in functionalities depending on what the journal is meant for. For example, **Item Journal**, **Phys. Inventory journal**, and **Output Journal** actually rely on the same real journal, that is, **Item Journal**.

Phys. Inventory Journal is meant to register the system inventory differences when a physical count is completed. It is an item transaction; that's why it's built on top of **Item Journal** but has some differences.

In a physical inventory, we count how many units we have in the warehouse. We know how many units we've counted, but we do not know how many units are registered in Dynamics NAV. That's why in **Phys. Inventory Journal**, we inform the real quantity we've counted (in the **Qty. (Phys. Inventory)** field), and the functionality of the journal decides whether to positively or negatively adjust the inventory in the warehouse.

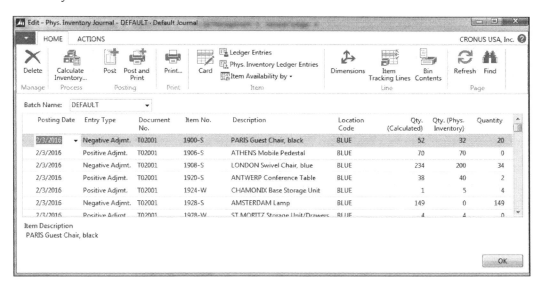

Output Journal is meant to register the stock increase of a manufactured item in the system when a production order is finished. It is again an item transaction and that's why it is built on top of **Item Journal**. However, the user will have to provide some extra information that is not usually entered in other kinds of item transactions, such as **Production Order** that is being posted, **Operation** in **Production Order**, or **Scrap Quantity**. The **Output Journal** line shows the user the fields that they have to fill in to post this transaction. These fields are not shown in other item journals.

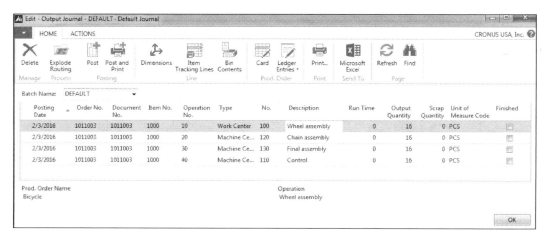

Once a journal is filled in with all the needed transactions, it has to be posted. Once it is posted, entries will be created and the journal lines will disappear (except for those that belong to **Recurring Journal**).

Entries

Entries are the result of a posted transaction and they are always related to a master record.

In the following table, you will find the most important entries in Dynamics NAV. You will also see the master tables they are related to:

Entry table	Related master table
G/L Entry	G/L Account
Cust. Ledger Entry	Customer
Vendor Ledger Entry	Vendor
Item Ledger Entry	Item
Res. Ledger Entry	Resource
Bank Account Ledger Entry	Bank Account

Entry table	Related master table
VAT Entry	Customer or Vendor
Job Ledger Entry	Job

Entries are created by a journal. **G/L Entries** are created by **General Journal**, which can also create **Cust. Ledger Entries**, **Vendor Ledger Entries**, **Bank Account Ledger Entries**, or **VAT Entries**. **Item Ledger Entries** are created by **Item Journal**.

In the following diagram, you can see which journal is responsible for creating which entry:

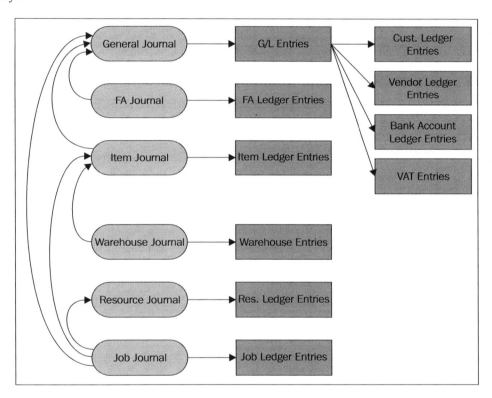

The image also shows that some journals, if needed, may call some other journals. So, the final result of the transaction will not only be the corresponding ledger entries for the journal that is being posted, but also ledger entries corresponding to a different journal.

For example, when posting an **Item Journal** transaction, Dynamics NAV will automatically post costs (depending on **Entry Type**) to the **Inventory** account, the **Inventory Adjustment** account, or the **Cost of Goods Sold** (**COGS**) account. The **General Journal** lines will be created and their posting route will be called from **Item Journal**.

Ledger entries in Dynamics NAV are the result of a transaction. They are the final stage of the transaction. In general, once a ledger entry has been created, it cannot be modified or deleted.

However, there is some information that must be updated on the posted ledger entries. For example, after you post a sales invoice, at some point the invoice will be paid if you want to stay in business. Therefore, **Cust. Ledger Entry** will have to be updated to reflect the new remaining amount for the invoice.

This is managed in Dynamics NAV using detailed ledger entries. Most entry tables in Dynamics NAV have a related detailed entry. Some information in the entry table is actually a calculation of the related detailed entries. So, there is no need to modify the original entry or even the related detailed entry. Changes are resolved adding new detailed ledger entries. This will allow the accounting department to have full traceability on the number of times the invoice is paid and/or any credits that has been applied to the invoice.

You will find only two exceptions to the norm:

- Fields used for the system's internal purposes (such as the open field found on some entry tables).
- Some specific fields that the user can modify manually, such as the **Due Date** field in customer and vendor entries or the **Shipment Agent Code** field in the shipments' header. Changes in these fields are handled in special codeunits.

Creating ledger entries

Let's see how this actually works step by step:

1. Using the CRONUS demonstration company, create a new sales invoice for customer number **10000, The Cannon Group PLC**. Create a line on the invoice for the item, **1000**, and **Bicycle**. The quantity of the line will be 1 PCS. You will find this in the following path:

   ```
   Departments/Sales & Marketing/Order Processing/Sales Invoices
   ```

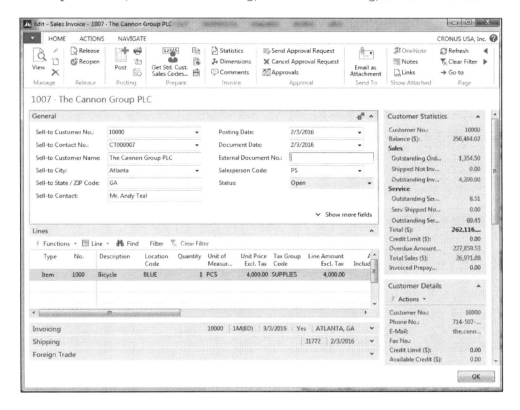

2. Post **Sales Invoice**.

3. Open **Customer Card** for customer number 10000, The Cannon Group PLC.

4. Click on the **Navigate** tab and then on **Ledger Entries** (or press *Ctrl + F7*).

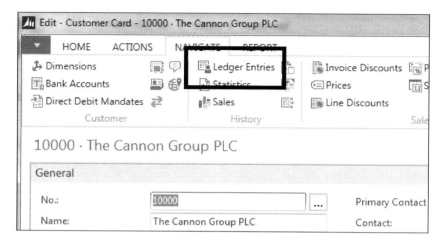

5. Locate the **Cust. Ledger Entry** value that corresponds to the invoice that has been posted. In this example, it is **Entry No. 2135**. The **Original Amount** for this entry is **4.000,00 with 200.00 sales tax**. The total of 4,200 is the same as the actual **Remaining Amount**. Yes, CRONUS sells expensive bicycles.

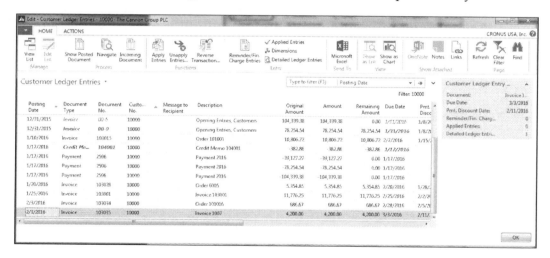

6. Open **Cash Receipt Journal**. You will find it in the following path:

```
Departments/Financial Management/Cash Management/Cash Receipt
Journals
```

7. Create a line in the invoice to indicate the partial payment of 2000 that was made February 16, 2016, using the following steps:

- Select **Payment** as the **Document Type**
- Select **Customer** as the **Account Type**
- Select customer number **10000** as the **Account No**
- Select **Invoice** as the **Applies-to Doc. Type**
- Select the invoice that has been posted on the **Applies-to Doc. No** field.

In this example, it is invoice **103035**.

Note that since the amount of the original invoice is **5.000**, the system has automatically set up the **Amount** field of the payment to **-5.000**. Change it to **-2.000** to partially pay the invoice. The **Amount** value in the **Cash Receipt Journal** field is negative because the payment of a sales invoice is, in accounting language, a credit amount and is translated in Dynamics NAV as a negative amount.

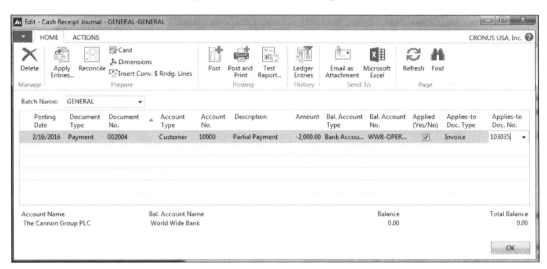

1. Post **Cash Receipt Journal**.
2. Open **Customer Card** for customer number **10000,** The Cannon Group PLC.
3. Click on the **Navigate** tab and then on **Ledger Entries** (or press *Ctrl + F7*).

Locate the **Cust. Ledger Entry** value that corresponds to the invoice that has been posted in the previous steps. You will also see **Cust. Ledger Entry** that corresponds to **Payment** we have just posted.

Note that **Remaining Amount** for **Invoice** has been updated after we posted the partial payment. **Remaining Amount** now shows **2.200,00**.

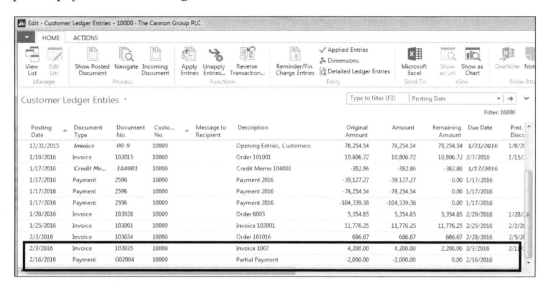

1. Click on the **Remaining Amount** field for the invoice.
2. The **View – Detailed Cust. Ledger Entries** page is opened.

There are two detailed entries for our **Invoice entry**:

*   The first one is the initial entry that corresponds to the **Invoice** entry with **Document No. 103035**

*   The second one is the entry that corresponds to the **Payment** entry that has **Document No. G02004**, which has been applied to the invoice

Remaining Amount for the invoice entry is the sum of these two detailed entries: **4.400 + (-2.000) = 2.200**.

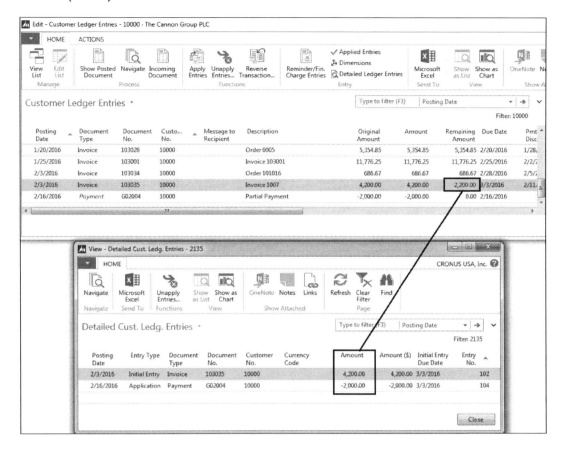

Not all **Ledger Entries** tables have a **Detailed Ledger Entry** table.

In the following image, you can see which **Ledger Entry** tables have a **Detailed Ledger Entry** table and the name of that **Detailed Ledger Entry** table:

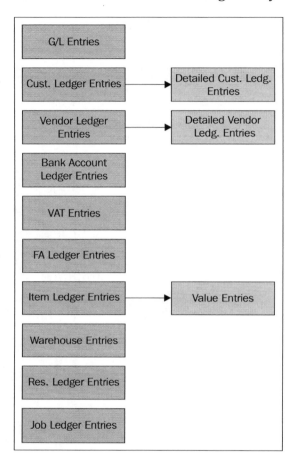

Combining all concepts

So far, we've covered master data, documents, journals, and entries. As we talked about each of these concepts, we explained a little bit of how they were connected to each other. Now we will see the general model that combines all four concepts.

The general data model looks somewhat like the following diagram:

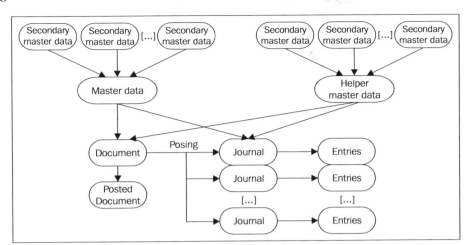

Master data and **Helper master data** are combined in **Document**. When **Document** is posted, its corresponding **Posted Document** is created. Also, **Journal** lines are created and posted. The **Journal** lines will end up in different **Entries**.

Master data and **Helper master data** can also be combined directly on **Journal** without using any document. These **Journal** lines will also end up in different **Entries**.

No save button

Dynamics NAV does not have any kind of **save** button anywhere in the application. So, data is saved into the database as soon as the user leaves the field.

Likewise, a record is inserted in its table right after the field (or fields) of the primary key. Some pages such as **Sales Line** and the different journals have the `DelayedInsert` property set to `Yes`, which means that the record won't be inserted until the user moves the cursor to the next line or the next record.

The main advantage

The major advantage is that users can create any card (for instance, **Customer Card**), any document (for instance, **Sales Order**), or any other kind of data without knowing all the information that is needed. Let's explain this with an example.

A new customer has to be inserted into the database. For Dynamics NAV, it is mandatory to fill in some information to actually be able to post any transaction with the customer. The mandatory fields are **Gen. Bus. Posting Group** and **Customer Posting Group**.

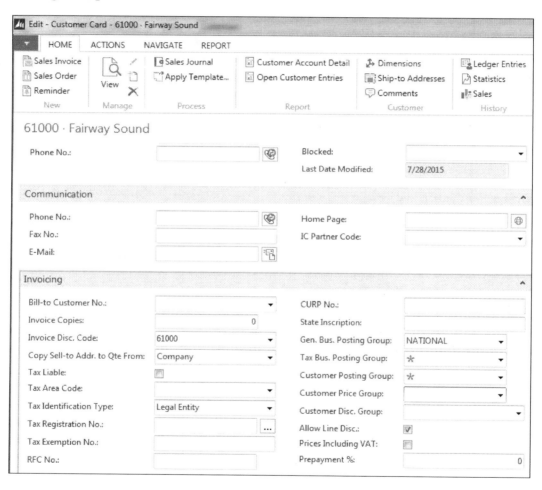

As you can see in the previous image, the **Customer Posting Group** field has not been filled for this customer. It doesn't matter right now; you can leave the card without losing the rest of the information that was introduced and come back to the card when you have figured out the **Customer Posting Group** that has to be used with this customer. The not-losing-the-rest-of-the-information part is important.

Imagine that there actually was a **Save** button; you would spend a few minutes filling in all the information and at the end, hit the **Save** button. At that moment, the system carries out some checks and finds out that one field is missing. It throws you a message saying that the customer card cannot be saved. So you basically have two options:

- To lose the information introduced until that moment, find out the posting group for the customer, and start all over again.
- To cheat. Fill the field with some wrong value so that the system actually lets you save the data. Of course, you can come back to the card and change the data once you've found out the right one.

Nothing will prevent any other user to post a transaction with the customer in the meantime.

When is the data verified?

How does Dynamics NAV verify the data that the user enters? Certainly not by someone looking over their shoulder. The data is verified when it is needed. In most cases, information in the master tables is needed when selecting a record either in a document or in a journal line, or when the posting routines are run.

Since customer number 61000 has a relevant field missing on its card, if you try to select this customer in **Sales Order**, you will get a runtime error that will say **Customer Posting Group must have a value in Customer No.=61000. It cannot be zero or empty**.

Some other data, such as the posting dates, will be checked when posting a transaction. You can set up your Dynamics NAV solution so that you only allow your user to post transactions using a specific range of dates. Posting dates can be restricted for the whole company or only to certain users.

Posting dates are an example of data that the system checks while posting a transaction. If posting dates are not allowed, an error message will be thrown saying **Posting Date is not within your range of allowed posting dates**.

The main drawback

There is one main drawback of validating the data this way. The problem will not occur until you try to post. An example would be when we have to post a shipment; the shipping agent is waiting with his truck and Dynamics NAV throws an error message because someone up the chain didn't properly do their job.

Problems like this can be mitigated by setting default values to the mandatory fields through modifications or through templates. However, the company should have the proper process or guideline in place for people to follow; the users should be responsible for their work. Basically, accountability is required.

In a way, this "drawback" is a benefit because there's no place for people to hide. Mistakes are reflected in a relatively short timeframe within your organization and you will be able to weed out who's good and who's not.

In our case, if the truck leaves and the warehouse person has to fill in the paperwork manually, you can go yell at the person responsible for setting up the data.

The posting routines

Dynamics NAV has one big key word (among others), called **post**. If you read the word post anywhere in an application or see the following icon, it means that if you click on the button, a routine will be run and this will lead to posted documents and posted entries that are on their last stage. It is the trusted data that won't change anymore. This is important for many IT and accounting audits.

As explained in *The data model* section of this chapter, Dynamics NAV has some tables called Entries (G/L Entries, Cust. Ledger Entries, Vendor Ledger Entries, Item Ledger Entries, and so on) that correspond to transactions related to master data. The only way to insert data into entry tables is through the posting routines. Numerous validations are carried out during posting routines as the system has to check whether all data is correct and that no inconsistencies exist.

One unique posting process usually creates multiple entries, and all of the entries are related and consistent to each other. For instance, when you post a sales invoice, the system needs to create the following entries (depending on what the invoice includes):

- **Customer Entries**: It is used to track all the transactions related to the customer.

- **Item Entries**: It is used if an invoice contains the items of which you need to reduce the stock of, plus if in the future you need to track all the transactions related to one particular item.

- **VAT (Tax) Entries**: You will need to report to the tax authorities, all VAT (tax) charged to your customers. Therefore, the VAT (tax) amount charged on every invoice has to be tracked.

- **General Ledger Entries**: Accounting rules say that when you issue an invoice, you have to record the related amounts on certain accounts. Dynamics NAV does this for you by creating G/L entries.

As explained in *The data model* section of this chapter, entries are created by reading information from a journal line. Therefore, if you choose to post a document, the first step that the system must follow is to create all the related journal lines. Then all the related entries have to be created. The following diagram shows the general schema:

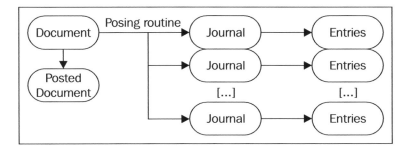

Posted data cannot be modified (or deleted)

Out of the box, posted data cannot be modified or deleted. Posted documents can be deleted, but only after a paper copy has been printed for manual archiving.

Not being able to modify or delete ledger entries data is one of the most basic requirements of any legitimate accounting software.

Frankly, no self-respecting accounting software will allow you to modify ledger entry data. Think about how trustworthy your financial data is if your auditors found out you can modify the financial ledger!

This may cause some frustration for the Dynamics NAV users who are used to a home-grown system or other off-the-shelf accounting software, where they can just void the data without any repercussions. This is usually not an issue when you only have one person using the system because they know exactly why a transaction needed to be "voided". When your business grows to a certain size, just voiding transactions will not only raise a slew of questions from your auditors, but also lead to inconsistent financial statements for you to run your business.

As mentioned earlier, there are a few exceptions where posted documents can be deleted or fields changed; they are as follows:

- Posted documents can be deleted after you have printed a paper copy for your ever hungry file cabinet. This feature cannot be used as a way to undo the document, as only the document is deleted but the corresponding ledger entries remain in the database.

 This feature was introduced back when database size was an issue. Document records were deleted to keep the size of the database small. However, with the current technology, this is not really an issue. Typically, I advise companies to not delete posted documents.

- Some specific fields can be modified by a user manually, such as the **Due Date** field in customer and vendor entries or **Shipment Agent Code** in the shipments header. Changes to these fields are handled by special codeunits.

You'll notice that none of the preceding exceptions deal with any dollar value or the transaction date. This is strictly implemented to maintain the integrity of your financial data!

As we have seen in the earlier sections of this chapter, when one document is posted, the result consists of several entries that are all consistent to each other and to the rest of the application data.

If data cannot be changed, how can users correct a mistake in the data? The solution is to post reversed documents or entries so that the net effect of the transaction is zero. This will give you a complete paper trail of what happened to a transaction and what actions are done to "void" that transaction.

Navigating through your data

In Dynamics NAV, it is extremely easy to navigate through data, remove default filters set by the system, and set your own filters to find or analyze your own data.

The Navigate functionality

You have probably seen the following **Navigate** button in many places in Dynamics NAV:

You can actually see it on every single page that shows posted transactions, either in **Posted Documents** and/or in ledger entry pages.

When you push the **Navigate** button, a page will be display magically showing all the related posted documents and entries to the record from where you hit the **Navigate** button. This means that if you are ever wondering which transactions were related to an entry, Dynamics NAV will do the hard work for you and find anything related to that particular document number.

Earlier in this chapter, we created and posted **Sales Invoice**. If we open **Posted Sales Invoice** and hit **Navigate**, the following navigation page will be opened:

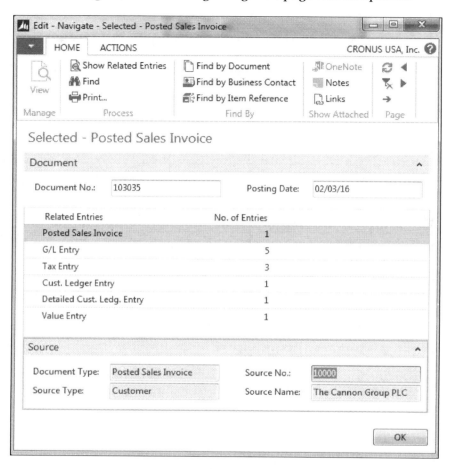

The navigation page is telling us that we can find a **Posted Sales Invoice** document, five **G/L Entry** records, three **Tax Entry** (VAT) records, one **Cust. Ledger Entry**, one **Detailed Cust. Ledg. Entry**, and one **Value Entry** table related to the **Document No.** field with the value of **103035** on the **Posting Date** field with the value of **2/03/2016**.

Basically, when you posted this invoice, all these documents and entries were created.

If we want to take a look at any of the documents or entries, we have to select the information we want to look at and click on the **Show** button.

> The **Navigate** feature is used within **Document No.** and **Posting Date**. The **Navigate** feature will show all the posted documents and entries that have used the same **Document No.** and **Posting Date**. If you use the same numbering rules for, let's say, sales invoices and purchase invoices, the **Navigate** functionality may show you information about all the **Sales Invoice** and **Purchase Invoice** tables that have the same **Document No.** and **Posting Date**, although they may have no relation at all.

Note that there are three different ways in which you can navigate for information: **Find by Document**, **Find by Business Contact**, and **Find by Item Reference**. By default, the **Find by Document** method is used. This navigates using internal document numbers. You can use the **Find by Business Contact** method to navigate using **External Document No.** (the **Customer PO** number or the vendor invoice number, for example) or use the **Find by Item Reference** method to navigate using serial or lot numbers.

> If you develop customized ledger entries or documents, do not forget to modify the **Navigate** functionality so that it also considers customized tables. You will have to add code in the `FindRecords` and `ShowRecords` functions found on the **Page** object that has the number 344.

Other ways to browse data

The **Navigate** functionality is extremely useful and is extended all over the application; it is used to drill down to detailed transactions of a specified entry. Instead of drilling down to the specific entries, sometimes, you just want to bring up a specific table related to the record you're looking at. For example, what if you want to bring up the customer card to check for some information when you're on the posted invoice document?

There is no need to close **Posted Sales Invoice** and exit out of whatever you're doing. The reason is because a relation exists; in the case of **posted sales invoice**, this is between **posted sales invoice** and the customer. The link is shown as a hyperlink on the page you are looking at. By clicking on the hyperlink, you will be directed to the right place.

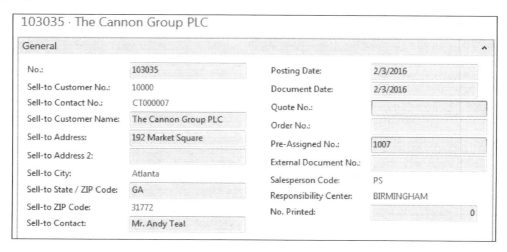

Take a look at the **General** fast tab of a posted sales invoice. The value of the **Sell-to Customer No.** field is showed as a hyperlink.

If you click on the hyperlink, a drop-down list is shown with the **customer** list, as follows:

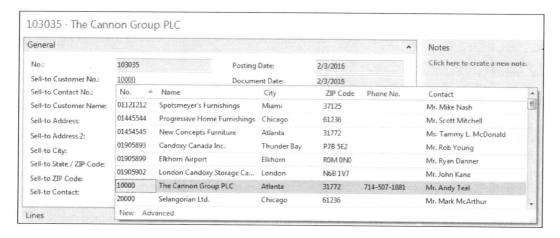

Clicking on the **Advanced** link in the lower-right part of the drop-down list will actually take you to the **Customer List** page and from there you can access **Customer Card**. You can achieve all of this using **Customer Card** without having to remember or write down the **Customer No.** value for which you wanted to check some information.

Hyperlinks are also shown when a value in a field is the result of a calculation. In this case, clicking on the hyperlink will open a page where the records taken into account during the calculation are shown.

Sorting on list pages

When you pull up a list page, you can dynamically do sorting based on any of the columns that are displayed. To sort a specific column of the list page, just click on the column header. Pull up the **Customers** list, and click on the **No.** column header:

No.	Name
01121212	Spotsmeyer's Furnishings
01445544	Progressive Home Furnishi...
01454545	New Concepts Furniture
01905893	Candoxy Canada Inc.

When the arrow on the column header is pointed up, it means that the list is sorted in ascending order. Now if you click on the column header again, the arrow will be pointed downwards. This means that the records are sorted in descending order.

You can click on any of the columns and the records will sort dynamically.

Filtering for the data you need

Sometimes you need to look for a set of information and you do not want to print it into a report. You just want to extract the data and do your own manipulations.

Fortunately, there are other ways to find data in Dynamics NAV. Applying our own filters in a page to display only the information we're looking for is a powerful tool that will save you thousands of consulting hours per year.

Imagine you're a brand new customer service representative and just want to get a list of all of the customers in your territory. You want to find all the **DOMESTIC** customers that are to be shipped from the **YELLOW** location.

You may examine all the reports that exist in Dynamics NAV and end up finding the one you need. But if you don't find it, don't worry; the following are the steps to do so:

1. Open the **Customer** page (**Departments/Sales & Marketing/Order Processing/Customers**).

2. Display the **Advanced filter** by navigating to **Customer | Advanced Filter**:

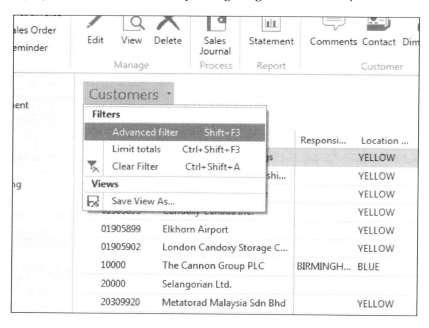

3. Click on **Add Filter** to add your own filters. A **Where** line is shown.

4. Select the field for which you want to apply a filter. In our case, we want to apply the filter on **Location Code** and **Customer Posting Group**.

5. The information we were looking for is now displayed, that is, all the customers that are to be shipped from the **YELLOW** location and are **DOMESTIC** customers.

At this point, you can copy and paste to Excel or simply click on Microsoft Excel on the ribbon and the data will be exported to Excel.

Saving views for the filters you've set

Assuming you need to frequently access the information based on the same filters that you set on the list. You can save the filters that you've set as an icon on your **Home** page:

1. Go back to the **Customer** list and set the filters and display the list of information you want.

2. Navigate to **Customer | Save View As**:

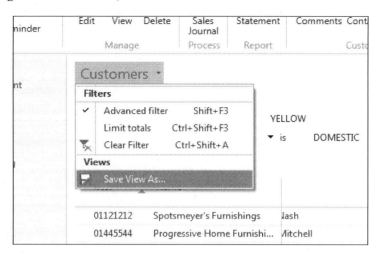

3. A popup will be displayed to allow you to change the description of your **View** and where you want to save it to. In our case, we can just save it to the **Home** page:

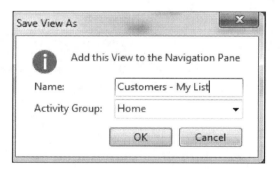

4. A message will be displayed asking you to restart the application. Once restarted, **Customer – My List** view will be on your **Home** page:

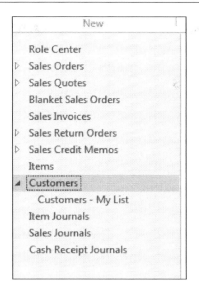

Real-time data gathering – the SIFT technology

Sum Index Field Technology (SIFT) is a built-in technology that exists in Dynamics NAV and is used for totaling.

In other ERP systems, totals, subtotals, and balances are calculated and stored somewhere. This calculation has to be redone over and over so that numbers are up-to-date.

In Dynamics NAV, if you're a developer you don't have to worry about calculating subtotals as it is done by SIFT. Creating a new subtotals field is as easy as indicating in the field properties that the field is **Flowfield** and specifying the formula in the field. After this, you will not have to worry about keeping it up-to-date.

As a user, you know that the balances for your G/L accounts, customers, vendors, or bank accounts are always displaying real-time information, similar to the other calculations done using SIFT. A few examples are quantity on hand of an item or all the customer statistics that are shown on the right-hand side of the screen when looking for or creating sales orders.

Everything leads to accounting

Accounting rules teach how to translate everything that happens in a company to an accounting language, that is, debits and credits.

Dynamics NAV has implemented these rules using posting groups, so the system can translate everything to the accounting language and post it to general ledger entries on the fly.

Posting groups are related to master data. When you create a new record in the master data (for instance, you create a new customer), you need to specify which posting group it belongs to.

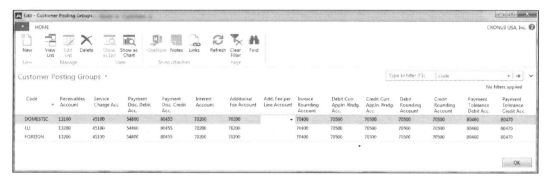

In the previous image, you can see the existing posting groups for customers. For each posting group, all the columns are filled with an account value. Dynamics NAV uses these accounts to post the general ledger entries anytime a transaction is made with a customer.

You can create as many posting groups as the amount of detailed information you need. In Europe, for example, you have to separate domestic customers, customers from the European Union, and foreign customers. This is why three customer posting groups exist on the CRONUS demo company.

The following posting groups exist, and each master data is related to at least one of these:

- Customer Posting Group
- Vendor Posting Group
- Job Posting Group
- General Posting Setup
- Bank Account Posting Group
- VAT (Tax) Posting Setup
- FA Posting Group
- Inventory Posting Setup
- Service Contract Account Group

Every time you post a transaction related to any master data record, general ledger entries will be created. This way accountants only have to bother about transactions that no other area in the company posts.

On some special occasions, the integration with accounting can be disabled. We can find an example of this in the **Fixed Assets** module. If the integration is disabled, it is the user's responsibility to ensure that the **Fixed Assets** entries are consistent with the amounts posted on the fixed assets accounts from the charts of accounts.

The Dynamics NAV database

Dynamics NAV 2016 stores its data in a Microsoft SQL database or Azure SQL. NAV 2009 and the earlier versions of Dynamics NAV used either a Microsoft SQL database or a native database for Dynamics NAV. The native database has been discontinued and is no longer available because it's antiquated and has limitations.

The database used by Dynamics NAV is a relational database but it does not fully implement the **referential integrity** concept that ensures that relationships between tables remain consistent. In Dynamics NAV, data integrity is maintained partially by the database engine itself and mainly by code. Sometimes, it is not even maintained.

 When developing new Dynamics NAV functionalities, consider data integrity inside your analysis and design work.

The TableRelation property

The **NAV Service Tier** (**NST**) uses the **TableRelation** property of fields in tables to maintain data integrity.

There are plenty of fields in Dynamics NAV tables that are related to other tables. In a sales invoice, for instance, the **Sell-to Customer No.** field is related to the **Customer** table.

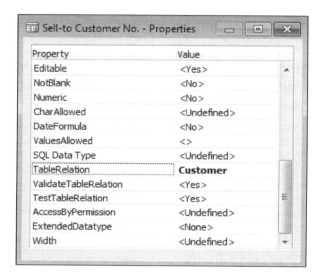

The relation is stated in the **TableRelation** property of the field. **Sell-to Customer No.** is related to the primary key field of the **Customer** table.

A relation is established for three important purposes, and two of them are related to data integrity:

- **To establish data integrity**: If **TableRelation** is defined, only values existing on the related table will be allowed to be written to the field. That is, you cannot create a sales invoice for a customer that does not exist.

  This rule can be omitted if **ValidateTableRelation** is set to **No**.

- **To maintain data integrity**: If a value is changed in the primary key fields of a related table, the change will be propagated to all the tables that have **TableRelation** with the first table. This means that if you rename a customer, all the existing sales invoices will change their **Sell-to Customer No.** field value so that the sales invoice points to the renamed customer (and not to the old value of **Customer No.**).

- **To enable the lookup functionality**: If **TableRelation** is defined for a field in a table whenever you are editing the value of that field, the system will allow you to pick up one of the possible values by showing a drop-down list.

The **TableRelation** properties may be as simple as the one shown for the **Sell-to Customer No.** field in the **Sales Header** table but they can also be more complicated. Conditional **TableRelation** properties can be defined, or you can apply filters to the relation.

TableRelation of the **No.** field in the **Sales Line** table is an example of a conditional **TableRelation**.

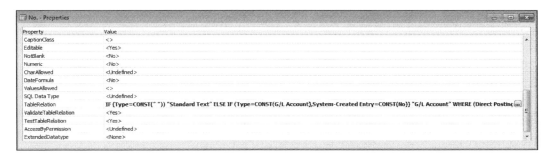

It's such a long **TableRelation** value that it is difficult to even read and understand in the **TableRelation** property. To take a better look at it, click on the **Assist Edit** button that appears at the rightmost part of the **Value** column for the **TableRelation** property.

An example of **TableRelation** with a filter can be found in the **Ship-to Code** field from the **Sales Header** table.

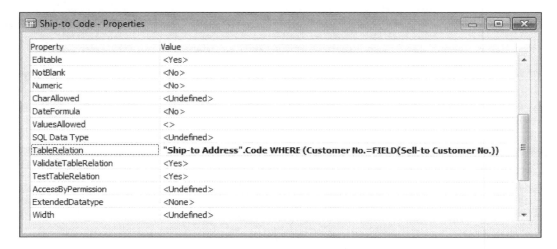

In this **TableRelation** table, a filter is applied, so we can only select **Ship-to Addresses** belonging to the customer for whom the sales document is created.

Coded data rules

Coded data rules are written in table and field triggers. They are used to enforce data integrity when it cannot be obtained with simple mechanisms, such as field types or table relations.

One of these data rules that you can see all over the application can be found in the `OnDelete()` trigger of most tables. In this trigger, conditions are usually checked to prevent the user from deleting certain information.

```
Table 14 Location - C/AL Editor                                    _ □ x
   1  Documentation()
   2
   3  OnInsert()
   4
   5  OnModify()
   6
   7  OnDelete()
   8  WMSCheckWarehouse;
   9
  10  TransferRoute.SETRANGE("Transfer-from Code",Code);
  11  TransferRoute.DELETEALL;
  12  TransferRoute.RESET;
  13  TransferRoute.SETRANGE("Transfer-to Code",Code);
  14  TransferRoute.DELETEALL;
  15
  16  WhseEmployee.SETRANGE("Location Code",Code);
  17  WhseEmployee.DELETEALL(TRUE);
  18
  19  WorkCenter.SETRANGE("Location Code",Code);
  20  IF WorkCenter.FINDSET(TRUE) THEN
  21    REPEAT
  22      WorkCenter.VALIDATE("Location Code",'');
  23      WorkCenter.MODIFY(TRUE);
  24    UNTIL WorkCenter.NEXT = 0;
  25
  26  OnRename()
  27
  28  Code - OnValidate()
100 %
```

In the `OnDelete()` trigger of the **Location** table, some conditions are checked using the **WMSCheckWarehouse** function. If some conditions make it impossible to delete the location, an error message will be shown and the action will not be taken.

In the `OnDelete()` trigger of tables, code also exists to ensure that related information is deleted as well. In the example, transfer routes for the location that is being deleted are deleted as well. The **WMSCheckWarehouse** function has also deleted the zones, bins, and bin contents of the location that was deleted.

If you're interested in learning more programming related aspects of Dynamics NAV, please refer to *Programming for Dynamics NAV*, also published by Packt Publishing.

Summary

In this chapter, you saw general considerations of Dynamics NAV and learned its philosophy. It is important for everybody to learn to work together since every part of Dynamics NAV is tied together one way or another. Application aside, implementing Dynamics NAV will give your employees an opportunity to understand exactly how your company operations happen, resulting in more productivity.

So far we introduced Microsoft Dynamics NAV 2016 in *Chapter 1, Introducing Microsoft Dynamics NAV 2016*, talked about the new features that the current version has introduced in *Chapter 2, What's New in NAV 2016?*, and we have now talked about the general philosophy of Microsoft Dynamics.

In the following chapters, we will talk about how we can implement this ERP in your fantastic company!

4
The Implementation Process – From the Reseller

In this chapter, we will learn about the Dynamics NAV 2016 implementation process from the perspective of a reseller or VAR (Value Added Reseller). This chapter will explain the meaning of implementation and show that there are different methodologies that you can apply.

In an implementation process, several people may get involved, each one playing their own role. We will learn what kind of roles can be found in a Dynamics NAV implementation and the job that can be expected from each role.

We will also see that the implementation process can be broken down into phases, and we will learn about the tasks included in each phase.

The main topics discussed in this chapter are:

- Defining what an implementation is
- Using methodology
- Roles involved in an implementation project
- The phases of the project

What is an implementation?

If you look for the definition of implementation, you will end up with something similar to the following, which has been taken from `http://searchcrm.techtarget.com/definition/implementation`:

> *"Implementation is the carrying out, execution, or practice of a plan, a method, or any design for doing something. As such, implementation is the action that must follow any preliminary thinking in order for something to actually happen.*
>
> *In an information technology context, implementation encompasses all the processes involved in getting new software or hardware operating properly in its environment, including installation, configuration, running, testing, and making necessary changes. The word deployment is sometimes used to mean the same thing."*

I especially like the part where it says: getting new software operating properly in its environment.

That is what needs to be done in a Dynamics NAV implementation process. Get the software (Dynamics NAV) to operate properly in its environment (the company that will use Dynamics NAV as their business management software).

One of the strongest selling points in Dynamics NAV is the ability to set it up any way you like. Often times, people take this flexibility to the extreme to the point of diminishing (or negative) return.

Companies are completely different from one another. They work completely differently as they have different processes and ways of doing business. Dynamics NAV, just as companies, can work in many different ways. Each company has to find its own way. And that is actually what will be done in the implementation process where you choose the way in which you want Dynamics NAV to work.

Dynamics NAV is a software product that requires you to set it up properly before you can start working with it. There are some areas that have to be configured, many others that have to be decided, master data that has to be introduced in the system, and a host of other decisions that have to be taken before a company can start using Dynamics NAV as their business software. Taking shortcuts in order to "save" on implementation cost will guarantee to cost the clients more in the long run.

Dynamics NAV, as many other business software products, provides a large stack of what is called horizontal functionality that may be useful for any company using Dynamics NAV, regardless of the business sector in which they work. It also provides the needed flexibility to adapt to any specific vertical requirement.

Vertical and horizontal solutions

A vertical solution is a stack of functionalities thought of and developed to cover industry-specific requirements of a business sector. Manufacturing companies need software solutions different from what a health care company needs, for example.

A horizontal solution is a stack of functionalities that every single company needs or can use, such as word processing or spreadsheet applications. In Dynamics NAV, application modules such as `Financial Management` are part of the horizontal solution, as they are useful and needed for every single company.

Apart from a host of horizontal functionalities, Dynamics NAV offers some out-of-the-box vertical application modules, such as the `Manufacturing` module, that will probably be used by manufacturing companies but not by retail companies, for instance.

All the out-of-the box application modules and functionalities that Dynamics NAV offers can be put together in what is called the **Standard Solution** or **standard software**. Don't take the word standard as something standardized by an international standards authority. That is not what standard means in this context. It actually refers to how Microsoft, based on the feedback of how companies use an ERP application of the necessary functionalities, that can be applied across most of the companies that uses Dynamics NAV.

If standard Dynamics NAV does not meet the specific requirements that a company needs, a large channel of Dynamics NAV partners exists, which may have developed a vertical solution. The solution probably complies with many of the requirements of what your client's industry needs.

You will find vertical solutions for as many business sectors as you may think of— retail, real estate, education, health care, non-profit— just to name a few. Custom development can also be done for a specific company to modify or extend Dynamics NAV functionality to meet the unique demands of your client's requirements.

In an implementation process of Dynamics NAV, you have to choose whether you will implement standard Dynamics NAV and/or a vertical solution offered by yourself or by any other company. You will have to choose which functionalities will be used, how they will be used, and know if development will be required, and then you will have to implement all of this by installing the product, develop what needs to be developed, and configure what's required.

After figuring out the framework that's needed for an implementation, you also need to load the initial data the company needs to start working with (primarily, their master data, such as their database consisting of customers, vendors, or items). Finally, you have to train the end users who will use Dynamics NAV, as they have to know how everything works and which tasks they are expected to perform in the system.

Methodology

Every implementation of Dynamics NAV is completely different from another one. The reason is because every company, no matter how similar of industry, is run differently. The company that is going to use the ERP software (usually called *the customer*) is different, the requirements are different, the scope is different, and even the team implementing it might be different. This brings a lot of uncertainty to the process and is the main reason why methodology has to be used.

Implementing Dynamics NAV is considered as working in a project environment. By definition, a project is a temporary endeavor undertaken to meet unique goals. The company implementing Dynamics NAV (usually called *the consultant*) is probably used to this kind of environment. On the other hand, the customer is probably used to working in an operational environment, where the same processes are repeated over and over. For the customer, implementing a new ERP system is like running in the jungle with dozens of options to take at each step and no idea about where to go. Therefore, methodology is not only going to help the consultant, but also the customer, understand exactly what's going on.

Methodology is not only applicable to the development and the implementation, but also to stuff such as how the project is going to be billed or how the project team is going to transfer the knowledge to the support department at the end of the project. You have to define some aspects before starting any project:

- **Billing**: A Dynamics NAV project means time and work investment before the go-live date. Usually, projects do not show results until the end. Even on Agile methodologies, you will need several iterations before the go-live date. Both the partner and the customer must be balanced in order to have the best relation possible. This can only be achieved by billing the project as it moves forward.

- **Estimating time and cost**: At the beginning of the project you will have to estimate the project, either in cost or time. Use templates to help you estimate and ensure that you don't forget any task.

  It is normal to think about the development time of a certain requirement and forget the time it takes to design it or implement it. It is also normal to forget the tasks related to managing the project, and it is time consuming.

For each requirement, you can use a template like the following one:

	Analysis	**Development**	**Test**	**Implementation**
Requirement 1	3h	10h	2h	2h
Requirement 2	1h	4h	1h	0.5h

Use this template to estimate all the requirements, even the ones that are going to be accomplished with standard functionality, because they will consume implementation time. Also, use this template (or a similar one) to estimate migration requirements.

Use another template for the rest of the tasks of the implementation. Write down all the tasks needed for the implementation and make sure to check them all for estimating a new project.

Some tasks that you should not forget are project management, software installation, training, support, and so on. To estimate the project management tasks, we use a percentage of the whole project estimation. It is up to you to fix this percentage, but it could be something like 10 percent. In a complex implementation you can also break down this task and perform the estimation from there.

- **Planning**: Determine how you will plan the project; planning both the phases and the everyday work. Visibility is important; therefore the whole team and the other people in your company have to be aware of the project plan.

  You might also need to use a tool such as Microsoft Project or Microsoft Excel to plan the whole project. You could then print the plan of the whole project and distribute it to the people who are going to be involved in this implementation.

Using MS Project vs. MS Excel

Both tools are great for planning. However, I find Excel a much better tool because it's something the customer is familiar with. Instead of teaching the customer MS Project, we can focus on determining which dates are important for which milestones.

The project plan should be shared with the customer as early as possible. This helps everyone plan their vacation and time off to ensure they are around when they need to be around.

- **Purchases**: Your project will, at least, involve the purchase of the customer's Dynamics NAV license. In some projects you will also have to buy other things, such as hardware if you are in charge of providing it.

  Determine when and how you are going to do all of your purchasing, and do it the same way in all your implementations.

- **Communication with the customer**: Communication is a very important part of any project. Determine how, who, and when you are going to communicate with your customers.

  It can be through meetings, e-mails, phone calls, or shared documents. Also decide on the single point of contact from the partner side as well as the customer side.

  If too many people from the partner side talk with too many people from the customer side, it can be chaotic and you will probably end up with inconsistencies.

- **Communication between the team**: This is also very important, especially if the team is placed at different locations. If someone has talked to the customer and has decided on something, the rest of the team must be made aware of it. One of the best ways to keep a tab on everything is to immediately follow up with an e-mail on what was decided, to both the customer and the parties involved as partners.

- **Development and testing**: Determine the strategy the company is going to use when developing and testing: how the code will be written and marked.

  If you have not defined this, you can end up with everybody developing on a local machine, marking their code in a completely different way, and having to invest a lot of time to put everything together.

- **Acceptance of the developments**: Your implementation methodology has to ensure that the customer accepts the developments as the project progresses. This involves delivering the bits and pieces of the project as soon as they're completed. Don't wait to show everything in the last week before the go-live date. If you do so, prepare yourself for a tough support phase with an unhappy customer.

- **Documentation**: Determine what has to be documented, the structure each document will have, and how it will be named.

  It may seem that this is a very bureaucratic process, but it can really be as simple as you want. By documentation we don't mean that each project has to generate a thousand pages of documentation, but that the few documents that are generated follow the same structure and are archived at the same place.

  Even on smaller projects, where only one person is involved, plan ahead so another person can come in and pick up where that one person left off if he/she goes on vacation.

- **Reporting and control**: Think about what kinds of reports you will have to generate and the kind of control that the project will have. You may want to control the project advance, the time, cost consumption, and so on. Invest time in your project to this area, even if the project seems to be okay, or you won't see the diversions until it's too late.

  To control the project advance, we recommend you to plan demo/training sessions, so that each developer can show his/her work to the rest of the team. These demo/training sessions have two purposes. One, the project gains visibility and is part of the communication between the team members that we talked about earlier. Two, it allows feedback from the team members on improvements needed in a project or whether a project is being done completely wrong.

There are different kinds of methodologies. The main ones are Waterfall and Agile. The Waterfall approach is the most used approach while implementing Dynamics NAV, but Agile gives better results, especially on software requirements. This is why Agile approaches have been gaining ground for the past few years.

In the next sections, we will cover both the approaches and learn how to use the best of both.

The Waterfall approach

The Waterfall model is a design process in which progress is seen as flowing steadily downwards (like a waterfall) through the phases.

The following diagram shows the typical representation of a Waterfall approach:

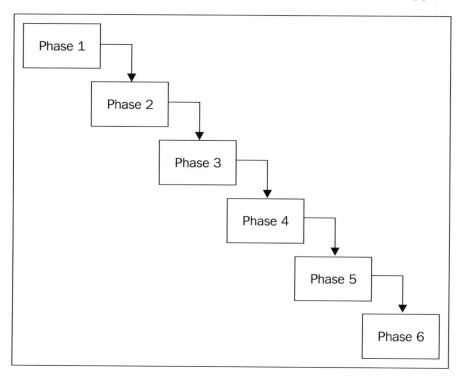

As you can see in the diagram, one phase does not start until the last one has finished. In the next section of this chapter, we'll talk about the phases of a Dynamics NAV implementation, which are presales, getting the requirements, analysis, development, deployment, and support. In our case, the analysis phase cannot start until all the requirements have been taken care of, and the development phase cannot start until all the requirements have been analyzed.

Companies have chosen this approach because it is the one that, theoretically, brings more certainty. Using this approach, the whole scope of the project is defined after getting the requirements, so it is easy to fix a cost for the project and fix an ending date. But, as we said, it is just theoretical. In reality, the requirements that are gathered at the beginning of the project may not be what you end up going live with. The reason is because in the earlier stages the customer does not know Dynamics NAV, but once they realize the potential of NAV, they will certainly want to change how they work for the better.

This is very similar to building or remodeling a house. In most cases, the owners want to make changes to what the architect drew because they see something that can totally make their house a lot better.

The Agile approach

The Agile approach is based on iterative and incremental development. It is typically represented like the following diagram:

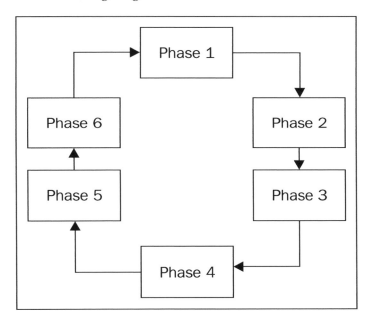

In this approach, you perform several iterations through all the phases before you reach the end of the project. With this approach, the customer needs to be more involved in the project and work more closely with the partner team.

The Agile approach is the best to meet the requirements and is able to more closely fit into the customers' needs. It is the approach that adds more value. However, it is hard to estimate time and costs at an early stage. And for the company implementing Dynamics NAV, not to exceed their budget may also be very important; in some cases even more important than the value added.

This is usually solved by establishing a win-win / lose-lose relation between the customer and the partner. Both parties agree with a desired cost. If the project ends up with less cost than expected, then both sides win. If the project ends up costing more than expected, then both sides lose.

We have worked for many years on projects implemented by following the Waterfall approach. The cost of the project is set up at the beginning of the project, and sometimes it can be tough to ask the customer for a revised budget.

With the cost already fixed, the customer always tries to get more value for the same price and the partner ends up lowering the quality for the same price. Fights between both happen when one party says that this is not what we agreed upon in the first place, and the other party argues that this was implicit in the requirements.

The win-win / lose-lose relation balances the equation between the value added and the final cost.

Using the best of both

To use the best of both approaches, you can have an initial getting the requirements phase, but with less detail than in the Waterfall approach. In this first phase, the requirements of all the areas are covered, so it helps the partner team to make an approximate estimation of the project cost and time. This helps the customer identify if the project fits their needs and also their budget. After that you loop through all the phases focusing on a few requirements at a time.

Of course, using this approach, the cost of the project is only an approximation; it may cost less or more.

If the project is finished with less cost than estimated, both the customer and the partner win, because they share the benefits of the savings. On the other hand, if the project costs more than expected, both have to share the cost overrun. This can be achieved by returning part of the savings to the customer, and compromising on the cost of the underestimated projects.

This kind of relation between the customer and the partner is new in the Dynamics NAV world and several cultural aspects must change inside the organizations, but we are sure that the results will be worth it.

Microsoft Dynamics Sure Step

Microsoft Dynamics Sure Step is a methodology designed by Microsoft, focused specifically on the implementation of all the stacks of Microsoft Dynamics ERP and CRM products in which Microsoft Dynamics NAV is included. The Sure Step process is available for both **On Premise** and **On the Cloud** deployments.

This methodology is not just a set of methods and a knowledge base about implementation projects. It consists of:

- Best practices that let the consultant know how an implementation task or a set of tasks should be performed to achieve the best possible result, or to avoid mistakes that have already been made by someone in the past.

- Tools that make it easier to perform the tasks by automating or streamlining time-consuming and error-prone tasks, such as organization and business process mapping.

- Templates that boost productivity by providing a documentation framework. Preparing documentation using these templates ensures that every important aspect of the documentation has been touched, and that nothing important has been missed.

The Sure Step methodology provides the two distinct implementation approaches we have been discussing, namely, the Waterfall approach and the Agile approach. We will define them in the following sections.

Project types based on the Waterfall approach

There are three types of Waterfall-based implementation project types. In addition, there is one Waterfall-based upgrade project type. Now, the four types of Waterfall-based implementation project types are as follows:

- The Rapid project type
- The Standard project type
- The Enterprise project type
- The Upgrade project type

The Rapid project type

This is, in theory, the fastest and most straightforward approach. The Rapid project type is designed for out-of-the-box implementations of Dynamics NAV solutions. This means that when you choose this method, you use Dynamics NAV as is without any customizations. It prescribes 14 activities from solution to "go-live".

In my personal experience, this is a terrible approach to NAV and I would never recommend any company to use this implementation method. Taking away customization from NAV is taking away one of the most powerful tools Dynamics NAV has to offer. It's like taking the balloons away from a clown. Without the balloons, the clown will just be scary.

The following is a screenshot of the Rapid project type, including the activities shown in the left navigation tree:

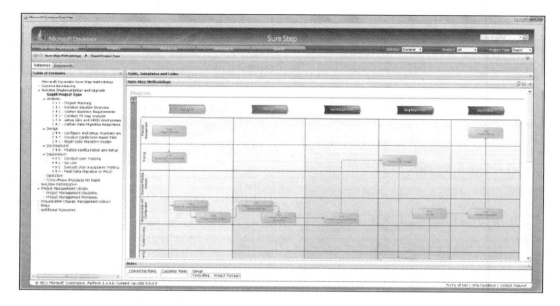

The Standard project type

This is typically used in most Dynamics NAV implementations for fixed price implementations. Using this method allows the Dynamics NAV partner to know and understand your business. It allows all your users to know your Dynamics partner as well so an accurate estimate can be established

The next screenshot is of the Standard project type in Sure Step:

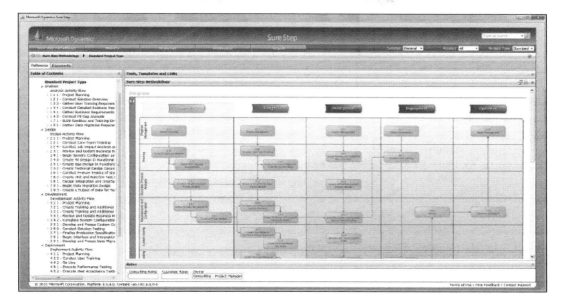

The Enterprise project type

This is the most detailed of all the Sure Step project types. This project type is
typically used in large organizations where multiple departments with multiple
heads of departments in multiple locations need to be involved in the project.
Basically, you should use this project plan if all the hands in the world need to be in
the cookie jar.

The following is a screenshot of the Enterprise project type in Sure Step:

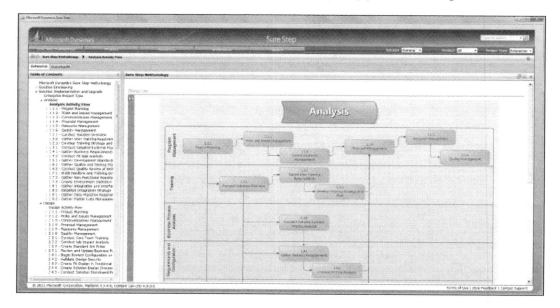

The Upgrade project type

This is a project type specially designed to address upgrade projects. It differentiates between technical upgrades and functional upgrades. A technical upgrade is meant to port an existing solution to a new product version. A functional upgrade is meant to not only port an existing solution to a new product version, but also to add new functionalities to the new product version.

The following is a screenshot of the Upgrade project type in Sure Step:

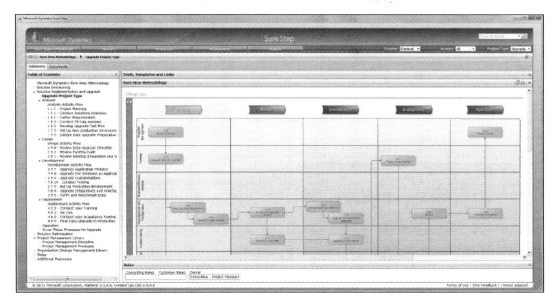

The Agile project type

This type is used to manage the Dynamics NAV implementations where the solution needs to fit very specific needs of the customer for whatever reasons. These customers are typically very involved with their partner, from specification design to development to testing.

The next screenshot shows the Agile project type in Sure Step:

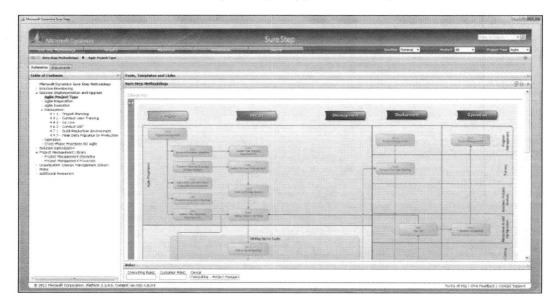

The Sure Step Agile project type has **Sprint** cycles to include the **Analysis**, **Design**, and **Development** phases.

A Sprint cycle is a set period of time during which specific work has to be completed and made ready for review. At the end of each sprint, you are adding value to the project by adding finished portions of the product. Usually, sprints last from one week to one month.

The Agile project type does have two phases, **Deployment** and **Operation**, at the culmination of the Sprint cycles. So, in this context, the Agile project type deviates from a strict Agile approach, and is fashioned as a blended approach for ERP/CRM deployments.

Roles

Implementing an ERP solution such as Microsoft Dynamics NAV 2016 in a company is not a trivial task. A lot of things have to be taken into account and a lot of things have to be done. That's why a lot of people have to get involved in the project, both in the company implementing Dynamics NAV, that is the partner, and in the company that will use Dynamics NAV as their management software, that is the customer.

Everyone will have a different and well-defined role in the project. In this section, we will try to explain who should get involved in the project and the tasks that they will be performing.

In the partner team, the following roles exist:

- Salesperson
- Project manager
- Business consultant
- Analyst
- Developer
- Implementer

In the customer team, we find the following roles:

- Project manager
- Key users
- End users

Note that one person can have multiple roles. It's not uncommon for an NAV partner to have one person that takes on all the roles mentioned earlier! It's also not uncommon for the customer to have one person who is the project manager, the key user, and the end user as well.

Salesperson

The salesperson acts even before the implementation project begins, but it is an important role as he or she is the one who defines the big lines of the project requirements and who creates expectations in the customer about what Dynamics NAV is and will be. We will discuss this in detail later on in this chapter.

Project manager

The most important role in the project is that of the project manager. Two project managers exist in an implementation project, one at the partner side and another one at the customer side. They have the maximum responsibility for the whole process of implementing Dynamics NAV.

The project managers define the scope of the project, the functionalities that will be implemented, the management of resources, and the timeline.

Business consultant

The first roles that come into play in the project are of the business consultants from the partner's team and the key users from the customer's team. These two roles define the business processes used by the customer, which of these processes will be done in Dynamics NAV, and how the system should behave.

While defining the business processes, the business consultant explains to the customer's key users whether these processes can be done in standard Dynamics NAV, if the processes exist in Dynamics NAV but are slightly different from those done by the customer (in which case, the customer may change its process to adapt to the Dynamics NAV process, or the Dynamics NAV process may be changed to adapt to the customer's process), or if the process doesn't exist at all in Dynamics NAV and will have to be developed.

The business consultant writes down a document (the **Project Requirements Document (PRD)** or the **Implementation Specifications**) in which all the business processes that have to be included in Dynamics NAV are explained. The document points out which business processes are covered by standard Dynamics NAV and which require development. When development is needed, the document has to explain the expected behavior of the development.

The PRD is the main document of the project. Once the business consultant has written it, the key users who defined the processes will have to read it and make sure everything important in their business is covered in the document.

The business consultant and the key users, with the aid of their respective project managers, have to agree on a final PRD as this is the document that describes the project and that will be used later on by the analyst and the implementer to get to a final solution.

The business consultant should be someone who knows about business, as he or she must be able to understand the customer's business processes and needs. The business consultant should also be someone who knows standard Dynamics NAV behavior and capabilities, as he or she must be able to distinguish whether a specific business process is covered by Dynamics NAV or not.

Often there are specialized business consultants in a specific area or functionality. For example, we can find financial business consultants and warehouse business consultants. Financial business consultants know about the business processes related to financial management and how the financial management functionality works in Dynamics NAV 2013, but they know nothing (or not too much) about warehouse management or any other business area. Warehouse business consultants know about the business processes related to warehouse management and how the warehouse is handled in Dynamics NAV 2013, but they know nothing (or not too much) about financial management or any other business area.

In some instances, several business consultants may be involved in a Dynamics NAV implementation project when several and completely different business areas are implemented.

Business consultants are often brought into the presales by the salesperson in order to help the customer define what is achievable within the customer's budget and timeframe.

Key users

The key users from the customer's side should be those who know the processes currently being followed in the company. They should be aware of the problems or inefficiencies the current processes have, and be willing to actively participate in the project.

The same way that more than one business consultant may get involved in the project, each one handling a specific business area, several key users may also participate in the definition of the project requirements, each one also handling a specific business area.

A common error regarding key users is to point out the heads of departments as the key users without analyzing whether they are the right people to play this role. Having good key users, just as having good business consultants, is vital to the deployment of the project, as they are the ones who will define the project, the needs, and the processes.

The key users have to be good communicators and should know their own processes. Sometimes, the heads of departments may know the *theory* of their own processes, but since they are not the ones doing them on a daily basis, they may not know the real processes (which may differ from the *theoretical* processes).

The heads of departments may or may not be good key users. We will discuss this in more detail in the next chapter, which will be dedicated to the implementation process at the customer's side.

Once the PRD is written and the project requirements are clear, both the analyst and the business consultant continue with the deployment of the project.

The business consultant will focus on all the standard functionalities of Dynamics NAV that the customer will use. The analyst will focus on all the functionalities of Dynamics NAV that have to be modified somehow or developed from scratch.

Some functionalities in Dynamics NAV can behave in multiple ways depending on how they have been configured. The business consultant is the person who defines the way in which the system has to be configured to meet the business process requirements reflected in the PRD.

Analyst

The analyst is the person who defines the way in which the standard functionalities of Dynamics NAV will be configured to meet the business process requirements defined in the PRD. The analyst also defines the way in which new functionalities will be developed and the way the customer's data will be migrated into the system.

To achieve this task, the analyst must be someone who knows the standard design of Dynamics NAV and the development capabilities of the system. Modifications have to be carefully designed because the right modification in the wrong area may cause inconsistencies in other areas or functionalities. It may also disable the future use of a standard functionality. In addition, new functionalities should be implemented using the same design philosophy as behind Dynamics NAV.

Developer

They are basically the coders.

Once the developments required to be done in the project are defined, the developer comes into the scene. The developer is the person who will develop the modifications and new functionalities defined by the analyst.

Once the developments are finished, the business consultant should test them to validate that they certainly meet the business process requirements defined in the PRD.

Implementer

At this point, everything is ready for the implementer to start working on the project. The implementer will configure the system as defined by the business consultant and will perform the data migration processes in test environments, using standard Dynamics NAV 2013 tools (defined later on in this book) or using tools defined by the analyst and developed by the developer.

Before going live, the implementer will validate all the business processes that will be running inside the system with the customer's key users, namely, the standard Dynamics NAV processes that have been configured, the processes that have been modified to meet the customer's requirements, and the processes that have been completely developed.

The implementer will be in charge of training the customer's end users about the usage of the system before the chosen go-live date.

The day the customer goes live, the implementer is the one who performs the data migration processes and for a defined period of time supports the customer's end users the day they begin using Dynamics NAV.

End users

The end user uses, on a daily basis, the final solution defined by the key users and the business consultants, developed by the developers, and implemented by the implementer.

The entire system is designed so that the end users can do their job using Dynamics NAV as their main tool. Usually, the end users get involved towards the end when the software is about to be rolled out, but they are the ones most affected since it affects their daily work.

Summarizing the roles

To summarize, the roles that are played in the implementer's game and the tasks these roles perform are categorized as follows:

- In the partner's team:
    - **The project manager**: Defines the scope of the project and the timeline. The project manager has the maximum responsibility of implementing the project.
    - **The business consultant**: Defines the business processes, gets the project requirements, and writes the main document of the project, the PRD, in which the customer's business processes that have to be covered by Dynamics NAV are explained, especially those that will require development. The business consultant also defines the way in which standard functionality has to be configured to meet the customer's business process requirements and validates the developments done by the developer.
    - **The analyst**: Defines the way in which the standard Dynamics NAV functionality will be modified, the way new functionalities will be developed, and the way the customer's data will be migrated into the system.
    - **The developer**: Develops the modifications and new functionalities defined by the analyst.
    - **The implementer**: Configures the system, validates the data migration processes, validates all the processes with the customer's key users, trains the end users on the usage of the system, performs the data migration tasks on the go-live date, and supports the end users for a defined period of time when the system is live.

- In the customer's team:
    - **The project manager**: Defines the scope of the project and the timeline. The project manager has the maximum responsibility of implementing the project.
    - **The key users**: Define the business processes, define the project requirements, and read the PRD document written by the business consultant.
    - **The end users**: Use on a daily basis the final solution defined by the key users and the business consultants, developed by the developers, and implemented by the implementer.

As we have defined, different roles exist both at the partner's side and at the customer's side. Each role performs a specific set of tasks. The same person, though, may play different roles in the same project. The business consultant in the partner's team may also be the implementer, for example.

Phases

The following section of this chapter will describe each phase in a Microsoft Dynamics NAV implementation, and the tasks each one includes. In a Waterfall environment, you can do one thing after another. In an Agile environment, don't forget to loop through all of them, especially the phases called getting the project requirements, analysis, development, and part of the task from the deployment phase.

It's especially important to define how the information will flow through all the phases to ensure that important information does not get lost.

Presales

This is the first contact between the partner and the customer — the big lines on which the project will be drawn.

This phase is usually executed by the sales or marketing people, with the help of a business consultant. Many companies think that at this stage the project hasn't started yet, so they don't think that this job is part of the project. But it actually plays a very important role.

Selling a project like a Dynamics NAV implementation is not just selling the software itself. It is not enough just to be aware of what the product can or cannot do. Part of successfully selling Dynamics NAV is instilling confidence in how you will approach the project.

Therefore, the salespeople need to sell not only the product, but also the methodology the company is using and the amount of work the customer will face in the next months. In addition, a good salesperson will discuss how the partner will help the customer face this challenge.

As the salespeople are part of the project, they have to identify fundamental aspects that will help the other members to do their job. A salesperson can help by identifying some of the risks of the project, for instance, mention the departments that have asked for a new ERP system, or someone from the customer's side who is not convinced about the need to change the ERP. They also have to identify if the customer processes are mature enough or need to be rethought. They are also responsible for properly identifying the key people in the customer's organization capable of doing this rethinking or figure out if they are expecting the partner to do it for them.

All this may completely change how the project will be approached. So it is important to identify it at earlier stages. At the end of this stage, a first cost and duration estimation must be done. It is important to be as close to reality as possible.

Getting the project requirements

This is the time for discussion between the partner and the customer. I mean the real deep down discussion, almost like a husband and a wife would. The business consultants and the key users will do a series of meetings in which the key users will explain to the business consultants the way they do business, the information they have to handle through their business processes, the reports they run, the users that are involved in the different stages of each process, and the problems they have with their actual business processes, and most importantly, how they expect the new system to help them solve their daily pains.

The business consultants will need to listen carefully to the key users and understand their pain points from their current operation. Only after understanding the customer's needs will they be able to design the right solution for the customer.

In order to do that, they not only have to be active listeners, but should also actively participate in the definition of the processes by asking all kinds of questions to the key users; namely, periodicity of the process, volume, amount of people involved, how automated it should be, how to handle exceptions to the process, how strict the process is, how important it is, and any other questions you may think of.

As they listen to the customer's processes' explanations, they should point out how this process is handled in Dynamics NAV to identify and mention as an evidence to everyone the differences between the customer's actual business process and the way it is handled in Dynamics NAV. This way, the customer may decide to change or reengineer its own processes or may ask to modify the behavior of Dynamics NAV to adapt to their predefined process.

With all the information gathered in the project requirements meetings, the business consultants should write a document in which the processes are explained and defined in as much detail as possible. This document should be reviewed by the key users so that everyone agrees that what was explained is what has been understood, and that all the decisions made in the project requirements meetings are reflected in the document.

As part of the project requirements, data migrations will also have to be handled and will include questions such as what kind of data will be migrated into Dynamics NAV, what volume of information this means, from where the data will be extracted and in which format, and so on.

To make sure everything has been talked through and defined, it is important for the business consultants to have a checklist of things to ask to the customer and use it in the project requirements meetings.

In this checklist, all Dynamics NAV functional areas should appear and have their own questions. Let's see an example of a checklist:

- **Financial Management**:
    - What are the tasks of the financial department?
    - Which chart of accounts is used? Is it sector specific?
    - How are posting accounts created?
    - Which kinds of transactions are posted? Can they be predefined or established as recurring transactions?
    - Which kinds of analytical information will have to be reported?
    - Does the company create accounting budgets? How often? Are they created over the chart of accounts or over analytical concepts?
    - What legal reporting does the company have to do? How often?
    - Does the company consolidate the accounting information with some other company in the same group?
    - Are additional currencies used?
    - How are banks managed?
    - Are fixed assets managed in the ERP system?
    - How many fixed assets has the company got?
    - Which depreciation method is used?
    - Do you keep maintenance track of your fixed assets?
    - Will the fixed assets have to be automatically imported in Dynamics NAV?

- **Marketing and Sales**:
  - ° Do you create your contacts in the ERP system?
  - ° Do you use a CRM system?

- **Customers and sales processes**:
  - ° How many customers do you have?
  - ° Is extra information about the customers needed in the customer card?
  - ° Do your customers have different shipment directions?
  - ° How do you classify your customers?
  - ° What is your sales process?
  - ° Do you invoice your customers per sales order they make or do you make a single invoice with multiple sales orders?
  - ° When do you invoice your customers?
  - ° Which documents are sent to the customers?
  - ° How are the sales prices established?
  - ° Are discounts applied to the customers?
  - ° Who introduces new sales orders in the system?
  - ° Do the sales orders require some kind of approval?
  - ° Which payment terms are applied to the customers?
  - ° Which payment methods are used to get the payments from the customers?
  - ° Do you ask your customers for prepayments of the sales orders?

- **Vendors and purchase processes**
- **Items and stock management**
- **Warehouse management**
- **Jobs and resources**
- **Manufacturing**
- **Service**
- **Human resources**

- **Others**:
    - ° Will Dynamics NAV receive information from some external application? A website, maybe?
    - ° Will Dynamics NAV have to send information to some external application?
    - ° In how many different devices will Dynamics NAV be used?

We have just written the functional areas of Dynamics NAV and a few examples of questions that can be asked for some of them. A complete checklist should be written for all the functional areas, and all those questions should be answered in the project requirements meetings.

Designing the solution

The solution design includes the configuration needed in standard Dynamics NAV functionality for it to behave in the way in which the customer's requirements are met. It also includes the technical analysis and design of modifications, the development of new functionalities, and the data migration tools that will be used to get the data into the system. Different things have to be taken into account for each type of design.

Configuration

All kinds of configurations have to be established in a Dynamics NAV implementation process:

- Posting groups will determinate how the documents and transactions will end up in an accounting transaction. There are several posting groups that have to be configured, such as the following:
    - ° General Posting Setup
    - ° Customer Posting Group
    - ° Vendor Posting Group
    - ° Fixed Assets Posting Group
    - ° Bank Account Posting Group
    - ° Inventory Posting Group
    - ° Inventory Posting Setup
    - ° VAT (Tax) Posting Setup
    - ° Currencies
    - ° Job Posting Group

- Series of numbers to be used in all the documents and the master data registers.
- The dimensions that will be used for analytical purposes.
- The allowed dimensions' combinations and the dimension priorities.
- The default dimension values for G/L accounts, customers, vendors, items, and so on.
- The following are the setup of all functional areas:
  - **General ledger setup**:
    - Allowed posting dates
    - The way addresses appear in printouts
    - The invoice rounding precision
    - The global and shortcut dimension codes
    - The payment tolerance
  - **Sales and receivables setup**:
    - The series of numbers to be used in the customers and sales documents
    - Whether it is mandatory to inform about an external document number in the sales documents
    - Whether stock out and customer credit warnings should be prompted to the user
    - Whether the posted invoices and credit memos should also create shipments and return receipts
  - **Purchases and payables setup**:
    - The series of numbers to be used in the vendors and purchase documents
    - Whether it is mandatory to include an external document number in the purchase documents
    - Whether the posted invoices and credit memos should also create receipts and return shipments
  - **Inventory setup**:
    - The series of numbers to be used in the items and item documents, such as transfer orders
    - Whether the cost and expected cost should automatically be posted to the general ledger

- ° Whether it is mandatory to use locations in item movements
  - ° **Warehouse setup**:
    - ° The series of numbers to be used in the warehouse documents
    - ° Whether receipt, put-away, shipment, and pick documents are required
  - ° **Manufacturing setup**:
    - ° The series of numbers to be used in the manufacturing documents and resources, such as work centers
  - ° **Jobs setup**:
    - ° The series of numbers to be used in jobs
    - ° Whether the job item costs should automatically be updated
  - ° **Resources setup**:
    - ° The series of numbers to be used in resources
    - ° Work types
    - ° Resource units of measure
- Item tracking codes if they are required.
- Payment terms for the customers and vendors.
- Payment methods for the customers and vendors.
- Configurations that will be used at the customer or vendor level, such as whether prices for a certain customer or vendor are VAT included or not.
- Configurations that will be used at item level like the costing method to be used or replenishment parameters.
- Approval workflows for the sales and purchases documents.

This is a list of typical and common configurations that have to be established in Dynamics NAV. But that's not all. There is a bunch of things that can be achieved in Dynamics NAV through configuration. Not only do those configurations have to be established on the implementation, but they also have to be documented so that the users apply the same configurations to items, customers, vendors, and so on, that are created in the future.

Modifying standard Dynamics NAV functionality

The modification of the standard Dynamics NAV functionality may be as simple as showing extra existing fields in some pages or as complex as altering the way in which the item costs or posting routines are managed.

All modifications have to be designed carefully so that they do not cause inconsistencies in other areas or functionalities and do not disable the future use of a standard functionality.

For example, if a modification is done regarding items, even if item variants are not used, make sure you take them into account to not disable the item variant functionality. Why? That's because you never know if the customer's business will change in the future and will require item variants.

We will discuss development in depth in *Chapter 8, Development Considerations*.

New functionalities

New functionalities should be designed complying with the design philosophy behind Dynamics NAV, as explained in *Chapter 3, General Considerations*.

These functionalities include using a master data table, using series of numbers to number your master data registers and your documents, writing a posting routine for your functionality, using non-modifiable ledger entry tables, and using posting groups if the new functionality has to end up in accounting transactions.

Data migration

For each kind of data that will be migrated into the system, we will have to define the tool to be used to achieve this task. In *Chapter 6, Migrating Data*, all kinds of details regarding data migration are explained.

Development

Once the analyst has defined the developments that have to be done, it's time for the developer to do his/her job.

The development should follow the standard way of development in Dynamics NAV, using the appropriate name convention for tables, captions, fields, pages, and all the other Dynamics NAV objects.

All kinds of developments should be clearly identified using the `Documentation` trigger than can be found in every single Dynamics NAV object, and also by using the comment lines in the code itself to identify where the developed code begins and where it ends.

Don't wait until the development has finished to validate it, and show it to the customer. Use prototypes for complex functionality development and show it to the customer as it gets developed. This way the design and development misunderstandings or mistakes can be identified in the early stages and corrected so that no one's time is lost.

Deployment

The deployment phase ends with the go-live day. A lot of work must be done before the system gets ready to start using it, and it is time to synchronize the entire job done in the previous phases. The best way to face this synchronization is to actually have some of the tasks done in the previous stages as provisional work. This way, major inconsistences can be found and fixed.

The deployment phase includes the following tasks:

- Software and hardware installation
- Configuration
- Data migration
- User acceptance testing
- End users training
- Go live!

Software and hardware installation

This task is all about installing the Dynamics NAV components on the server side, and installing the Dynamics NAV client on the required machines. Also make sure that Dynamics NAV is accessible from all the required devices.

In big implementations, with lots of users using Dynamics NAV from different locations, a load test must be performed. A load test simulates the amount of transactional operations and concurrency pressure that the system will face. The load test will help you determine whether the hardware was properly sized and configured or not.

We recommend you to install the Dynamics NAV test environment at an earlier stage in the project, so that you can release functionality to the customer as it gets developed. It will help you with the final user acceptance test and will allow you to improve your development.

Configuration

Dynamics NAV includes many tables that include the word "setup" in their names. They are the base to define how each module will behave, so they need to be properly configured. There are also all sorts of supplementary setups, including posting groups, payment methods, dimensions, security roles, and so on.

If you are going to release your developments to the customer periodically, not just at the end of the project, then you will have to execute the configuration task at the beginning of the project. This way the customer can see and test the development with an environment that is similar to the one they will find once they start using the system. If you do so, you will also help the people doing the development. It's easier to develop using a development environment similar to the production one.

Don't think that if you do it at the beginning of the project, you will have to do the same job twice. The company you set up at the beginning cannot be used for production, since test transactions and documents will be posted during development and testing. However, you can always copy all the tables, except entries, posted documents, and master data. There are more than 200 tables that can be considered as part of the Dynamics NAV configuration.

We've done this dozens of times and it's something that really helped us in our implementation, so we encourage you to try it.

Data migration

Chapter 6, Data Migration, explains in detail what has to be taken into account to perform data migration. In many cases, the data will have to be transformed or adapted in order to use it in Dynamics NAV.

The data migration task should be performed twice. The first time should be done in the test environment, so that the user acceptance test can be performed using real data. The second data migration is done the day before the go-live day. You can also do the first data migration at the beginning of the project. This way you will help the developers do their job with real data which will help them understand the company they are developing for.

Since data migration requires the partner to work closely with the customer, an early data migration will help both the partner and the customer to get used to working together. It will also help the customer to get more involved with the project right from the beginning.

User-acceptance test

All the work is done and the system is ready to go live. During development, each individual functionality has been tested several times, and also on every release, the users test the system. One more test is required, the one that tests the whole system. All the processes have to be tested, from the initial input, going through all the stages, to the last output. You also need to test if the data generated during each process fits their analysis and reporting requirements.

This test is the last chance to find out if something is wrong and needs to be adjusted. Detecting an issue during the acceptance test and fixing it before going live may save a lot of money.

It's after this test that both the partner and the customer have to agree that everything is ready to go in production. Do not go live if anyone is not comfortable after the test.

End users' training

Last but not the least, the end users have to be trained. They are the ones who are actually going to use the system, so they need to know how it works. Many of them will see Dynamics NAV for the first time during the training. If possible, make them practice with the system during the training.

The training shouldn't be taken too early, or they will easily forget what they have been told.

Go-live!

Finally, the go-live is here. We need to perform the final data migration, validate this data, and start working!

Post Implementation Support

As you can probably guess by now, Dynamics NAV is not like installing Microsoft Office. It's not a static software where the vendor installs it and then leaves. It's a constantly evolving organism that must be maintained because the customer's business will always face new challenges that require more out of Dynamics NAV.

The support phase starts on the go-live day when Dynamics NAV is ready and all the users start to intensively use the system.

No matter how hard you try during the training (try it hard anyway), the users will have a lot of doubts and they need someone by their side. So for the first couple of weeks, depending on the size of the implementation, someone from the partner side is going to be at the customer's office to help them resolve issues as they come up.

But this is not only about functional questions and problems. It would be easy if it was only functional questions and problems. Actually, the support phase is the hardest one! During this phase you will also have to handle the following issues:

- **Old tasks from previous phases**: You will be carrying over a few tasks from the previous phases that weren't important enough to stop the go-live. But the day you start, those tasks become very important all of a sudden. Those tasks become important because the users don't feel comfortable with the new process. They may have a hard time adapting to the new way of doing things. The rate at which the users adapt to the new processes varies, depending on the individuals. Not only extreme patience has to be practiced, empathy from the support person will need to be observed as well.

- **System stabilization**: Even if testing had been done before the "go-live", you can expect the users to find bugs in your developments once they intensively start using the system. Some setups may be wrong as well. You will have to handle and fix all these kinds of issues.

- **Data stabilization**: A massive data migration had been done right before the go-live and a lot of other data had been configured or entered by hand.

  Although the data has been checked before going live, issues with the data will also appear. For the next few weeks, you will have to spend time to stabilize that data.

Summary

In this chapter, we saw that an implementation is a process to get the software to operate properly in a company. To do so, we need to use a methodology that will take us from the beginning to the end of the project, not only on the technical part of the project, but also in the other aspects such as billing the project, effort estimating, planning, and communication.

We saw different methodology approaches, such as the Waterfall approach and the Agile approach, and how they are addressed in Microsoft Dynamics Sure Step.

We also saw the phases and the activities included in a typical Dynamics NAV implementation project.

In the next chapter, we will learn some tips about the implementation process on the customer side.

5
The Implementation Process on the Customer Side

In order to have a successful implementation of Microsoft Dynamics NAV, the company for which NAV is implemented has to actively participate in the project.

In this chapter, we will cover the following aspects of the work a company should do to implement an ERP system such as Microsoft Dynamics NAV:

- Define goals
- Define internal processes
- Define requirements for the new ERP system
- Involve end users
- Follow up the entire process of implementation

We will explain the theory of all these points, and we will also follow up the entire process with a very specific example from a real-world implementation.

Definition of goals

Implementing Dynamics NAV as your ERP system is not a turnkey project. Purchasing and implementing Dynamics NAV is not like installing Microsoft Office, for which you run the `Setup.exe` file and be done with it. Implementing Dynamics NAV is a process, and with such a process, you need people that are involved in the process to actively participate in all phases of the implementation. How involved the client's team is will affect the final result of the implementation.

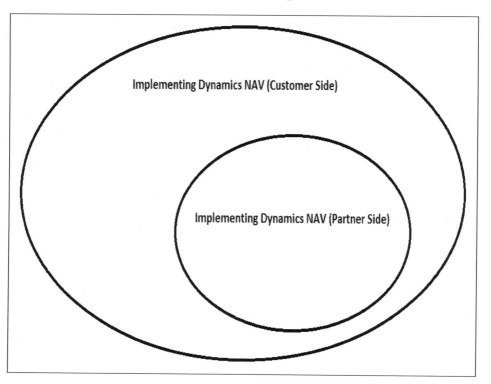

In the preceding diagram, you can see that implementing Dynamics NAV on the partner side is a project that can be framed within a larger project—the implementation of Dynamics NAV at the customer's side. Depending on the scope of the project, the amount of work on each side may differ.

As in any project, the definition of goals is essential to measure whether the project succeeds or not. Goals have to be clearly defined at the beginning of the project and all parties must agree on them. If you don't define clear goals, you may find yourself working as hard as you possibly can and still never able to satisfy your boss or end users.

It not uncommon to define goals such as "improve the sales process". The question is by how much does it have to be improved? How is the improvement going to be measured? When are you going to measure it? Honestly, most of these questions do take more time than it's worth to measure. Most of the time, the measurement of these goals is just a gut feeling. However, if they are defined clearly by your customer, measurements can be achieved.

Measuring goals

Before defining goals that are measurable, you and your partner should clearly agree on how the goals are to be measured, before and after. For example, if a goal is to reduce the number of chargebacks from a customer within 6 months, then it would be as simple as looking at the G/L accounts that you post the chargebacks to.

Some goals are tougher to measure, for example, if a goal is to increase productivity for the workforce, it may not be as simple as running some financial reports. For goals like these, it's recommended to define what does "increase productivity" mean? Is it to reduce the printed documents? Is it to reduce the time between customer service calls? Once that's defined, the next question would be how to quantify and measure the goal.

When defining a goal, it should be **SMART**, as shown in the following image:

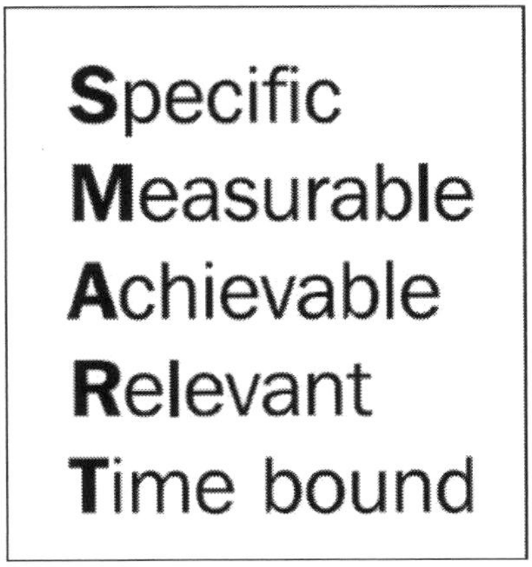

Specific
Measurable
Achievable
Relevant
Time bound

Define different goals for your company and for the partner that is going to implement your Dynamics NAV. Each party will be responsible for different parts of the projects and their goals must be specific to the area they are responsible for. If the definition of the goals is clear enough, it will help everybody to focus on the tasks that will help to accomplish them. This is something that will benefit any party involved in the project.

Let's now take a specific example from a real-world Microsoft Dynamics NAV implementation. The example is from a company that provides public and private health care services. This company uses a specific health care software and an accounting software. With the explosive growth this company experienced, they needed something more robust to accommodate the changes for their company for now and the future as well.

They want to start out by replacing the accounting software, which only keeps track of accounting information. Through careful software selection, they made the right choice and selected Microsoft Dynamics NAV. As we described in the earlier chapter, Dynamics NAV is not just an accounting application, it is actually an ERP system that can do several business functions within an organization.

The main goal that this company wants to accomplish with Dynamics NAV is to make their departments stick to a budget. This budget will be established at the beginning of the year for each service that the departments offer. Nowadays, they do not have a detailed budget per service and they do not keep track of costs per service.

Making the departments stick to a budget is not actually a goal. It's not something specific or time bound; it is a general vision of where to go. To accomplish this vision, several goals that point in the same direction will have to be accomplished, one at a time.

The goals to accomplish that vision could be as follows:

- Being able to define budgets per service
- Determine the service to which every cost applies
- Being able to compare budgets and real costs
- Get a report of costs for a specific service

Let's take that last goal to get a report of costs of a specific service. It is still a goal but it is not a SMART goal. It is specific, measurable, achievable, and relevant; however, there is no timing for the goal. Let's write down the goal in a different way: get a report of costs for a specific service at the end of each month. This is definitely a much a better goal.

Defining the internal processes

Once the goals of the project are clear, and when the company knows what they want to accomplish with their brand new ERP, it's time to go into details and write down all the company processes one by one that will have to be done or supported by Microsoft Dynamics NAV.

When you think about your processes, don't just expose what they should theoretically be. Ask the people who are actually carrying out those processes about what they really do. Also ask about the exceptions to the processes, as handling exceptions for a normal process usually requires more time from end users.

You may want to take this opportunity to eliminate exceptions for a normal process by changing how the process works. Exceptions are basically processes that are created to do something that a normal process does not accommodate. So essentially, the user has to pay special attention and spend extra time to handle these exceptions. What's worst if they start building exception processes on top of exception processes, that's when we really talk about wasting time.

If an exception happens a lot, then it should be incorporated into a normal process. If not, then I would try my best to eliminate this exception, either through changing the process or setup company policies so these exceptions do not occur.

Questions to be asked

For each process, at least the following questions have to be answered:

- What is the desired outcome of the process?
- What are the start and end points?
- What activities are performed?
- What is the order of the activities?
- Who performs the activities?
- What information is required (documents)?
- How often is this process done?
- What is the importance of the process?

Take the example of your sales process. What is the start point for your sales orders? Customers pick up the phone, call you, and tell you exactly which items they want in what quantities. Or maybe you receive the orders by e-mail, or customers submit them in a website, or the order is submitted through EDI, or maybe your salesperson visits your customers and gets the sales order, or the customers ask you for sales quotes that finally get accepted (and thus converted into a sales order) or rejected, or you have blanket sales orders for a certain period of time and you do not receive any further sales orders.

In reality, it may be a combination of all of these and other methods to get sales orders into the system. It's your responsibility, not your consultant's, to know and understand how you receive sales orders and properly document them so an 8-year old can read your document and know exactly how you receive orders into the system.

After sales orders are received, you will probably check them for the following: do you have a minimum sales order amount? Do you sell your items per unit or per box? If you sell per box, you probably have to check whether the quantities asked by customers are multiples of quantities per box. Do you establish a credit limit for your customers? If so, before serving the order, you may want to check whether the credit limit has been exceeded. You may also want to check the *requested delivery date*. Is it possible to serve the customer in time or should you talk to them and negotiate a different delivery date?

Once the sales order has been revised and accepted, it has to be executed. What does this mean? How do you prepare your shipments? Do you group orders per customer so that multiple orders are prepared and served together? Do you pick up items of all the orders of the day together and then pack them separately per order or per customer in the preparation area? Do you attach the sales shipment document to the pack? Which carriers do you use? Do you primarily ship LTL (Less Than Truckload) or small parcel?

And finally, in the sales invoice document, how do you process your invoices: do you post an invoice per sales shipment at the same time the sales shipment is done, a sales invoice per sales order, or a single sales invoice per customer at the end of the month including all the sales orders served in the current month?

Now that we have a bunch of questions and their answers, it is time to write it all down. While writing down your processes, you may come across new questions that have to be asked and answered. For example, you may know that your process has two sequential activities, but you may not have a clear picture of what triggers the beginning of the second activity. This is probably a good question to ask to the people involved in the process.

Writing your processes in a structured way—preferably using any kind of business process modeling diagrams or workflows—will help you and other people to understand them and will also allow you to rapidly measure how simple or complex a process is, identify bottlenecks and redundant work, and basically, where the weakness of the process lies so that it can be improved.

Let's go back to our example of getting a report of costs for a specific service. This process was done in the company before the implementation of Microsoft Dynamics NAV. It wasn't done monthly though, as it took too long and it was done manually. By asking the people involved in the process, we found out the following:

- **Desired outcome**: The cost amount of a specific service in a specific year.
- **Start point**: The service contract has reached its end.
- **End point**: The cost amount of a specific service in a specific year.
- **Activities and their order**: The following is the list of activities performed:

    1. Prepare a list of the vendors that provide goods to this service.
    2. Go through all the purchase invoices of the vendors in the list prepared in the first activity.
    3. Determine whether the purchase invoice is complete or in a high percentage, attributable to the service that is being analyzed.
    4. If it is attributable to the service that is being analyzed, write down the purchase invoice amount in a spreadsheet.
    5. Ask the head of the department providing the service who (and in what percentage of their time) works for the service.
    6. Calculate the costs of human resources attributable to the service. Write down the calculated amount in a spreadsheet.
    7. Get the total purchase invoice amount corresponding to general supplies or costs (water supply, energy supply, phone, general insurances, and so on). Because of the actual accounting practices, this amount can be found in a specific general ledger account.
    8. To the service being analyzed, attribute a percentage of the total amount obtained in the previous activity. The percentage attributable to the service will be calculated based on the human resources that work on it and the surface the service uses from the entire company's surface.
    9. Sum up all the amounts on a spreadsheet.

- **People who perform the activities**: All the activities are performed by a person in the administration department.

- **How often is it done**: It is done four or five times per year; each time for a different service.

- **Importance**: It is a very important process, as this report will be used when negotiating with the public authorities the income that the company will receive to perform this public service for the following years.

We can write down the activities, their order, and the relations with other activities using a flow chart. It will look similar to the following diagram:

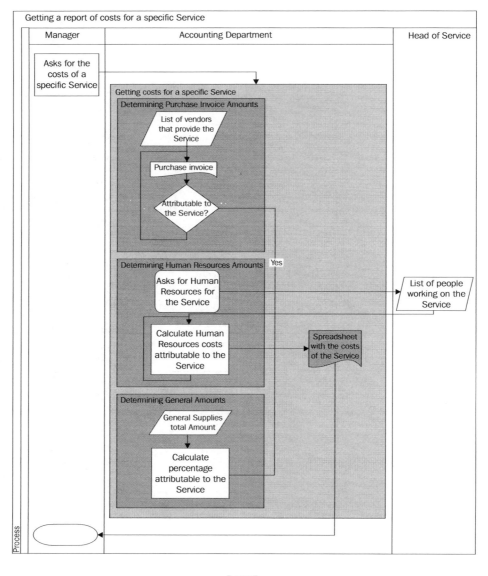

Improve before automating

IT tools allow us to automate all kinds of tasks with the aim of reducing time and errors. But not everything should be automated. An inefficient and complex process can be sped up using some kind of automation but it will still be an inefficient and complex process. Because of its complexity, the cost (in terms of time, validations, and money) of automating the process will be probably greater than expected.

In addition, trying to automate an already messed up process will only make your process quickly more messy.

It is much better to improve your business processes and think about automation once they are good and efficient.

You should also think about the importance of the process and about how often that process is done. A process that is done dozens of times per day is probably worth automating while a process that is done once a year may not be the best candidate for automation.

The process in our example has to be clearly improved before any kind of automation is applied to it. We cannot just take it as it is and automate only some of the activities.

The longest activity is the process of going through all the purchase invoices and determining whether they are attributable to a specific service. The human decision part probably cannot be automated now or in the near future.

Getting the requirements

How do I know what my requirements are? Well, if the internal processes have been defined, this should be an easy question to answer. You should start by the most important and frequent processes and move on to the least important or infrequent processes. The important and frequent ones should be handled by the ERP while the least important and infrequent processes may or may not be handled by the ERP depending on your goals and the budget for the implementation.

Talk to the consultants who will be implementing Dynamics NAV for your organization. Tell them how your process looks like, who is involved in it, what information is required, and so on. They will tell you how this specific process is resolved in Dynamics NAV.

If the way Dynamics NAV handles the process meets the way you handle the process, you've struck gold! You will be able to keep on doing what you're already doing without any kind of modification in the behavior of the application. This is a requirement that may not need any work at all or at the most, may need some tweaking.

If the way Dynamics NAV handles the process does not meet the way you handle the process, two possible options exist: modify the behavior of the system to meet your requirements, or change the way you handle your process to meet Dynamics NAV's way of doing things. You may even consider an option that combines the best of both options.

Is it okay to switch to the way Dynamics NAV handles the process? What will this involve? Will a different kind of information be needed? Who will have to be responsible for the process? Will it be the same people or different people? Will the steps or activities of the process be done in the same order or in a different order than before? Will all of this fit with the other processes? What will be the cost of changing the way we handle a specific business process?

On the other hand, is it possible to modify Dynamics NAV to handle the process in a different way? What would such a modification imply? How much development work will be needed to modify the behavior of the system? What will be the cost of changing the way Dynamics NAV handles a unique business process?

By doing this exercise with all your processes, one by one, you will end up with your list of requirements.

Back to our example of reporting the costs of a specific service. There is something in Dynamics NAV called **dimensions**. Dimensions are actually meant to be able to analyze any information in Dynamics NAV according to a specific value of a dimension.

One way to resolve the reporting goal in our example is to set up a dimension that will be called **service**. The values of this dimension will be all the different services the company provides.

The service dimension can then be set up as mandatory in all the general ledger accounts that are used to post expenses. This means that before an expense is posted, whether it is a purchase invoice or any other expense such as salaries, insurances, and so on, someone has to determine the service in which the expense is attributed. If this is not determined prior to the posting of the expense, an error message will be raised. That is, you will not be able to account your expense if you do not attribute it to a service.

This completely changes the process. At the moment, assignment to services are determined a while after the expense has been accounted or are never determined if no one asks for the costs of a specific service. But having all this information can automate the process of getting an amount for a specific service in a specific period of time. If the information is in the system, a report can be automated using the appropriated reporting tools.

Once you have the whole explanation of the standard functionality provided in Microsoft Dynamics NAV, the best option in the example is to change the way the process is handled and use the Dynamics NAV way.

Two requirements will come up as follows:

- Set up a dimension called service and make it mandatory in all general ledger accounts that are used to post expenses
- Develop a report to get the total expenses amount for a specific dimension value in a specific period of time

The first requirement will only require configuration work. The second one can be addressed through configuration (setting up the appropriate analysis view, a feature in Dynamics NAV to report the general ledger amounts based on the dimension values) or a custom report can be developed.

Change management

Not changing your company's management team!

Implementing a brand new ERP means a lot of changes within an organization. The first change is the software the company is using. This will affect the people that use the ERP intensively and they will be probably worried about the project and how it will affect their daily tasks.

But this is not the only change that the company will face. While changing the ERP, you will probably change some processes or you could even change who is responsible for doing certain tasks. Usually, these changes are not easy to make. You will have to take some actions in order to reassure people and help them during the change process.

For example, on an implementation project I was involved with recently, the company had an employee whose major task was to post all the sales invoices in the system after the user "checks" whether everything is correct with the invoice before posting.

With the implementation of Dynamics NAV, it was proposed that it made more sense that the warehouse staff post the invoice along with the shipment so that the invoice can go along with the shipment. Now, that particular employee will probably feel that they are going to lose their job, so they may start avoiding the project instead of helping the implementation.

We had to assure the employee that their position will evolve. Instead of checking each order for their pricing, address information, and so on one by one, the employee will now be responsible for setting up accurate pricing into the Customer Sales Price, maintain the different addresses in the Ship-to Address, and maintain their credit up to date. This means that instead of checking each order one by one (sometimes up to a thousand orders a day), they will be managing the setup data for the customer. This was a much better use of their time and it definitely increased their productivity. The checking is done beforehand, not at the time of posting.

The first thing you need to do to face a change in management is to identify all the stakeholders of the project. After that, you need to analyze their needs and their expectations from the project. You will also have to determine whether they support the project or not and what actions you can take to change their position.

Usually, communication is the easiest way to face changes. Keep all the stakeholders informed on what the project is all about, why the company has decided to implement Dynamics NAV, how will it affect them, and how the project is advancing.

If communication is not enough for some stakeholders, you will need to take other actions. Getting them involved is usually a good way to change their vision of the project. Think carefully about how you are going to handle all those changes. People are the most valuable asset you have to make a project a success.

Get involved in testing the system

When a project starts, a consultant will take all the requirements needed to implement Dynamics NAV and determine which of those requirements will be covered with the standard application and which ones will be developed for you.

Implementing Dynamics NAV for a company is a unique process since it is going to cover specific needs of your company. Even for similar companies, there will be many differences in the process that will make the implementation unique. No matter how much experience the implementer has in the companies of your sector, you and the people in your organization are the best testers to verify that everything works as defined.

Usually, the implementer will setup a second Dynamics NAV server for you so that you can test the system before it goes to production. The consultants and developers will conduct their own test before delivering the solution but it is also important that you invest time in testing whatever you have received. Any issue found before the go-live day is much easier to solve than when it's used in a production environment.

Ask different people with different tasks within your organization to test the system. This way, all the areas will be covered by different people and the more eyes you can have over on the application, the more issues you will usually find than if just one person was testing all the areas.

Testing with real data is one of most accurate tests you could do. Before you start testing, you may want to insist your NAV partner to create an environment loaded with your data first. This way, when the users are doing testing, it's more "real".

Involve end users

The end users are actually the people who will be using Dynamics NAV on a daily basis. The project will truly succeed if they fully utilize the system. And they will only fully utilize the system if they believe it's reliable and find that it makes their job easier.

For all of this to happen, it is important that they get involved in all the steps of the implementation from the very beginning. They may not have a high position within the company, and they may not have the power to take certain decisions but they definitely have a lot to say.

When we talked about the definition of the internal processes, we said that you had to ask yourself and your people what were your processes, the activities inside each process, and the information used by the process. We also said that the real processes should be considered and not just the *theoretical* processes. The ones who actually know the real processes and activities are the end users. If their input is not taken into consideration, and you do not involve them, you will not be working with complete information and thus, you will not be able to define your real requirements.

Even if the final solution really meets all the requirements defined in the project, if those are not well-defined requirements, the project will fail as the end users will not find it useful. Instead, they will keep doing their extra processes and keeping their own information in spreadsheet files. In fact, it will make your existing process even worse.

The definition of the processes and requirements is the most important part in which the end users should get involved. If they get involved in defining how they work and how the system should behave, they will really find the system useful and actually embrace it.

But that's not the only part of the implementation process in which they should get involved. It is also important that they participate in the testing process, especially in those functionalities that have been either modified or completely developed. If they participate in the testing process, they might find errors or any other kind of improvements that could be done to make everything easier. If they bring it to your attention, the Dynamics NAV implementers will be able to fix or improve the process. If they do not get involved in this process, they may find errors or improvements once the functionalities are live but they might never tell you. Instead, they will create exception processes for their daily job that will make everything less efficient and more chaotic.

Summary

In this chapter, we saw how to handle the implementation of Dynamics NAV from a customer's perspective. We've covered a few areas but the whole idea is that you, as a customer, have to manage the implementation as a project. The implementer cannot do all the work for you. People within your organization will have tasks and responsibilities assigned, and you will have to monitor and control all those tasks.

Do get involved with the project management and with the project's progress in order to make the project successful.

In the following chapter, you will see how a company may have data in other applications (their old ERP system, spreadsheet files, and so on) and how it can be massively imported to Microsoft Dynamics NAV.

6
Migrating Data

Microsoft Dynamics NAV, since its 2013 release, is completely configured and tuned. A range of brand new functionalities have been developed and everything is ready for you to go live. There's only one thing missing in the database - the data!

In this chapter, we will see which tools can be used in Dynamics NAV to migrate data into the system and how to convert the data to meet NAV requirements. We will look at tools such as:

- RapidStart Services
- XMLport
- User defined tools

We will also see what kind of data is commonly migrated to Dynamics NAV and which strategies can be used to migrate it. The kind of data and strategies are listed as follows:

- Master data
- Open entries
- Historical data
- Open documents

Tools to migrate data

There are several ways to migrate data into Microsoft Dynamics NAV. You choose the method depending on what is to be migrated and whether any additional processes need to be carried out on the provided data to meet the Dynamics NAV requirements.

We'll go through the different tools available in Dynamics NAV to migrate the data. We'll also explain how to write our own tools if the ones provided out of the box do not meet our requirements or expectations.

RapidStart Services

RapidStart Services is a new feature of Microsoft Dynamics NAV that was released in Dynamics NAV 2013. It allows you to configure your company data using out-of-the-box features that are built in. Microsoft Dynamics NAV also allows streamlined importing of opening balances into journals, and also allows you to open documents with dimensions.

With RapidStart Services, you can set up the tables involved in the configuration process of new companies. You can create a questionnaire to guide you and your customers through the collection of setup information. Your customers have the option of using the questionnaire to set up application areas on their own, or they can open the setup page directly and complete the setup there. Most importantly, RapidStart Services helps you, as a customer, prepare the company with default setup data that you can fine-tune and customize. Lastly, when you use RapidStart Services, you can configure and migrate existing customer data, such as a list of customers or items, into the new company.

The RapidStart Services tools can be found under **Department | Departments | Administration | Application Setup | RapidStart Services for Microsoft Dynamics NAV**.

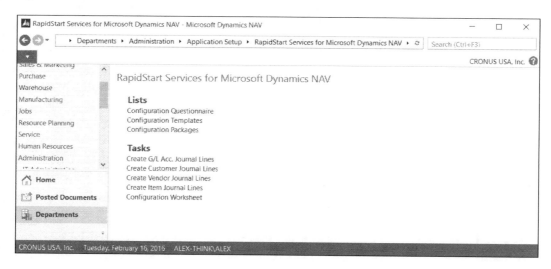

The following components can be used to set up a new company:

- Configuration wizard
- Configuration packages
- Configuration worksheet
- Configuration templates
- Configuration questionnaire

Let's work through these components by following a step-by-step example. Before starting with the example, you need to create a new company, and you may have an easier time if you change your role to that of **RapidStart Services Implementer**.

In this example, we will do the following:

1. Create a new company using PowerShell
2. Change our profile to **RapidStart Services Implementer**
3. Use the configuration wizard
4. Create a data configuration package
5. Apply the configuration package

Creating a new company using PowerShell

The following steps will guide you through to creating your new company within PowerShell:

1. Start the Microsoft Dynamics NAV 2016 Administration Shell (make sure to right-click on the icon and select **Run as Administrator**).
2. Type in `New-NAVCompany`.
3. Let's name the new company `My New Company`.
4. For **ServerInstance**, type in the same server instance as you're using to connect to Dynamics NAV. If you installed with the default settings, type in `DynamicsNAV90`, otherwise, run the Microsoft Dynamics NAV 2016 Administration and check the services that are running.

5. Push *Enter* and wait for a few seconds until the system finishes creating the company. When the process is done, as shown in the following screenshot, it will bring you back to the PowerShell command prompt.

```
PS C:\WINDOWS\system32> New-NAVCompany

cmdlet New-NAVCompany at command pipeline position 1
Supply values for the following parameters:
CompanyName: My New Company
ServerInstance: DynamicsNAV80
PS C:\WINDOWS\system32>
```

6. Open the Windows client.

7. Click on the Dynamics icon found on the upper-right corner of the page, and click on the **Select Company** option.

8. On the **Select Company** page, as shown in the following screenshot, choose **My New Company**. Then click on **OK**.

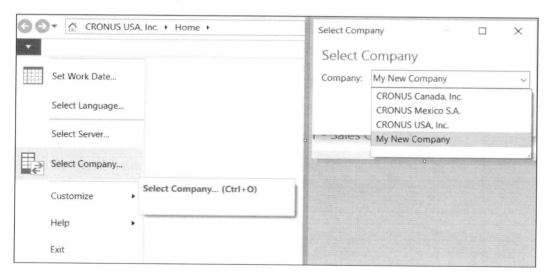

You have now entered in the **My New Company** section.

Changing the profile to RapidStart Services Implementer

Follow the ensuing steps for changing **User Personalization**:

1. Open the **User Personalization** page, found under **Departments | Administration | Application Setup | Role Tailored Client | User Personalization**.

2. Double click on the **RAPIDSTART SERVICES** profile to bring up the card page.

3. Click on the **Default Role Center** checkbox shown as follow:

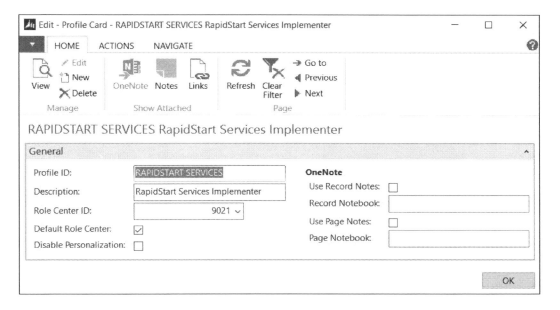

4. Close the Windows client and open it again. Your **Role Center** now looks like the following screenshot:

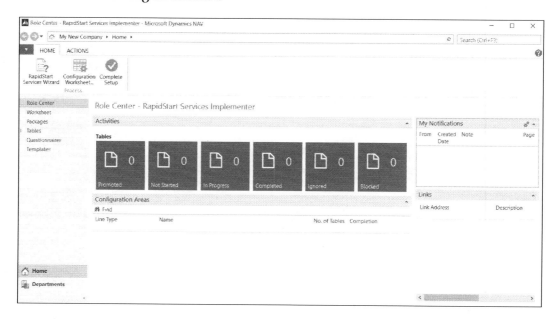

Now that we have a new company and we have selected the **RapidStart Services Implementer** role, we are ready to use all the components of the RapidStart Services tool to set up our company.

Using the configuration wizard

The configuration wizard is used to quickly configure a new company. Click on the **RapidStart Services Wizard** option found on the ribbon bar.

A new page will open where you will be able to enter basic information about the new company. You can also load your company logo by right clicking on the **Picture** box.

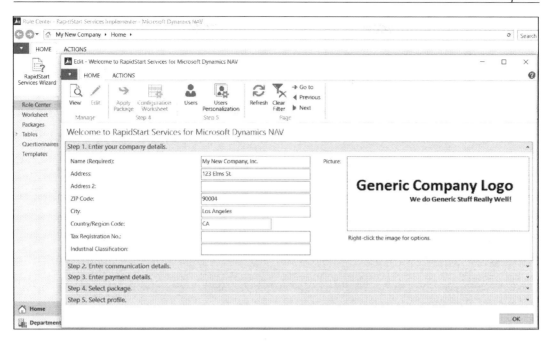

You can go through all the tabs of the page, entering the required information. The **Select Package** tab is mentioned in the *Applying a configuration package* section, next.

Creating a data conversion package

There are more than 200 tables that can be considered as configuration tables. If you intend to utilize all the features in Dynamics NAV, you need to fill them in when you create a new company.

You will find almost 50 tables with the word *setup* as their description, but there are many other tables that can also be considered as setup tables. Here you can see a list of some setup tables:

- **Posting Groups**: There are 10 tables located here
- **Journal Batch** and **Journal Template** tables: More than 20 tables are located here
- **G/L accounts**, **Account schedules**: Almost 10 tables are present here
- **Payment terms**, **Payment methods**, **Currencies**, **Languages**, **Countries** and **Regions**, **Post codes**, **Series**, and so on: These are the other setup tables without the word *setup* in their description

Having to edit all these tables manually on each implementation can take a long time. Fortunately, this is where RapidStart package can help by speeding up this process.

The best approach is to create a configuration package for the data on the configuration tables and then apply it on each new implementation, like a template.

You can create one configuration package per functional area. For example, you can create one package for the manufacturing functionalities and one package for the finance functionalities. Another approach can be to create one package for each type of data. For example, you can create one package with the data related to all the posting groups found in the application and one package for all the master data.

In this section, we will see how to create a configuration package and also how to apply it to a new company.

Creating a configuration package

In this section, we are going to create a new configuration package with all the posting groups tables found on the application. Since posting groups refer to general ledger accounts, we are also going to include the chart of accounts in our package.

Follow these steps to create the new configuration package:

1. Select a company containing the data that you want to include in your configuration package. Then, change the company back to our demonstration company, **CRONUS USA, Inc.**.

2. From the **RapidStart Services Implementer** role center, click on the **Packages** option.

3. Click on the **New** button on the ribbon bar. The **Config. Package Card** page opens. Fill in the fields in the **General** tab, as shown in the following screenshot:

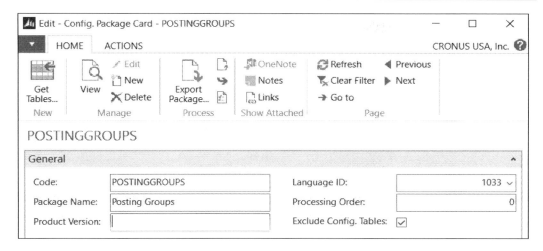

4. Add tables to the package by creating new lines on the **Tables** tab, as shown in the following screenshot. You will only have to fill in the **Table ID** column.

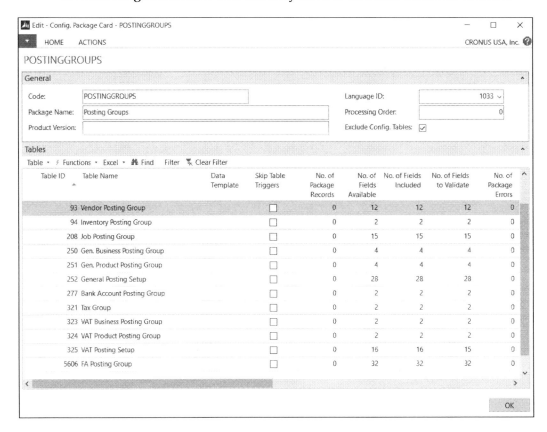

5. When you insert a table in the package, all the table fields are included by default. In some cases, you may want to exclude certain fields from the package. Select the **G/L Account** line and click on **Table | Fields**. On the **Config. Package Fields** page, uncheck the **Include Field** column for the **Global Dimension 1 Code** field and the **Global Dimension 2 Code** field. This will also remove the **Validate Field** checkbox. Push **OK** to close the page.

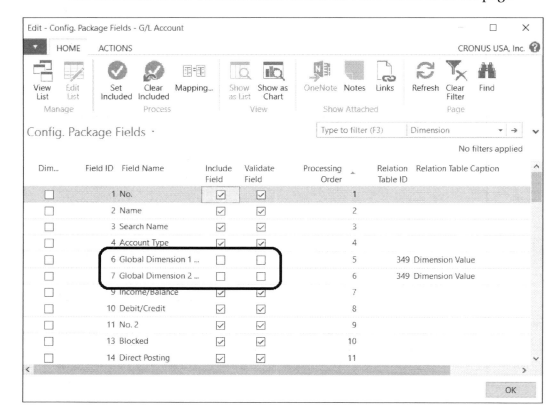

6. Click on the **Export Package** option on the ribbon bar. This will create a RAPIDSTART file that you can save. Go ahead and save the file somewhere on your computer so we can import it into **My New Company**.

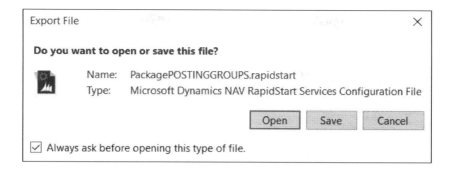

Applying a configuration package

In the previous section, we created a new configuration package. In this section, we are going to apply this package to the company **My New Company**; the new company we created earlier in this chapter.

Follow these steps to apply the configuration package:

1. On the Windows client, open the company **My New Company**.

2. From the **RapidStart Services Implementer** role center, click on the **RapidStart Services Wizard** option.

3. On the **Select package.** tab, select the configuration package that you created in the previous section.

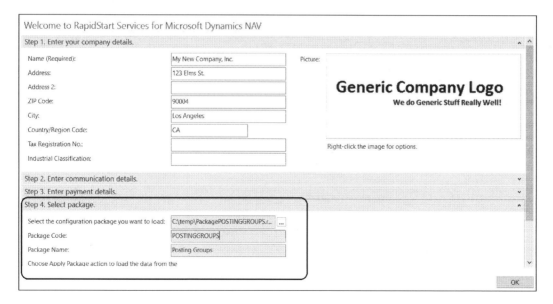

4. Click on the **Apply Package** option found on the ribbon bar. When the process is done, you will get a confirmation message.

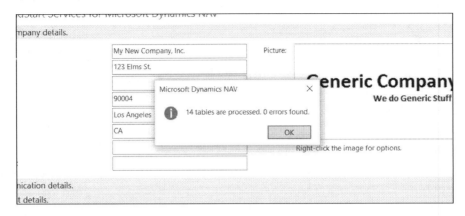

The data contained in the configuration package has now been imported to the new company. You can also import packages from the packages page we saw while creating the configuration package.

Configuration worksheet

In the previous section, we created a configuration package and imported all the tables and fields that were within that package. But what if we want to migrate specific tables but use the same field setups in the package? For the purpose of eliminating the need for creating a different configuration package for each table that we want to convert, this is where the configuration worksheet comes in.

The configuration worksheet allows you to migrate specific tables using a specific configuration package that we setup in the previous step. You can plan, track, and perform your own data imports instead of asking developers to create XMLports to import data into NAV.

For those of you who have used the previous versions of Dynamics NAV, the configuration worksheet is the old migration tool with some new features.

The configuration worksheet is used to create the structure of tables that need to be imported with the company data. You will be able to export this structure to Microsoft Office Excel, fill in the data, and then import it back to Dynamics NAV. This makes it easy for companies to copy and paste information from another ERP system. This is also very handy if you're going to be importing data from existing Excel sheets that the users are working with.

Basically, the configuration worksheet allows you to select and choose specific tables to import/export using the configuration package.

Let's explore how the configuration worksheet works by importing the Customer table and all the related tables into our new company.

Creating the migration structure

Make sure you're currently working in My New Company. As described previously, we must first open the configuration package and setup a new package.

1. Click on **Packages** from the home page, or you can access it by going to **Departments | Administration | Application Setup | RapidStart Services** for Microsoft Dynamics NAV/Configuration Packages.

2. Click on **New** to create a new package and name it CUSTOMER.

3. In the lines area, type in 18 for the **Table ID** field.

4. Click on **Table** in the lines area and select the fields. Doing so will automatically populate the fields that are defined in the table, which can be seen in the following screenshot:

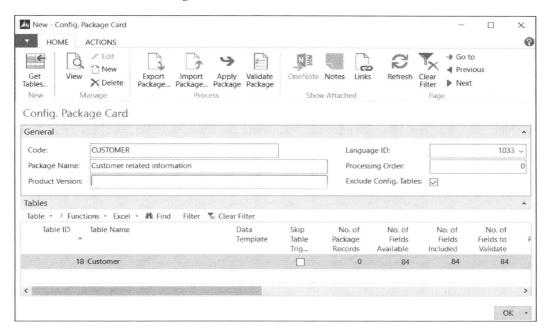

5. Now that we've created the configuration package, we are ready to assign this package to a configuration worksheet.

Perform the following steps to define the tables in a configuration worksheet:

1. Open the configuration worksheet from the **RapidStart** role center.

2. Create a line for table **18, Customer**. You only need to fill in the **Line Type** field and the **Table ID** field.

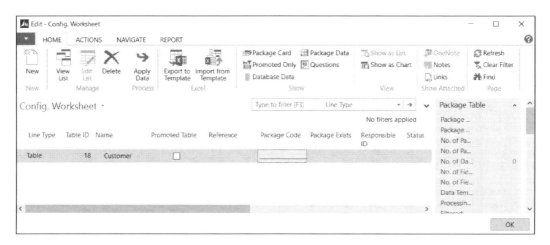

3. Click on **ACTIONS** and select **Assign Package**.

4. Select the **CUSTOMER** package and click on **OK**.

BOOM! We're done! You're now ready to use this configuration to copy the customer data from CRONUS to My New Company. All you need to do is click on the **Copy Data from Company** button to copy the customer data over.

We proceed by performing the following steps:

1. Click on the **Copy Data from Company** button under **Actions**.

2. Click on **Copy Data** from the prompt.

3. Push **Yes** on the confirmation message.

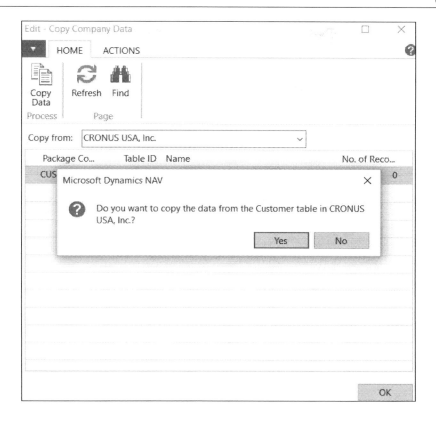

4. After the data is copied over, you can click on the **Database Data** from the **Config. Worksheet**, or go to **Customer List** to see the customer information that has been copied over.

Copying related tables

Dynamics NAV is built based on a relational database. In the case of the `Customer` table, there are a lot of tables that are related; for example, `Payment Terms Code`. Just copying over the `Customer` table will not allow us to function property on our new company.

Prior to RapidStart, you would've had to find out all the tables that the `Customer` table is related to by going into the Development Environment. Fortunately, there's a function called **Get Related Tables** in the **Config. Worksheet** and the configuration package that takes care of this for us.

Select the **Customer** record from the **Config. Worksheet** and click on **Get Related Tables**. This will populate all the related tables onto our worksheet.

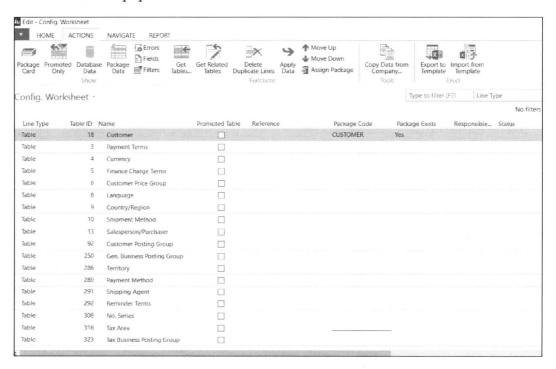

One thing you'll notice after you get the related tables is that **Package Code** is all blank. To assign a package to all the records, do the following:

1. Highlight all the lines.
2. Click on **Assign Package**.
3. Select the **CUSTOMER** package.
4. Click on **OK**.

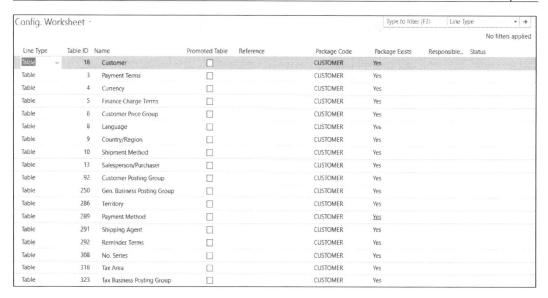

Assigning the package to the tables on the worksheet will also populate the fields that are related to the tables.

Using Excel templates

We used the **Copy Data from Company** function to copy the data from a company that's setup within Dynamics NAV. Suppose we want to migrate the data from an external source. We wouldn't want to use the copy data functionality because that data is not even in Dynamics NAV yet!

We can utilize Dynamics NAV to export the structure that we've defined on the configuration package and configuration worksheet into Excel. Then you can either copy/paste the data, or manually enter the data into Excel and import it back in to NAV. To do so, perform the following steps:

1. Go to the **Config. Worksheet**.
2. Highlight **Payment Terms** (you can highlight more lines if you want to export them into the same Excel sheet).

3. Click on **Export to Template**.

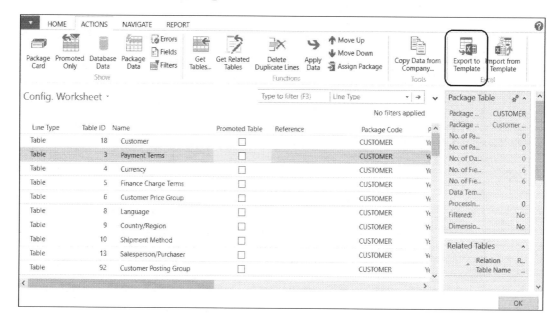

4. Give the file a name and save it somewhere on your computer.

5. After the file is saved, open the Excel file and fill in the information without modifying the column structure.

 If you need to modify the column structure, make sure to update the **Processing Order** field in the **Config. Package** field. This will change the order in which the fields are read.

6. Fill the Excel sheet as shown in the following screenshot:

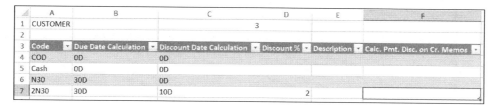

7. Save and close the Excel sheet and go back to the configuration worksheet. We will import what we've filled in into My New Company.

8. Click on **Import from Template**. Select **Yes** from the prompt and choose the Excel sheet that you saved in the preceding step.

9. When the data is imported from Excel, Dynamics NAV will put it in the holding spot called **Package Data**. Click on the package data from the configuration worksheet to check what was imported. The following screenshot shows the `Payment Terms` package data:

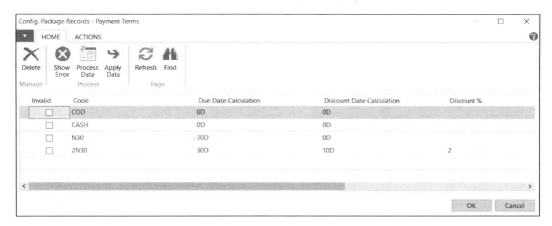

10. Once you've confirmed that this is indeed what you want, click on **Apply Data**. This will create the records in our database. If we open the **Payment Terms** table, we will see the records created in `My New Company`.

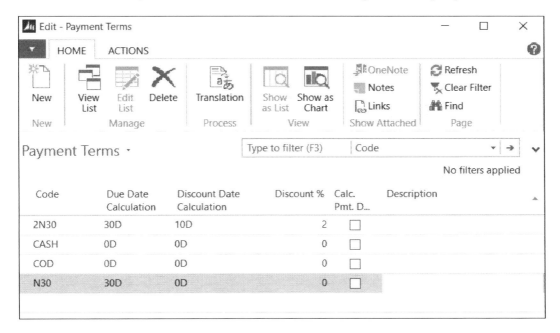

Configuration templates

Templates are used to default data on some fields when we import data into Dynamics NAV. There are some mandatory fields in Dynamics NAV which do not exist on the dataset that you're importing the data from, using the configuration templates; we will be able to default these mandatory fields.

You usually create templates for the master data, such as customers, vendors, and items master data.

 You can also use data templates for daily operations to create records that are based on templates.

In this section, we are going to see how to create a configuration template and how to use it while importing data into Dynamics NAV.

Creating a configuration template

Each template consists of a header and lines. On the header, you specify the table related to the template. On the lines, you specify which fields are included in the template and their default values. Following is an example of a template setup for DOMESTIC customers in CRONUS USA, Inc.:

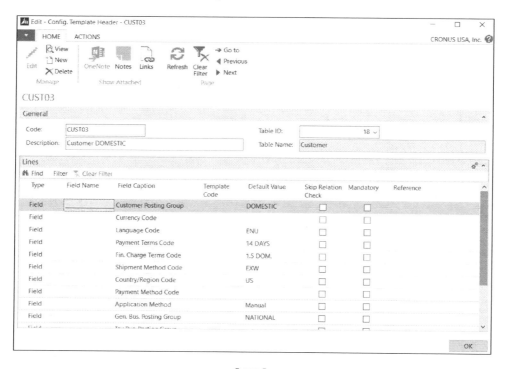

Let's create a new template on our own and apply it to an existing configuration package. While you're in `My New Company`, do the following:

1. Open the **Templates** page and click on the **New** button.

2. In the **Code** field, enter a unique ID for the template. Let's name it CUSTTERM. In the **Description** field, enter a description.

3. In the **Table ID** field, enter the table to which this template has been applied. In our case, it will be table **18**.

4. Create a new line and select the **Field Name** field. The **Field List** window displays the list of fields in the table. Since we want to default the **Payment Terms** to **N30**, select the **Payment Terms** field and then click on the **OK** button.

5. In the **Default Value** field, enter N30.

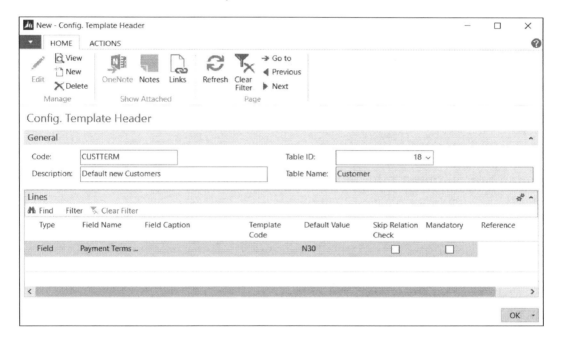

Using configuration templates

Using configuration templates with RapidStart Services is as simple as selecting the template we want to use on a line of a configuration package. The following steps will demonstrate this:

1. Open the **Packages** page.

2. From the list of packages, open the **CUSTOMER** package we created earlier in this chapter.

3. Find the **Customer** table included in the package. In the **Data Template** field, select the template that we created in the previous section.

And we are done! When importing new customers using the package, the template will be applied, as can be seen in the following screenshot:

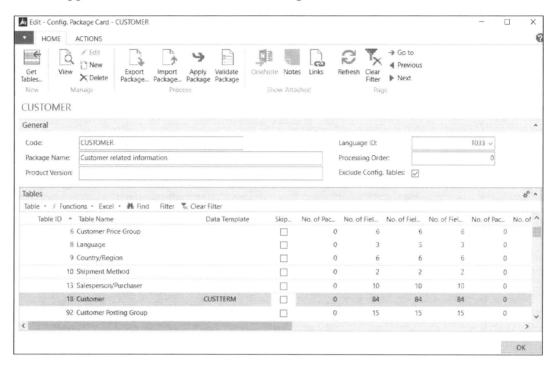

Configuration questionnaire

The configuration questionnaire is used to collect data from the users to help configure a new company. You can create a list of questions and provide it to the users as an Excel or an XML file. When the user completes the questionnaire, you import the file into the new Microsoft Dynamics NAV company and then apply it to the database.

The idea behind the configuration questionnaire is to allow the NAV partner to bypass speaking to customers directly and automate the setup. Why on earth would any partner do this to a customer? Simple, if your NAV solution is so vertical that you can practically set it up blindfolded, you can probably write down all of your knowledge and have the system set itself up.

Follow the steps described in the following section to create and complete a configuration questionnaire.

Creating a configuration questionnaire

Follow the steps listed in this section to create a configuration questionnaire:

1. Open the **Questionnaire** page and click on the **New** option.

2. Provide a code and a description.

3. Click on the **Questions Areas** option found on the ribbon bar.

4. In the **Code** field, enter a code for the question area.

5. In the **Table ID** field, choose the ID of the table for which you want to collect information.

6. Click on the **Update Questions** option found on the ribbon bar. Each field in the table is added to the questionnaire with a question mark following its label. You can rephrase the label to make it clear how the question should be answered. For example, if a field is called **Name,** you can edit it to state What is the name of <data being collected>. As needed, you can also delete the questions that you do not want to include in the questionnaire.

7. Repeat these steps to add additional question areas.

In the following screenshot taken from CRONUS USA, Inc., you can see an example of a questionnaire for the inventory setup area:

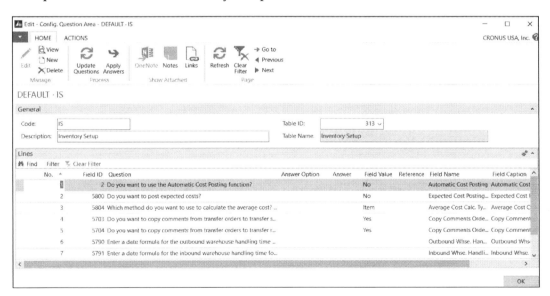

Completing the configuration questionnaire

Once you have the configuration questionnaire thought out, you can export it to Excel and send it off to the customers to fill in. Change to the CRONUS USA, Inc. company to see a list of the premade questions.

1. Open the CRONUS USA, Inc. company.

2. Open the **Questionnaire** page, click on the **Export to Excel** option found on the ribbon bar, and save the file.

3. Complete the configuration questionnaire by entering the answers in the Excel workbook. There are worksheets for each of the question areas that have been created for the questionnaire. Save the file.

4. Back in the questionnaire, click on the **Import from Excel** option. Select the XLSX file that you have saved.

5. Click on the **Question Areas** option, and select one question area to begin the process of validating and applying the answers to the setup questionnaire.

6. After the validating process is complete and the answers to the whole questionnaire are applied, click on the **Apply Answers** option of the **Questionnaire** page.

7. To apply answers for a specific question area, click on the **Apply Answers** option from the **Question Areas** page.

Summarizing RapidStart Services

We have already covered RapidStart Services. Before moving to another tool to migrate, there are a few things you should know about RapidStart Services:

- RapidStart Services can be used both for importing and exporting data. It is not a tool reserved just to import data when you first start working with Microsoft Dynamics NAV.

- RapidStart Services does not only insert new data into the database, it can actually be used to modify the data as well. This functionality can be used as a "find and replace" substitute that was sorely missed by users using the classic client. To modify the data, first export it to an Excel template, modify whatever needs to be modified, and import the data again. The tool will perform the following actions:

  ° Create a new record in the corresponding table if no record exists with the same values on the primary key fields as the imported record.

  ° Update a record in the corresponding table if the record imported already exists in the table. The record will be updated with all the information coming from the imported record.

- RapidStart Services consumes a lot of time while importing and exporting data. It took us 1 minute to import 5,000 customers and almost 5 minutes to apply them. However, importing that exact same data using an **XMLport** (the next tool we will explain) took us just a couple of seconds.

Using XMLports to migrate data

An XMLport is a Microsoft Dynamics NAV object type used to import and export data encapsulated in XML format. Fixed text and variable text formats are also available on an XMLport to import and export data from a plain text file, just as we used to do with **dataports** (a Dynamics NAV object type that has been discontinued in the previous release of the application). XMLports have their own designer, **XMLport Designer**, which can be found in **Object Designer**, as shown in the following screenshot:

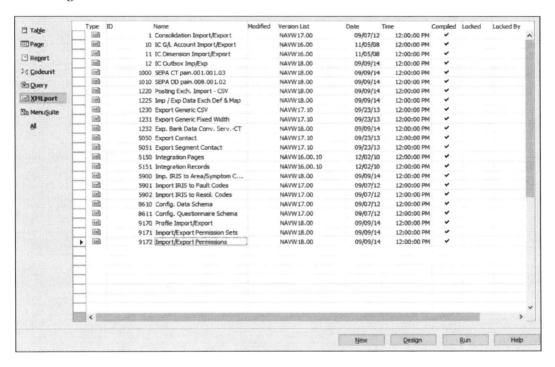

By using XMLport Designer, we specify all the XML tag names and their types (element or attribute). We also map these tag names to data structures (tables, records, or fields) in the Dynamics NAV database.

We will create an XMLport to import customers, just as we did in the *Configuration worksheet* section. By performing the same example with both the tools, we will be able to compare them and have some elements to decide which one we should use in our migrations.

We will be importing the following data into the Customers table:

- Name
- Address
- City
- Salesperson code
- Payment terms code

The XMLport structure

To understand the XMLport structure, we will create a new XMLport as an example, using the following steps:

1. Open the Dynamics NAV Development Environment.
2. Navigate to **Tools | Object Designer** (or press *Shift + F12*).
3. Select XMLport.
4. Click on the **New** button (or press *Alt + N*).
5. XMLport Designer will open with an empty XMLport.
6. Create the structure shown in the following screenshot:

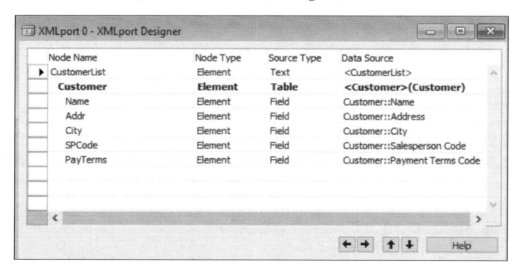

7. Save the XMLport by clicking on **File** | **Save** (or press *Ctrl + S*).

8. Give your XMLport an ID, 50001 and a name, Import Customer Data.

9. Click on the **OK** button.

The additional elements are indented using the → icon and not by using the *Spacebar*. There are many details on programming Dynamics NAV in the Development Environment. I highly recommend *Programming Microsoft Dynamics NAV 2015* published by Packt Publishing.

The following are the elements of our XMLport:

- The **Node Name** column indicates the tag names that will be used in the XML document

- The **Node Type** column is where we indicate which type of tag it will be, whether element or attribute

- The **Source Type** column is from where we can select whether the mapping of the element or attribute is with a text source, a table source, or a field source

- The **Data Source** column is where we indicate the text for the text sources, the Dynamics NAV table for the table source types, and the Dynamics NAV field for the field source types

> For both the table and field source types, we can click on the up arrow that appears in the column to select the appropriate Dynamics NAV data structure. When a table source type is selected, a list of Dynamics NAV tables is shown. When a field source type is selected, a lookup field appears for us to select a field in any of the tables selected as a table source type on the XMLport. When using a text source type, the information imported from the XML document is put in a text variable with the name specified in the **Data Source** column. This variable can be used as a global C/AL variable.

Child nodes have to be indented under their parent elements using one indentation per level. To indent the elements, use the left and right arrows that can be found in the lower right corner of the **XMLport Designer** window. Nodes have to be entered in the exact same order in which they appear in the XML document.

If you check the XMLport properties by placing the cursor on the first empty line of the XMLport and clicking on **View** | **Properties** (or pressing the *Shift + F4* key combination), you will see a property called **Format**, which is set to **xml**. The other options for this property are variable text and fixed text. By selecting either variable text or fixed text, you will be able to import/export data in a plain text format rather than in an XML format. Let's leave this property alone for now.

Running the XMLport

We will be importing a file called `Customer.xml` that has the following structure and data:

```
<?xml version="1.0" encoding="UTF-16" standalone="no"?>
<CustomerList>
  <Customer>
    <Name>GDE Distribución S.A.</Name>
    <Address>Plaza del mercado 192</Address>
    <City>Barcelona</City>
    <SalespersonCode />

    <PaymentTermsCode>N30</PaymentTermsCode>
  </Customer>
  <Customer>
    <Name>Sellafrio S.L.</Name>
    <Address>Rambla de Teruel 153</Address>
    <City>Sabadell</City>
    <SalespersonCode />
    <PaymentTermsCode>COD</PaymentTermsCode>
  </Customer>
</CustomerList>
```

To import the file, follow these steps:

1. Open the Dynamics NAV Development Environment.
2. Click on **Tools | Object Designer** (or press *Shift + F12*).
3. Select the **XMLport** option.
4. Click on the **Run** tab (or press *Alt + R*).
5. The Windows client will open, and the **Edit – Import Customer Data** page will also open.
6. Select the **Import** tag in the **Direction** field.
7. Click on the **OK** button.
8. Navigate to the XML file you want to import and click on the **Open** tab.
9. The file will be imported.

Check the customer list to see the records that have been created by the XMLport. You will notice that the **OnInsert** and **OnValidate** triggers for each of the fields have been run (each customer has a number, so the **OnInsert** trigger has been run, and the field **Search Name** has been filled in, which means that at least the **OnValidate** trigger for the **Name** field has been run as well).

Writing code inside the XMLport

With an XMLport you can write your own code to handle multiple situations. You can either write data on multiple Dynamics NAV tables or create secondary records while importing the master data.

In our example, you can write code to create new payment terms if the payment terms code filled for one customer does not exist on the database.

XMLports also offer the capability of importing data into different Dynamics NAV tables that have a link relation between them, such as in a **Sales Order** table. In a **Sales Order** table, data has to be imported into the **Sales Header** and **Sales Line** table, which have a header/line relation through the **Document Type** and **Document No.** fields.

The document structure

Imagine we have an XML document, like the one shown in the following screenshot, that we want to import into Dynamics NAV:

```xml
<?xml version="1.0" encoding="UTF-16" standalone="no" ?>
<SalesOrder>
  <Header>
    <SalesHeader Date="18/01/12">
      <CustomerName>Deerfield Graphics Company</CustomerName>
      <Lines>
        <SalesLine>
          <ItemNo>LS-10PC</ItemNo>
          <Quantity>12</Quantity>
          <UnitOfMeasureCode>BOX</UnitOfMeasureCode>
          <UnitPrice>57</UnitPrice>
          <LocationCode>WHITE</LocationCode>
        </SalesLine>
        <SalesLine>
          <ItemNo>LS-150</ItemNo>
          <Quantity>8</Quantity>
          <UnitOfMeasureCode>PCS</UnitOfMeasureCode>
          <UnitPrice>120</UnitPrice>
          <LocationCode>WHITE</LocationCode>
        </SalesLine>
      </Lines>
    </SalesHeader>
  </Header>
</SalesOrder>
```

We analyze the XML document tag structure and decide that we will have to import the data into the **Sales Header** and **Sales Line** tables, and we design an XMLport with the following structure:

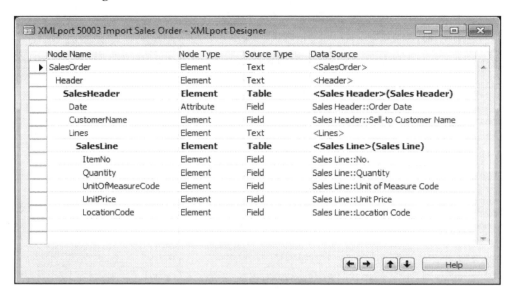

In this XMLport structure, we have used all the XML tags detected on the XML document and we have mapped them to Dynamics NAV tables (the **SalesHeader** element is mapped to the **Sales Header** table and the **SalesLine** element is mapped to the **Sales Line** table) and Dynamics NAV fields in the corresponding tables.

Note that the **Date** tag, which has been mapped to the **Order Date** field of the **Sales Header** table, has a node type of attribute. We have designed it that way because, while analyzing the XML document, we can see the **Date** tag as an attribute of the preceding tag, **SalesHeader**.

```
<SalesHeader Date="18/01/12">
```

The following screenshot shows the properties page of **SalesLine**. In the properties of the **SalesLine** tag, which is mapped to the **Sales Line** table, we have indicated that this tag has a link relation with the **Sales Header** table, we have specified which fields offer the link in the **LinkFields** property, and we have set the **LinkTableForceInsert** property to **Yes**. This means that we force the record on the link table (**Sales Header**) to be inserted before we start writing anything in the linked table (**Sales Line**).

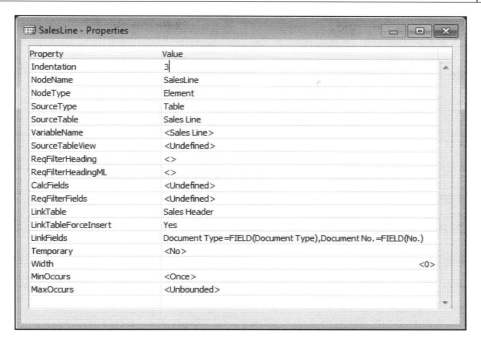

Filling data not included in the XML file

The data provided to you may not be enough. Different software have different fields that they consider mandatory and Microsoft Dynamics NAV is no different. Therefore, we will need to write some code to fill-in those fields that do not appear in the XML document but are needed in Microsoft Dynamics NAV to create a `Sales Order` table.

For example, we will have to fill-in the **Document Type** field in both the **Sales Header** and **Sales Line** tables. We will also have to fill in the **Type** field in the **Sales Line** table. In addition, we will need to find the customer number as only the name of the customer appears in the XML document, but in Dynamics NAV we will have to inform the **Sell-to Customer No.** field as well. Now, declare the global variables as shown in the following screenshot:

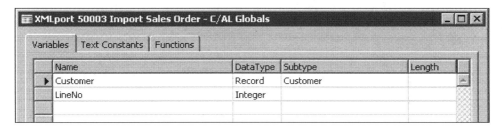

When initializing the **Sales Header** record, assign **Order** as the **Document Type** field and assign an initial value of **10000** to the global variable **LineNo**.

```
XMLport 50003 Import Sales Order - C/AL Editor                              _ □ X
  SalesHeader - Import::OnAfterInitRecord()
  "Sales Header"."Document Type" := "Sales Header"."Document Type"::Order;
  LineNo := 10000;
```

Assign the **Document Date** field the same value as the **Order Date** field.

```
XMLport 50003 Import Sales Order - C/AL Editor                              _ □ X
  Date - Import::OnAfterAssignField()
  "Sales Header".VALIDATE("Document Date","Sales Header"."Order Date");
```

Find the customer number by setting a filter on its **Name** field and assign it to the **Sell-to Customer No.** field, as shown in the following screenshot:

```
XMLport 50003 Import Sales Order - C/AL Editor                              _ □ X
  CustomerName - Import::OnAfterAssignField()
  Customer.SETRANGE(Name,"Sales Header"."Sell-to Customer Name");
  IF Customer.FINDFIRST THEN
    "Sales Header".VALIDATE("Sell-to Customer No.",Customer."No.");
```

When initializing the Sales Line record, assign Order as the Document Type field, Item as the Type field, and the value of the global variable LineNo as the Line No field. Then the increment variable LineNo should be used in the next line.

```
XMLport 50003 Import Sales Order - C/AL Editor                              _ □ X
  SalesLine - Import::OnAfterInitRecord()
  "Sales Line"."Document Type" := "Sales Line"."Document Type"::Order;
  "Sales Line".Type := "Sales Line".Type::Item;
  "Sales Line"."Line No." := LineNo;
  LineNo := LineNo + 10000;
```

Save and compile the XMLport with the number 50003 and the name Import Sales Order.

Run the XMLport and take a look at the **Sales Order** that has been created:

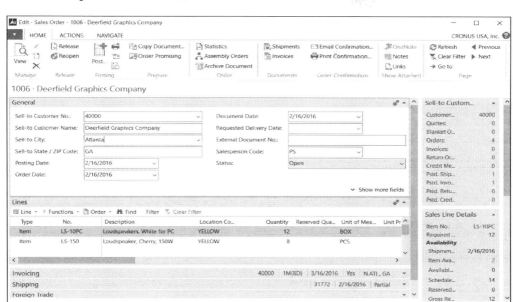

Note that this is a very fast example of how to write code in the XMLport. As previously mentioned, to get a complete guide on programming for Dynamics NAV, refer to *Programming Microsoft Dynamics NAV 2015* published by Packt Publishing.

Validation order may change our data

Everything seems to be fine except the dates, which were set to `01/18/12` in the XML document but have the value `2/16/2016` in the `Sales Order` table.

The reason is because although the order and document dates were first set to `01/18/2012`, but when the `OnInsert` trigger for the `Sales Header` table was run, they get defaulted to `Work Date`, which was `02/26/2016`. How do we know this? You can turn on the debugger (which will be covered in *Chapter 11, Debugging,* of this book) and follow through the code, or just ask a NAV developer.

Either way, we will have to change something in our XMLport to prevent this behavior. What we will do is save the `Order Date` field in a global variable and validate it against the `table` field after the `OnInsert` trigger is run.

Create a global variable named OrderDate as the Date field. Modify the code in the XMLport to insert the highlighted code lines in the Date - Import::OnAfterAssignField() trigger.

```
XMLport 50003 Import Sales Order - C/AL Editor
Date - Import::OnAfterAssignField()
  "Sales Header".VALIDATE("Document Date","Sales Header"."Order Date");
  OrderDate := "Sales Header"."Order Date";
```

Also add the highlighted code line in the SalesLine - Import::OnAfterInitRecord() trigger.

```
XMLport 50003 Import Sales Order - C/AL Editor
SalesLine - Import::OnAfterInitRecord()
  "Sales Header".VALIDATE("Order Date",OrderDate);
  "Sales Header".VALIDATE("Document Date",OrderDate);
  "Sales Header".VALIDATE("Posting Date",OrderDate);
  "Sales Header".MODIFY(TRUE);

  "Sales Line"."Document Type" := "Sales Line"."Document Type"::Order;
  "Sales Line".Type := "Sales Line".Type::Item;
  "Sales Line"."Line No." := LineNo;
  LineNo := LineNo + 10000;
```

When the Date tag is assigned to the Order Date field, we can also assign it to the variable named OrderDate.

When the sales line record is being initialized (it means the OnInsert trigger for the table Sales Header has already been run), we once again assign the saved date to the Order Date, Document Date, and Posting Date fields and we modify the Sales Header record.

Back in Microsoft Dynamics NAV, if we take a look at the Sales Order table that has been created, we will see that, finally, all the data is correct.

Writing your own tools

The tools provided by Microsoft Dynamics NAV to import data only allow you to import data in a very specific Microsoft Office Excel format, in an XML format, or in plain text.

What if you have the data in a completely different format? In that case, you have two options:

- Manually manipulate the document you have, to give it the format expected. This may be a good option for a one-time import process. Manual manipulation of data and formats may lead to errors, but if you just have to do it once, do it carefully, take your time, and check everything afterwards. The time consumed in doing all this work will probably not be as much as developing a tool to import the data, so yes, it is probably a good option.

- Write your own tool to import the data. Make your tool meet the exact format as it appears in the original document, so no manual manipulation of data is needed.

 You can use a **codeunit**, a report, or even a page to write your own code. You will find several examples in the Dynamics NAV code on how to read from files or how to use the `Excel Buffer` table to read from an Excel file. Use variables of type `record` for as many tables as you have to import data to.

We will not be giving any examples on how to develop a tool to import data as it is not within the scope of this book. We just wanted to point out that this is always an option, although if possible, it is better to use the tools provided by Dynamics NAV. That will probably save you a lot of time.

Converting data from the old system to Dynamics NAV's needs

The company's legacy system will probably have a very different data structure. However, in the meantime, a conversion process must be done. In this section, we'll explain a few tips to convert data to meet Dynamics NAV's needs.

In most of the Dynamics NAV tables (including all master and document tables), the primary key uses a code field type. The code field type is alphanumeric and is stored in the database in uppercase characters. You can write either numbers or characters in a **Code** field. If a code contains only numbers, people expect the data to be ordered by a number. But Dynamics NAV does not act this way. A code is always sorted by a character, even if it only contains numbers. This may confuse the user, so using fixed-length number codes is recommended. Let's look at this with an example:

Number Sort	Dynamics NAV Sort	Fixed length Sort
1	1	01
2	10	02
3	2	03
10	3	10

As you can see, if you use fixed length codes, the way these codes are sorted in Dynamics NAV is the same as the number sort. Therefore, we recommend that you identify those codes in the old system data and convert them before importing the data into Dynamics NAV.

Fields particular to Microsoft Dynamics NAV

In Dynamics NAV, posting groups are used in the master tables (customers, vendors, items, banks, fixed assets, and other such master tables) to identify which accounts must be used while posting entries related to them. This information may not be available in the old system or may need to be transformed. For instance, the company could be using a system that uses one single account for each customer. In Dynamics NAV, just a few accounts are necessary, so you may have to figure out which posting group fits all the master data the best.

You also need to know which fields are mandatory for each master table in order to use its registers. For instance, a customer needs to have the **Customer Posting Group** field filled, in order to create a new order; also, items need the **Base Unit of Measure** field. You may not find this information in the old system, but you need to define how to fill these fields during the migration process.

In general, find all Dynamics NAV required fields and also the fields required by the company's business logic, determine how they are going to be filled, and fill them during the migration process.

Master data

Master data can be defined as information key to the operation of a business that is often non-transactional but supports transactional processes and operations.

Customers are a good example of master data. Data about customers (their names, addresses, phone numbers, and so on) is not transactional data but will support a transactional operation, for example, a sales order for a customer.

Microsoft Dynamics NAV has several master data tables, namely, **Customer**, **Vendor**, **Item**, **Contact**, **Resource**, **Fixed Asset**, and so on. Each master data table is the primary table in an application area. The Customer table is the main table in the sales application area, while the **Vendor** table is the main table in the **Purchases** application area.

Secondary tables, such as Sales Prices, also support transactions just as the master tables do. You will also need to take the secondary tables into account while migrating the master data.

The master and secondary tables that will be used in Microsoft Dynamics NAV have to be identified and a migration plan has to be defined in order to get all this information into the system.

The migration plan for the master data tables includes:

- The table name and number
- The list of fields that will be migrated and their possible values (if applicable)
- The format in which the data will be presented
- The possible requirement of data manipulation before importing it to Dynamics NAV
- The tool that will be used to import the data
- The date on which a migration test will be done
- The go-live migration date
- The person responsible for providing the data
- The person responsible for importing the data into Microsoft Dynamics NAV
- The person responsible for testing and validating the migrated data

To import the master data into Microsoft Dynamics NAV, use the tool that best meets your requirements for importing the master data into the Dynamics NAV database.

Open entries

Open entries are transactions that haven't reached their final status yet, and are not included in the *Open documents* section. You can only post open entries when the corresponding master data is already imported. In a common scenario, the open entries include:

- **Customer entries**: It means all the money each customer owes on the day of the migration; basically, accounts receivable
- **Vendor entries**: It means all the money the company owes to each of their vendors on the day of the migration; basically, accounts payable
- **Bank entries**: It means the money the company has in each bank account
- **Item entries**: It means the stock the company has in each location on the day of the migration
- **Accounting balances**: It means the balance that each account has on the day of the migration
- **Fixed asset entries**: It means all the company's assets with their initial cost and the amount depreciated, as on the day of the migration

All these entries must be posted through their corresponding journal and must use a specific posting date. The posting date must be at least one day prior to the migration date. For instance, if you choose to go live on January 1st, you should use December 31st as the posting date for all the open entries. This way, we will start off with a fresh year with the new data and it reflects when you actually start off with a new system. The easiest way to migrate the open entries is to use the configuration worksheet described earlier in this chapter.

Customer entries

Customer entries refer to all the money that each customer owes on the day of the migration. We need to create at least one customer entry to summarize all the money that the customer owes. If the company wants to control the due dates from Dynamics NAV for the open entries, we need to create at least one summarized entry for each due date, or we can create one entry for each pending invoice.

The minimum information needed is as follows:

- **Posting date**: Use one day before the migration day for all the entries.
- **Account type**: Use the `Customer` option for all the entries.
- **Account number**: Use the customer code given to the customer.

- **Document number**: You can use the invoice number extracted from the old system, or you can give it a document number such as OPENING.

- **Description**: Give the entry a description. You can use the invoice description extracted from the old system, or you can give a description such as Opening Entries to all the entries.

- **Currency**: Leave it blank if the amounts are in local currency. Write the currency code otherwise. Keep in mind that if a currency code is filled, the amounts must be in that currency.

- **Amount**: It's the money the customer owes. Write a negative amount if it's the company which owes money to the customer, either because of credit memos or advance payments.

Other information that can be provided are as follows:

- **Document date**: In case you create one entry for each pending invoice, the document date corresponds to the date of the original invoice

- **Due date**: In case you create one entry for each pending invoice, the due date corresponds to the date when the customer has to pay his debt

- **Payment method**: In case you create one entry for each pending invoice, the payment method corresponds to how the debt will be paid

Actually, you can provide information for any field included in the Gen. Journal Line table. However, for migration purposes, the previously listed fields are enough.

Let's see with an example how to migrate the customer entries. We'll just take the minimum information needed. The following steps are involved while migrating a customer entry:

1. Provide an Excel template; we'll use RapidStart Services. The data has to be imported into the General Journal to create the customer entries when posted.

2. Create an Excel template for the table 81 and include the fields Account Type, Account No., Posting Date, Document No., Description, Currency Code, and Amount. Refer to the *Create the migration structure* section in this chapter for more information on this step.

3. Ask someone in the company to fill in the template, extracting data from the old system using the extraction tools available. You are a Dynamics NAV expert, and you may not know how the data is stored in the old system, so don't try to do it yourself.

> Remember that your job is to import data into Dynamics NAV the way Dynamics NAV expects it. It is the company's responsibility to assure that the data is consistent and of good quality.
>
> As a Dynamics NAV expert, you are responsible for filling in the fields corresponding to the primary key of the table. In this case, these are the `Journal Template Name`, `Journal Batch Name`, and `Line No.` fields.

4. Once the template is completely filled, it's time to import it to Dynamics NAV and apply it. Refer to the *Migrate your data* section in this chapter for more information on this step.

5. Open the General Journal. The data is almost ready to be posted. Once posted, Dynamics NAV won't allow you to delete or modify the created entries, so take your time before posting. Check, check, and check your work. Once you are done, check it again. Also ask the user who provided you the information to check it. Use this checklist:

Question	Answer
Does the Total Balance shown in the Journal correspond with the total Accounts Receivable?	
Does your Accounts Receivable match that of the General Ledger A/R account?	
Does each Customer owe the Amount shown in its Journal line?	

> Do not check it with the template you just imported; you will easily get a positive answer. Instead, ask someone in the company to check it with their old system. If you added extra fields to the template, add at least one question for each new field.

Once the lines are posted, new customer ledger entries will be created. G/L entries will also be created. When a new `Gen. Journal Line` table is created, Dynamics NAV copies the posting group from the customer card to the `Gen. Journal Line` table. The receivables account found in each posting group is used to determine which account must be used to post the amount each customer owes. Now, add another question to your checklist:

Question	Answer
Group all the lines by posting group. Get the receivables account for each posting group. Will each account receive the expected amount?	

Since G/L entries will be created, the accounting rules must be followed. One rule says that any transaction must be balanced. The sum of the debit amounts in each line must equal the sum of the credit amounts. The following screenshot shows the **General Journal** page of the **Default Journal Batch**:

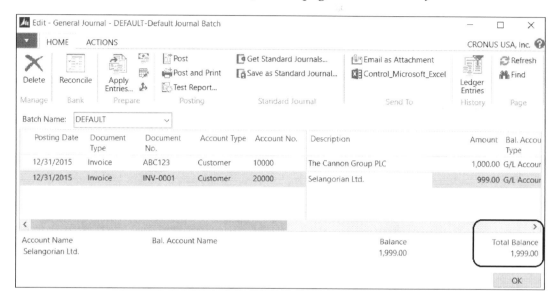

In Dynamics NAV, the **Total Balance** entry shown at the bottom of the **General Journal** field must be **0**.

6. In our example, the total available balance is **1,999.00**. We need to perform an extra step to make it **0** and balance the whole transaction. There are a few options we can use to accomplish this. Let us explain two of these options which we are aware of:

    ○ Fill in the **Bal. Account Type** field with **G/L Account**.

    ○ Fill in the **Bal. Account No.** field with the receivables account on the customer posting group assigned to each customer. In the example, both customers have the domestic customer posting group. The receivables account for them is **13100**.

Note that there are some accounts where you will not be able to directly post into. This is because Dynamics NAV has a mechanism to prevent accounts included in any posting group from receiving entries directly. You will have to skip this control in order to post the customer open entries. Go to the account card and uncheck the **Direct Posting** field. Don't forget to check it again when the migration process is over!

Your journal lines will now look like the following screenshot, and the transaction will be balanced and ready to post:

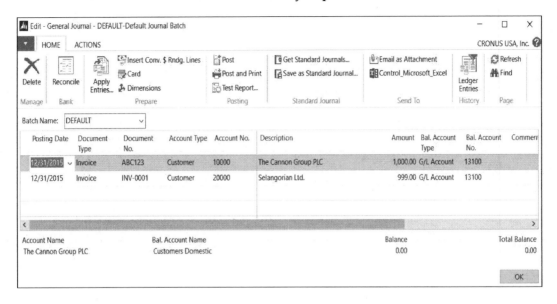

Of course, these two new fields can be added to the migration template to fill them at the outset.

Let's look at the general ledger entries that have been created after the posting process:

As you can see, the same account has been used. The balance of the account is **0.00**, even though it has four entries. If you run a balance report, you will see that no amount is shown in the **Accounts Receivable** line. It feels weird, doesn't it? Don't worry, this will be solved once the balance open entries are imported.

 In the company CRONUS USA, Inc., the open entries are posted balancing the transactions this way.

7. We are done for the accounts receivable! You can repeat this process as many times as you want.

Vendor entries

Vendor entries are pretty much the same as customer entries. Just follow the steps described in the previous section. There are a few differences explained as follows:

- When you fill in the data migration template, the account type must have the vendor value
- You have to reverse the sign of the amounts
- The balancing account will be found in the **Payables Account** field in the **Vendor Posting Group** table

Bank entries

Bank entries are pretty much the same as customer entries. Just follow the steps described in the previous section. The few differences are explained as follows:

- When you fill in the data migration template, the account type must have the bank account value
- The balancing account will be found in the **G/L Bank Account No.** field in the **Bank Account Posting Group** table

Item entries

Item entries are a bit different from the entries described so far. First of all, another journal must be used – the item journal. Also, you can choose whether the posting of the item entries creates general ledger entries or not.

The data migration tool has limitations here, so follow the recommendations to work around them.

The minimum information needed is:

- **Posting date**: Use one day before the migration day for all the entries
- **Entry type**: Use **Positive Adjmt.** for all the entries
- **Document number**: You can use a generic document number, such as OPENING
- **Item number**: Use the item code given to the item
- **Location code**: Leave it blank if the company is not using locations; otherwise, write the location code
- **Quantity**: Fill in the quantity in terms of the base unit of measurement of the item
- **Unit cost**: Fill in the unit cost in the base unit of measurement of the item

Note that the **Item Journal Line** table contains a field called **Unit of Measure Code**. So, you can use a different unit of measurement and therefore the quantity and unit cost will refer to the new unit. When you import data using RapidStart Services, the OnValidate trigger of each field is run. By default, the fields are validated in the same order that they are declared in the table.

The **Unit Cost** field has the field number **17**, whereas the **Unit of Measure Code** field has the field number **5407**. The **Unit Cost** field will be validated before the **Unit of Measure Code** field. If you fill in the **Unit of Measure Code** field in the template, code will be run. In this particular case, the unit cost will be recalculated and you will not get the unit cost you filled in the template.

To avoid this situation, you have to change the default validation order, as explained in the *RapidStart Services* section.

Usually, the automatic cost posting is disabled, since in most scenarios it is not recommended that this functionality should be used.

To check whether the automatic cost posting is disabled, go to **Departments | Financial Management | Inventory | Setup** and open the **Inventory Setup** page. There is a field called **Automatic Cost Posting**. If this field is not checked, the functionality is disabled.

Even if, in your case, the automatic cost posting must be used, disable the functionality while posting the initial item open entries. The cost will be posted in the corresponding account later on, when the accounting balances are imported.

Run the data migration tool to import the data into the item journal and post it. The item entries will be created.

Fixed-asset entries

Migrating fixed assets is a bit tricky. Here, we are not talking just about the assets that have pending depreciation but all the active assets in the company. Two types of entries have to be posted: cost entries and depreciation entries. Plus, there is more than one account involved with a singular asset. You can post the fixed asset entries from two different journals:

- The General Journal will post the fixed asset entries as well as the general ledger entries

- The fixed asset journal will only post the fixed asset entries; the general ledger entries will not be posted

We will now explain how to post the fixed asset entries using the fixed asset journal. Accounting entries related to them will be posted while importing the accounting balances later on.

To use the fixed asset journal, you must uncheck the G/L integration for the acquisition cost and the depreciation. Go to **Departments | Financial Management | Fixed Assets | Setup | Depreciation Book**. Open the **Depreciation Book Card** page and uncheck the fields, as shown in the following screenshot:

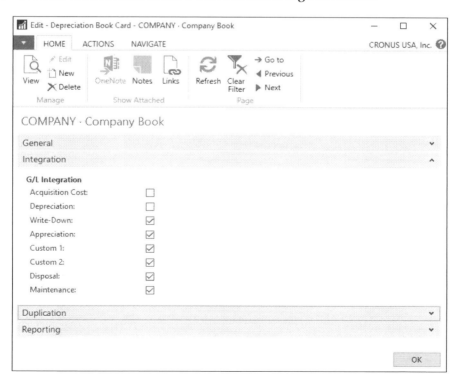

From the fixed asset journal, the minimum information needed for the acquisition cost entries is:

- **FA posting date**: Use one day before the migration day for all the entries
- **Document number**: You can use a generic document number, such as OPENING
- **FA number**: Use the fixed asset code given to the asset
- **FA posting type**: Use the **Acquisition Cost** value
- **Amount**: Fill in this field with the amount of the original invoice

Import this information using the data migration tool and post it.

From the fixed asset journal, the minimum information needed for the depreciation entries is as follows:

- **FA posting date**: Use one day before the migration day for all the entries
- **Document number**: You can use a generic document number, such as OPENING
- **FA number**: Use the fixed asset code given to the asset
- **FA posting type**: Use the depreciation value
- **Amount**: Fill in this field with the total amount already depreciated for each asset
- **Number of depreciation days**: Count 30 days for each month depreciated

Import this information using the data migration tool, and post it. Do not forget to check the G/L integration again in the Depreciation Book Card. If you have been using a temporary account in the previous sections, we recommend that you post the general ledger entries for the fixed assets entries that you just posted.

Summarize all the asset acquisition cost entries, grouped by posting groups. In the General Journal, create one line for each posting group. Use the acquisition cost account found in the FA posting group. Use the FA - Opening Cost entries account to balance the whole transaction.

Do the same with the depreciation entries and use the FA - Opening Depreciation entries account to balance the transaction.

General Ledger balances

General Ledger balances are the backbone of all open entries. When the accounting balances are posted, everything else must match. It is like putting in the last piece of a puzzle. The sad part is that sometimes you find that your last piece does not fit. Don't worry about this right now; at the end of this section, we will explain how to check whether everything is okay and how to solve problems.

While other open entries could be imported and posted in many iterations, the accounting balances must be posted all at once because the whole transaction must be self-balanced. Follow the steps described in the *Customer entries* section of this chapter, but keep in mind these few differences:

- When you fill in the data migration template, **Account Type** must have the G/L account value
- If an account has a debit amount, the amount for that account must be positive
- If an account has a credit amount, the amount for that account must be negative

Make sure that the amount you are about to post is the same as the sum of all the corresponding entries. You can run the following reconciliation reports:

- **Aged Accounts Receivable**: This report and the **Aged Accounts Payable.** report can be found at **Departments | Financial Management | Receivables | Reports and Departments | Financial Management | Payables | Reports** respectively

- **Inventory to G/L Reconcile**: This report can be found at **Departments | Financial Management | Inventory | Reports**

No standard reconciliation report for the bank accounts or fixed assets exists, so you will have to check it yourself.

Since accounting must always be balanced, if the reconcile reports show any difference, it will mean that some other account does not have the correct balance. Find this other account and you will find the solution to your problem.

Historical data

When moving from an ERP system to another ERP system such as Microsoft Dynamics NAV, a lot of companies want to import their historical data into the new ERP. For example, the companies may want to import all the inventory entries made for the previous year for statistical purposes; or, if they start working with Microsoft Dynamics NAV in the middle of a fiscal year, they may want to import all the G/L entries made in the old system for the current fiscal year.

In Microsoft Dynamics NAV, this kind of data is stored in ledger entry tables. If you have to conduct a migration of such data, never import it directly into the ledger entry tables. Use journals instead, and post the data. This way, Microsoft Dynamics NAV will create the ledger entries for you in a consistent way.

For the item ledger entries, for instance, not only is the item ledger entry created, but the value, item register, item application entries, and other entries are created as well. If a journal is used, all these entries will consistently be created for us and we won't have to worry about anything.

Several journals exist in Microsoft Dynamics NAV. Choose the right journal for the ledger entries that have to be imported. If item ledger entries have to be imported, use the item journal. If G/L entries have to be imported, use the General Journal. Some journals use the same underlying table but have specific values in some fields or use specific fields to differentiate what they're used for. General Journals and Recurring Journals use the same **Gen. Journal Line** table, and item journals and revaluation journals use the same **Item Journal Line** table.

If you have to import data into these tables, make sure the right fields are being filled and that the right options are used.

A good idea would be to create some journal lines manually, through the interface provided by Microsoft Dynamics NAV, and compare these lines with the ones created through an import process. This way, we will know whether we are missing something in our import process code and will be able to correct it.

Open documents

The day a company moves to Microsoft Dynamics NAV, they can start creating all kinds of documents in the system for their daily work: sales orders, purchase orders, production orders, and so on.

There may be cases where some documents on the old system have not yet been completed; for example, sales orders that have not yet been shipped, purchase orders that have not yet been received, or production orders that have yet not been finished.

What should be done with all these documents?

The first recommendation is to have the least possible open documents on the old system on the day you start working with Dynamics NAV. Make sure the customer calls their vendor, informs the production team, and notifies the shipping team that during this date all open orders should be closed in their legacy system.

For those documents that could not be finished before migrating to Dynamics NAV, there are a few strategies you can follow:

- Finish them in the old system and recreate the movements in Dynamics NAV. This will mean doing double the manual work and some manual checks, and asking the users to function somewhat differently from how they have been taught to in Dynamics NAV. All of this added to the fact that the users may still not be 100 percent comfortable with the new system may lead to some errors. But it may be an option to be taken into account.

  How should the users act if this is the chosen option?

  When an open sales order is shipped in the old system, you will have to do a negative adjustment in Dynamics NAV to reflect the inventory decrease. No sales shipment will exist in NAV though; the person responsible for posting the sales invoices will not have the information in NAV for what to invoice. He will have to check the old system and do a manual invoice in Dynamics NAV. This will be done using a G/L account and not the item number since we do not want the inventory decrease to be posted again while posting the invoice.

  You can think of similar strategies for all other kinds of documents that still exist on the old system and that will be finished at some point.

- Create them in Dynamics NAV and finish them in the new system. This strategy may also involve some manual work, extra checks, and acting differently for these documents. You can create all the open documents in Dynamics NAV using any of the migration tools explained in this chapter, keeping in mind that:

  - If a sales order line, for instance, has already been partially shipped in the old system, only the pending quantity should be transferred to Dynamics NAV.
  - In some cases, most of the lines of a document may have been finished, but the document could be open because of a still pending single line. In this case, only this line should be transferred to Dynamics NAV.
  - For tracing purposes, whenever it is possible, try to create the documents in Dynamics NAV using the same document number they were given on the old system.

- If the documents are created in Dynamics NAV, you will be able to finish them without having to do any extra work or extra checks. You will be able to proceed as normal in Dynamics NAV.

- You will probably have to do an extra check and extra work with all the partially finished documents. Let's imagine you have a partially shipped sales order on the old system. Only the pending lines and quantities are transferred (and finished) in Dynamics NAV. Imagine the company does not post the invoice for the sales order until the sales order has been completely shipped. The sales order (and sales shipment) in Dynamics NAV will not have complete information about the original sales order. To be able to post the sales invoice in Dynamics NAV, you will have to use the sales shipment existing in NAV, but you will also have to complete the sales invoice with information that is in the old system.

Open documents can be handled, but they imply extra work. This is actually why our recommendation was to try to finish as many documents as possible in the old system before migrating.

You can also think of some other strategies. For example, you could have created the open documents in Dynamics NAV in a way in which no extra work was needed in any of the processes to actually finish the document.

In the sales order case, you could have created the pending lines for the pending quantities and also the lines already shipped but not yet invoiced.

For those last lines, you could have used G/L accounts instead of items. After creating them in Dynamics NAV, they should be posted. This way, we have a scenario in which:

- The complete information of the sales order exists in Dynamics NAV
- Posting the already shipped but not yet invoiced lines as G/L entries does not lead to wrong inventory information for the items
- Posting the already shipped but not invoiced lines creates a sales shipment that you will be able to use while doing the sales invoice (although in Dynamics NAV, the sales shipment may be given a different document number from what was given in the old system, which may lead to mistakes or misunderstandings)

Even more elaborate strategies can be used. Think of all the possible strategies, analyze them, and determine how much work is needed in the migration process (define the data to be imported, the migration tool to be used, and so on), how much work is needed by the users to finish those documents, and so on. After analyzing all of them, choose the one that best meets your requirements.

Choosing a go-live date

If you ask any accountant which date to choose to start working with Dynamics NAV, they will always answer "January 1". The reason behind this answer is that, for most companies, January 1 is the beginning of their fiscal year. It has advantages, no doubt, but it also has drawbacks. The year has 364 additional days to work, but limiting yourself this much is not worth the hassle and stress.

In this section, we will see the pros and cons of going live at the beginning of a fiscal year versus going live on any other date. With all this information, you should be able to choose the best date in your case and know the consequences of your choice.

Going live at the beginning of the fiscal year

All companies analyze information at least annually. Among other reasons, because the tax authorities require certain documentation submitted annually as balance sheets. Starting to use Dynamics NAV at the beginning of the year has another major advantage; there is no need to do anything special to get annual information. There is no need to seek information in two different systems and add it somewhere, and then repeat this process every time you need to analyze the information.

We are not just talking about accounting. Accounting information is the easiest to add. This is because accounting is an area where everything is regulated, and so there will not be many differences between the old system and Dynamics NAV. No major problem here. But there are other areas where it may be impossible to obtain information from the old system. We will never have complete information in the first year.

Let's see an example. Imagine a company that sells items. In their old system, the company had no way to classify the items by category, but in Dynamics NAV, they do. Now they want to analyze the sales by item category. As you can imagine, there will be no way to have complete information on an annual basis as the old system did not have this information. Therefore, the only way to get complete information from any area is migrating at the beginning of a fiscal year.

As you can see, the major (and the only) advantage here is having complete information on an annual basis for analytics and statistics purposes.

What cons do we have?

A project is, by definition, a temporary endeavor with a defined beginning and end, undertaken to meet unique goals and objectives. Implementing Dynamics NAV is a project. At the beginning of the project you have some requirements which give you the details of the amount of work needed to accomplish it. Along with the resources available, you can perfectly plan when each task must be done in order to get the entire job done before January 1. However, when it comes to software projects, changes in requirements are on the agenda all the time.

Each project has three main constraints that must be balanced: time, cost, and scope. This is known as the iron triangle.

In order to keep the triangle balanced, any change in one of the sides modifies at least one of the other sides. Therefore, any change in the requirements (scope) produces a change in the cost, the time, or in both of them.

If you choose January 1 as the migration day, the time side will be pretty difficult to change. You will have to wait a whole year for it to be January 1 again. Your other option is to increase the cost side. You can put in more resources to help finish the project on time. But this is not an easy solution. Resources are not always available, plus you will have to teach them what the project is all about. Wouldn't it be easier if you could just go-live two weeks later?

Another con is that the month prior to the go-live date is quite busy, both at the implementer's and at the customer's ends. All the training has to be done, all the development has to be tested, and the new requirements usually come at the end! Plus, usually the customer is asked to leave as few things pending as possible, and complete most of the tasks. This again means extra effort. Besides, December is not the best time of the year to ask people for extra effort. It's Christmas, kids are off school, and moms and dads want to be with their children playing with the new toys Santa brought them.

Okay, there are not that many cons on the list. Just two, but they are important enough to consider another date.

Going live in the middle of a fiscal year

Here the pros and cons are just the opposite of those in the case we discussed earlier.

The main advantage is that the starting date can be moved. Don't get us wrong; it does not mean that you can play with the date with no consequences. Your customer will always ask you to be committed with a date. But in case of some change within the iron triangle, you will always have the chance to negotiate a change on the time side to balance the triangle.

It is better to go live a few days late with guarantees than do it on time if some new feature hasn't been implemented or tested yet.

Choose a date, bearing in mind what your customer's busiest time of the year is and try to avoid it. As we mentioned earlier, the month before the go-live date is a pretty busy month. Actually, the month after it is also a very busy one.

The main con is that, in some cases, the company won't have complete information, on an annual basis, during the year they start to work with Dynamics NAV. But don't worry, you also have the option of doing an extra job to mitigate it. You can post historical data, such as accountant entries or item entries, into Dynamics NAV. Read the *Historical data* section in this chapter for more information. If you choose to migrate the historical data, the main con of going live in the middle of a fiscal year is gone and only the pros stay.

So, there is no reason not to choose a date different from January 1.

Summary

Several kinds of data may be imported into Microsoft Dynamics NAV. There are different ways to import that data into Microsoft Dynamics NAV and a variety of ways to present that data.

Do you remember anything about statistical classes? Let's remember some basics:

Several x Different x Many x A bunch = Too many options

This means that the migration processes should be carefully designed and planned. Everyone, both at the partner and at the customer end, should know what will be migrated, how it will be migrated, when it will be migrated, who is responsible for retrieving or filling in the data, how the data has to be presented, and what the result in Microsoft Dynamics NAV will be.

The tools that can be used, the way you can use them, and the kind of data that is commonly migrated has been covered in this chapter. We hope all of this helps you to plan all your migration processes.

In the next chapter, we will learn how to upgrade Dynamics NAV from the previous versions to Dynamics NAV 2016.

7
Upgrading Microsoft Dynamics NAV

In the previous chapters, we covered the implementation process of Microsoft Dynamics NAV for new customers or companies that had not used Microsoft Dynamics NAV before.

What about companies already using Microsoft Dynamics NAV that want to upgrade to the latest version?

Upgrading to a newer version of Dynamics NAV, unfortunately, is not like upgrading Microsoft Office where it can be done with clicks of buttons. It's a project that has to be planned and executed carefully.

In this chapter, we will explain the migration process coming from almost all the previous versions of the application. We will go through the steps that should be done and the tools that are out there to help us execute the upgrade process.

The topics covered in this chapter are as follows:

- An explanation of the upgrading philosophy in Dynamics NAV
- A brief checklist of all the steps required to upgrade from the previous versions
- An in-detail explanation of all the steps pointed in the checklist
- The tools that must be used in the upgrade process
- The tools that can be used in the upgrade process to make the whole process easier

Upgrading philosophy

Prior to the release of Dynamics NAV 2015, upgrading was a tremendous project that required hundreds (sometimes thousands) of hours to bring you to the latest version.

The reason why the upgrade required a lot of time was because of modifications done in your database; essentially, the less you modify, the faster the upgrade. In fact, if you need to upgrade from versions prior to Dynamics NAV 2013, you may see similar estimates as during a new implementation.

Microsoft Dynamics NAV can be used with no customization at all, but that's almost unheard of. That's like buying a Ferrari and only driving it at 25 miles per hour. Once the users discover the power of Dynamics NAV and how flexible the software is, they will want to make changes to give them a competitive edge in their industry. It's like the users suddenly discover the power of the force.

One of the greatest selling points for Dynamics NAV is the ease of making changes to the software. There is no need for other applications to edit the application code since Dynamics NAV has its own code editor. There is no need for full compilations of code projects, and there's no need for deployment of the new solution since modifications can be done on the fly and they get to the end users right away.

They can be minor customizations, such as adding an existing field to a page or creating a new field in an existing table. They can be mid-size customizations, such as modifying some minor standard behavior. Or they can be major customizations, such as developing a whole new functionality or changing the way the major standard functionalities behave.

When you get a new version of Microsoft Dynamics NAV and a new application code file, a merge process has to be done to ensure that customizations done in a specific version of Microsoft Dynamics NAV are carried out into the new version of the application. The upgrade process can be done automatically with the PowerShell upgrade since Dynamics NAV 2015.

However, even with the automated PowerShell upgrade, some steps in the merge process and data migration process will have to be done manually by a Microsoft Dynamics NAV developer because of conflicts in the automated process.

Upgrades prior to Dynamics NAV 2013

An upgrade project from versions prior to Dynamics NAV 2013 can be an easy task or a large project. It really depends on the amount of modifications that are done and the version of Dynamics NAV you are upgrading from. The basic principle is that the older the version, the more involved it will be for you and your company.

Summarizing, the processes to upgrade versions prior to Dynamics NAV 2013 are:

1. Backup your existing database (of course)
2. Compare and manually merge the codes that are modified to the latest version of Dynamics NAV
3. Convert the database to the version you're upgrading to by opening it in the new version of the software
4. Import the merged objects (new version objects with customizations) to your current database
5. Run the processes to upgrade your data

All these steps are done manually and some steps are very time consuming. There are horror stories of developers pulling all nighters just so they can execute the next step in the upgrade process.

It's not a very good use of time and money for both the partner and the customer. But this was how it was done when I was younger.

Upgrades from Dynamics NAV 2013 forward

With the release of Dynamics NAV 2015, Microsoft introduced the PowerShell upgrade that automates the code merging as well as the data upgrade. In order to take advantage of the PowerShell upgrade process, you need to be at least on Dynamics NAV 2013.

There are some limitations to the automated upgrade. This is listed on MSDN at `https://msdn.microsoft.com/en-us/library/mt600251(v=nav.90).aspx`.

Basically, what it says is the following:

- If the names of your old variables are used in the newer version as a function or statement, you must change them before you upgrade
- If your old code calls functions that do not exist anymore in the newer version, you must verify that the upgrade codeunits migrate data correctly
- If the code you're coming from causes some fields on the table to be dropped, you'll need to make sure that it doesn't
- If your company name uses special reserved characters in NAV, such as [~ @ # $ % & * ( ) . ! % - + / = ?], then rename the company before proceeding
- Make sure the system tables are in English

In the following section, we will do a checklist of the steps that have to be taken to upgrade to the latest version of Microsoft Dynamics NAV; from every version since Navision Attain 3.60. We will do that in the reverse order; we will first explore the checklist of actions to upgrade from Microsoft Dynamics NAV 2013 which is the minimum version you must be on in order to initiate the automated PowerShell upgrade and then work to cover the other versions prior to Dynamics NAV 2013.

Upgrading process checklist

As mentioned, using the PowerShell upgrade is only supported from Dynamics NAV 2013 forward. There are ways to use PowerShell upgrade if you're running earlier versions, but that will be beyond the scope of this book. So, the simple rule is to get to at least Dynamics NAV 2013 to make your upgrade easier in the future.

If you are on older versions, the official documentation tells you to follow the Microsoft Dynamics NAV upgrade guide for the respective versions for details. Essentially, if you are coming from versions previous to X, you will have to follow guide Y, and so on. If you follow all the steps detailed in all the guides, it will take a long time. Hence the rule that the older the version you're on, the more time consuming and more complex is the upgrade.

But there is good news. If you are planning to upgrade from the older versions, you can skip some steps since the ultimate goal is to get to the latest version. In this section, we will look at the steps you need to follow to upgrade from Version 3.60 to Dynamics NAV 2016. You can use this section as a checklist for your upgrade process.

The steps that you will have to follow to upgrade from any version to Dynamics NAV 2016 can be spread out into three groups:

- Preparing to upgrade
- Upgrading the application code
- Upgrading the data

The first group will be the same for all the versions. The second and third groups will be different depending on which version you intend to upgrade to Microsoft Dynamics NAV 2016.

We will first enumerate the steps for the preparing to upgrade group, and then enumerate the steps in the other two groups depending on the version.

Upgrading from 2013, 2013 R2, or 2015

If you're currently using these versions, good for you! The PowerShell upgrade is ready for you to use. There are three steps you will need to follow to get to NAV 2016. They are:

1. Convert the database
2. Upgrade the application code
3. Upgrade the data

Technical upgrade (converting the database)

Before anything can be done, you need to make sure your database is converted. Simply put, this just means that the foundation of the database has to be to the standards of NAV 2016.

Make sure your existing database works. This is done by using **Build Server Application Objects** that can be found from the **Microsoft Dynamics NAV Development Environment**.

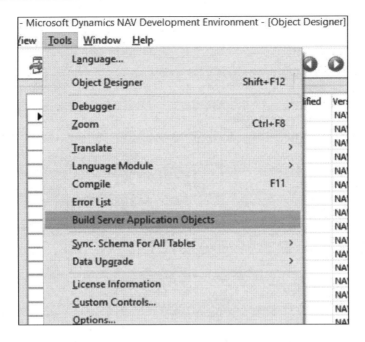

This step essentially converts the code you've written in C/AL into C# for Dynamics NAV middle tier.

Upload your Dynamics NAV 2016 license using the Development Environment. The license can be obtained from your Dynamics NAV partner or by logging into **CustomerSource**, a portal for Dynamics NAV customers. Once you have the license file (usually with a file extension of `.flf`), you can upload the license file onto your server by going to **Tools | License Information**.

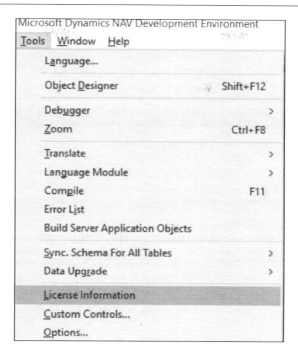

A new screen will pop up. Click on **Upload** and select the `.flf` file, and then your license will be updated to the latest version.

Start the Dynamics NAV 2016 Development Environment and open your old database. A warning message will appear to confirm your actions to convert the database.

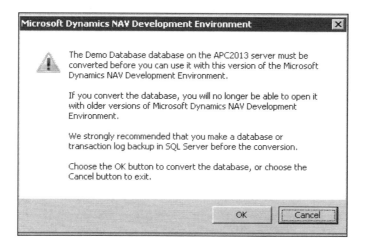

As the warning suggests, make sure you really want to proceed. There's no turning back!

After the process completes in a few minutes, you will receive the following message, basically telling you that you're ready to connect the new service tier to the database:

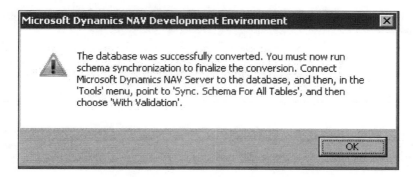

You now have your database with NAV 2013 functionalities that have the NAV 2016 foundation.

Connecting the Dynamics NAV Server

After the database has been converted, we will need to setup the service tier to connect to the upgraded database.

Start the Dynamics NAV 2016 administration, select the **Dynamics NAV Server** that was installed when you installed Dynamics NAV, and edit the **Database Name** to the name of your database.

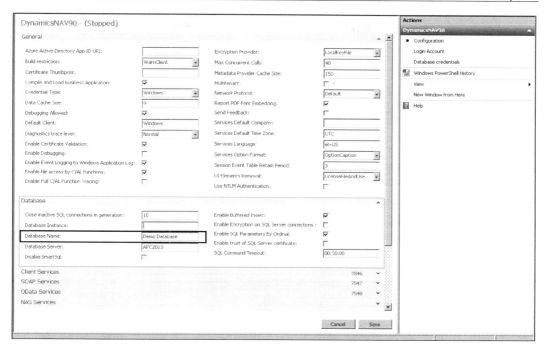

If you want further information on how to configure the service tier for Dynamics NAV, go to `https://msdn.microsoft.com/en-us/library/hh165851(v=nav.90).aspx`.

Once you've changed the database the service is pointing to, start the Dynamics NAV service.

> Make sure the user on the service has sufficient permission on SQL Server or else the service will not start.

Once the service is started, go back to the Development Environment for Dynamics NAV 2016 and synchronize the schema so the database matches with the service tier.

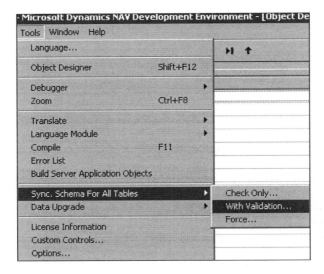

You will be prompted with a message and the ability to select the Dynamics NAV service you want to sync the schema with.

Once the schema is synchronized, click on **Build Server Application Objects**. This will push what we've done to the service tier.

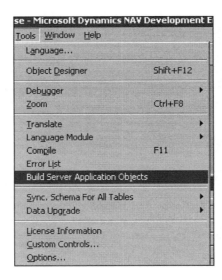

Not too much coding here and we're done! You've now done what's called a technical upgrade. Basically, upgrading the platform without upgrading the application code or the data.

Application code upgrade

After the technical upgrade of the database to Dynamics NAV 2016, you will need to upgrade the application code.

The application code is basically where the functionalities in Dynamics NAV reside. Without upgrading the application code, you will not be able to utilize the new features with the new version.

To upgrade the application code using PowerShell upgrade, you will need the following:

- The original unmodified Dynamics NAV 2013 objects in text format. Note that if you've applied any hotfix into the application code, then you will need that version with the hotfix applied.
- Your current modified database objects in text format.
- The objects from the new version in text format.

Before you proceed to export the objects, let's first create the folders on your computer to store the files:

This will allow us to easily see what is being done and where.

In order to get the objects for these databases, you will need the original unmodified Dynamics NAV 2013 (with any hotfixes), your current NAV database, and a new Dynamics NAV 2016 database.

If you're using versions NAV 2013 R2 and prior, then in order to get these objects in text format, you will need a developer's license. In the object designer, you can export the objects by clicking on **File | Export**, then selecting the proper export format:

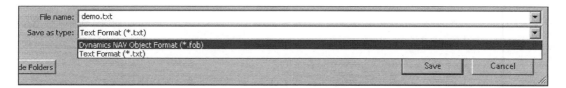

If you're using NAV 2015 or a newer version, you can use the ExportObjects cmdlet to start the Dynamics NAV 2016 Development Shell:

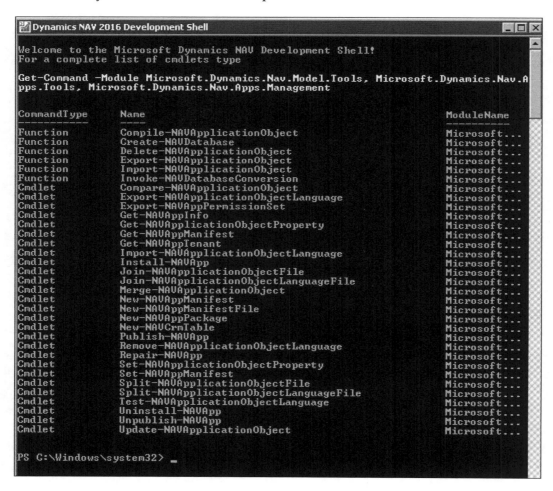

The cmdlet we want to use is `Export-NAVApplicationObject`. You will need the following when you run this command:

- The Dynamics NAV service name
- The database name
- The directory where you want to export the object in text format to

Once you've obtained the information, type in the information in the PowerShell as the following screenshot shows:

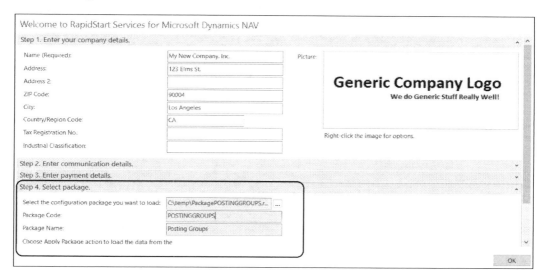

In this example, we're exporting the objects from the database that we did the technical upgrade on. You will need to repeat this process for the unmodified NAV 2013 database (after you do the technical upgrade) and the unmodified NAV 2016 database, and save it to the appropriate folders that we defined earlier.

Merging the code

The next step is to merge the modifications that you've done to your existing database into the new Dynamics NAV version.

The cmdlet we will use is `Merge-NAVApplicationObject`. In this example, the files are put into the appropriate folder in a sub path called `upgrade`.

```
PS C:\Windows\system32> merge-navapplicationobject

cmdlet Merge-NAVApplicationObject at command pipeline position 1
Supply values for the following parameters:
OriginalPath[0]: c:\upgrade\original\original.txt
OriginalPath[1]:
ModifiedPath[0]: c:\upgrade\modified\modified.txt
ModifiedPath[1]:
TargetPath[0]: c:\upgrade\target\target.txt
TargetPath[1]:
ResultPath: c:\upgrade\result\result.txt

Summary:
  Merge operation processed 1129 application object(s) with a total of 1 indivi
  dual change(s). 100.0% of individual modifications were automatically merged.

Details:
  Processed 1129 application object(s):

    Merged        1 objects - with changes in MODIFIED that were successfully m
                              erged with any changes from TARGET into RESULT.
    Conflict      0 objects - with changes in both MODIFIED and TARGET that cou
                              ld only be merged partially.
                              Partially merged objects and corresponding .CONFL
                              ICT files are added to RESULT.
                              This also includes objects that are deleted in MO
                              DIFIED/TARGET and changed in TARGET/MODIFIED.
    Inserted      0 objects - in MODIFIED that do not exist in TARGET and are i
                              nserted into RESULT.
    Deleted       0 objects - that exist in ORIGINAL, but do not exist in MODIF
                              IED and are unchanged in TARGET.
    Unchanged  1128 objects - in TARGET which are not changed in MODIFIED and a
                              re copied from TARGET to RESULT.
                              This also include objects deleted in both MODIFIE
                              D and TARGET and objects unchanged in MODIFIED an
                              d deleted in TARGET.
    Failed        0 objects - that could not be imported, such as an object tha
                              t is not valid or that contains
                              unsupported features.

  Processed 1 individual changes:

    Conflict      0 changes
    Merged    100.0% of all changes

To see detailed explanation of these, type: "get-help Merge-NAVApplicationObjec
```

You can select multiple files to merge. If there is only one file, you can push *Enter* to go to the next file it's asking for.

After the merge is done, it will list out what was merged, what has conflicts, what was inserted, and what was removed from the code. If there are any conflicts, they will be kept in the `Conflicts` folder in the `Result` folder. The conflicts will need to be resolved manually.

Importing the merged code

The merged file will be stored in the `Results` folder. You can now import the merged objects into your fresh Dynamics NAV 2016 database. You can do this by using the `Import-NAVApplicationObject` cmdlet.

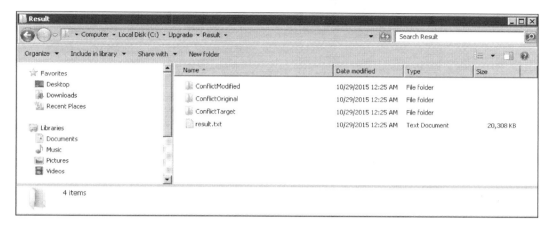

Once the merged code is imported successfully, you will need to start the Dynamics NAV 2016 Development Environment and select all the objects and click on **Tools | Compile**.

Any errors that may come up will need to be resolved manually.

Congratulations! You've now upgraded the application code to the latest version of Dynamics NAV.

Upgrading the application data

So we did a technical upgrade by converting the foundation to NAV 2016, and then we upgraded the application code so the functionalities are now in NAV 2016. The last step of the process is to upgrade the data so it utilizes the NAV 2016 functionalities.

First we will need to import the upgrade to the toolkit that's included in the Dynamics NAV installation files. These `.FOB` or object files are located in the `UpgradeToolKit` folder. Within the folder, you may see `Data Conversion Tools` or the `Local Objects` folder. If you see the `Local Objects` folder, you will want to use the contents in that folder since it's localized for your region.

Import the object into NAV by going to the Development Environment and clicking on **File | Import**.

The file you choose will depend on the version you're coming from:

- `Upgrade700900.US.fob`: If you're upgrading from Dynamics NAV 2013
- `Upgrade710900.US.fob`: If you're upgrading from Dynamics NAV 2013 R2
- `Upgrade800900.US.fob`: If you're upgrading from Dynamics NAV 2015

```
PS C:\Windows\system32> import-navapplicationobject

cmdlet Import-NAVApplicationObject at command pipeline position 1
Supply values for the following parameters:
Path[0]: c:\upgrade\result\result.txt
Path[1]:
DatabaseName: Demo Database

Confirm
Import application objects from C:\upgrade\result\result.txt into the Demo
Database database. If you continue, you may loose data in fields that are
removed or changed in the imported file.
[Y] Yes  [A] Yes to All  [N] No  [L] No to All  [S] Suspend  [?] Help
(default is "Y"):
```

Once the objects are imported, we can run the upgrade by clicking on **Tools | Data Upgrade**. Then choose **Show Progress**.

Once the process is complete, we're totally done!

Automating upgrading using PowerShell

As previously mentioned, there's a totally hands - off approach to upgrade to NAV 2016 using PowerShell scripts. Fortunately, Microsoft has provided sample scripts on automating that can be found in the installation files in the `WindowsPowerShellScripts\ApplicationMergeUtilities` directory.

Configuring these scripts will be beyond the scope of this book. The scripts basically follow the same principle as the steps that are described in this section.

You can read more about these scripts at `https://msdn.microsoft.com/en-us/library/dn414687(v=nav.90).aspx`.

Upgrading from 2009, 2009 SP1, or 2009 R2

You need to get to at least NAV 2013 in order to get to NAV 2016. Upgrading to Dynamics NAV 2013 is officially supported only from those versions. In this section, we will enumerate the steps that have to be performed to upgrade from these versions.

Upgrading the 2009 application code

The steps that have to be performed to upgrade the application code from Dynamics NAV 2009 to Dynamics NAV 2013 are listed as follows:

1. Get the objects' versions.

2. Convert the old objects' version files to Microsoft Dynamics NAV 2013 format.

3. Compare your database objects to the standard objects of your current version to determine the objects that have been customized.

4. Carry out your customizations to the new standard code for the new version of Microsoft Dynamics NAV.

> You can use any generic text-comparing application to do this job. It will be easier, though, if you use an application specifically designed for Microsoft Dynamics NAV, such as **MergeTool**, which will be explained later in this chapter.

5. If you have a Microsoft Dynamics NAV 2009 classic client installation, transform your own forms to pages.

6. If you have a Microsoft Dynamics NAV 2009 classic client installation, carry out your customizations on the existing forms and into its corresponding page object.

7. Transform your reports to the new report definition of Microsoft Dynamics NAV 2013.

8. Revise and modify your customized code for better performance in Microsoft Dynamics NAV 2013.

Upgrading the 2009 data

Data and field structure has changed between Microsoft Dynamics NAV 2009 and Microsoft Dynamics NAV 2013. That's why a data upgrade process has to be run. The data upgrade is done in two steps: one still in the old version and the other in the new version. The data conversion process can be seen in the following figure:

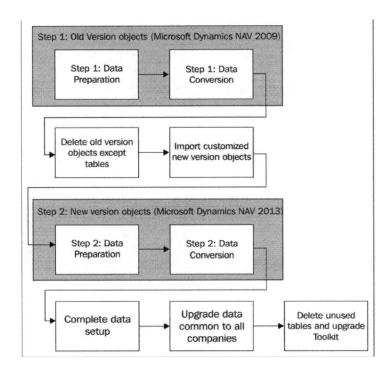

Follow these steps to perform the data conversion process:

1. In your old customized database, import the file called Upgrade Step 1 Objects.
2. Run the data conversion process for the objects of the old version.
3. Create a new Microsoft Dynamics NAV 2013 database.
4. Restore the database that was being upgraded.
5. Import all the customized Microsoft Dynamics NAV 2013 objects.
6. Import the file called Upgrade Step 2 objects.
7. Run the data conversion process for the objects of the new version.
8. Delete the upgrade toolkit objects.

Upgrading from 5.0 or 5.0 SP1

To upgrade to Microsoft Dynamics NAV 2013 from any Microsoft Dynamics NAV 5.0 version, you will have to upgrade first to Microsoft Dynamics NAV 2009, and then follow the upgrade steps to upgrade from Microsoft Dynamics NAV 2009 to Microsoft Dynamics NAV 2013.

Even if having to upgrade first to NAV 2009, a full upgrade to the intermediate version will not be necessary. For example, you will not need to upgrade your application code to NAV 2009. The application code can be upgraded directly to Dynamics NAV 2013. You don't need to perform the data upgrade process while upgrading from Dynamics 5.0 to Dynamics 2009 since there is no table structure changes between these two versions.

Upgrading the 5.0 application code

The steps that have to be performed to upgrade the application code from Dynamics NAV 5.0 to Dynamics NAV 2013 are listed as follows:

1. Import both your customized application code and the standard application code of your current version in a Dynamics NAV 2009 database. Compile all the objects. Use those objects that are converted to Dynamics NAV 2009 format for comparing and merging purposes.

2. Get the objects' version (exporting them from the Dynamics NAV 2009 database).

3. Compare your database objects to the standard objects of your current version to determine the objects that have been customized.

4. Carry out your customizations to the new standard code for the new version of Microsoft Dynamics NAV.

> You can use any generic text-comparing application to do this job. It will be easier, though, if you use an application specifically designed for Microsoft Dynamics NAV, such as MergeTool, which will be explained later in this chapter.

5. Transform your own forms to pages.

6. Carry out your customizations on the existing forms to their corresponding page objects.

7. Transform your reports to the new report definition of Microsoft Dynamics NAV 2013.

8. Revise and modify your customized code for better performance in Microsoft Dynamics NAV 2013.

Upgrading the 5.0 data

Data and field structure has changed between Dynamics NAV 5.0 and Dynamics NAV 2013. That's why a data upgrade process has to be run. However, the data and field structure did not change at all between Dynamics NAV 5.0 and NAV 2009. So the data upgrade tools available for NAV 2009 also apply to NAV 5.0. The only extra thing you will have to do is to convert your database to Dynamics NAV 2009. The data conversion process can be seen in the following figure:

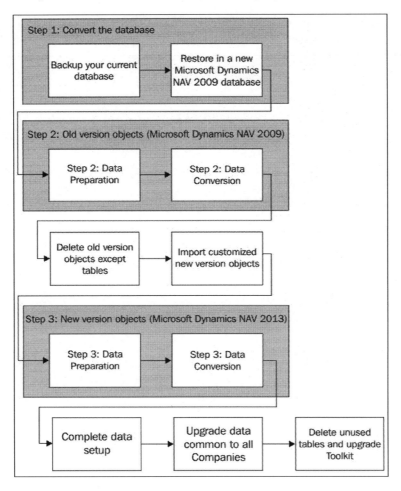

The steps required to upgrade the data are listed as follows:

1. Create a new Microsoft Dynamics NAV 2009 database.
2. Restore your Microsoft Dynamics NAV 5.0 database in the new 2009 database.
3. Import the file called `Upgrade Step 1 Objects`.
4. Run the data conversion process for the objects of the old version.
5. Create a new Microsoft Dynamics NAV 2013 database.
6. Restore the database that was being upgraded.
7. Import all the customized Microsoft Dynamics NAV 2013 objects.
8. Import the file called `Upgrade Step 2 objects`.
9. Run the data conversion process for the objects of the new version.
10. Delete the upgrade toolkit objects.

Upgrading from 4.0, 4.0 SP1, 4.0 SP2, or 4.0 SP3

To upgrade to Dynamics NAV 2013 from any Microsoft Business Solutions–Navision 4.0 version, you will have to upgrade first to NAV 2009, and then follow the steps to upgrade to Dynamics NAV 2013.

Even when having to upgrade to Dynamics NAV 2009 first, a full upgrade to the intermediate version will not be necessary. For example, you will not need to upgrade your application code to the intermediate version. The application code can be upgraded directly to Microsoft Dynamics NAV 2013.

You will, however, need to do a data upgrade though, from Microsoft Business Solutions–Navision 4.0 to Dynamics NAV 2009. To do so, an application code upgrade from 4.0 to 2009 will be needed. It will not be a complete code upgrade, however. Only the application code corresponding to the definition of all the tables' structures will have to be upgraded. This will be explained in detail in the upgrade steps in detail.

Upgrading the 4.0 application code

The steps that have to be performed to upgrade the application code from Microsoft Business Solutions–Navision 4.0 to Dynamics NAV 2013 are listed as follows:

1. Import both your customized application code and the standard application code of your current version in a Microsoft Dynamics NAV 2009 database. Compile all the objects. Use those objects that are converted to Microsoft Dynamics NAV 2009 format for comparing and merging purposes.

2. Get the objects' version (exporting them from the Microsoft Dynamics NAV 2009 database).

3. Compare your database objects to the standard objects of your current version to determine the objects that have been customized.

4. Carry out your customizations to the new standard code for the new version of Microsoft Dynamics NAV.

 You can use any generic text-comparing application to do this job. It will be easier, though, if you use an application specifically designed for Microsoft Dynamics NAV, such as MergeTool, which will be explained later in this chapter.

5. Transform your own forms to pages.

6. Carry out your customizations on the existing forms to their corresponding page objects.

7. Transform your reports to the new report definition of Microsoft Dynamics NAV 2013.

8. Revise and modify your customized code for better performance in Microsoft Dynamics NAV 2013.

9. Compare your database table objects to the standard table objects of your current version to determine the changes in the data structure.

10. Carry out your customizations to the table object's data structure. This will be similar to the standard table object's data structure of Microsoft Dynamics NAV 2009.

Upgrading the 4.0 data

Data and field structure has changed between Microsoft Business Solutions–Navision 4.0 and Microsoft Dynamics NAV 2013. That's why a data upgrade process has to be run. However, the data upgrade tool available is only to upgrade from NAV 2009 to NAV 2013. Data and field structure also changed between Microsoft Business Solutions–Navision 4.0 and Microsoft Dynamics NAV 2009. We will first have to upgrade our data to Dynamics NAV 2009 data and field structure, and then we will be able to finish the upgrade process to Microsoft Dynamics NAV 2013.

The data upgrade from NAV 4.0 to NAV 2009 is very similar to the one described for NAV 2009 to NAV 2013. The steps are exactly the same, but the *upgrade* objects will be different. The data conversion process can be seen in the following figure:

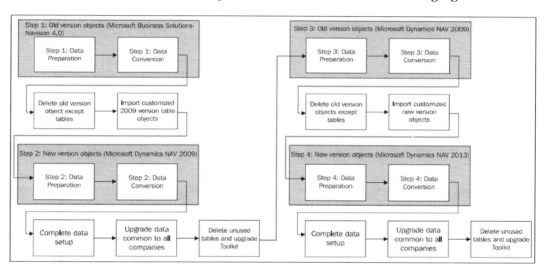

The steps required to upgrade the data are listed as follows:

1. In your old customized database, import the file called `Upgrade Step 1 objects` from the upgrade toolkit found in the Microsoft Dynamics NAV 2009 installation media.

2. Run the data conversion process for the objects of the old version (Microsoft Business Solutions–Navision 4.0).

3. Create a new Microsoft Dynamics NAV 2009 database.

4. Restore the database that was being upgraded.

5. Import the customized Microsoft Dynamics NAV 2009 table objects.

6. Import the file called `Upgrade Step 2 objects` from the upgrade toolkit found in the Microsoft Dynamics NAV 2009 installation media.

7. Run the data conversion process for the objects of the new version (Microsoft Dynamics NAV 2009).

8. Delete the upgrade toolkit objects.

At this point, the data upgrade from Microsoft Business Solutions–Navision 4.0 to Microsoft Dynamics NAV 2009 has been completed. From now on, the data upgrade to Microsoft Dynamics NAV 2013 will have to be done.

1. In the Microsoft Dynamics NAV 2009 database, import the file called `Upgrade Step 1 objects`.

2. Run the data conversion process for the objects of the old version (Microsoft Dynamics NAV 2009).

3. Create a new Microsoft Dynamics NAV 2013 database.

4. Restore the database that was being upgraded.

5. Import all the customized Microsoft Dynamics NAV 2013 objects.

6. Import the file called `Upgrade Step 2 objects`.

7. Run the data conversion process for the objects of the new version (Microsoft Dynamics NAV 2013).

8. Delete the upgrade toolkit objects.

Upgrading from 3.60 or 3.70

To upgrade to Microsoft Dynamics NAV 2013 from any Navision Attain 3.xx version, you will have to upgrade first to Microsoft Dynamics NAV 2009 and then follow the upgrade steps to upgrade to Microsoft Dynamics NAV 2013.

Even when having to upgrade to Dynamics NAV 2009 first, a full upgrade to the intermediate versions will not be necessary. For example, you will not need to upgrade your application code to the intermediate versions. The application code can be upgraded directly to Microsoft Dynamics NAV 2013.

You will, however, need to do a data upgrade though, from Navision Attain 3.xx to Microsoft Dynamics NAV 2009. To do so, an application code upgrade from 3.xx to 2009 will be needed. It will not be a complete code upgrade, however. Only the application code corresponding to the definition of all the tables' structures will have to be upgraded. This will be explained in detail in the upgrade steps in detail.

Upgrading the 3.60 or 3.70 application code

The steps that have to be performed to upgrade the application code from Navision Attain 3.60 or 3.70 to Dynamics NAV 2013 are listed as follows:

1. Import both your customized application code and the standard application code of your current version in a Microsoft Dynamics NAV 2009 database. Compile all the objects. Use those objects that are converted to Microsoft Dynamics NAV 2009 format for comparing and merging purposes.

2. Get the objects' version (exporting them from the Microsoft Dynamics NAV 2009 database).

3. Compare your database objects to the standard objects of your current version to determine the objects that have been customized.

4. Carry out your customizations to the new standard code for the new version of Microsoft Dynamics NAV.

 You can use any generic text-comparing application to do this job. It will be easier, though, if you use an application specifically designed for Microsoft Dynamics NAV, such as MergeTool, which will be explained later in this chapter.

5. Transform your own forms to pages.

6. Carry out your customizations on the existing forms to their corresponding page objects.

7. Revise and modify your customized code for better performance in Microsoft Dynamics NAV 2013.

8. Compare your database table objects to the standard table objects of your current version to determine the changes in the data structure.

9. Carry out your customizations in the table objects data structure to the standard table object data structure of Microsoft Dynamics NAV 2009.

Upgrading the 3.60 or 3.70 data

The data and field structure has changed between Navision Attain 3.xx and Microsoft Dynamics NAV 2013. That's why a data upgrade process has to be run. However, the data upgrade tool available is only to upgrade from NAV 2009 to NAV 2013. The data and field structure also changed between Navision Attain 3.xx and Microsoft Dynamics NAV 2009. We will first have to upgrade our data to a Microsoft Dynamics NAV 2009 data and field structure, and then we will be able to finish the upgrade process to Microsoft Dynamics NAV 2013.

The data upgrade from NAV 3.xx to NAV 2009 is very similar to the one described for NAV 2009 to NAV 2013. The steps are exactly the same, but the upgrade objects will be different. The data conversion process can be seen in the following figure:

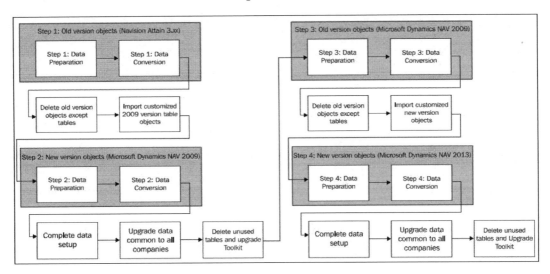

The steps required to upgrade the data are listed as follows:

1. In your old customized database, import the file called `Upgrade Step 1 objects` from the upgrade toolkit found in the Microsoft Dynamics NAV 2009 installation media.

2. Run the data conversion process for the objects of the old version (Navision Attain 3.xx).

3. Create a new Microsoft Dynamics NAV 2009 database.

4. Restore the database that was being upgraded.

5. Import the customized Microsoft Dynamics NAV 2009 table objects.

6. Import the file called `Upgrade Step 2 objects` from the upgrade toolkit found in the Microsoft Dynamics NAV 2009 installation media.

7. Run the data conversion process for the objects of the new version (Microsoft Dynamics NAV 2009).

8. Delete the upgrade toolkit objects.

At this point, the data upgrade from Navision Attain 3.xx to Microsoft Dynamics NAV 2009 has been completed. From now on, the data upgrade to Microsoft Dynamics NAV 2013 will have to be done.

1. In the Microsoft Dynamics NAV 2009 database, import the file called `Upgrade Step 1 Objects`.

2. Run the data conversion process for the objects of the old version (Microsoft Dynamics NAV 2009).

3. Create a new Microsoft Dynamics NAV 2013 database.

4. Restore the database that was being upgraded.

5. Import all the customized Microsoft Dynamics NAV 2013 objects.

6. Import the file called `Upgrade Step 2 objects`.

7. Run the data conversion for the objects of the new version (Microsoft Dynamics NAV 2013).

8. Delete the upgrade toolkit objects.

Upgrading steps to NAV 2013

In the preceding sections, we saw all the steps that you have to follow in order to upgrade from the older versions of Dynamics NAV to Dynamics NAV 2013. In this section, we will explain all those steps in more detail.

Preparing to upgrade

No matter what your current version of Microsoft Dynamics NAV is, before you can upgrade to Microsoft Dynamics NAV 2013, a migration to SQL Server is needed if you are using a native database as it is no longer available.

A test of the database is also needed before starting the upgrade process. In this section, we will explain how to perform these two processes.

Migrating to SQL Server

Microsoft SQL Server (on its 64-bit version) is the only database supported in Microsoft Dynamics NAV 2013. The native database is gone. If you are using a native database in the older versions of Microsoft Dynamics NAV, you should upgrade to SQL before you start the upgrade process to Microsoft Dynamics NAV 2013.

The steps to upgrade to SQL Server will not be explained in this book. You can use the official Microsoft Dynamics NAV documentation to do that.

Testing the database

This is a required step to upgrade to Microsoft Dynamics NAV 2013. The steps to test the database are as follows:

1. Open your current database in the classic client (testing the database can be done in any version of Microsoft Dynamics NAV; if you are upgrading to Microsoft Dynamics NAV 2013 from any version prior to Microsoft Dynamics NAV 2009, you can do the test of the database in your current version).
2. Go to **File | Database | Test**.
3. The **Test Database** form will open.
4. Click on the **Options** tab.
5. Select the file's output and enter or browse to a path and filename.
6. Click on the **General** tab.
7. Choose **Normal** to test everything except the field relationships between the tables.
8. If the test fails, follow the workflow for repairing damaged databases.
9. Open the **Test Database** form again (**File | Database | Test**).
10. Choose **Custom** and then check **Test field relationships between tables** to test the field relationships between the tables.
11. This will determine if there is any data inconsistency in your database. You should determine whether errors detected in this test will affect the upgrade process.
12. Compile all the objects in the database. Repair the objects that are not compiling correctly.

Upgrading the application code

Customers typically want all the customizations that had been implemented in their old Microsoft Dynamics NAV databases to be implemented in their new Microsoft Dynamics NAV 2013 database.

To achieve this goal, a sequence of development actions, intended to fully transfer the functionality of a customer's solution to the latest version of Microsoft Dynamics NAV, have to be performed.

Getting object versions

When working with code upgrade, it is important to analyze and process the changes by comparing and evaluating three separate versions of the Microsoft Dynamics NAV database:

- **The old base version**: This is the standard version of the current version of the Dynamics NAV database
- **The old custom version**: This is the old base's database plus the customer's changes and add-on solutions
- **The new base version**: This is the standard version of the Microsoft Dynamics NAV 2013 database

Follow these steps to obtain the three `.txt` files:

1. Open the standard Microsoft Dynamics NAV database of your current version.
2. Navigate to **Tools | Object Designer** (or press *Ctrl + F12*).
3. Click on **All** to see the list of all the application objects.
4. Select all the objects (clicking on the upper-left corner of the grid will select all the objects).
5. Go to **File | Export**.
6. Select the destination folder and give the file the name `OldBase.txt`.
7. Open your current customized Microsoft Dynamics NAV database.
8. Navigate to **Tools | Object Designer** (or press *Ctrl + F12*).
9. Click on **All** to see the list of all the application objects.
10. Select all the objects (clicking on the upper-left corner of the grid will select all the objects).

11. Click on **File | Export**.

12. Select the destination folder and give the file the name `OldCustom.txt`.

13. Open the standard Microsoft Dynamics NAV 2013 database.

14. Navigate to **Tools | Object Designer** (or press *Ctrl + F12*).

15. Click on **All** to see the list of all the application objects.

16. Select all the objects (clicking on the upper-left corner of the grid will select all the objects).

17. Go to **File | Export**.

18. Select the destination folder and give the file the name `NewBase.txt`.

19. At this point, you should have three `.txt` files named `OldBase.txt`, `OldCustom.txt`, and `NewBase.txt`.

Converting objects to the Dynamics NAV 2013 format

There is a tool called `TextFormatUpgrade2013` that is explained later in this chapter, in the *Upgrading tools* section. Right after the `OldBase.txt` and `OldCustom.txt` files are obtained, they have to be converted to the format used in Microsoft Dynamics NAV 2013.

This will make comparisons to the new standard application code (the `NewBase.txt` file) much easier.

New custom objects that do not exist in the standard application but only in the customized application (custom objects in the range of 50,000 to 99,999 or in add-on ranges) cannot be directly imported in Microsoft Dynamics NAV 2013 in a `.fob` file (`.fob` is the extension of Dynamics NAV object files). Doing so will cause the application to crash as soon as the objects are accessed. For these objects, you have to use the `TextFormatUpgrade2013` tool to do the appropriate formatting change, import them in Microsoft Dynamics NAV 2013 in text format, and compile the objects in Microsoft Dynamics NAV 2013.

Refer to the *Upgrading tools* section to know what exactly the tool does and how to use it.

Carrying out customizations to the new version

As explained in the *Upgrading philosophy* section, carrying out customizations to the new version is actually the main point of the whole upgrade process.

There are a couple of ways to achieve this:

- Rewriting your customizations from scratch in Microsoft Dynamics NAV 2013
- Using any merge tool to follow a compare-and-merge process to finally get the customized code into Microsoft Dynamics NAV 2013

As the implementer, feel free to use the approach that best suits your needs. You can probably go for the rewriting method when just a few customizations exist, and use the compare-and-merge one when the old database has been customized a lot.

Where do draw the line between a few and a lot? We really don't know.

To rewrite your customizations, you will probably want to use a text compare tool to compare your old base application code to your new base application code. That way, you will understand what the differences are and you will be able to write them again on a Microsoft Dynamics NAV 2013 database.

To do a compare-and-merge process, you need a tool that allows you to compare three text files at the same time (`OldBase.txt`, `OldCustom.txt`, and `NewBase.txt`) and automatically create the new application code (`NewCustom.txt`).

In the *Upgrading tools* section, we will talk about comparing the text tools and about MergeTool, which can be used for the purpose of the current section. Refer to them to get a detailed view of how to use them to carry out customizations to a new database.

Transforming forms to pages

The object type *form* is no longer available in Microsoft Dynamics NAV 2013. The process of transforming forms to pages had to be done when upgrading to Microsoft Dynamics NAV 2009 with an RTC installation.

If you intend to upgrade to Microsoft Dynamics NAV 2013 from Microsoft Dynamics NAV 2009 with an RTC installation, just skip this section. It's not for you.

For those using a classic installation in any previous version of Microsoft Dynamics NAV, this is a required step. Your own forms have to be transformed to pages. Also, the standard customized forms should be transformed to pages to carry out the customization done in the form to the standard page.

There isn't a form-transformation tool specific for Microsoft Dynamics NAV 2013. The form-transformation tool that was released with Microsoft Dynamics NAV 2009 can be used.

Refer to the *Upgrading tools* section to learn more about the form-transformation tool.

Transforming reports

The report definition had already changed in Microsoft Dynamics NAV 2009 compared to the previous versions of Microsoft Dynamics NAV. In Microsoft Dynamics NAV 2013, the report definition changes again. So, no matter which version you are upgrading to Microsoft Dynamics NAV 2013 from, you will have to go through a report-transformation process.

The report-definition changes in Microsoft Dynamics NAV 2013 include the following:

- The report sections and section triggers are no longer available
- The request form is no longer available
- The RDLC definition of reports has changed

With the release of Microsoft Dynamics NAV 2013, a tool for report transformation included in the Microsoft Dynamics NAV 2013 Development Environment has been shipped. This is the tool to use. It can be used for reports in Microsoft Dynamics NAV 2009 that have both a classic definition and an RDLC definition and for reports in Microsoft Dynamics NAV 2009, or any previous version, that only have a classic definition.

Refer to the *Upgrading tools* section to get detailed information on how to use this tool.

Upgrading the data

The steps explained to upgrade your data have been summarized to reflect the most important steps involved in the process. There are many other minor steps that are required to successfully upgrade your data to Microsoft Dynamics NAV 2013. A complete list of all the steps can be found in the official documentation provided by Microsoft, which can be downloaded from PartnerSource or CustomerSource from `https://mbs.microsoft.com/customersource/downloads/servicepacks/msdyn_nav2013rtmdownload_cs.htm`.

In this link, navigate to the *Microsoft Dynamics NAV 2013 Documentation* section and download the *Upgrade Quick* guide.

If you are upgrading from Microsoft Business Solutions–Navision 4.0 or from Navision Attain 3.xx, download that same guide, but from the Microsoft Dynamics NAV 2009 download page, which is available at `https://mbs.microsoft.com/customersource/downloads/servicepacks/microsoftdynamicsnav2009r2.htm`.

Follow the steps described on these documents to perform the data upgrade.

If you are upgrading from Microsoft Business Solutions–Navision 4.0 or from Navision Attain 3.xx, then to do the first data upgrade to Microsoft Dynamics NAV 2009 you will not need a full application code upgrade to Microsoft Dynamics NAV 2009. You really only need to do an application code upgrade to Microsoft Dynamics NAV 2009 for your table objects; and even for those, you don't have to upgrade all your code but only your own customized fields.

Just compare your old database version object tables to the Microsoft Dynamics NAV 2009 standard object tables to determine which fields were created by customization and create those same fields in a Microsoft Dynamics NAV 2009 database. There is no need to upgrade any other application code.

Upgrading tools

There are several tools that help us in the upgrading process. Some of them must be used at some point of the upgrade process (such as the text format upgrade tool). Some others can be used to help us in the upgrade process, but are not mandatory (such as MergeTool). In this section, we will explain them all.

Upgrade toolkit

The upgrade toolkit is included in the Microsoft Dynamics NAV 2013 installation media.

For the W1 version of Microsoft Dynamics NAV 2013, the upgrade toolkit only includes two folders: `Data Conversion Tools` and `Object Change Tools`. For country versions, it also includes an extra folder: `Local Objects`.

In both the `Data Conversion Tools` and `Local Objects` folders, there are two `.fob` files that have to be used in the data upgrade process. If you are upgrading an old W1 version database, the objects found in `Data Conversion Tools` should be used. If you are upgrading any old localized version database, use the objects under the `Local Objects` folder instead.

Dynamics NAV is used throughout the world. Every country and region has a localized version of Dynamics NAV, or a version that complies with the local government or tax regulations. Make sure you utilize the right version for your country.

In the *Upgrading the data* section, outlining the different versions of Microsoft Dynamics NAV, we have explained at what point these objects have to be imported and used.

In the `Object Change Tools` folder, there is a `.exe` file that helps us transform our new customized objects that have a Dynamics NAV 2009 object definition into objects with a Dynamics NAV 2013 object definition.

Text format upgrade

As part of the upgrade toolkit, there is a folder called `Object Change Tools`, which contains a tool called `TextFormatUpgrade2013`. This tool has to be used during the application code upgrade process.

There are several object properties, parts, triggers, text in code, and so on, that are no longer available in Microsoft Dynamics NAV 2013. Some of them have been replaced by other properties, parts, or triggers. Some of them have just been removed.

As part of the code upgrade to Dynamics NAV 2013, we have to get rid of all the old stuff and get a *clean* object for the new application version.

The text format upgrade tool does the following:

- Replaces the `LookupFormID` table and page property with `LookupPageID`
- Replaces the `DrillDownFormID` table property with `DrillDownPageID`
- Replaces the text form with the text page on the value of former table properties `LookupFormID` and `DrillDownFormID`
- Replaces code `FORM.RUN(FORM::` and `FORM.RUNMODAL(FORM::` with `PAGE.RUN(PAGE::` and `PAGE.RUNMODAL(PAGE::`
- Replaces all form variables declared in the application code with a page variable, taking the same variable ID and name
- Deletes the whole definition of the request form in reports
- Replaces the `UseRequestForm` XMLport property with `UseRequestPage`
- Replaces the value form with the value page in the `MenuSuite` property, `RunObjectType`
- Replaces the `RunFormLink` page property with `RunPageLink`

- Replaces the `CardFormID` page property with `CardPageID`
- Replaces the `RunFormView` page property with `RunPageView`
- Replaces the `SubFormLink` page property with `SubPageLink`
- Replaces the `RunFormMode` page property with `RunPageMode`

We may have skipped some individual replacements, but we are pretty sure you got the idea. Actually, to summarize, what the tool does is the following:

- Replaces all references to the former form object with the page object in the following:
    - Object properties
    - Application code
- Deletes the definition of request form in reports

So now, how do we use this tool? Well, it is a command-line tool that can just take one parameter, so it's pretty easy to use! Just follow these steps:

1. Open the Microsoft Dynamics NAV 2009 database.
2. Select all the objects except forms and dataports.
3. Export them in the `.txt` format.
4. Open the command-line interface.
5. Execute the following command:

    `TextFormatUpgrade2013.exe <PathToTheTxtFileOrFolder>`

    - Which can, for instance, be:

        `TextFormatUpgrade2013.exe C:\ImplementingDynamicsNAV2013\OldCustom.txt`

    - Or just:

        `TextFormatUpgrade2013.exe C:\ImplementingDynamicsNAV2013\`

    - In this second case, we have just specified the folder containing the different `.txt` Dynamics NAV files (`OldBase.txt` and `OldCustom.txt`) and the tool will convert all the text files inside the folder during the same execution.

6. The tool will start its execution. Wait for the process to finish.
7. The result of the execution of the tool will be a text file with the same name as the original text file, but it will be stored in a directory called `Converted` inside the directory where the original file was.

8. You can now use these new text files for merging purposes by following the instructions explained in the previous sections. If you use the old text files instead, any comparison to the new standard application code of Microsoft Dynamics NAV 2013 will result in hundreds or thousands of modifications, purely because of object property changes, even if the object has not changed between the two versions. Using these new files instead, will let us just compare *real* object modifications.

Form transformation

For those who upgrade to Microsoft Dynamics NAV 2013 from Microsoft Dynamics NAV 5.0 or previous versions, or from Microsoft Dynamics NAV 2009 in a classic environment, you have to know that your form objects have to be transformed to pages. Customizations done in the standard form objects have to be carried out to the corresponding standard page object and new custom form objects have to be fully transformed to new custom page objects.

This process is not new for Microsoft Dynamics NAV 2013. It was already a requisite if you wanted to upgrade to Microsoft Dynamics NAV 2009 in an RTC environment.

There was a form-transformation tool available with Microsoft Dynamics NAV 2009. You will find the tool in the Microsoft Dynamics NAV 2009 installation media, in a folder called `TransformationTool`.

There is no form-transformation tool shipped with Microsoft Dynamics NAV 2013. So, if you have to transform forms into pages, you will have to use the tool shipped with the 2009 version.

We will not explain how to use this tool in this book. If you have never used the tool and want to learn how to use it, you can consult the online help available at `http://msdn.microsoft.com/en-us/library/dd338789.aspx`.

Report transformation

With Microsoft Dynamics NAV 2009, a new way of reporting was introduced: **Reporting Definition Language Client-side (RDLC)**. The old way of reporting, the classic way, was kept for compatibility reasons to use it with the classic client. That is, in Microsoft Dynamics NAV 5.0 and previous versions, only classic reporting was available; in Microsoft Dynamics NAV 2009, hybrid reporting was available (reporting in classic and RDLC at the same time); and now, in Microsoft Dynamics NAV 2013, only RDLC reporting is available.

For RDLC in Microsoft Dynamics NAV 2009, classic sections were the base to construct the layout of the report, and Report Viewer 2008 was used. In Microsoft Dynamics NAV 2013, the base of the RDLC layout is not the classic report structure anymore (because it has disappeared). The new report structure is the report dataset. Along with that, RDLC 2005 (the RDLC version used in Microsoft Dynamics NAV 2009) has been upgraded to RDLC 2008, and the report viewer used is the 2010 version.

All of this means that the old reports done in the previous versions of Microsoft Dynamics NAV 2013 will not run anymore in the new version. They have to be converted to the new report format and structure.

The method of upgrading reports to Microsoft Dynamics NAV 2013 differs for hybrid reports (those that have both a native Dynamics NAV and a RDLC definition) and classic reports (those that only have a native Dynamics NAV definition).

Upgrading hybrid reports

The steps required to upgrade a hybrid report to Microsoft Dynamics NAV 2013 are the following:

1. Export the hybrid report in .txt format from the Microsoft Dynamics NAV 2009 database.

2. Use the text format upgrade tool described earlier in this section to transform its definition to a Microsoft Dynamics NAV 2013 format.

3. Import them in the Microsoft Dynamics NAV 2013 database.

4. Compile the imported reports. The reports must be compiled in order to finish the report transformation. If there is any report that does not compile because it refers to tables, fields, or any structure that does not exist in Dynamics NAV 2013 anymore, make the report compile by redefining it.

5. In the Microsoft Dynamics NAV 2013 Development Environment, go to **Tools | Upgrade Report**.

   When the **Upgrade Report** tool is run, the report data is upgraded to a valid Microsoft Dynamics NAV 2013 dataset definition and the layout is upgraded to RLDC 2008.

6. Save and compile the report.

Upgrading classic reports

The steps required to upgrade a classic report to Microsoft Dynamics NAV 2013 are the following:

1. Export the classic report in `.txt` format from the Microsoft Dynamics NAV 2009 database.

2. Use the text format upgrade tool described earlier in this section to transform its definition to a Microsoft Dynamics NAV 2013 format.

3. Import them in the Microsoft Dynamics NAV 2013 database.

4. Compile the imported reports. The reports must be compiled in order to finish the report transformation. If there is any report that does not compile because it refers to tables, fields, or any structure that does not exist anymore in Dynamics NAV 2013, make the report compile by redefining it.

5. In the Microsoft Dynamics NAV 2013 Development Environment, go to **Tools | Upgrade Report**.

6. When the upgrade report tool is run, the report data is upgraded to a valid Microsoft Dynamics NAV 2013 dataset definition, the request form is deleted, and the RDLC 2008 layout is generated by using the layout suggestion tool.

7. Manually adjust the RDLC layout in Visual Studio.

8. Manually create a request page if needed, or use the form-transformation tool to transform the former request form into a request page.

9. Save and compile the report.

Comparing text tools

To upgrade your application code to a new version of Microsoft Dynamics NAV, you have to compare your customized application code with the old original standard application code to determine which customizations have been made and where they have been made.

A second comparison has to be done, between the old original standard application code and the new original standard application code to determine what differences exist between these two versions, so that we can decide whether the old customized objects can still be used (if the original object hasn't changed) or if the customization has to be manually carried out to the new version of Dynamics NAV.

There are several generic compare text tools that you can use for this purpose. A web search will present you with several tools that you can use. We will not explain any of these tools here. We just want to point out that you can use any of them for application code upgrade purposes.

MergeTool

MergeTool is a third-party application that can be used for free by Microsoft partners. This application is developed inside Microsoft Dynamics NAV. Using this application to help you out in your application code upgrade will probably save you a lot of time in analyzing text, as it will let you concentrate only on the real customizations.

When using any generic text compare tool, you have to deal not only with customizations but also with object structure changes that may exist between a Microsoft Dynamics NAV version and its preceding versions. Dealing with object structure changes is useless.

Downloading MergeTool

MergeTool can be downloaded from `www.mergetool.com`. In the download section of the web page, you will find a ZIP or RAR file containing all the objects of the application. Download it onto your hard disk and unzip the file.

The version of MergeTool at the time of writing was MGT1.30.37. This version contains four `.fob` files that can be imported into Microsoft Dynamics NAV 2013, two help files, one Microsoft Visio file, and one readme file.

Installing MergeTool

The steps to install MergeTool are as follows:

1. Create a new Dynamics NAV 2013 database.
2. Open the Development Environment for the new database.
3. Open the **Object Designer** page by navigating to **Tools | Object Designer** or by pressing *Shift + F12*.
4. Navigate to **File | Import**.
5. Select the `MGT1.30.37 NAV7 B33451.fob` file.
6. A message will be prompted saying that all the objects have been examined and no conflicts were found. Choose **Yes** to import all the objects.

The steps to install the help files for MergeTool are as follows:

1. Copy the file `addin_e.hh` to the folder `C:\Program Files\Microsoft Dynamics NAV\70\Service\ENU` in the server where Microsoft Dynamics NAV 2013 services are installed.

2. Copy the file `addin_e.chm` to the folder `C:\Program Files\Microsoft Dynamics NAV\70\RoleTailored Client\en-US` in all the PCs where the Microsoft Dynamics NAV 2013 client is installed.

3. Restart the Microsoft Dynamics NAV 2013 service.

4. Restart the Microsoft Dynamics NAV 2013 client.

Using MergeTool

MergeTool allows us to compare our customized application code with the old standard application code and merge the customizations to the new standard application code, creating a new customized application code.

Follow the steps explained in the upgrade steps in detail.

1. Get the object's version to get the files `OldBase.txt`, `OldCustom.txt`, and `NewBase.txt`.

2. Open your Microsoft Dynamics NAV MergeTool database.

3. Open the MergeTool menu by navigating to **Departments | MergeTool**.

4. In this menu, you will find everything that can be done with MergeTool.

5. We will start by importing the old base version of our current Microsoft Dynamics NAV database. That is, the `OldBase.txt` file.

Importing the old base version

To import the old base version, follow these steps:

1. Click on **Versions**.

2. Click on the **Import Object Text File** process option that appears on the ribbon bar.

3. Select the `OldBase.txt` file, give this version a name in the **Version** field, and put a checkmark on **Navision Version**.

4. Click on **OK**.

5. The text file will be imported.

6. In the example we are using, the old version is a Microsoft Dynamics NAV 2009 R2 database. This version has **4,232** different objects (excluding forms and dataports), which get reflected in the version list of MergeTool once the file is completely imported.

Importing the old custom version

We will now import our old customized database, that is, the `OldCustom.txt` file:

1. Click on the **Import Object Text File** process option that appears on the ribbon bar.

2. Select the `OldCustom.txt` file, give this version a name in the **Version** field, select **OLDBASE** in the **Based on Navision Version Code** field and also in the **Compare Old Version** field, and select **Delete Equal Objects**.

3. Click on **OK**.

4. The text file will be imported.

When importing the old custom version, we have selected a version in the **Based on Navision Version Code** and **Compare Old Version** fields and have also selected **Delete Equal Objects** because this will allow us to concentrate only on the customizations done on the base code.

By selecting **Based on Navision Version Code**, the import process will skip those objects in our custom version that do not exist in the base version. The objects that exist in a custom version but do not exist in its base version are objects that have been created for the customization. You don't need to compare them to anything; you will just import those in the new custom database. That's why we skip them.

By selecting **Compare Old Version** and **Delete Equal Objects**, the import process will first compare the custom objects against those in the base version and, if they have not changed at all, will skip them. As we saw in the first import process, a Microsoft Dynamics NAV database has thousands of objects. In a customization, probably not all of them have been customized. Probably only a few dozens or even some hundreds of objects have been modified, but all 7,000 objects are not customized. We want to skip objects that have not been modified because we want to concentrate only on those that have actually been modified.

Once the old custom version has been imported, compared against the old base version, and equal objects have been deleted, our old custom version has only 927 objects. Only 927! We don't need to go through all 4,232 objects for the application code upgrade. We only need to concentrate on those 927 that have actually been modified. That's great! That will save us a lot of time!

But we can further reduce these 927 objects by a little. How is that? Well, sometimes it happens that you open an object in the design mode through the **Object Designer** page because you want to check something. You finally leave the object without modifying anything at all, but the editor asks you whether you want to save the changes made to the object or not. If you say yes, the object properties such as Date and Time will be modified. Since there is something that has changed, even if it's just those object properties, MergeTool determines that you will have to compare and merge those objects. Wouldn't it be great to be able to delete those objects from comparison so that only real modifications have to be compared and merged?

This is possible with MergeTool. That's cool, right?

Let's see how to delete objects that have only object property changes (date, time, and version list):

1. Navigate to **Departments | MergeTool | Versions**.
2. Click on the **Navigate** tab that can be found on the ribbon bar.
3. Click on **Find Object Properties Changes**.
4. The **Find Object Properties Changes** process will open.
5. Select the version **OLDCUSTOM** in the **Version** field.
6. Select **Delete Objects**.
7. If we go back to the **Versions** list, only **914** objects are on the **OLDCUSTOM** version now. That means that 13 objects had only object properties changes and have been removed. Great! As we go on, we will be saving more and more time. Now we will only have to concentrate on 914 objects!

Importing the new base version

Now it is time to import the new base version, that is, the NewBase.txt file.

1. Click on the **Import Object Text File** process option that appears on the ribbon bar.
2. Select the NewBase.txt file, give this version a name in the **Version** field, place a checkmark on **Navision Version**, and select **OLDCUSTOM** in the **Must Exist** in **Version** field.
3. Click on **OK**.
4. The text file will be imported.

5. When importing the new base version, we have selected a version in the **Must Exist in Version** field because this will allow us to concentrate only on the customizations done on the base code. In previous steps we saw that only 914 objects were really modified or new in the custom application code used in that example. For the new version, we only want to import these 914 objects. Microsoft Dynamics NAV 2013 has 4,053 objects. But we only want to focus on the 914 that were modified or are new in our custom version. For the rest of the objects, we will use the standard objects of Microsoft Dynamics NAV 2013. By selecting the **OLDCUSTOM** version in the **Must Exist in Version** field, we are telling MergeTool that we only want to import the new object of the new version if it was an object modified in our custom version.

6. Only 182 objects are shown in the new base version. This means that 732 objects that were modified in the old custom version do not exist anymore in Microsoft Dynamics NAV 2013 or they were new customized objects.

7. The main thing is that now we have just a few objects to concentrate on. Our customizations on those objects will have to be carried out to the new application code version.

8. To do so, the first thing we need to know is if the standard code for these 182 objects has been modified at all. If there are no modifications in the standard code, carrying out our customizations will be easy. If there are modifications in the standard code, we will have to take a closer look to see how to carry out our customizations to the new objects.

Comparing the old base and new base versions

Let's first compare the old base and new base versions:

1. On the ribbon bar, click on **Compare Objects**.
2. Select **OLDBASE** in the **Old Version** field.
3. Select **NEWBASE** in the **New Version** field.
4. Click on **OK**.
5. The compare process will start.
6. A message saying that the versions have been compared will appear once the compare process has finished.
7. Click on **OK**.

Take a new look at the **Versions** list. Contrast fields have been updated. A contrast is a group of code lines that have some differences (change in code, added code, or deleted code) respective to the two versions. MergeTool does not treat modifications on a line-by-line basis. It actually treats modifications as groups of line codes.

Imagine that the modification in an object consists of creating a new function with hundreds of code lines and a call to that function from within the same object. There aren't hundreds of modifications for the hundreds of code lines added. There are only two modifications: added code for the definition of the function and added code for the call to that function. It's easier to deal with two modifications than with hundreds of modifications. And that's what MergeTool does.

MergeTool groups contrasts in **Contrast Headers**. There is one contrast header per object in the new base version. Each contrast header may have several contrasts inside.

NEWBASE was compared against **OLDBASE** and it tells us that there are **182** contrasts:

- **Equal Contrast Headers – 9**: These contrasts correspond to **9** whole objects out of the 182 new base version's contrasts that have not changed at all.

- **Changed Contrast Headers – 168**: These contrasts correspond to 168 objects that have changed.

- **New or Added Contrast Headers – 5**: These contrasts correspond to **5** objects that are new in **NEWBASE** (they did not exist in **OLDBASE**). Even if they did not exist in **OLDBASE**, they did actually exist in **OLDCUSTOM**. Otherwise they would not be on **NEWBASE**, because of the import options we have selected. Standard objects that were not in **OLDBASE** but were in **OLDCUSTOM**, now remain the same in **NEWBASE**. This may seem weird, but it's not. They probably correspond to hot fixes or new functionalities released by Microsoft that we have applied to our customized version of Microsoft Dynamics NAV and that were not part of the original standard code for our old version of the application.

We can navigate to the contrast to analyze the differences. To do so, click on the type of contrast you want to analyze (for all, click on the **Contrast Headers** field; for equal contrasts, click on the **Equal Contrast Headers** fields; for changed contrasts, click on the **Changed Contrast Headers** field; for new contrasts, click on the **New Contrast Headers** field) and the list of contrasts will be shown. Select then the specific contrast you want to analyze and click on **Lines** (log), which can be found on the ribbon bar.

We can see what a contrast looks like. The code lines in green remain the same in both the versions (**Line Status** is **Equal**). The code lines in red tell us what the code was in the old version (**Line Status** is **Before**). The code lines in orange tell us what the code is in the new version (**Line Status** is **After**).

In the example, a line of code has been replaced by three lines of code. The three lines of code are involved in the change but there is only one change—a local variable has been defined for an action in **Page 143 Posted Sales Invoices**.

In the **Contrast Headers** list, we can see how many groups of changes exist between the two versions. In the example, we have 182 contrast headers (objects) with a total of 4,018 groups of changes: 330 changes in properties groups, 2,368 changed groups, 893 inserted groups, and 427 deleted groups.

We definitely do not want to deal with all 4,018 groups of changes by manually looking at all the differences in code. We want MergeTool to deal with them automatically and just let us decide on those that cannot be merged automatically by the application. That's what we are going to do in the last part of this section.

Merging all versions

We will go back to the version list page of MergeTool and we will follow these steps:

1. Click on the **Merge Version** action that can be found on the ribbon bar.
2. Select **OLDBASE** in the **Old Base** field.
3. Select **NEWBASE** in the **New Base** field.
4. Select **OLDCUSTOM** in the **Custom Version** field.
5. Write **NEWCUSTOM** in the **New Custom Version** field.
6. Give this new version a description in the **New Custom Version Description** field.
7. Put a checkmark in the **Skip if Manual Merge** field. We select this option because on the first merge we want MergeTool to automatically merge everything that can be merged without our intervention. In the second run, we will uncheck this option to deal with those changes that MergeTool cannot automatically deal with.
8. Leave the rest of the options to their default value.
9. Click on **OK**.
10. The merge process will start.

11. When the merge process is completed, a message will appear saying that the NEWCUSTOM version has been created and the number of objects that require manual merging.

12. Click on **OK**.

13. If we go back to the MergeTool version list, we will see that a new version, **NEWCUSTOM**, has been created with a few objects—the ones that were completely merged automatically.

14. We will now do a second run of the merge process, unselecting the **Skip if Manual Merge** field. Once the merge process starts again, the process will prompt a page with all the versions (the old base code, the old custom code, the new base code, and the new merged custom code) when a manual merge is required. After MergeTool merges the changes to the new merged custom code, we have to decide if we accept the merge or if we want to do any extra modification. Let's see an example of this.

The first subpage corresponds to the old base code. Earlier, we had the assignation of a value to a field, then a record was inserted into the database, and finally the call to a function to store document dimensions.

The second subpage corresponds to the new base code. In the new application code, there is an extra code line between the assignation of a value to a field and the insertion into the database, and the call to a function to store document dimensions has disappeared.

The third subpage corresponds to the old custom base code. To see the whole customization, we will have to scroll through the subpage. The customization consists of a group of 11 code lines added between the assignation of a value to a field and the insertion of the record into the database.

The fourth subpage corresponds to the new custom code. There is a conflict. The custom code inserts the code lines in a specific place and the new code inserts different code lines in the same place. MergeTool cannot automatically merge this because the tool cannot decide if only the custom-added code lines have to be inserted, if only the new code lines have to be inserted, or if both the added code lines have to be inserted in the new custom version; and, in this case, in which order.

Let's take a better look at the fourth subpage, at the proposal made by MergeTool in the following screenshot:

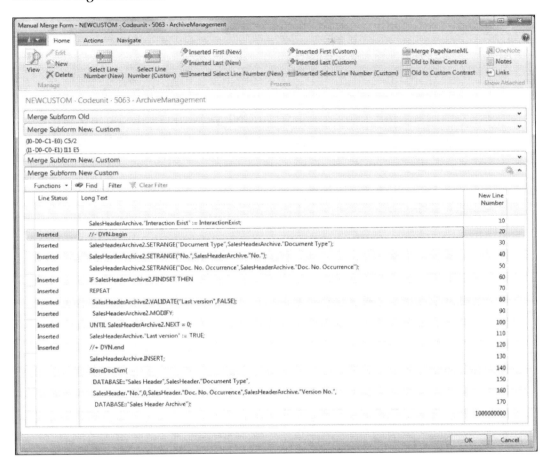

As you can see, the merge proposal consists of using only the customized code. Even the old call to the `StoreDocDim()` function has been used in the custom-merged code. MergeTool has made this proposal because of the option **Default Manual Merge Lines** used in the merge options, which we left to its default value, **Custom**. That is, we have actually told MergeTool to use the custom version for the first proposal when merging lines manually.

In this particular example, we actually want both the groups of added lines (the ones coming from the old customization version and the ones coming from the new base version) to be added to the new customized version, and we want the call to the function to be deleted from the new customized version, as this function is no longer available in Microsoft Dynamics NAV 2013 because of the dimension functionality redesign.

The way to move the code lines from any version to the new customized version in MergeTool is through the **New Line Number** field that can be found in any of the subpages. If there is a number in the **New Line Number** field in any line code of the three first subpages, which correspond to the three code versions used for the merge process, that line will show up on the fourth subpage, in the new customized code. The number used in this field will determine the order in which the code lines will be shown in the fourth subpage.

In this particular example, we want to do the following:

1. Delete the **New Line Number** field values on the third subpage (custom version) for lines 140 to 170. That is, we do not want the call to the `StoreDocDim()` function to be in our new customized version.

2. Leave the proposed **New Line Number** field values as is, on the third subpage for lines 20 to 120. That is, we want our 11 customized code lines to be in our new customized version.

3. Give a value of **15** to the **New Line Number** field on the second subpage (new version), to the second line:

    ```
    SalesHeaderArchive.COPYLINKS(SalesHeader);
    ```

4. To do so, we will use the functions found on the **Actions** tab of the ribbon bar.

5. In the **New Lines** action, there are several functions to assign a value to the **New Line Number** field to code lines in the second subpage, the one corresponding to the new base version.

6. In the **Custom Lines** action, we will find the same functions but they apply to the code lines in the third subpage, the one corresponding to the old custom version.

7. The final result is the one that can be seen in the following screenshot:

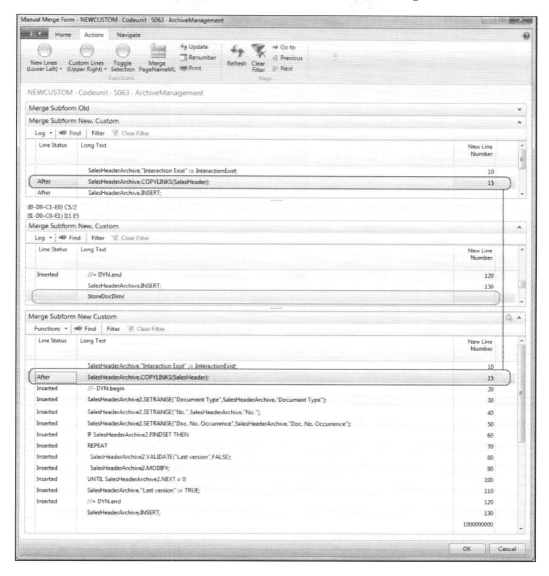

8. In the new custom version, we have our customized code and we have the code line added in the new version, and the call to the `StoreDocDim()` function is not there anymore.

9. Once we are done, we will click **OK** and MergeTool will move on to the next merge conflict.

Exporting the new custom version

Once we are done with the whole merge process and we have a good new custom version, we can go back to the MergeTool versions list and export this version as a .txt file. To do so, there is an action in the **Actions** tab of the ribbon bar, called **Export Object Text File**. Select **NEWCUSTOM** as the version to export and select a destination folder and file name.

Importing the new custom version to a Dynamics NAV 2013 database

The last part of the merge process is to get a new database, with all the new objects, and import into that database the .txt file we have just exported with the customizations merged into the new code version. After importing the .txt file, we will have to compile all the objects and solve any additional issues that may exist.

And that's it! We have a brand new full application code with standard objects for all those objects that we have not modified in the old version and with the customizations carried out to this new version.

We still have to import into this new database the new objects created in our customization. To do so, we will first have to do the following:

- Transform form objects to pages
- Transform reports to the new RDLC definition

Summary

Upgrading used to take a considerable amount of time and effort. With the release of Powershell upgrade, it doesn't have to be so. Companies that already use Microsoft Dynamics NAV will want to get to, at least, Dynamics NAV 2013, so upgrading in the future can be easier. To do so, they have to go through an upgrade process to get their current implementation to the latest version. In this chapter, we covered upgrading to NAV 2016 by using Powershell to upgrade from NAV 2013. Even upgrading to Microsoft Dynamics NAV 2013 is only supported from Microsoft Dynamics NAV 2009. We also explained how to upgrade from the previous versions of the application.

In the next chapter, we will be talking about developing in Microsoft Dynamics NAV 2016.

8

Development Considerations

Almost every Dynamics NAV implementation will have some development. The customized code must fit inside the standard code within Dynamics NAV and it should look like it was a part of the standard NAV. This makes it easier for the users to understand how the customized modules work and for the partners to support it. A good initial development also makes any future change easier and more efficient, for both the customer and the partner.

In this chapter, we will go through the main development considerations you should take into account while developing for Dynamics NAV. The topics covered in the chapter are:

- Setup versus customization
- The data model principles
- How the posting processes are developed
- Where to write customized code
- How to write customized code

Setup versus customization

Dynamics NAV offers many configuration options within all of its modules. These options make Dynamics NAV work differently in each company depending on the option selected; for example, you could define that your locations will use warehouse documents for shipping or process shipping directly from the sales order.

When you set up a new company, you will find more than 200 tables that can be considered setup tables. You will find the setup table of each module, its journals, and its sections. In addition, there are global setups such as the accounting periods, the payment terms, and dimensions.

You will find there are hundreds of setup options in the base Dynamics NAV product. This is not including the thousands of add-ons that are available to NAV. The combination of all these options leads to millions of possibilities.

It is really difficult for a person who does not work with Dynamics NAV full time to be aware of all these options and the impact that a single option can have on the system. Even some Dynamics NAV consultants or developers may not know the consequence of certain settings in Dynamics NAV without research.

A good consultant or developer will not fall into the temptation of starting to develop right away. Before this, it is important to invest time to understand exactly what the client company needs and why. In conjunction, investigate all the setup options in Dynamics NAV that are related to the client's core business. For example, if the client is a manufacturing company, the partner better make sure they thoroughly understand the basic manufacturing principles and the manufacturing functionality in Dynamics NAV and how it can be applied to the client's business based on their requirement.

How can we discover and know how all the features work? Basically, there are three options: read, research, and ask for help.

- **Read**: Microsoft now publishes all the documentation with regards to Dynamics NAV online in MSDN. You do not need a subscription to MSDN in order to view it. In fact, when you search anything on the functionality of Dynamics NAV, one of the results may point to the MSDN article. For example, for the current release, Dynamics NAV 2016, the full documentation can be found at `https://msdn.microsoft.com/en-us/library/hh173988(v=nav.90).aspx`.

  Not only does the MSDN article go through all the technical aspects of the product, it also shows you step-by-step instructions on the functional aspects of the program, that is, how to create a new sales order.

- **Research**: This is one of the best ways to discover all the features that Dynamics NAV can offer, in a step-by-step manner. Every time a customer raises a need, do investigate. Do not start to develop a new feature; before that, you must try to fulfill the need using the standard options. For example, if the need of your customer is related to items, start by looking at each single field in the item table. If you don't know what a certain field is used for, use tools to help you see where the field is used and why.

- **Ask for help**: Dynamics NAV has a large online community that can help you with a specific problem. Microsoft has an official community called Microsoft Dynamics Community (`https://community.dynamics.com/`). This community can be accessed from the Dynamics home screen by displaying **Connect Online** from the **Customize This Page** option.

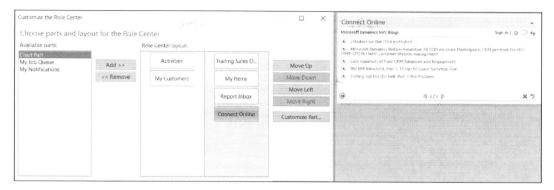

There are also paid online communication groups such as the Dynamics NAV user group (www.navug.com) and free online communities such as MIBUSO (www.mibuso.com) and Dynamicsuser.net.

Our recommendation is to ask the community just after you have tried to solve it yourself. You can state the problem by explaining what you have tried so far. Generally, the community will be more receptive if you have tried first, rather than you throwing the question without investigating beforehand. You must understand that the community is there to help you, not to work for you.

Lastly, if you still can't get the help you need, pay for the help by contacting your partner. Or if you're a partner, contract a NAV person with better knowledge than what your company has. Investing in training is better than paying for mistakes down the road.

As we have seen, it is important to invest time in finding ways to use the standard features before starting to develop. This implementation project will be easier and you will also increase your knowledge of the product, which will be very useful in your future projects.

For the customer, the benefit is also clear. Apart from saving the cost of unnecessary developments, you will also save the grief of creating unnecessary business processes because the solution was not fully thought through.

Data model principles

After analyzing the standard functionality, if there needs to be custom development, it is important to develop the solution with the same structure that Dynamics NAV uses in its modules.

The users that are going to use the functionalities are users that are also going to use the standard parts of the application. To avoid confusing them, it is essential to use the same philosophy and the same structure everywhere. This way, once a user knows one part of the application, he/she can intuitively use the other modules.

This is something that will also help us; we do not have to reinvent the wheel every time. There is no need for us to consider how to structure our data on each development. Take the existing structure as your basis, and just grow its functionality to meet your needs. With this, we are not only making the developer's life easier, but also the life of others who will participate in the project, such as the consultant, the implementer, the trainer, and the person who will support the customer once they start to run with Dynamics NAV. To develop our own application, using the principles and structure of what already exists, it is important to know what already exists. This is what we will cover in the next section.

Basic objects

In Microsoft Dynamics NAV 2016, you can find seven basic object types. They are as follows:

Object	Description
Table	This object is used to store data in the database. Most of the time it is within this object that data is validated or calculated so that it follows the business rules described in each application area. Understanding tables is the key to using all the other objects.
Page	This object is used to display data to the users. Pages allow the users to add records to a table, and to view and modify the records. Pages can also be exposed as web services so that the other applications can also read, insert, modify, or delete data, just like the users do.
Report	These objects are mostly used to summarize and print detailed information by using filters and sorting, selected by the users. On some occasions, reports are also used to batch process data.
XMLport	This object is used to export and import table data in XML format.
Codeunit	This object is used to group code of a particular functional area.
MenuSuite	This object contains the menus that are displayed in the Department page. It is the user's door to access the functionalities of a certain area.
Query	This object is used to specify a set of data from the Dynamics NAV database.

Even if we talk about objects, it is important to note that Dynamics NAV is not object-oriented, but object-based. You have seven object types that you can use, but you cannot create new object types. This may seem limiting, but it also makes development work much easier.

Each object is created using a specific designer. For example, tables are created using **Table Designer**, pages are created with **Page Designer**, and so on.

To open the Development Environment, you have to install **Dynamics NAV Development Environment**. Open it and navigate to **Tools | Object Designer** (or press *Shift + F12*). The following window will open:

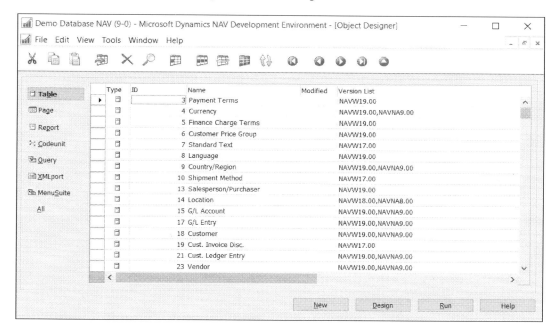

On the left-hand side, you will find a number of icons representing the different objects available. On the right-hand side, you will see a list of all the existing objects of the object type selected. In the previous screenshot, we can see a list of objects of the `Table` type.

All application objects are identified by an ID number. There are, however, restrictions about which numbers can be used while creating application objects. As a general rule, when you are developing for a customer, you use ID numbers between 50000 and 99999 when creating new objects, although you will have to check the exact IDs that can be used for a specific customer license. You will be allowed to modify the standard objects, but you cannot create them.

To modify an existing object, you must select it and then click on the **Design** button. This will open the object in its corresponding designer. In the following screenshot, we can see the **Table 18 Customer - Table Designer** window:

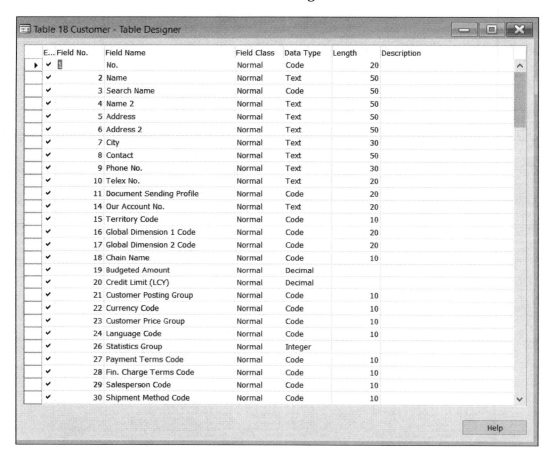

Object elements

Each object has its own attributes. A table contains properties, triggers, fields, and keys, which are related to each other, as we can see in the following image:

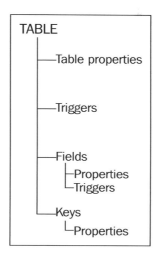

To access the table properties, scroll down from the **Table Designer** and put the cursor on an empty line at the bottom of the **Table Designer**. Then navigate to **View | Properties**, or click on the properties icon on the toolbar, or press *Shift + F4*. The **Table - Properties** window opens and shows the properties of the table. In the following screenshot, the developers can view and modify the properties for the Customer table:

To access the triggers from the **Table Designer**, go to **View | C/AL Code** (or press *F9*). The following window will open, showing all the triggers of the table, including the field triggers:

```
Table 18 Customer - C/AL Editor
  1  Documentation()
  2
  3  OnInsert()
  4  IF "No." = '' THEN BEGIN
  5    SalesSetup.GET;
  6    SalesSetup.TESTFIELD("Customer Nos.");
  7    NoSeriesMgt.InitSeries(SalesSetup."Customer Nos.",xRec."No. Series",0D,"No.","No. Series");
  8  END;
  9  IF "Invoice Disc. Code" = '' THEN
 10    "Invoice Disc. Code" := "No.";
 11
 12  IF NOT InsertFromContact THEN
 13    UpdateContFromCust.OnInsert(Rec);
 14
 15  DimMgt.UpdateDefaultDim(
 16    DATABASE::Customer,"No.",
 17    "Global Dimension 1 Code","Global Dimension 2 Code");
 18
 19  OnModify()
 20  "Last Date Modified" := TODAY;
 21
 22  IF (Name <> xRec.Name) OR
 23    ("Search Name" <> xRec."Search Name") OR
 24    ("Name 2" <> xRec."Name 2") OR
 25    (Address <> xRec.Address) OR
 26    ("Address 2" <> xRec."Address 2") OR
 27    (City <> xRec.City) OR
 28    ("Phone No." <> xRec."Phone No.") OR
100 %
```

Field properties can be accessed from the **Table Designer**. Put the cursor on the field you want to check and then navigate to **View | Properties**, or click on the properties icon on the toolbar, or press *Shift + F4*.

The **Properties** window for the selected field opens, as shown in the following screenshot:

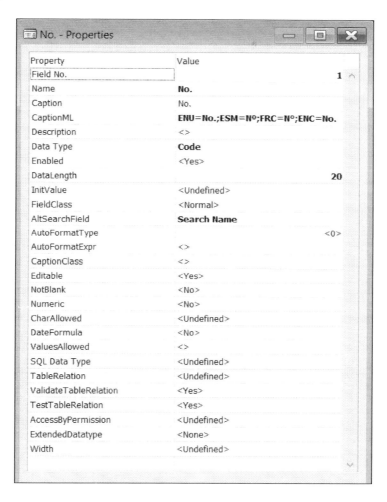

The properties that are changed from the default settings will be highlighted in bold. Keys can be accessed from the **Table Designer** by navigating to **View | Keys**, as shown in the following structure:

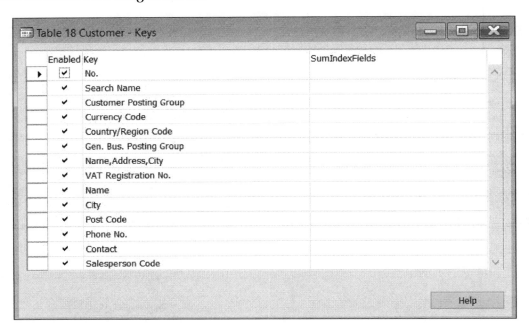

The properties of the keys can be accessed the same way you accessed the table properties or the field properties. Select the key you want to check, and navigate to **View | Properties**. Not all the objects have the same elements as the ones shown for the tables, but they have similar elements that can be accessed in a similar way.

How tables are structured

Tables are the most fundamental objects among any databases. They store records that are collected through pages; for example, customers, sales, and inventories. These records are then presented to the users through pages and reports.

The table's structure is the base of the structure of the whole application. We have already covered the table structure in *Chapter 3, Dynamics NAV – General Considerations*, but we will go a bit deeper in this section. In the standard application, we find different kinds of tables that are used for different purposes:

- **Master tables**: We will find master tables in each area of the application; they are the ones that are used to store the more important information of each module. In the sales area, the most important table is the `Customer` table; in the purchase area, it is the `Vendor` table; and in the warehouse management module, the `Item` table is the most important table. Therefore, they are called master tables.

- **Secondary or subsidiary tables**: These are the tables that store secondary data, usually related to the master table, or that can be selected from a master table. An example of a secondary or subsidiary table is the `Customer Price Group` table. This table contains the distinct price groups that are set up in the `Company` table. A value from this table can be selected and assigned to a customer from the `Customer` table.

- **Setup tables**: All the modules have their own setup table; different options can be selected to specify how the module is going to work.

- **Document tables**: We always find the document tables in pairs, because a document always has a `Header` table and a `Lines` table. Orders, shipments, or invoices are all examples of documents. The documents can also be divided between live documents and posted documents. The posted documents are stored in different tables that cannot be edited, but can be deleted.

- **Entry tables**: Entry tables are used to keep track of all the transactions related to a master table. On the `Customer ledger Entry` table, for instance, we can find an entry for each invoice, credit memo, or payments for a single customer.

- **Register tables**: Register tables are used to keep track of entries created on the same posting process. For instance, the posting of a single sales invoice creates different G/L entries (an entry in the customer account, another in the sales account, another in the VAT account, and so on). All these entries are grouped in the `G/L Register` table as they all belong to the same posting process, the posting of a specific sales invoice.

- **Journal tables**: These are the tables that the posting process uses to create entries. It is the system that introduces data as a previous step on the journal tables while posting a document. The user can also manually introduce data on a journal table if he wants to post a transaction without a document. We can find many processes that create data on journal tables but don't post them. The user is responsible for checking that data and finally posting it. That's what the calculate depreciation process does. For each fixed asset, it calculates the corresponding depreciation, and creates a line that reflects those calculations. The user has to go to the journal, review the lines, and post them.

Understanding table structures

The best way to understand a concept is to see it in practice. This is why we are going to analyze the structure of the tables in a particular area, the warehouse management area.

Master tables

The master table of the warehouse management area is the `Item` table. It holds the main data in this area and everything else relates to it. Usually, the primary key of a master table is a field named `No.`. Typically, a series number is used to assign a new `No.value` each time a new item is created. The field `No.` gets replicated on different tables to refer to a specific item.

Secondary tables

In the item card, you will find fields that can be filled by selecting data from a secondary table, such as the `Base Unit of Measure` field that can be filled by selecting data from the `Item Unit of Measure` table. For each item, you can indicate its sales price on the `Sales Price` table, which is also a secondary table.

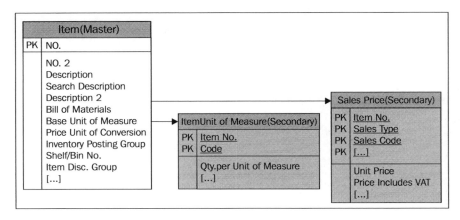

Any table (it doesn't matter if it's a master table, a secondary table, a setup table, or any other kind of table) can be used in the other application areas. The `Sales Price` table, which we've seen, is also a secondary table of the sales area.

In the preceding example, we've only seen a couple of secondary tables related to the `Item master` table. We'll find many other secondary tables, such as the `Item Category` table, the `Product Group` table, the `Tariff Number` table, the `Item Tracking Code` table, and the `Item Variant` table, just to give a few examples.

Setup tables

The setup table of the warehouse management area is called the `Inventory Setup` table. The number series used to code the items can be set up on this table. In addition, other information such as whether we want the item cost to get automatically posted to the general ledger or not is controlled through here. Other setup tables also affect how the warehouse management area works. For instance, in the `General Ledger Setup` table, you can indicate the rounding precision of the unit prices of the items in the `Unit-Amount Rounding Precision` field.

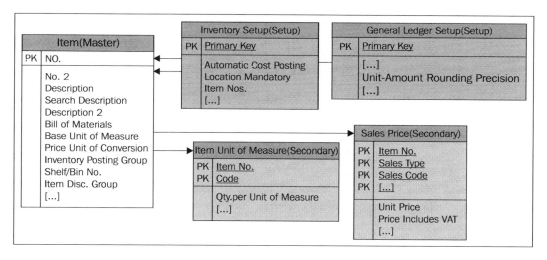

Document tables

Now it's time to start using the item on documents, to purchase or sell them. The item can now be used on the lines of a document. In the following example, we will use a sales order to put in an item line in the sales order. There are other sales documents where an item can be used, such as the sales quote, the sales invoice, the sales return order, or the sales credit memo. In fact, all these sales documents are stored on a single document structure composed of the `Sales Header` table and the `Sales Line` table. Each one is identified by the `Document Type` field that is part of the primary key of the tables.

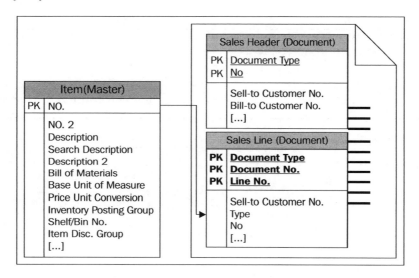

When an item is used in a document, not only is the item number stored in the `Sales Line` table, but many other fields from the `Item` table are also copied. Fields such as the `Inventory Posting Group` field, the `Description` and `Description 2` fields, the `Gen. Prod. Posting Group` field, or the `VAT Prod. Posting Group` field—just to name a few—are copied from the `Item` table to the `Sales Line` table.

It may seem redundant; why are all these fields copied if the information is already stored in the item card? Well, this information is copied for two reasons. Firstly, this information is considered default data; and secondly, it gets copied to allow the users to change a field value on a specific order. As an example, you can change the item description, the sales unit of measure, or the item description on a specific order. Other fields, such as `Inventory Posting Group`, are also replicated on the `Sales Line` table, but the users cannot modify their value. It may take some time between creating the order and finally posting it. In the meantime, the item configuration may have changed. However, it is not acceptable for a specific order to post something different to when it was created, which is probably when the user checked it.

The same is true for the item price. When we create a sales order for the item, the system calculates and proposes a price for the item. This is the price we configure, either on the item card or in the `Sales Price` table. We tell our customer the selling price so that he can approve the order before we ship the item. Imagine that in the meantime, the item price changes. We all agree that the new price is for the new orders. It will be unacceptable for the system to change the existing price without warning.

Copying data from the master table to a document table is part of Dynamics NAV philosophy. It is something that we can find in all the application areas and in all the documents. It has a clear pro: it makes the system flexible. It also gives us a lot of traceability. It also has a con: any change on a master table is not reflected immediately. The existing document lines keep the old configuration. The user has to refresh the line if the new configuration is needed. From our experience, some users have difficulty understanding this. They don't know when to refresh a line. During training, we will have to invest time to tell them and make sure they understand when to refresh a line. When the order is ready and the item has been shipped to the customer, the order can be posted. The posting routines, which are explained later on, are in charge of verifying that all data is correct and creating all the required entries to reflect the transaction.

Concerning documents, a shipment is created by inserting records on the `Sales Shipment Header` and `Sales Shipment Lines` tables. In the next step, the invoice will be created by inserting the records on the `Sales Invoice Header` and `Sales Invoice Lines` tables.

Records representing the shipment and the invoice are almost the exact copies of the original order. Take a look at the fields found on the `Sales Line` table, which is shown in the following screenshot:

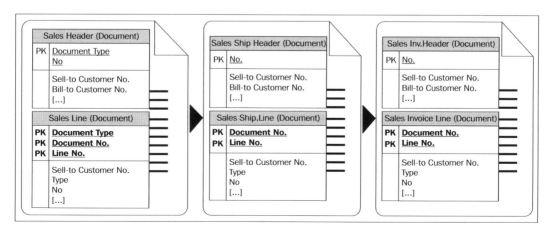

Now take a look at the fields found on the `Sales Shipment Line` table, which is shown in the following screenshot:

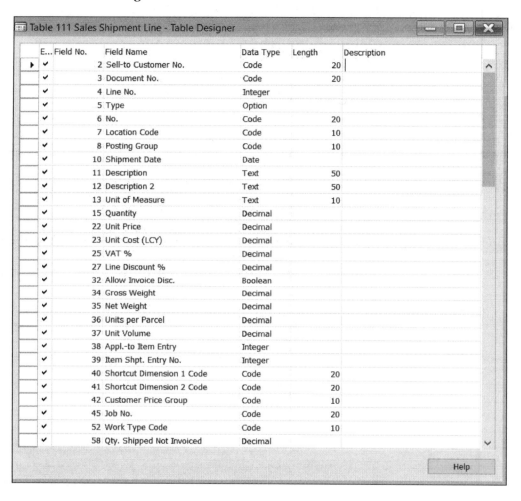

As you can see, we can find almost the same fields, with the same name and the same type. The most important part is that the fields have the same value in the `Field No.` property. This is important because to copy values from one table to another, the `TRANSFERFIELDS` instruction is used. This instruction copies the fields based on the `Field No.` property. For each field in the `Record` (the destination) table, the contents of the field with the same `Field No.` property in the `FromRecord` (the source) table will be copied, if such a field exists. Note that in order for the function to work, the fields that are being transferred need to have the same data type. You cannot transfer a text value into a date field. You will receive an error if the field type is different when this function is called.

So, if you create a new field on the `Sales Line` table and you need to copy the value of the field along the different documents, you just have to create the same field with the same `Field No.` property on the tables where the documents are stored. There is no need for extra coding.

There are other document tables related to the warehouse management area. For instance, the `Transfer Header` and `Transfer Line` tables, with their corresponding historical documents `Transfer Shipment Header`, `Transfer Shipment Line`, `Transfer Receipt Header`, and `Transfer Receipt Line`. Historical documents are part of the Dynamics NAV protected tables. Data on the protected tables cannot be changed and nor can you directly insert new records on these tables; the posting routines are the ones in charge of inserting data in these tables.

To refresh our memory, so far we have covered the types of tables that are shown in the following diagram:

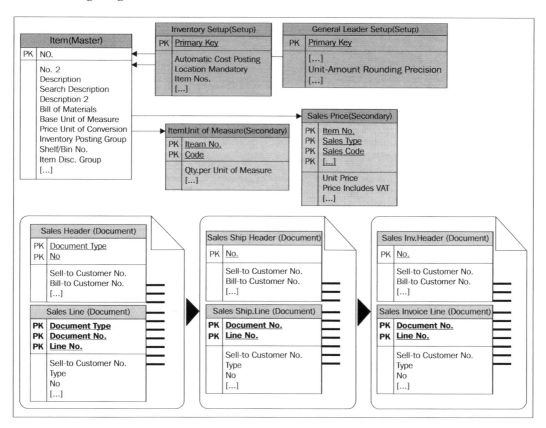

Only the `Entry` and `Journal` tables are left and we will cover them in the following section.

Entry tables

As we have mentioned, the purpose of entry tables is to keep track of all the transactions done with a master table. Each time we purchase an item, we have to record the stock increase. Every time we sell an item, we have to record the stock decrease. It gives us valuable information about the item, such as the inventory quantity we have at any time.

One might think that we don't need an entry table to determinate the stock. When we purchase or sell, we create the appropriate purchase and sales document. Theoretically, we can just add all the purchases and sales document lines and get the same data. Again, we seem to be duplicating information. It is true that for one transaction the same information has to be copied to a lot of tables. However, in each case we want to see the information in a different way. Also, the tables that are used for sales and purchases documents are different; to get the stock, we will have to search between multiple tables. This will make the whole system slower.

Another element to consider is that on some occasions we need to register an item transaction but have no documents. What if we break an item? Or if an item "magically" disappears? We need to decrease the item stock but there is no document to reflect this. In this case, we will want to create a new record in the table entry without creating a purchase or sales document.

Some master tables will need more than one entry table. This is the case of the warehouse management area, where we find the Item Ledger Entry and Value Entry tables. The Value Entry table is used to store the costing details related to each item ledger entry.

Item Ledger Entry (Entry)		Value Entry (Entry)	
PK	**Entry No.**	**PK**	**Entry No.**
	Item No. Posting Date Entry Type [...]		Item No. Posting Date Item Leader Entry Type [...]

The primary key for all the entry tables is a field called Entry No., which is an auto-incremental integer. All the entry tables also have a field named Posting Date.

Additionally, when new records are inserted on the entry tables, the system also creates new records on tables called `Register`. In the warehouse management area, we find the `Item Register` table. The `Item Register` table is used to keep track of when entries are created (regardless of the posting date), which user created them, and also how many entries have been created for each transaction. The `Item Register` table can be considered a secondary table.

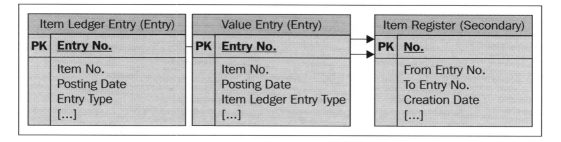

Journal tables

Last but not the least, we find the journal tables. Journal tables are very important since they contain most of the business logic of the application. All the posting processes found on the application are based on journal tables. In the warehouse management area, we find the `Item Journal Line` table.

If the posting is made from a document, the posting process converts the document lines to journal lines by creating temporary registers on the `Item Journal Line` table. The user can also manually create lines on the `Item Journal Line` table and then post them, without using a document at all.

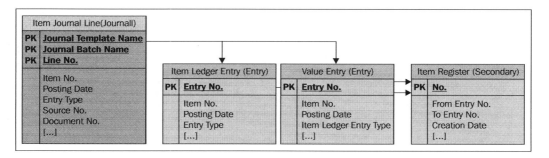

The final picture

And at last, we can see the final picture of how the tables are structured in Dynamics NAV, as shown in the following diagram:

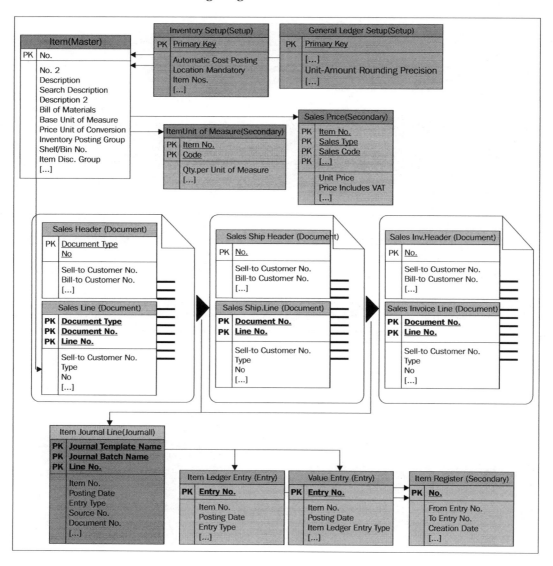

You will find many other secondary tables, setup tables, document tables, and entry tables that are not shown in the diagram, but the structure remains the same.

Remember that all the existing areas in the applications follow this structure; therefore users are used to it. Keep this structure in mind while building your own applications.

The structure of pages

In the previous section, we saw the tables' structure and how important it is to keep the same structure in all the areas to help the users understand how the area works. Pages are also important; they are the objects through which the users interact with Dynamics NAV. The users do not see tables, but pages. Thus, maintaining consistency in the page structure is vital for the user to perceive the consistent application structure. In the standard application, we find different kinds of pages that are used for different purposes, such as:

- **Role center pages**: This is the first page that the users see when accessing Dynamics NAV. Depending on each user's role, the page shows a quick view of the work that the user is responsible for.

- **Card pages**: Card pages show data from a single table and also from a single record. All the master tables have a card page associated with them, which is also the only way to insert, edit, or delete records. Some secondary tables with sufficient entities (many fields) also use card pages.

- **List pages**: List pages show multiple records from a single table. For each card page, you will find a list page that shows data from the same table. In fact, the users access the card page from the list page. These pages are not editable and are only used to show data, not to modify or delete it. Most secondary tables don't have a card page, but all of them have a list page. When no card page can be found for a table, the list page is editable. We are allowed to insert, modify, or delete records from the list page.

- **Document pages**: These pages are used to show the two tables related to a document: the header and the lines. Document pages are used to show data related to the header, and they include a link to a ListPart page where the lines are shown.

- **ListPart pages**: ListPart pages are pages with the same characteristics as those of a list page, but the difference is that they are always used inside other pages.

- **Worksheet pages**: These pages are based on a template, batch, or name structure and have a control for selecting a template, batch, or name. Journals are a good example of worksheet pages.

- **ConfirmationDialog pages**: These are pages that pose a question to the user, have no input fields, and require that the user select **Yes** or **No**.

- **NavigatePage pages**: These pages are used for wizards, which consist of a number of user input screens or steps linked together, enabling the users to carry out infrequently performed tasks.

Understanding page structures

As in the previous section, we will analyze the structure of pages in a particular area, the warehouse management area.

Role center pages

The following screenshot shows the default role center page for a user who has the sales order processor profiles assigned:

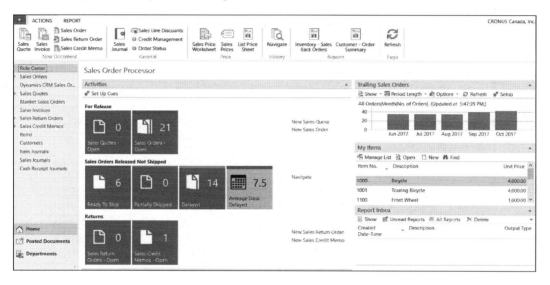

The role center page has a central area called **Activities**. This area contains a few cues that provide a visual indicator of the work that a user has to do each day. Cues are different for each role. The **Activities** area also contains actions so that the user can start new transactions right from the role center.

Card pages

Card pages show data from a single table and also from a single record. In the following screenshot, you can see the **Item Card** page. It contains all the fields that can be stored in the `Item` table, except for a few fields that are used for internal purposes.

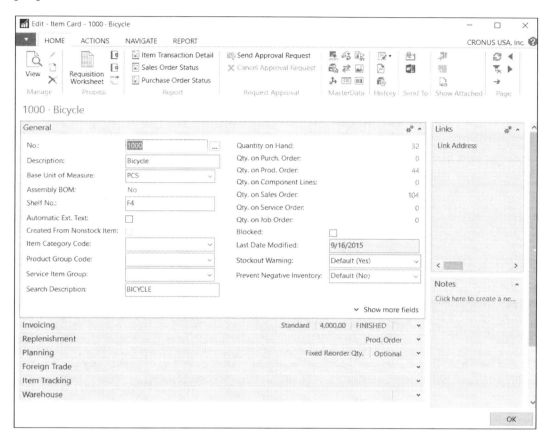

Data is shown in different tabs, grouping fields that are used for similar purposes. In the **Item Card** page, we can find all these tabs: **General**, **Invoicing**, **Replenishment**, **Planning**, **Foreign Trade**, **Item Tracking**, and **Warehouse**.

If you need to create your own card page, keep a similar structure. Keep in mind that all the cards start with a tab called **General**. The card pages are always editable, which means that the user can insert, modify, or delete data on this page. Only a few fields are not editable, such as the `Last Date Modified` field. But you don't have to define this as an editable page because it is a property of the field in the table where you define whether a field is editable or not.

There is one exception to this. If one field has to be editable only in certain circumstances, you cannot define it on the table. You will need to do that on the page.

Find the **Planning** tab from the item card. Note that fields such as **Safety Stock Quantity** can only be editable with certain values from the **Reordering Policy** field.

When the **Reordering Policy** field has no value entered into it, the **Safety Stock Quantity** field is not editable. This is recognizable because the field has a grey background. When you change the value to `Lot-for-Lot`, the **Safety Stock Quantity** field becomes editable. You can identify it because the fields have a white background.

As we mentioned earlier, this behavior has to be coded from the card page. Follow these steps to see how it is achieved in the item card page:

1. Open Dynamics NAV Development Environment
2. Navigate to **Tools | Object Designer**

Find **Page 30 Item Card** and click on the **Design** button.

Navigate to **View | C/AL Code**. The following screenshot shows what you will see:

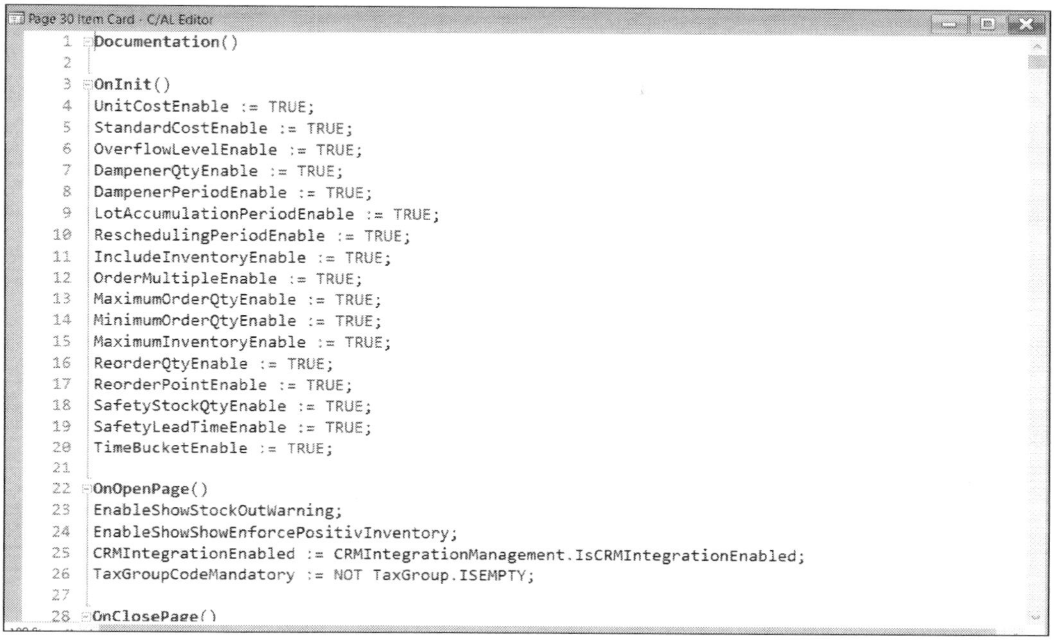

```
Page 30 Item Card - C/AL Editor
  1  Documentation()
  2
  3  OnInit()
  4  UnitCostEnable := TRUE;
  5  StandardCostEnable := TRUE;
  6  OverflowLevelEnable := TRUE;
  7  DampenerQtyEnable := TRUE;
  8  DampenerPeriodEnable := TRUE;
  9  LotAccumulationPeriodEnable := TRUE;
 10  ReschedulingPeriodEnable := TRUE;
 11  IncludeInventoryEnable := TRUE;
 12  OrderMultipleEnable := TRUE;
 13  MaximumOrderQtyEnable := TRUE;
 14  MinimumOrderQtyEnable := TRUE;
 15  MaximumInventoryEnable := TRUE;
 16  ReorderQtyEnable := TRUE;
 17  ReorderPointEnable := TRUE;
 18  SafetyStockQtyEnable := TRUE;
 19  SafetyLeadTimeEnable := TRUE;
 20  TimeBucketEnable := TRUE;
 21
 22  OnOpenPage()
 23  EnableShowStockOutWarning;
 24  EnableShowShowEnforcePositivInventory;
 25  CRMIntegrationEnabled := CRMIntegrationManagement.IsCRMIntegrationEnabled;
 26  TaxGroupCodeMandatory := NOT TaxGroup.ISEMPTY;
 27
 28  OnClosePage()
```

Only a few lines of code are present for the non-editable fields, but no code for inserting or deleting a record or when validating a field.

List pages

List pages show multiple records from a single table. For each card page, you will find a list page that shows data from the same table. In fact, the users access the card page from the list page. These pages are not editable and are only used to show data, not to modify or delete it.

The following screenshot shows the item list page:

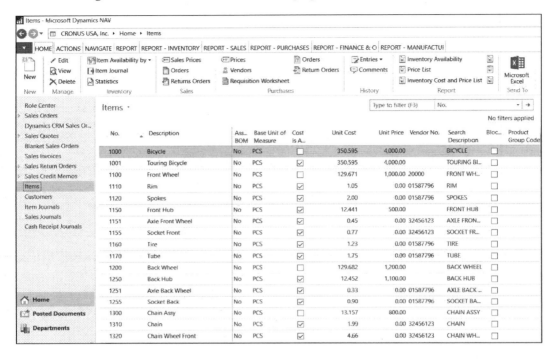

The list pages show fewer fields than the card pages. Only the most important fields of each master table are shown in the list.

All options that can be found on the **Actions** pane can also be found on the item card page. Therefore, while creating a new option, remember to make it accessible from the list page and also from its corresponding card page.

Most secondary tables don't have a card page, but all of them have a list page. When no card page can be found for a table, the list page is editable. We are allowed to insert, modify, or delete records from the list page.

This is the case of the **Item Units of Measure** page, which can be accessed from the **Actions** pane, the **Navigate** tab, the **Item entry**, and the **Units of Measure** icon. You will find the option both from the item card and the items list.

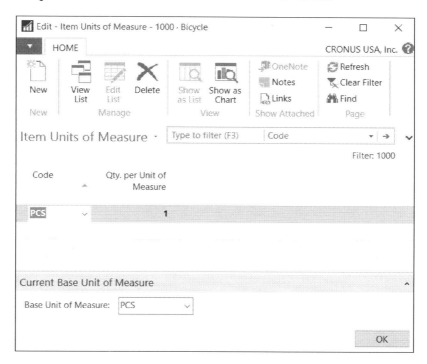

Those list pages need to show all the fields (except internal use fields) to the user, so that he/she can fill them with the required data. By default, the **Item Units of Measure** page shows only two fields, but many others are also available to the user.

Put the cursor anywhere on the header of the table, where it says the name of the fields. Right-click on the mouse and select the **Choose columns** option as shown in the following screenshot:

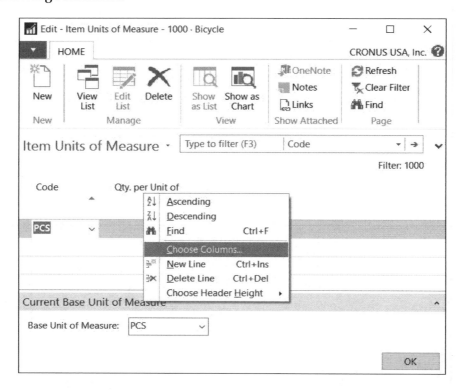

A new window opens and allows the user to customize the page. On the **Available columns** grid, you will find all the fields that are available for the page but are not shown at the moment, as shown in the following screenshot:

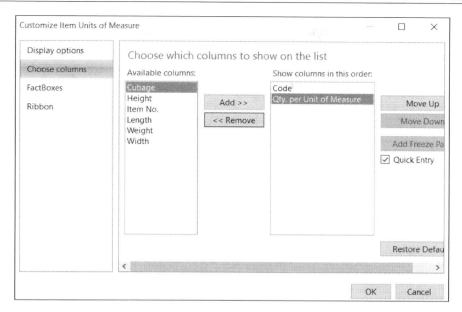

Select one of them and click on the **Add >>** button. Do the same with all the remaining fields, and then click on the **OK** button. You will end up with the **Item Units of Measure** page, as shown in the following screenshot:

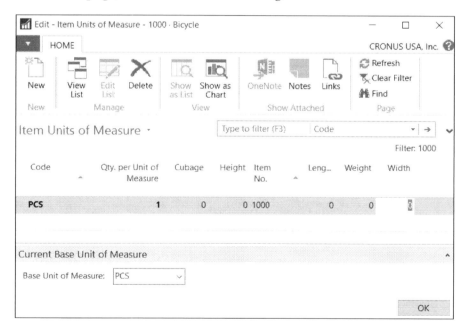

So remember that if you want a field from a secondary table to be filled by the users, you have to make the field available from the list page. With the master tables, you will have to make the field available from the card page and then decide if the new field is important enough to make it available on the list page.

Document pages

These kinds of pages are used to show the two tables related to a document: the header and the lines. The document pages are used to show data related to the header, and they include a link to a ListPart page where the lines are shown.

An example of this is on the sales order page:

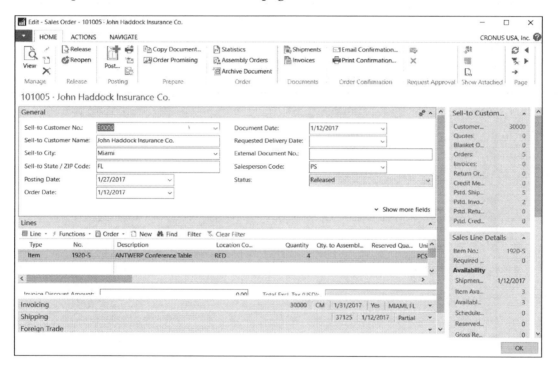

As with the card pages, the users access the document pages from a list page. The actions and related information found on the document page and its corresponding list page must remain the same while adding new options.

The document pages are organized in tabs, like the card page. The only difference is that the **Lines** tab shows another page—a ListPart page that is embedded into the document part.

On the right-hand side of the preceding screenshot, you can find a few tabs showing data related to the document, the customer, or the item on the order. These tabs are a particular type of page, called **CardParts**. These pages are associated to the **FactBox** pane of the document page.

ListPart pages

ListPart pages are pages with the same characteristics as of a list page, but the difference is that ListPart pages are always used inside other pages. Actions can also be defined for ListPart pages.

In the example of the sales order page listed previously, the line area where you enter the items are created using the ListPart pages.

Worksheet pages

Worksheet pages are based on a template, batch, or name structure and have a control for selecting a template, batch, or name. Journals are a good example of worksheet pages, but there are other worksheet examples such as the account schedule or the requisition worksheet functionality. The following screenshot shows the **Item Journal** page:

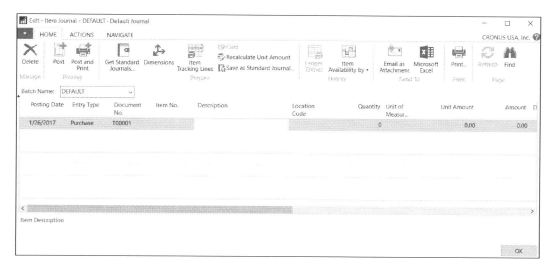

The **Item Journal** page is based on a batch and has a control for selecting the batch name. Only the lines associated with the selected batch are shown in the page. It's similar to the header-lines structure. In this case, the header is the batch and has only one field, its name.

The users can create as many batches as needed on each journal.

Different batches on a journal can be set up as a distinction between the journal adjustments for different people. In the **Item Journal Batches** page, the No. Series field, the Posting No. Series field, or the Reason Code field can be filled for each batch. You will find other options on other journals.

Another reason for creating different batches on the same journal is that different people can input data on the same journal but in different batches. Doing so, the users will not disrupt each other's work.

ConfirmationDialog pages

ConfirmationDialog pages are pages that pose a question to the user, have no input fields, and require that the user selects the **Yes** or the **No** button.

The **Check Availability** page shown in the following screenshot is a good example of a **ConfirmationDialog** page:

This page will pop up when the quantity filled in a line, either a document line or a journal line, is bigger than the current availability of the item.

NavigatePage pages

These pages are used for wizards, which consist of a number of user input screens or steps linked together, enabling the users to carry out infrequently performed tasks.

Dynamics NAV has a functionality called **Navigate**, and the page that shows this functionality is a NavigatePage type of page.

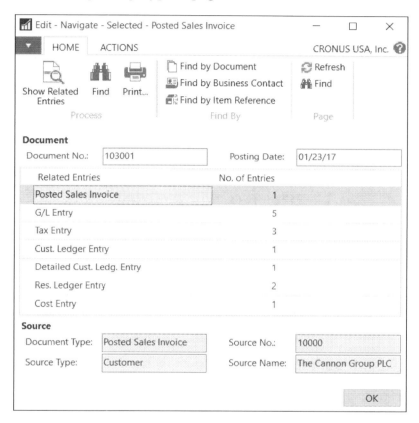

The **Navigate** functionality shows all the documents and entries posted using the same document number on the same posting date. This is a very useful way to see all the entries of a particular transaction that has been posted. If you create your own entry or posted document tables, don't forget to add them to the Navigate functionality.

The posting process

The posting process is the most important process in Dynamics NAV. It commits the data entered by the users into the financial ledgers. There are a few different posting processes; however, they all follow the same structure. The posting process runs through a lot of code from a lot of functions. In fact, many functions are executed many times. This section does not cover the posting process in depth, instead, it shows the overview of the codeunits and how they are structured.

There are several posting routines, one for each journal table and one for each group of documents. All posting routines use more than one codeunit. In Dynamics NAV, you can find more than 80 codeunits with the word *post* in their description. That's quite a few!

Let's see a couple of examples of the posting's codeunits structure. The first example is posting codeunits for sales documents. In the second example, we will see posting's codeunits for **General Journal** lines.

The codeunit structure for sales posting

The sales posting routine starts with four codeunits. The following diagram shows the schema that shows how each codeunit relates to one another:

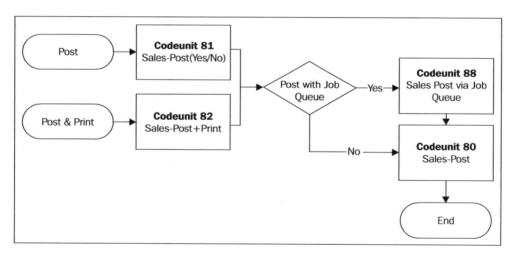

A user can start the posting process by selecting the **Post** or the **Post & Print** action, which will run **Codeunit 81 Sales-Post (Yes/No)** or **Codeunit 82 Sales-Post + Print** respectively. Both codeunits perform the same action; the only difference is that the **Codeunit 82 Sales-Post + Print** prints the posted sales document at the end.

Both codeunits ask a confirmation from the user and check whether the post with the job queue is activated. If the post with the job queue is activated, they call the **Codeunit 88 Sales Post via Job Queue**, which is an automatic process to post documents when the system is not busy.

When the record in the queue is processed, **Codeunit 80 Sales-Post** is called in order to end the posting routine. If the post with the job queue is not activated, **Codeunit 80 Sales-Post** is called from **Codeunit 81** or **Codeunit 82**.

Codeunit 80 Sales-Post is the most important one. It checks the data, inserts records into the historical document tables, and creates all the required journal lines. It also calls the posting routines for the journal lines. You will find similar structures in the other document-posting routines.

The codeunit structure for General Journal posting

The General Journal routine consists of seven codeunits. The following screenshot shows us the schema of how each codeunit relates to each other:

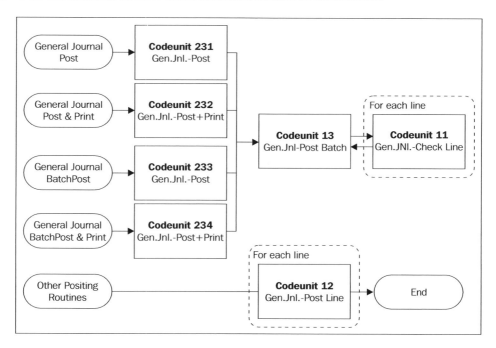

The general journal posting routine can start from several places. Either from a general journal page or a general journal batch page. When the user clicks on **Post** or **Post & Print**, this will run one of the following codeunits: **Codeunit 231 Gen. Jnl.- Post, codeunit 232 Gen. Jnl.-Post + Print, codeunit 233 Gen. Jnl.-B.Post**, or **codeunit 234 Gen. Jnl.-B.Post + Print**.

All these codeunits ask for confirmation from the user, and codeunits 232 and 234 also print the posted entries at the end. After that, they all call **codeunit 13 Gen. Jnl.-Post Batch**. This codeunit checks the consistency of all the lines individually, by calling **Codeunit 11 Gen. Jnl.-Check Line**. **Codeunit 13** also checks that all the lines in the transactions are balanced, and if so, it inserts some secondary data into the records.

Finally, **codeunit 13** calls **codeunit 12 Gen. Jnl.-Post Line** for each line. **Codeunit 12** is the one in charge of creating the corresponding ledger entries. If some other posting routines need to post **General Journal Lines**, they do so by calling **Codeunit 12** directly.

Where to write customized code

While writing your own customized code for Dynamics NAV, it is important to choose where to write that code. Code can be written in different places and the application will still work as you had intended. Unfortunately, not all places are good choices. Depending on where you write your code, it may be easier or more difficult to expand or change functionality. In this section, we will give you some guidelines for choosing where to write your code.

Validating fields

When a field is filled, a special trigger runs the `OnValidate` trigger of the field. For a given field, you will find an `OnValidate` trigger on the page where the user enters the data and also on the table itself. Whenever possible, write your code on the `OnValidate` trigger of the table.

A field can be shown on multiple pages. If you choose to validate the field on the page, you will have to replicate your code in all the pages where the field is shown. This will make your code difficult to maintain.

Batch jobs

Batch jobs are written using a Report object. Typically, batch jobs are not to be done for all the records on a table, but for a set of them. In most cases, it is the user who selects what set of data has to be processed. The Report objects are the ones that best suit these requirements, since they have an interface that allows the users to select options or filter the data.

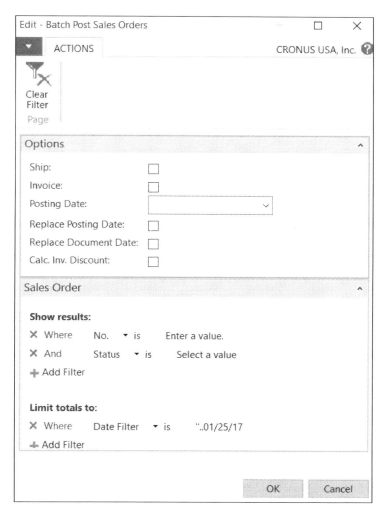

The previous screenshot is an example of a **Batch Post Sales Order** report. It is used to post multiple sales orders at once. As we can see in the screenshot, there is an **Options** tab, and a **Sales Order** tab that allows the users to filter the data.

In this section, we saw where to write customized code. Besides following the guidelines given in this book, there are other options that will help you choose where to write your code. When you need to write a new functionality, you can search for a similar functionality on the standard application and try to mimic the structure.

Formatting customized code

Your customized code should look like the standard code. Keep in mind that any code you write today will probably be maintained by others in the future. If you follow your own programming conventions, we are pretty sure you'll find them easier to write and read. Unfortunately, others may not be used to your conventions, so you'll be making their lives a lot harder.

All Dynamics NAV developers are used to reading code from the standard application. If everyone writes customized code like the standard application does, everybody will only be able to read their own code. To make it easy to maintain an application, it is important to follow a few strict guidelines while writing C/AL code. The standards can be found in the C/AL programming guide. The guide can be found published on MSDN at:

```
https://msdn.microsoft.com/en-us/library/dd355277(v=nav.90).aspx.
```

Summary

In this chapter, we saw that Dynamics NAV offers many configuration options and workarounds that we should use before starting to write our own code. If you need to write customized code, it is important to do it following the same structure as the standard application, to avoid confusing the users. The structures of the tables and the pages are the most important ones, and we've seen them in depth.

The posting process, or posting routines, are the ones in charge of creating historical documents and entries. If you need to modify them, you have to be careful and know what you are doing. That's why we have explained the main idea of posting routines. Last but not least, we saw where and how to write customized code on the Dynamics NAV objects.

In the following chapters, we will see how to implement functional changes on existing and running Dynamics NAV implementations.

9
Functional Changes on Existing Implementations

The world changes constantly, therefore, the demands for every company that's interested to keep doing business will need to change with it.

A company may require functional changes on their Microsoft Dynamics NAV implementation as more and more demands from external parties they do business with. The new project may not be an implementation project, but some of the steps that have to be taken on an implementation project also apply. There are some other things to take into account and this chapter will explain how to handle a project like this one by analyzing the actions to be performed by using four examples of a functional change in Dynamics NAV:

- The Requisition Worksheet
- Fixed Assets
- Item Tracking
- Extending a customized functionality

General guidelines

Depending on the requirement, the functional changes will be different. Some will just require a few actions to complete the change; others may require many actions, which is not just on the functionality being changed. There are a few things to take into account when implementing a functional change. In this section, we will provide some general guidelines. Later on, we will follow the guidelines for all the examples of the chapter.

The following figure shows the general steps that should be performed to implement a functional change:

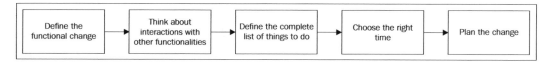

1. The first step is to clearly define the functional change
2. Think about how this change will affect existing Dynamics NAV functionalities and whether those functionalities will need to be changed as well
3. Define a list of all the actions that will have to be completed to be able to implement the functional change
4. Choose the right time to implement the change
5. Actually implement the change into the system

What is a functional change?

A functional change in a Dynamics NAV implementation is to start using an application functionality not used before, or to change the way certain application functionalities were used in the past.

Here are some examples of some new functionalities that a company might want to explore after Dynamics NAV is implemented.

The Requisition Worksheet

Imagine a distribution company that purchases items from its vendors and sells those same items to its customers. This company does not have any kind of automation on its purchase order creation process. It manually determines when purchase orders have to be created, for which items, and in what quantities.

The aim of automating this process, to reduce the time invested in purchase order creation, is that the company wants to start using the **Requisition Worksheet** based on the replenishment parameters established in every item. This function will calculate the replenishment needs of the company and allow the user to automatically create the corresponding replenishment purchase orders.

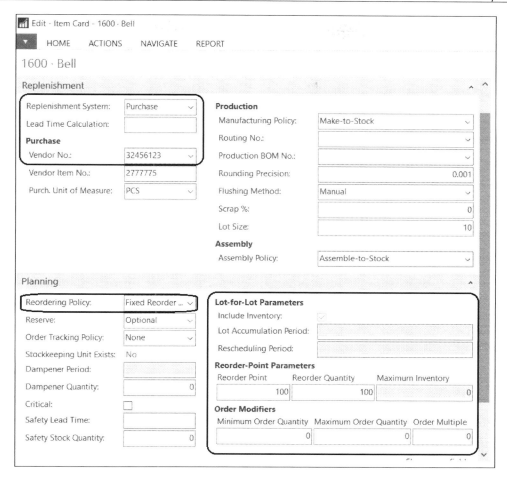

Fixed Assets

You could also think of a company that has never used the **Fixed Assets** functional area and has been keeping its fixed assets by posting manual accounting transactions using the **General Journal**. The company may want to start using the **Fixed Asset** functionality to better manage its fixed assets and automating some of its depreciation entries.

Item Tracking

A company may have been working with items for a long time, but now it has developed new products and the company wants to start keeping track of their lot and serial numbers.

Extending a customized functionality

Sometimes, the existing functionality may not meet what your business needs. In this case, customization will be required. The custom requirements will be as follows:

- Volume Discounts were calculated for each sales invoice line, according to a set of predefined rules, and they were stored as **Volume Discount Ledger Entries**.

- When thousands of **Volume Discount Ledger Entries** existed in the system, the company wanted to be able to apply those ledger entries to other ledger entries, so that they could know which entries are still open, partially open, or closed. This is similar to how an application of **Customer Ledger Entries** or **Vendor Ledger Entries** works in standard Dynamics NAV.

Interactions with other functionalities

If you have to make a functional change in a Dynamics NAV implementation that has been working for a while, the questions that should be answered are: Does the functionality being changed (or that will begin to be used) have interactions with other Dynamics NAV functionalities? What are those interactions? How will the other functionalities have to change?

The Requisition Worksheet

The Requisition Worksheet has interactions with the **Purchase** functionality of Dynamics NAV, since purchase orders can be created as the result of running the Requisition Worksheet.

However, it also has interactions with items (as they hold the replenishment parameters that the Requisition Worksheet will use), (since the Requisition Worksheet will check this functionality to get the demand of items), and with other functionalities that represent the demand of items (item transfers between locations, production components, service orders, and so on), and again with the Purchase functionality (since the Requisition Worksheet will check this functionality to get the supply of items) and other functionalities that represent the supply of items (item transfers between locations, inventory, production, and so on).

The answer to the question of how those functionalities will have to change, in the case of using the Requisition Worksheet, is that they do not have to change at all. Not in standard Dynamics NAV at least.

What will definitely have to change is the way users create purchase orders. The old procedure will not be used anymore, as it will be replaced by a new procedure.

Fixed Assets

The **Fixed Assets** functionality interacts with the **Financial Management** functionality.

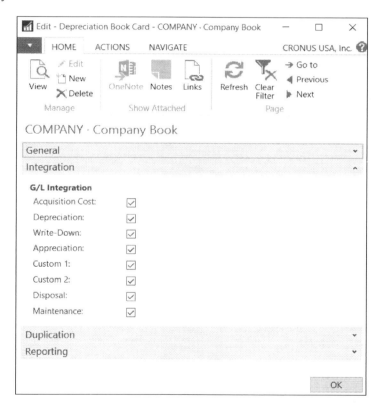

The **Acquisition Costs** and **Depreciation** of the company's fixed assets have probably already been posted to the **General Ledger** by posting manual transactions using the **General Journal**. But this will have to change in the future. Those transactions will not be posted anymore by creating manual transactions, but using standard functionality offered by the Microsoft Dynamics NAV Fixed Assets module. The accounting procedure will have to be changed.

Fixed Assets also interact with Microsoft Dynamics **Sales** and **Purchases** functionalities, as fixed assets can either be sold or purchased using those functionalities. The user's procedures to post those transactions will change when the new functionality starts being used.

Item Tracking

The **Item Tracking** functionality interacts with all the Dynamics NAV areas that use items to post item transactions, such as:

- Sales and marketing
- Purchase
- Warehouse
- Manufacturing
- Jobs

Every single item posting a transaction will have to change since Item Tracking will have to be informed prior to posting. Examine all places where you use items. Very often items have some kind of customization in Microsoft Dynamics NAV. When determining interactions with other Microsoft Dynamics NAV functionalities, take into account those customizations. They may not have been developed to support **Item Tracking**.

Item Tracking also interacts with Item Ledger Entries. Even if the actual inventory of an item is 0, Dynamics NAV will not allow you to start using **Item Tracking** that involves either **SN Specific Tracking** or **Lot Specific Tracking** if the item has had any kind of movement in the past.

This is a big problem for most companies, as the only way (without customizing Dynamics NAV) to start using **Item Tracking** for already used items is to use the official workaround, which involves the following steps:

1. For the item in question, reduce the quantity in hand to 0 by making a negative adjustment.

2. Rename the item in question.

3. Create a new item and give it the name of the original item.

4. Set up an Item Tracking Code for the new item.

5. For the new item, increase the quantity in hand to the original amount by making a positive adjustment.

Companies don't like this workaround. It involves a lot of work and a lot of problems:

- This workaround involves doubling your list of items (if **Item Tracking** has to be used in all items).

- It involves "losing" your item's history (entries, orders, and so on), as this will be under the renamed item and not under the new item.

- When renaming, not only the history of the item will be renamed, but also all kinds of related data (units of measure, sales and purchase prices, sales and purchase discounts, item variants, extended texts, cross references, stockkeeping units, bill of materials, and so on) and other documents. However, not only historical documents (posted documents) will point to the renamed item, but pending documents as well. So you will have to go to all pending documents, one by one, and change the **Item No.** field so that the new item is shipped, received, or manufactured instead of the old one. You will also have to check bills of materials where that item was used, because you probably also want to point it to the new item.

- Creating a new item involves not only creating the item itself, but also its related data (units of measure, sales and purchase prices, sales and purchase discounts, item variants, extended texts, cross references, stockkeeping units, bill of materials, and so on).

If you have to do this for thousands of items and you have a lot of data related to your items and a bunch of pending documents, then completing all those steps can take many hours (even days).

You could also think about customization. Do not check whether **Item Ledger Entries** exist for the item and allow the Item Tracking functionality to be turned on. If you do so, we recommend a lot of testing work. If Microsoft Dynamics NAV doesn't allow this change to be made, it is probably because the application has not been designed to do it under those circumstances. If you plan on turning on **Item Tracking** on your existing items without using the official workaround and allowing it through customization, test the application so that no data inconsistency is introduced due to the change.

By testing, you may find odd behaviors that you will have to take into account in the future.

For instance, an undo action on a **Sales Shipment** posted prior to the change (so posted without any **Item Tracking** information) may not work as expected. There is no tracking information for the undo action to use, but the item now requires this information. The standard functionality of Microsoft Dynamics NAV hasn't been designed to allow the user to introduce **Item Tracking** information when undoing a **Sales Shipment**. The posting action will require **Item Tracking** but there will be no way to introduce that information, so there will be no way to undo a **Sales Shipment** posted prior to the change.

Let's actually take a look at that situation in a step-by-step example. We will create a new item (with no **Item Tracking**) and post a purchase order for it. We will also post a sales order for that same item. Having **Item Ledger Entries** for the item, we will enable the **Item Tracking** functionality for it and will try to undo the **Sales Shipment** to see what happens.

Creating a new item

Follow the given steps to create a new item:

1. Navigate to the item list.
2. On the **Home** tab, click on **New** to create a new item.
3. Place the cursor on the **No.** field on the **General** tab.
4. Press *Enter*. Microsoft Dynamics NAV will give you a new item number. The item number in this example is `70061`.
5. Enter the following information for the item:

Tab name	Field name	Field value
General	Description:	Item Tracking Test
General	Base Unit of Measure:	PCS

Tab name	Field name	Field value
Invoicing	Gen. Prod. Posting Group	MISC
Invoicing	VAT Prod. Posting Group	TAX25
Invoicing	Inventory Posting Group	RESALE
Invoicing	Tax Group Code	MATERIALS

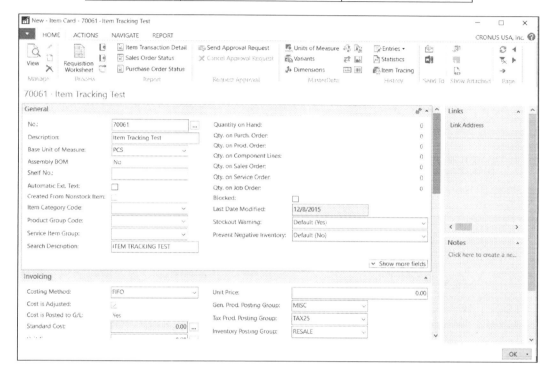

Creating and posting a purchase order for the new item

Follow the given steps to create and post a purchase order for the new item:

1. Navigate to the **Purchase Order** list.

2. On the **Home** tab, click on **New** to create a new purchase order.

3. Place the cursor on the **No.** field on the **General** tab.

4. Press *Enter*. Microsoft Dynamics NAV will give you a new purchase order number.

5. Enter the following information for the purchase order:

Tab Name	Field Name	Field value
General	Buy-from Vendor No.:	10000
Lines	Type	Item
Lines	No.	70061
Lines	Location Code	BLUE
Lines	Quantity	10
Lines	Direct Unit Cost Excl. VAT	1

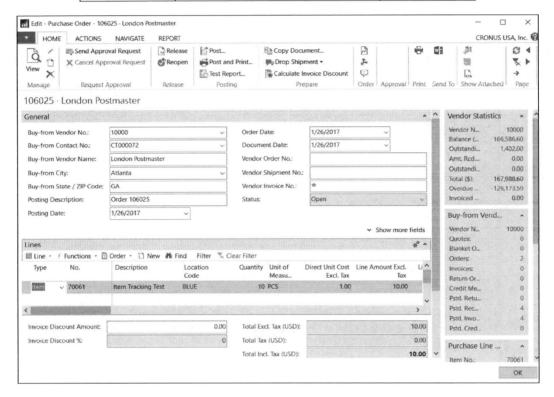

6. Make sure the **Qty.** to **Receive** field in the line has a value of **10**.

7. On the **Home** tab, click on **Post** to post the purchase order.

8. A dialog will open with the options **Receive, Invoice,** and **Receive** and **Invoice**. Select **Receive** and click on **OK**.

9. The purchase order has been posted (received).

Creating and posting a sales order for the new item

Follow these steps to create and post a sales order for the new item:

1. Navigate to the **Sales Order** list.
2. On the **Home** tab, click on **New** to create a new **Sales Order**.
3. Place the cursor on the **No.** field on the **General** tab.
4. Press *Enter*. Microsoft Dynamics NAV will give you a new **Sales Order** number.
5. Enter the following information for the sales order:

Tab Name	Field Name	Field value
General	Sell-to Customer No.:	20000
Lines	Type	Item
Lines	No.	70061
Lines	Location Code	BLUE
Lines	Quantity	2
Lines	Unit Price Excl. VAT	1.5

6. Make sure the **Qty.** to **Ship** field in the line has a value of 2.
7. On the **Home** tab, click on **Post** to post the sales order.
8. A dialog will open with options **Ship**, **Invoice**, and **Ship** and **Invoice**. Select **Ship** and click on **OK**.
9. The **Sales Order** has been posted (shipped).

Turning on Item Tracking for the new item

Follow these steps to turn on **Item Tracking** for the new item:

1. Navigate to the items list.
2. Select item **70061**.
3. On the **Home** tab, click on **Edit**.
4. The **Edit – Item Card** for item **70061** opens.
5. On the **Item Tracking** tab, enter the **LOTALL** value in the **Item Tracking Code** field.

6. An error message will be displayed:

```
You cannot change Item Tracking Code because there are one or more
ledger entries for this item.
```

This step-by-step example was meant to show you a problem you may encounter if you turn on **Item Tracking** on an item that had one or more **Item Ledger Entries**.

If you test around, you will probably find many other problems. If you do customizations, you will need to know all the problems you may encounter in the future.

Extending a customized functionality

In this example, we will talk about a customized functionality in which **Volume Discounts** were calculated for each sales invoice line, according to a set of predefined rules, and stored as `Volume Discount Ledger Entries`.

The functionality had to be extended to allow users to apply those ledger entries to other `Volume Discount Ledger Entries`, so that they could know whether `Volume Discount Ledger Entries` were completely open, partially open, or closed.

In this case, there are no interactions with other Dynamics NAV functionalities. The interaction is actually with the customized **Volume Discount** functionality itself.

Since the functionality was developed to follow the same philosophy behind **Customer Ledger Entries** or **Vendor Ledger Entries**, the extension of the functionality had to follow the same philosophy as well.

This means creating a `Detailed Volume Discount Ledger Entry` table (similar to tables `Detailed Cust. Ledg. Entry` or `Detailed Vendor Ledg. Entry`) and then creating extra fields, the most important ones being **Remaining Amount, Open**, and **Amount To Apply** in the already existing `Volume Discount Ledger Entry` table.

For all of this to work, the development of the functionalities' extension had to:

- Insert a `Detailed Volume Discount Ledger Entry` of type **Initial Entry** when inserting a `Volume Discount Ledger Entry`
- Develop the functionality to be able to select which **Volume Discount Ledger Entries** have to be applied

- Develop the posting process of **Volume Discount Ledger Entries'** applications, which should include:

    ° Inserting **Detailed Volume Discount Ledger Entries** of type **Application**

    ° Updating the field **Open** for the corresponding **Volume Discount Ledger Entries**

That is great and the extended functionality will work for new **Volume Discount Ledger Entries**. But, what happens with existing **Volume Discount Ledger Entries**? They do not have a **Detailed Ledger Entry** of the **Initial Entry** type. And their **Open** field will indicate **No** (the default value for fields of type **Boolean**), but some of the existing **Volume Discount Ledger Entries**, especially the newest ones at the moment of implementing the new functionality, are probably open, so their **Open** field should actually indicate **Yes**.

When implementing the new functionality, some actions will have to be performed to create **Detailed Volume Discount Ledger Entries** for all existing **Volume Discount Ledger Entries**. And a process will have to be run so that only existing **Volume Discount Ledger Entries** that are indicated will be open.

Writing a to-do list to implement a change

Several actions will have to be performed to implement a functional change. All of them will have to be written down so that everyone is aware of what has to be done for the new functionality to work properly.

The Requisition Worksheet

Let's examine the Requisition Worksheet implementation. The actions that have to be performed are as follows:

1. Study the different reordering policies Microsoft Dynamics NAV offers.

2. Determine which replenishment parameters apply to each reordering policy. Notice that some replenishment parameters are not editable when you select a specific reordering policy. This means that those parameters do not apply to the selected reordering policy.

3. The **Maximum Inventory** field is non-editable when the **Fixed Reorder Qty.** reordering policy is selected.

4. Establish which reordering policies will be used in every group of items. Different kinds of items will probably be the best fit in different reordering policies.

5. Calculate the appropriate replenishment parameters for every item using statistical information of sales or any other information.

6. Set the **Vendor No.** for every item.

7. Set the **Lead Time Calculation** for every item.

8. If the company manages different locations and replenishment parameters are different for every location, create **stockkeeping units** and inform the replenishment parameters in the stockkeeping unit card rather than on the item card.

9. If the company uses item variants and replenishment parameters are different for every variant, create stockkeeping units and inform the replenishment parameters in the stockkeeping unit card rather than on the item card.

10. If the company uses both different locations and item variants, create stockkeeping units per variant and per location.

That's a lot of clicks and some of them may require a lot of time and effort to complete. As you go on, you may find several other actions that have to be done. Write them all down so that nothing is forgotten. Consider using flow charts for a clearer picture of what has to be done and in which order, if the order matters.

If you have a reasonable amount of items, this project will not be difficult or time consuming.

If you have thousands of items, you may want a Dynamics NAV developer to help you out with some of the steps, especially in the calculation of the replenishment parameters. You could think of an algorithm to calculate and inform replenishment parameters in your items or stockkeeping units and ask a Dynamics NAV developer to develop it for you.

Fixed Assets

Imagine a company that has been using Microsoft Dynamics for a while. This company has never used the **Fixed Assets** functionality. Now they want to start managing their fixed assets with Dynamics NAV.

How many actions do you think will be needed to complete the project? Let's go through them:

1. Get a list of the fixed assets. This may require that you perform a **Fixed Asset Physical Inventory** in your company.

2. Check the existing FA posting groups. Modify the existing FA posting groups if they do not meet your accounting requirements, or create new ones if you need to. To do so, navigate to **Departments/Financial Management/ Administration** and click on **FA Posting Groups**.

3. Study the different depreciation methods Microsoft Dynamics NAV offers. The **Depreciation Method** field can be found on a fixed asset card; the options for this field are shown in the following screenshot:

4. Choose the appropriate **FA Posting Group** for each fixed asset in your list.

5. Choose the appropriate **Depreciation Method** for each fixed asset in your list.

6. Determine **Depreciation Starting Date** and **Depreciation Ending Date** for each fixed asset in your list.

7. Determine **Acquisition Cost** for each fixed asset in your list.

8. Manually create all the fixed assets in Microsoft Dynamics NAV or choose a data migration tool and format to create fixed assets from an archive.

[You will find more information about data migration tools in
*Chapter 6, Migrating Master Data, Pending Entries, Pending Documents
and Historical Data.*]

9. Uncheck all G/L integrations of all depreciation books your company will
   be using. Fixed asset movements have to be posted with the acquisition cost
   and depreciation that your fixed assets have had prior to using the Microsoft
   Dynamics NAV **Fixed Asset** functionality. We do not want all of those
   movements to be posted to the **General Ledger** because they have probably
   already been posted to the **General Ledger** by posting manual transactions.
   That is why we want to uncheck all kinds of integrations between fixed
   assets and the **General Ledger**.

10. Use the **FA Journals** to post an **Acquisition Cost** movement for each fixed
    asset. You can either create the lines in the **FA Journal** manually or use a data
    migration tool to create them from an archive.

11. Use the FA Journal to post depreciation movements for each fixed asset. You
    can either create the lines in the FA Journal manually or use a data migration
    tool to create them from an archive.

12. Make sure both acquisition costs and depreciation movements match with
    transactions previously posted to the **General Ledger**.

13. Check the G/L integrations again of all the depreciation books your
    company will be using.

In this example, 13 actions had to be completed to implement this functional
change. All the steps can be done by an end user using standard Dynamics NAV
functionality.

If you have a reasonable amount of fixed assets, this project will not be difficult or
time consuming.

If you have thousands of fixed assets, you may want a Dynamics NAV developer to
help you out with some of the steps, especially in the creation of thousands of FA
Journal lines to post acquisition costs and depreciations.

Item Tracking

In this example, we are talking about turning on **Item Tracking** for existing items that have at least one **Item Ledger Entry**. This is a casuistry in which Dynamics NAV will not allow us to turn **Item Tracking** on.

In the previous section, we already talked about some of the steps that will have to be performed for this to be possible. We will follow the official workaround to implement this functional change, as we have seen that some other solutions can lead to data inconsistency, unpredictable behavior, or some other functionalities not working as expected.

Let's write down the list of actions we need to perform in order to turn on **Item Tracking** for existing items that have at least one **Item Ledger Entry**:

1. Reduce the quantity in hand to zero by making negative adjustments of all items for which **Item Tracking** will be turned on.
2. Rename all those items.
3. Create new items and give them the name of the original items.
4. Create and configure related data for the new items that include:
    - Units of measure
    - Sales prices
    - Sales discounts
    - Purchase prices
    - Purchase discounts
    - Vendors
    - Item variants
    - Extended texts
    - Translations
    - Cross references
    - Stockkeeping units
    - Bill of materials
    - Substitutions
    - Dimensions
    - Customized related data
5. Set up the **Item Tracking Code** for the new items.

6. Do a physical inventory of those items, specifying quantities and their tracking (serial number, lot number, and expiration date).

7. Increase the quantity in hand of the new items by making positive adjustments in which quantities and tracking will have to be specified.

8. Review open documents and change the item number to point to the new item instead of the renamed one, so that the item that will be shipped, received, or manufactured is actually the new one and not the renamed one.

   ° Sales documents

   ° Purchase documents

   ° Service documents

   ° Transfer orders

   ° Manufacturing documents

   ° Job planning lines

   ° Item journals

   ° Warehouse journals

   ° Requisition Worksheets

Extending a customized functionality

In this example, we are talking about a customized functionality in which **Volume Discounts** were calculated for each sales invoice line, according to a set of predefined rules, and stored as **Volume Discount Ledger Entries**.

The functionality had to be extended to allow users to apply those ledger entries to other **Volume Discount Ledger Entries**, so that they could know whether **Volume Discount Ledger Entries** were completely open, partially open, or closed.

In the *Interactions with other functionalities* section, we said that this extension actually had only interactions with the functionality itself, and we have already pointed out some of the actions that will have to be performed, such as creating **Detailed Volume Discount Ledger Entries** of the **Initial Entry** type for all existing **Volume Discount Ledger Entries** and doing a big initial application of **Volume Discount Ledger Entries** so that only real open **Volume Discount Ledger Entries** indicate so on their **Open** field.

The actions to be performed in this example are as follows:

1. Develop the extended functionality as per requirements.

2. Develop a process that will create **Detailed Volume Discount Ledger Entries** of the **Initial Entry** type for all existing **Volume Discount Ledger Entries**.

3. Develop a process that will set the recently created **Open** field to **Yes** in the table **Volume Discount Ledger Entry**.

4. Determine which existing **Volume Discount Ledger Entries** are actually open and what **Remaining Amount** they should have.

5. Implement the development change.

6. Execute the process that will create **Detailed Volume Discount Ledger Entries** of the type **Initial Entry** for all existing **Volume Discount Ledger Entries**.

7. Execute the process that will set the recently created **Open** field to **Yes** in the table **Volume Discount Ledger Entry**.

8. Use the new **Volume Discount Application** functionality to do a big initial application posting so that at the end of this process, only real open **Volume Discount Ledger Entries** are marked as open and they have the correct **Remaining Amount**.

Choosing the right time

It is important to choose the right time to make a functional change on an existing Dynamics NAV implementation. Some functional changes can be implemented at any time. Some of them may require a lot of time and no users to be working and changing data; you may want to choose a weekend for that. Some others could be implemented at any time, but to keep a better track of the time at which it began to work differently, you might want to choose the start of a fiscal year or the start of a month.

The important thing is to think about it, analyze it, and choose the right time for every functional change implementation.

The Requisition Worksheet

Using the **Requisition Worksheet** to automatically calculate and plan the replenishment of items is something that could be done at any time. It could even be done progressively, starting with a few items to get familiar with the requisition functionality and adding new items to this process by progressively configuring their replenishment parameters.

In this case, the right time is anytime, whenever you are ready for it.

Fixed Assets

In the previous section, when talking about the actions required to start using the Microsoft Dynamics NAV Fixed Assets functionalities, we said that fixed assets' movements will have to be posted with the acquisition cost and depreciation — the fixed assets without G/L integration before starting to utilize them and the fixed assets' functionality to calculate your depreciations.

Item Tracking

If you turn **Item Tracking** on for your items, it is because you want or need to be able to have traceability of your products.

Choose an appropriate time to do so because you will have to know when your traceability begins and that before that date there is no traceability at all.

You may have a legal requirement that says that after a specific date, traceability will be mandatory for the kind of items you sell or manufacture. If this is the case, that date will probably be the right time.

If this is not the case, or you have a period of time to implement it, you will have to choose a specific date. The beginning of a fiscal year or the beginning of a specific month are dates that are easy to remember for anyone. They could be good candidates.

But you also have to take into account that turning **Item Tracking** on, especially if it has to be done for a large number of items, or if you have a lot of data related to your items or a lot of pending documents, is something that will be time consuming. You will have to rename old items, create new items, create their related data, and go through all pending documents. You will also have to reduce the quantity in hand of the old items and do a physical inventory of the new items to write down their tracking, and be able to increase the inventory of the new items and assign them the right tracking.

Even if you develop a process to rename items, create new items and all their related data and go through all pending documents. You have to know that this will be a time-consuming process if that has to be done for a lot of items, because the renaming instruction in Dynamics NAV takes an extremely long time to execute.

There is something else to take into account. When doing all of this, you do not want any users to be posting any item entries as they will either be locked up as the process is running, or they may transact on an item that may not have all of the settings completed yet.

Keeping all of this in mind, you will probably have to choose a time to implement the change on items outside regular working times: a long weekend or a holiday period.

You could also choose to implement **Item Tracking** progressively, a few items at a time. That will take a shorter time per partial implementation, so it will be easier to find the time to do it, but the global process will take longer and there will not be a single date on which **Item Tracking** functionality was turned on.

Extending a customized functionality

In this example in which a functionality of **Volume Discounts** — which has **Volume Discount Ledger Entries** — wants to be extended by adding application functionality similar to how applications work both in **Customer Ledger Entries** and **Vendor Ledger Entries**, any time is good to implement the change. Whenever it is developed and ready to go live will be considered a good time to implement this change.

The only thing to take into account is that the list of **Open Ledger Entries** has to be prepared for the initial application to be done. Some manual work will have to be done to post this initial application, but there is no need for the users to stop working with the system.

Planning the change

Good planning (and actually sticking to it) is something you always need. As we have seen, some implementations may require a lot of actions to be done, some of them before the new functionality is implemented, some during the implementation process, and some others right after the implementation process is completed. Some implementations can even be done progressively, so they could last weeks or even some months.

Everything has to be planned and scheduled so that all needed work for the implementation of the functionality is ready on the chosen date to go live.

Take the to-do list written in the previous section and determine the following for each action:

- Determine when the action has to be performed:
  - Before the implementation date
  - During the implementation process
  - After the implementation process is completed

- Estimate the time that will be needed to complete the action

- Establish relations between actions (some actions have to be completed so that other actions can start; some actions have no relations with other actions, so two or more actions can be performed simultaneously)

- Determine the date on which the actions should be completed

- Determine the person or persons responsible to perform the action

The Requisition Worksheet

Let's take the actions required for this implementation and determine relations between them, estimation of time, and when they should be performed. In the example, we will not be determining the due date and the people responsible for the action.

The estimation of time will depend upon the number of items the company implementing this functionality may have.

1. Study the different reordering policies which Microsoft Dynamics NAV offers:
   - **When**: Before the implementation
   - **Estimation of time**: 1 day
   - **Previous action**: None

2. Determine which replenishment parameters apply to each reordering policy:
   - **When**: Before the implementation
   - **Estimation of time**: Half a day
   - **Previous action**: Action 1

3. Establish which reordering policies will be used in every group of items:
   - **When**: Before the implementation
   - **Estimation of time**: 1 day
   - **Previous action**: Action 2

4. Calculate the appropriate replenishment parameters for every item using statistical information of sales or any other information:
    - ° **When**: Before the implementation
    - ° **Estimation of time**: 3 days
    - ° **Previous action**: Action 3

5. Set **Vendor No.** for every item:
    - ° **When**: Before the implementation
    - ° **Estimation of time**: 1 day
    - ° **Previous action**: None

6. Set **Lead Time Calculation** for every item:
    - ° **When**: Before the implementation
    - ° **Estimation of time**: 1 day
    - ° **Previous action**: None

7. If the company manages different locations, and replenishment parameters are different for every location, create stockkeeping units and inform the replenishment parameters in the stockkeeping unit card rather than on the item card:
    - ° **When**: Before the implementation
    - ° **Estimation of time**: Half a day
    - ° **Previous action**: None

8. If the company uses item variants and replenishment parameters are different for every variant, create stockkeeping units and inform the replenishment parameters in the stockkeeping unit card rather than on the item card:
    - ° **When**: Before the implementation
    - ° **Estimation of time**: Half a day
    - ° **Previous action**: None

9. If the company uses both different locations and item variants, create stockkeeping units per variant and per location:
    - ° **When**: Before the implementation
    - ° **Estimation of time**: Half a day
    - ° **Previous action**: None

Fixed Assets

Let's take the actions required for this implementation and determine relations between them, estimation of time, and when they should be performed. In the example, we will not be determining the due date and the people responsible for the action.

The estimation of time will depend upon the number of fixed assets the company implementing this functionality may have.

1. Get a list of fixed assets:
   - **When**: Before the implementation
   - **Estimation of time**: 2 days
   - **Previous action**: None

2. Check the existing **FA Posting Groups**.

   Modify the existing **FA Posting Groups** if they do not meet your accounting requirements or create new ones if you need to:
   - **When**: Before the implementation
   - **Estimation of time**: Half a day
   - **Previous action**: None

3. Study the different depreciation methods which Microsoft Dynamics NAV offers:
   - **When**: Before the implementation
   - **Estimation of time**: Half a day
   - **Previous action**: None

4. Choose the appropriate **FA Posting Group** for each fixed asset in your list:
   - **When**: Before the implementation
   - **Estimation of time**: Half a day
   - **Previous action**: Actions 1 and 2

5. Choose the appropriate **Depreciation Method** for each fixed asset in your list:
   - **When**: Before the implementation
   - **Estimation of time**: Half a day
   - **Previous action**: Actions 1 and 3

6. Determine **Depreciation Starting Date** and **Depreciation Ending Date** for each fixed asset in your list:
    ◦ **When**: Before the implementation
    ◦ **Estimation of time**: 1 day
    ◦ **Previous action**: Action 1

7. Determine the acquisition cost for each fixed asset in your list:
    ◦ **When**: Before the implementation
    ◦ **Estimation of time**: 1 day
    ◦ **Previous action**: Action 1

8. Create all the fixed assets in Microsoft Dynamics NAV:
    ◦ **When**: Before or during the implementation
    ◦ **Estimation of time**: Half a day
    ◦ **Previous action**: Actions 1 to 7

9. Uncheck all G/L integrations of all depreciation books your company will be using:
    ◦ **When**: During the implementation
    ◦ **Estimation of time**: Half an hour
    ◦ **Previous action**: None

10. Use the **FA Journals** to post an acquisition cost movement for each fixed asset:
    ◦ **When**: During the implementation
    ◦ **Estimation of time**: Half a day
    ◦ **Previous action**: Actions 8 and 9

11. Use the **FA Journal** to post depreciation movements for each fixed asset:
    ◦ **When**: During the implementation
    ◦ **Estimation of time**: Half a day
    ◦ **Previous action**: Action 11

12. Make sure both acquisition costs and depreciation movements match with transactions previously posted to the **General Ledger**:
    ◦ **When**: During the implementation
    ◦ **Estimation of time**: Half a day
    ◦ **Previous action**: Action 11

13. Check G/L integrations again of all the depreciation books your company will be using:

    ○ **When**: After the implementation
    ○ **Estimation of time**: Half a hour
    ○ **Previous action**: Action 12

Item Tracking

Let's take the actions required for this implementation and determine the relations between them, the estimation of time, and when they should be performed. In the example, we will not be determining the due date and the people responsible for the action.

The estimation of time will depend upon the number of items the company implementing this functionality may have.

1. Reduce the quantity in hand to zero by making negative adjustments to all items for which **Item Tracking** will be turned on:

    ○ **When**: During the implementation
    ○ **Estimation of time**: Half a day
    ○ **Previous action**: None

2. Rename all those items:

    ○ **When**: During the implementation
    ○ **Estimation of time**: 1-2 days
    ○ **Previous action**: Action 1

3. Create new items and give them the names of the original items:

    ○ **When**: During the implementation
    ○ **Estimation of time**: Half a day
    ○ **Previous action**: Action 2

4. Create and configure related data for the new items:

    ○ **When**: During the implementation
    ○ **Estimation of time**: Half a day
    ○ **Previous action**: Action 3

5. Set up the **Item Tracking Code** for the new items:
   - ° **When**: During the implementation
   - ° **Estimation of time**: Half a day
   - ° **Previous action**: Action 3

6. Do a physical inventory of those items, specifying quantities and their tracking (serial number, lot number, and expiration date):
   - ° **When**: During the implementation
   - ° **Estimation of time**: 1 day
   - ° **Previous action**: None

7. Add the quantity on hand of the new items by making positive adjustments in which quantities and tracking will have to be specified:
   - ° **When**: During the implementation
   - ° **Estimation of time**: Half a day
   - ° **Previous action**: Action 6

8. Review open documents and change the **Item No.**: field to point to the new item instead of to the renamed one, so that the item that will be shipped, received, or manufactured is actually the new one and not the renamed one:
   - ° **When**: After the implementation
   - ° **Estimation of time**: Half a day
   - ° **Previous action**: Action 2

Extending a customized functionality

Let's take the actions required for this implementation and determine relations between them, the estimation of time, and when they should be performed. In the example, we will not be determining the due date and the people responsible for the action.

The estimation of time will depend upon the number of **Volume Discount Ledger Entries** the company implementing this functionality has.

1. Do the required development of the extended functionality:
   - **When**: Before the implementation
   - **Estimation of time**: 4 days
   - **Previous action**: None

2. Develop a process that will create **Detailed Volume Discount Ledger Entries** of the **Initial Entry** type for all existing **Volume Discount Ledger Entries**:
   - **When**: Before the implementation
   - **Estimation of time**: Half a day
   - **Previous action**: Action 1

3. Develop a process that will set the recently created **Open** field to **Yes** in the table **Volume Discount Ledger Entry**:
   - **When**: Before the implementation
   - **Estimation of time**: Half a day
   - **Previous action**: Action 1

4. Determine which existing **Volume Discount Ledger Entries** are actually open and which **Remaining Amount** they should have:
   - **When**: Before the implementation
   - **Estimation of time**: 1 day
   - **Previous action**: None

5. Implement the development change:
   - **When**: During the implementation
   - **Estimation of time**: Half an hour
   - **Previous action**: Action 1

6. Execute the process that will create **Detailed Volume Discount Ledger Entries** of type **Initial Entry** for all existing **Volume Discount Ledger Entries**:

    ◦ **When**: During the implementation
    ◦ **Estimation of time**: Half an hour
    ◦ **Previous action**: Action 5

7. Execute the process that will set the recently created **Open** field to **Yes** in the table **Volume Discount Ledger Entry**:

    ◦ **When**: During the implementation
    ◦ **Estimation of time**: Half an hour
    ◦ **Previous action**: Action 5

8. Use the new **Volume Discount Application** functionality to do a big initial application posting so that at the end of this process, only real open **Volume Discount Ledger Entries** are marked as open and they have the correct **Remaining Amount**:

    ◦ **When**: After the implementation
    ◦ **Estimation of time**: Half a day
    ◦ **Previous action**: Action 4

Summary

In this chapter, we have seen that Microsoft Dynamics NAV implementations are not only for companies that have never used this ERP before and that will start doing it. An implementation can also be done for companies already using Dynamics NAV. They will not be complete implementations, of course, probably just the implementation of a new module or functionality. There are some things to take into account in these kinds of implementations. We have talked about them using different examples.

In the next chapter, we will be talking about reporting in Microsoft Dynamics NAV and how to analyze the data stored in the database.

10
Data Analysis and Reporting

Data analysis and reporting is an important part in the management of a company. Having a system where you can do accounting, invoicing, warehouse management, and all kinds of tasks a company does is great. Dynamics NAV is a good data entry system and offers ways to provide a flow to the information and make it available when it is needed to complete the company's processes. Sales processors enter the sales orders, which are then available to the warehouse employees so that they know what has to be shipped. Once the warehouse employees are done with the shipping, the invoicing people have the needed information to make the invoice.

But companies also need to be able to analyze all this information. Do we ship our orders on time? Which item category is the most profitable? Are our departments generating value for the company? We have to be able to answer these kinds of questions. That is what analysis and reporting can do.

In this chapter, we will see the tools available to analyze Dynamics NAV data, both inside and outside the application.

This chapter covers the following topics:

- Analyzing data using filters and FlowFilters
- Statistics
- Charts
- Reports
- Analysis views
- Account schedules
- Extracting Dynamics NAV data
- Report development

Using filters and FlowFilters

A good and powerful way to view and analyze data is to use **filters** and **FlowFilters** inside the application.

We have explained the use of filters in the *Navigating through your data* section in *Chapter 3, Dynamics NAV – General Considerations*. Refer to that chapter to get some examples on how to use filters to analyze your data.

In that same chapter we explained what the SIFT technology is and how to define fields on tables to use that technology. What we did not explain in that chapter is that FlowFilters can be applied over the fields defined to use SIFT to narrow-down the calculated results. That is actually what we will be explaining now.

We will be looking at the **Chart of Accounts** page to explain how to apply FlowFilters and the results they produce.

1. Enter `Chart of Accounts` in the search box of the Dynamics NAV Windows client.
2. Select **Chart of Accounts**.
3. The **Chart of Accounts** page will be shown.

    The following screenshot shows part of the **Chart of Accounts** page. The fields that are shown are **No.**, **Name**, **Net Change**, and **Balance** because these are the relevant fields for this example.

Chart of Accounts ·

No.	Name	Net Change	Balance
10000	**ASSETS**		
11000	**Current Assets**		
11100	**Liquid Assets**		
11200	Cash	306.64	306.64
11400	Bank, Checking	4,386.79	4,386.79
11500	Bank Currencies	10,886.31	10,886.31
11600	Bank Operations Cash	405,032.77	405,032.77
11700	**Liquid Assets, Total**	420,612.51	420,612.51
12000	**Securities**		
12100	Bonds	18,278.46	18,278.46
12200	Other Marketable Securities		
12300	**Securities, Total**	18,278.46	18,278.46
13000	**Accounts Receivable**		
13100	Customers Domestic	946,072.71	946,072.71
13200	Customers, Foreign	464,359.14	464,359.14
13300	Accrued Interest	57,337.20	57,337.20
13350	Other Receivables	3,129.30	3,129.30
13400	**Accounts Receivable, Total**	1,470,898.35	1,470,898.35

The fields **Net Change** and **Balance** are FlowFields that use the SIFT technology. They both show the sum of G/L entry amounts for the different accounts.

Now that we are on a page that uses FlowFields, let's apply FlowFilters and look at the results.

4. Click on **Chart of Accounts** and select **Limit totals** (or press *Ctrl + Shift + F3*).

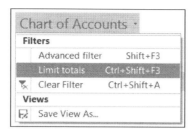

The **Limit totals** to part will be shown.

5. Select **Date Filter** and set **01/01/17..12/31/17** as the filter.
6. The **Net Change** field will be updated.

Not all FlowFilters apply to all FlowFields; however, FlowFilters only apply to FlowFields. In the preceding example, we saw that after applying a date FlowFilter, the **Net Change** field got updated and now shows only the sum of G/L entry amounts in the specified period, while the **Balance** field has remained the same. This is because of the definition of the fields. The definition of the **Net Change** field states that the calculation of this field will take into account a date filter, while the **Balance** field does not.

Limit total is the place where a user can apply FlowFilters. It can be found in all the application pages where a FlowFilter is available, and also in the **Filter** section of reports, which will be seen later in this chapter.

Creating views

We have seen how to apply filters and FlowFilters to the application. But once we leave the page and come back to the same page, the filter is gone. We have to apply the same filter or FlowFilter over and over again if we want to see the same results. Wouldn't it be great if we could save the applied filters so that we could apply them as many times as we wished without having to select the fields we want to filter and writing the filter expression again? This is possible with Dynamics NAV Views.

To create a View, follow the given steps:

1. Follow the steps from the previous section to apply a FlowFilter to the **Chart of Accounts** page.

2. Click on **Chart of Accounts** and select **Save View As...**.

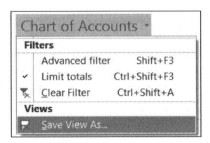

The **Save View As...** dialog will open.

3. Enter **Chart of Accounts - 2017** in the **Name** field and select **Home** in the **Activity Group** field.

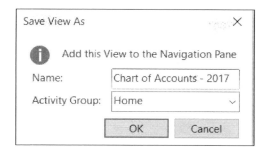

4. Click on **OK**.

5. The View will be saved.

Every time you want to see your saved View, follow the given steps:

1. Click on **Home**.

2. Click on your saved View.

Statistics

All master data have one or more statistical page associated where the most important statistical information about the record is shown.

Statistics can be found under the **Navigate** tab of the ribbon.

Follow the given steps to view **Customer Statistics**:

1. Type Customer in the search box of the Dynamics NAV Windows client.

2. Select **Customers**. The customers list will be shown.

3. Click on the **Navigate** tab of the ribbon.

4. Select **Statistics**. The **Customer Statistics** page for the current selected customer will be shown. This page shows the most important economic information about the customer.

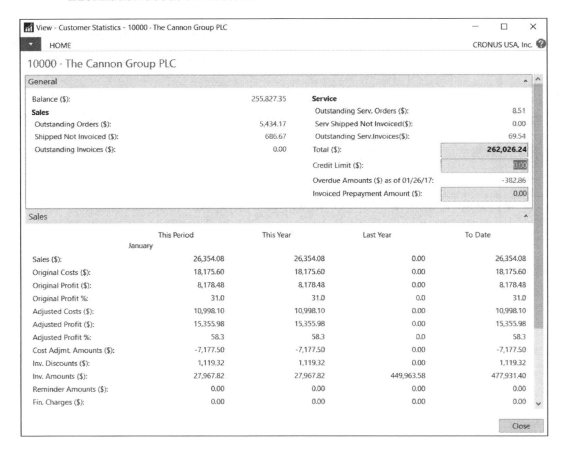

Other statistics pages offer dynamical information, such as the **Customer Sales** statistics that show, for example, the sale for that customer for a specific period. To open the **Customer Sales** statistics page, follow the given steps:

1. Type `Customer` in the search box of the Dynamics NAV Windows client.
2. Select **Customers**. The customers list will be shown.
3. Click on the **Navigate** tab of the ribbon.
4. Select **Sales**. The **Customer Sales** page for the current selected customer will be shown. This page shows the customer sales on time basis.

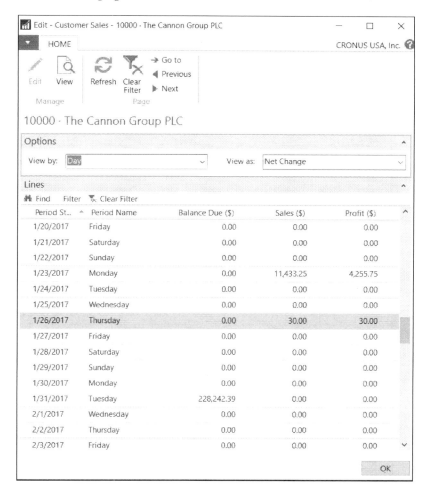

Charts

Graphical information is always useful when analyzing data. Dynamics NAV offers various ways of viewing data in a graphical way.

The Show as Chart option

Whenever the information shown on the screen can be viewed as a chart, the **Home** tab of the ribbon will contain a section called **View** where the users can switch the view of the information from **List** to **Chart**, and vice versa.

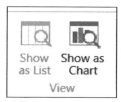

Let's see an example of how to build a chart based on the customer list:

1. Type Customer in the search box of the Dynamics NAV Windows client.

2. Select **Customers**. The customers list will be shown.

3. Click on **Show as Chart**. An empty chart will be shown. We will have to select a measure and the dimensions we want to use to build our chart.

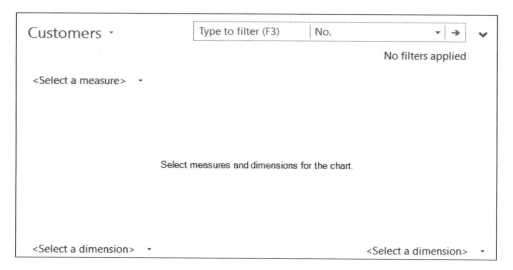

4. Select **Sales ($)** as the measure.
5. Select **Country/Region Code** as the dimension on the right of the chart.
6. The chart will be drawn.

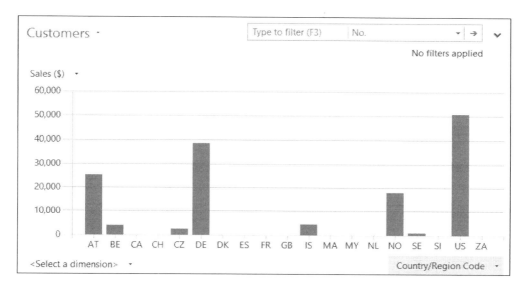

We can quickly see that US is the country where our sales are concentrated.

Adding charts to the Role Center page

Dynamics NAV has a set of predefined, generic charts that can be added to the **Role Center** page.

To add a chart to the home page, follow the given steps:

1. Click on **Home**.

2. Click on the Application icon, choose **Customize**, and then **Customize This Page**. The **Customize the Role Center** window will open.

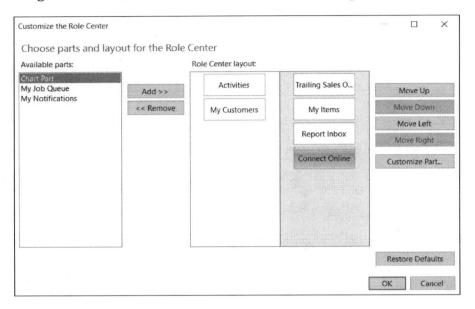

3. Select **Chart Part** from the **Available parts** field and click on the **Add** button.

4. A **Blank Chart** will appear in the **Role Center layout** field.

5. Select **Blank Chart** and click on the **Customize Part** button. A list of available charts will appear.

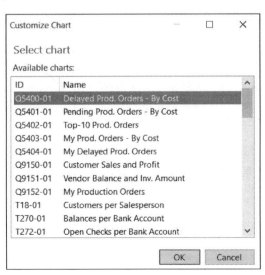

6. Select the **Customer Sales and Profit** chart.

7. Click on **OK**.

8. Click on **OK** to close the **Customize the Role Center** window.

9. The selected chart will be displayed on the **Role Center** page.

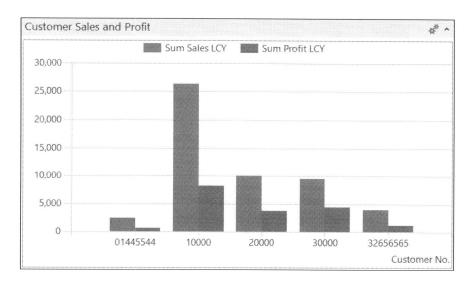

 The data in this chart is displayed after the customers on the **My Customer** list. If you have no customers on the **My Customer** list, this chart will show no data.

Creating and configuring charts

If the predefined generic charts are not enough for you, you can define other generic charts and make them available to all the users, so that they can add your chart to their **Role Center** page.

To create and define a generic chart, follow the given steps:

1. Type `Generic Charts` in the search box of the Dynamics NAV Windows client.

2. Select **Generic Charts**. The **Generic Charts** list will be shown.

3. Click on **New** to create a new generic chart.

4. Give the new generic chart an ID (`MYCHART`) and a name (`My Chart`).

5. Select **Table** as **Source Type**.

6. Select **18** as **Source ID**.

7. In the **Required Measure** row, select **Sales (LCY)** in the **Data Column** field, **Sum** as **Aggregation**, and **Column** as **Graph Type**.

8. In the **Optional Measure** row, select **Profit (LCY)** in the **Data Column** field, **Sum** as **Aggregation**, and **StepLine** as **Graph Type**.

9. Select **Country/Region Code** in **X-Axis Field**. The entire configuration of the generic chart is shown in the following screenshot:

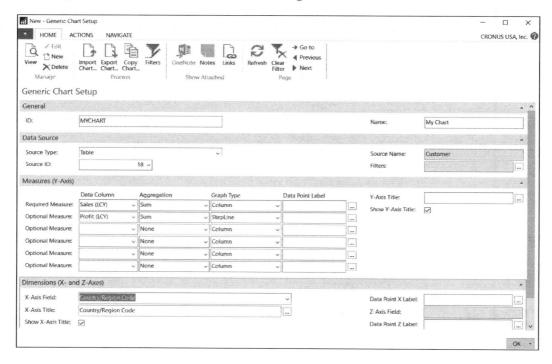

10. Click on **OK**.

A new chart is now created and configured. Follow the steps in the previous section to add this new chart to your **Role Center** page. The following screenshot shows the defined chart:

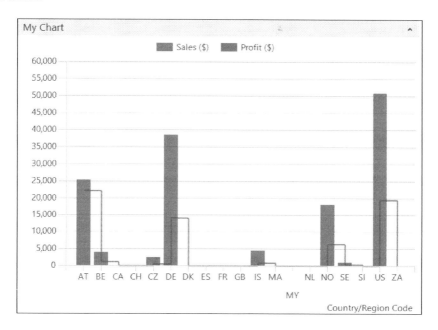

Using reports

Dynamics NAV has a bunch of reports that can be used out of the box. Some other reports may have been added by a partner and can also be used.

The first thing you need to know to be able to execute the application reports is where to find them.

Finding reports

To find the application reports, follow the given steps:

1. Click on **Departments** and then select any functional area; **Sales & Marketing,** for instance.

2. The main menu for the selected functional area will appear on the screen. Every item you can find inside a menu for an application area has a category associated with it. In the menu, there is a way to view the items according to their category. The following screenshot illustrates the existing categories in Dynamics NAV:

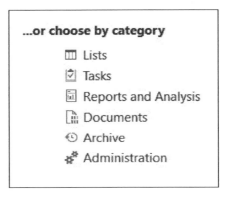

3. Select **Reports and Analysis**.

4. All items under the **Reports and Analysis** category for the functional area selected will be shown.

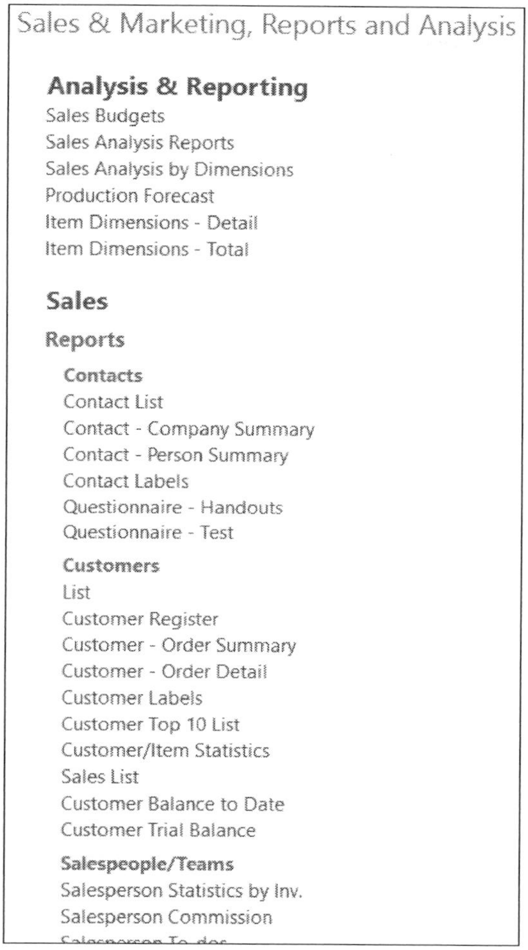

```
Sales & Marketing, Reports and Analysis

  Analysis & Reporting
  Sales Budgets
  Sales Analysis Reports
  Sales Analysis by Dimensions
  Production Forecast
  Item Dimensions - Detail
  Item Dimensions - Total

  Sales
  Reports
    Contacts
    Contact List
    Contact - Company Summary
    Contact - Person Summary
    Contact Labels
    Questionnaire - Handouts
    Questionnaire - Test
    Customers
    List
    Customer Register
    Customer - Order Summary
    Customer - Order Detail
    Customer Labels
    Customer Top 10 List
    Customer/Item Statistics
    Sales List
    Customer Balance to Date
    Customer Trial Balance
    Salespeople/Teams
    Salesperson Statistics by Inv.
    Salesperson Commission
    Salesperson To-dos
```

But reports are not only found on the main menu. They can also be found in many application pages where only the reports that are valuable for the data shown on the page will be found.

Follow the given steps to see an example:

1. Click on **Departments**, then choose **Sales & Marketing**, and then choose **Sales**.

2. Click on **Customers** to open the customers list. In the **Home** tab of the ribbon, a section called **Report** contains the most relevant reports regarding customers.

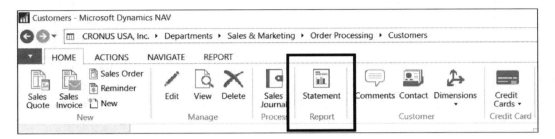

On the **Report** tab of the ribbon, the reports regarding customers will be shown and grouped according to the application area to which they belong.

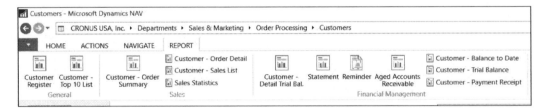

Running reports

Now that we have found all the available reports, it is time to execute them and see what kind of information they show. To execute a report, follow the given steps:

1. Click on the report that you want to execute. For instance, click on **Customer Top 10 List**.

2. The **Request** page for the report will be shown. The following screenshot shows the **Request** page for the **Customer Top 10 List** report:

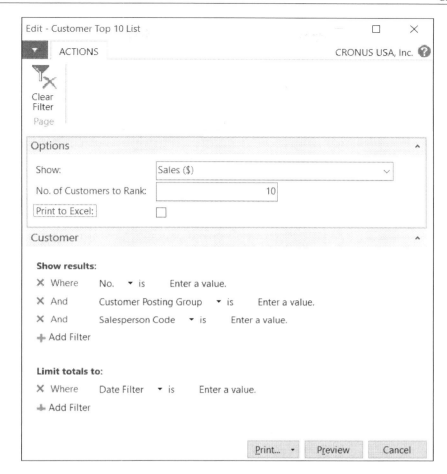

3. Request pages for reports have three different sections:

    ○   **The Options section**: Here the users can choose among different
        options to define the behavior of the report. This section is always
        called **Options** and is shown as the first section of a report request
        page. The **Options** section may not be shown in some reports if the
        report actually has no options for the user to select.

        In the **Customer Top 10 List** report, the **Options** section is shown
        and the users have three different fields (**Show**, **No. of Customers
        to Rank**, and **Print to Excel**) to define what they want to see (using
        the **Show** field), how many customers they want to list (using the
        Quantity field), and if they want to print to Excel in a specific format
        written into the report.

     °   **The Filter sections**: Here the users can apply filters over their data so that the report only shows the data the users are interested in. The **Filter** sections may take different names depending on which data the filters can be applied to. In the **Customer Top 10 List** report, the **Filter** section is called **Customer** because the filters will be applied over the `Customer` table.

The **Filter** sections are always shown after the **Options** section. A report may have no **Filter** sections if there are no filters that the users can apply to the data shown in the report, or may have several **Filter** sections if the report combines data from multiple tables and filters can be applied over the data of the different tables.

The **Customer Top 10 List** report has a single **Filter** section, **Customer**, but the **Customer – Order detail** report, which can be found under the **Reports and Analysis** category of the **Sales & Marketing** functional area, has two **Filter** sections, **Customer** and **Sales Order Line**.

     °   **The Buttons section**: Here the users can choose to either **Print** the report in different formats (print it using one of the available printers in the system by using the **Print** option, print the report into a PDF archive by using the PDF option, print the report into a Microsoft Word archive by using the **Microsoft Word** option, or print the report into a Microsoft Excel archive by using the **Microsoft Excel** option), **Schedule** the report to be printed at a later time, **Preview** the report on the screen, or **Cancel** the execution of the report.

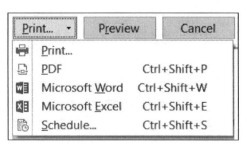

 All four existing options on the **Print** button can also be found afterward on the **Preview** screen.

4.   Click on **Preview** to see the results of the report on the screen.

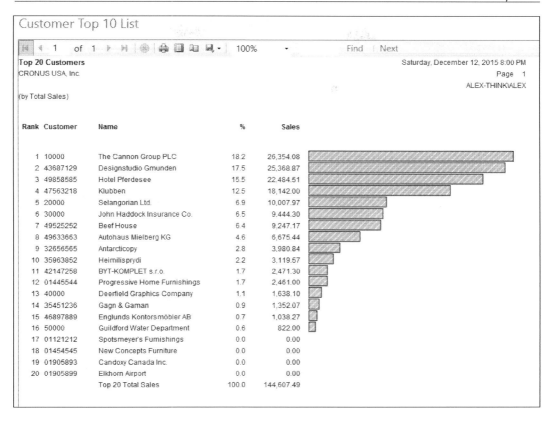

Types of reports

Reports in Dynamics NAV have several purposes:

- Reports are used to print information from the database in a structured way
- Reports are used to print documents, such as the **Sales Invoice**
- Reports are used to automate recurring tasks, such as updating all the prices in an item list

There are different types of reports available in Dynamics NAV.

List reports

A list report is intended to print a list of records from a table, usually a table containing master data or secondary master data. Each column contains a field from the table. Most of the data is printed from that table and sometimes brought in or calculated from the other tables. The name of the list report is usually the name of the table followed by the term `List`.

The following are examples of list reports:

- Customer List
- Inventory List

Test reports

A test report is printed from unposted transactions, such as entries in a journal or sales/purchase documents. The purpose of this kind of report is to test each line of the journal according to the posting rules so that all errors can be found and fixed before posting. If you try to post and the posting routine encounters an error, the posting routine will stop and will show the first encountered error. If several errors exist, they will be shown and, thus, corrected one at a time. A test report will show all the existing errors. The name of the test report is usually the name of the corresponding Journal, followed by the term `Test`.

The following are examples of test reports:

- General Journal – Test
- Resource Journal – Test

Posting reports

A posting report prints from a register table. It lists all the transactions (ledger entries) that are posted into the register. This kind of report can be very useful for auditing. The name of the posting report is usually the name of either the register table or the master table of the corresponding ledger entries.

The following are examples of posting reports:

- G/L Register
- Job Register

Transaction reports

A transaction report has the following characteristics:

- It lists all the ledger entries for each record in the ledger table.
- It contains a subtotal for each master table record, and a grand total for all the tables printed.
- It is used to view all the transactions for a particular master record.
- It has no standard naming convention. A transaction report usually has one or more data items, including the master and the corresponding ledger table.

The following are examples of transaction reports:

- Detail Trial Balance
- Customer – Detail Trial Bal.

Document reports

A document report prints a document, such as a **Sales Invoice** or a **Purchase Order**. Document reports have a different layout than all the other reports. The header information of the document is printed as if filling out the document at the top of the page and is repeated on every page. The information on the lines of the document resembles other kinds of reports because it is printed in rows and columns. These types of reports are typically modified for every implementation because each company will want the documents sent out to vendors and customers to have their own unique design.

The following are examples of document reports:

- Sales – Invoice
- Order

Report selection

A user can select which document report will be printed with each document type. To view and select the document reports that will be printed with each document type, follow the given steps:

1. Type `Report Selection` in the search box of the Dynamics NAV Windows client.
2. Select **Report Selection Sales**. The **Edit - Report Selection - Sales** window will open.

The following screenshot shows that report number **10076** in the NA (North America) version, which is called **Sales - Quote**, will be used to print the sales quotes:

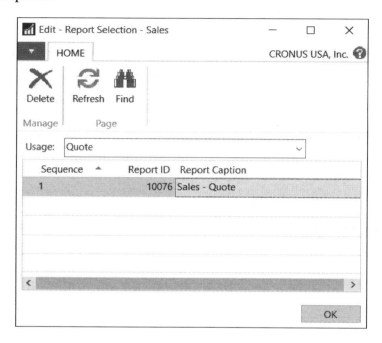

By selecting other usages (**Order, Invoice, Credit Memo, Shipment, Order Archive**, and so on), you will be able to see and choose which report(s) to print for each type of sales document.

By default, there is usually only one report selected for each type of document, but you can add more reports to the list so that more than one record is printed for each document type.

Other reports

Most reports consist of a tabular listing with records listed horizontally and each field displaying in its own column. Many times, there is a group heading or total to split the lines among various categories and to subtotal the lines by categories.

The following are examples of other reports:

- Customer/Item Sales
- Vendor/Item Purchases

Account schedules

The account schedules functionality is part of the **Analysis & Reporting** section of the **Financial Management** area. It is meant to create customized financial reports based on the **General Ledger** information, the **Budget** information, or on the analysis views information. Account schedules can group data from various accounts and perform calculations that are not possible directly on **Chart of Accounts**.

When defining account schedules, both the information that will be displayed on rows and columns can be defined.

Just to see how it works, we will create a simple account schedule that will compare the budgeted amounts versus the real amounts. To do so, we will follow the given steps:

1. Navigate to **Departments/Financial Management/Reports and Analysis** and choose **Account Schedules**.
2. Click on **New** to create a new account schedule.
3. For the new account schedule, select **EXAMPLE** as **Name**, **Comparing budget versus actual** as **Description**, and **ACT/BUD** as **Default Column Layout**.
4. Click on **Edit Account Schedule**. An empty page will open. We will define our account schedule on this page.
5. Define the account schedule as shown in the following screenshot:

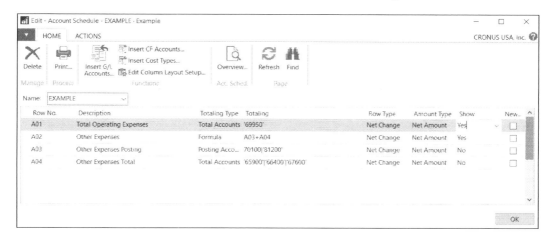

- ° The first row gets the net amount of account **69960**; a totaling account that summarizes all the operating expenses.

- ° The second row uses a formula to sum up the results of rows **A03** and **A04**. This is because the other expenses couldn't be summarized together in a single account schedule row, as some of the other expenses are summarized in **Chart of Accounts** on totaling accounts, but there are a couple of other expenses that have to be taken directly from the posting accounts.

- ° The third row gets the net amount of other expenses from the posting accounts. The posting accounts used are **70100** and **81200**. As this row is only used for calculation purposes and is not intended to be shown in the report, the **Show** field has been set to **No**.

- ° The fourth row gets the net amount of other expenses from totaling accounts. The totaling accounts used are **65900**, **66400**, and **67600**. As this row is only used for calculation purposes and is not intended to be shown in the report, the **Show** field has been set to **No**.

The account schedule is fully defined now. The account schedule defines the rows that will be shown in the report.

Columns are defined at **Column Layout**. In the preceding example, we used an existent column layout called **ACT/BUD**. Let's see what this column layout will show.

6. On the **Edit – Account Schedule** page, where we were defining our account schedule, click on the **Actions** tab and then click on **Edit Column Layout Setup**. The **Edit – Column Layout** page will open.

7. Select **ACT/BUD** for the **Name** field.

8. The **ACT/BUD** column layout definition will be shown:

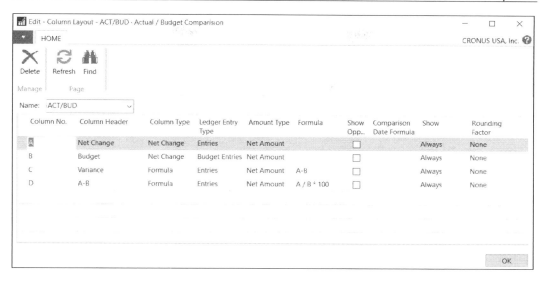

- ° The column layout defines that the report will have four columns called **Net Change**, **Budget**, **Variance**, and **A-B**

- ° The **Net Change** column will show the net amount for the G/L entries

- ° The **Budget** column will show the net amount for the budget entries

- ° The **Variance** column will show the difference between the first and the second column

- ° The **A-B** column will calculate the percentage that the first column represents versus the second column

Now that we have both the account schedule and the column layout defined, it is time to see the results of our account schedule.

9. Navigate to **Departments/Financial Management/Reports and Analysis** and select **Account Schedules**.

10. Select the account schedule that we have created in this section.

11. Click on **Overview**.

12. The report will be shown on the screen.

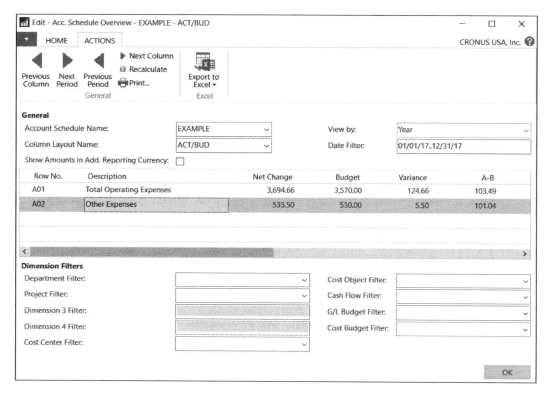

The results can be seen in different time periods and filters can be applied over the calculation to get a more refined dataset that you may be looking for. The results can be exported to Excel and can also be printed.

Analysis views

Analysis views are used to analyze the information about dimensions from general ledger entries, budgets, and cash flow forecast entries.

Let's first have a look at what dimensions are, and then we will be able to see how to analyze the information that dimensions provide using analysis views.

Understanding dimensions

A dimension can be seen as information linked to an entry, something like a tag or a characteristic. The purpose of dimensions is to group entries with similar characteristics so that you can report on the data in a way that is meaningful to the company. Each company can define its own dimensions according to how they need to analyze their data.

Posted entries and posted documents can contain analyzable dimension information as well as budgets. The term dimension is used to describe how analysis occurs. A two-dimensional analysis, for example, would be sales per area. You can also apply more than two dimensions when posting a document or a journal. This will allow you to carry out a more complex analysis, for example, sales per sales campaign, sales per customer, or group per area.

Each dimension can have unlimited dimension values that are subunits of the dimension. For example, a dimension called `Department` can have subunits called `Sales`, `Administration`, and so on. These departments are dimension values.

Dynamics NAV supports unlimited dimensions. This means that you can create as many dimensions as needed according to how you are currently categorizing areas of the business. However, even if you can create unlimited dimensions, there are some restrictions on how they are stored and how easy it is to access their information.

In Dynamics NAV, all dimensions are stored in special dimension tables. Some dimensions are also stored in fields inside the table they refer to. We can group dimensions in three categories according to their access level (how easy it is to access them):

- **Global dimensions**: Their value is stored on special dimension tables and also on fields inside the table they refer to. We can use up to two global dimensions.

- **Shortcut dimensions**: Their value is stored on special dimension tables. Although the value is not stored inside the table they refer to, in some occasions they are shown on pages as if they were stored on the table. We can use up to eight shortcut dimensions. Two of them correspond to global dimensions.

- **The rest of the dimensions**: Their value is only stored on special dimension tables.

Setting up new dimensions

Imagine that in our company we have two different divisions: one responsible for selling items and another responsible for renting items. We decide to use dimensions to analyze the results of each division. So, we are going to create a dimension called **DIVISION**.

To create new dimensions, access **Departments | Financial Management | Setup | Dimensions** and follow the steps described in this section:

1. Click on the **New** icon found on the ribbon bar.

2. Create a new dimension by assigning some values, as shown in the following screenshot.

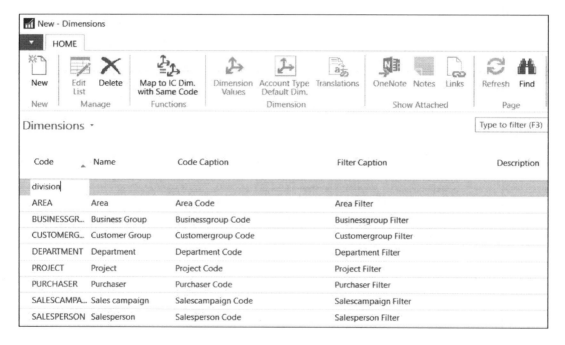

3. Click on the **Dimension Values** icon found on the ribbon bar. A new page will open.

4. Create two different dimension values by giving them the values shown in the following screenshot:

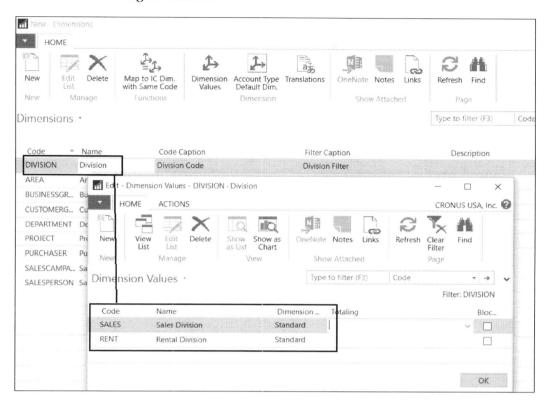

Categorizing dimensions

We have already created a new dimension along with its dimension values. Now we must determine if it is going to be a global dimension, a shortcut dimension, or one of the rest of the dimensions.

To do so, open **General Ledger Setup** by navigating to **Departments/Financial Management/Setup/General Ledger Setup**. Select the **Dimensions** tab.

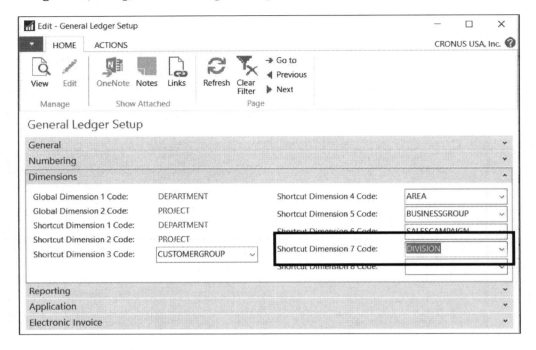

In the company CRONUS USA Inc., global dimensions are already defined. The company has already defined up to six shortcut dimensions.

Select **DIVISION** in the **Shortcut Dimension 7 Code** field, to define our new dimension as a shortcut dimension.

Accessing dimensions

As we said earlier in this chapter, the difference between global, shortcut, and the rest of the dimensions is how easy it is to access them.

We are going to see how to access the **DEPARTMENT** global dimension, the **DIVISON** shortcut dimension, and the **SALESPERSON** dimension, which is one of the rest of the dimensions.

To see how dimensions can be accessed to fill them when creating documents, follow the given steps:

1. Open the **Sales Invoices** page that you will find by navigating to **Departments/Sales & Marketing/Order Processing/Sales Invoices**.

2. Click on the **New** icon found on the ribbon bar to create a new sales invoice.

3. In the **Sell-to Customer No.** field, select customer **62000**.

4. Create a line for item `1000` to sell 1 PCS.

5. On the **Lines** tab, click on the setup icon and select **Choose Columns....**

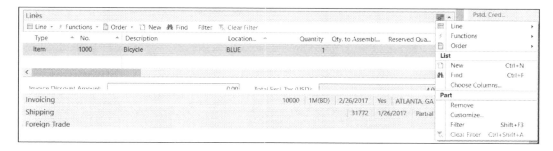

6. Add **Department Code** and **Division Code** in the column titled **Show columns in this order**. Then click on **OK**.

   Salesperson Code cannot be selected because it is not a global dimension or a shortcut dimension.

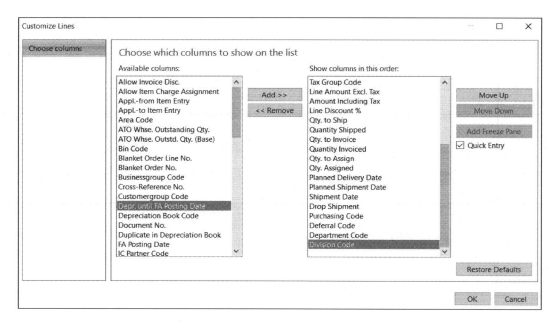

7. Back to the sales line, fill in the value **Sales** for the **Department Code** field. Also fill in the value **Sell** for the **Division Code** field.

8. To fill in a value in the **Salesperson Code** field, click on **Line** and then **Dimensions** to open the **Edit Dimension Set Entries** page.

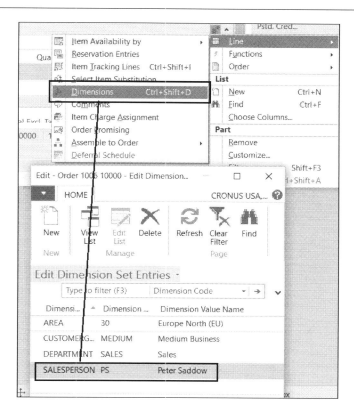

9. Post the **Sales Invoice**.

10. Open the **Posted Sales Invoices** page. You will find it by navigating to **Departments | Sales & Marketing | History | Posted Sales Invoices**. Locate the invoice we have just posted and open it by double-clicking on it.

11. Open the **Customize Lines** page, as we did in step 6.

12. Add **Department Code** in the column titled **Show columns in this order**. Note that you will not find **Division Code** available in the column titled **Available columns**.

    This is because Division is a shortcut dimension. As we said earlier, shortcut dimensions are, in some occasions, shown on pages as if they were stored on the table. Usually they are shown in pages meant to enter information, but not on pages meant to show posted information.

13. Access all the dimensions by clicking on **Line** and then **Dimensions**, as we did in step 8.

Creating an analysis view

As we have seen, there are several dimensions that are not easily accessed by the users, especially when the document or the entry has been posted. This is when we need to analyze the data.

Analysis views are specially meant to access all the dimensions in the same easy way, in groups of a maximum of four dimensions at the same time. The four dimension groups may seem a limitation, but it is not, since we can create as many analysis views as needed combining all the dimensions we want.

With an analysis view, we can view data from the general ledger. Entries are grouped by criteria, such as:

- G/L accounts
- Period
- Business units
- Up to four dimensions

In other words, if a G/L entry has been posted to a particular account with one of the four dimensions selected, the G/L entry information will be included in the analysis view as an analysis view entry. You can also include G/L budget entries in an analysis view to compare reality and budget.

Follow the given steps to set up an analysis view:

1. Open the **Analysis Views** page by navigating to **Departments/ Administration/Application Setup/Financial Management/Dimensions/ Analysis Views**.

2.   The **Analysis Views** page will open showing the existing analysis views.

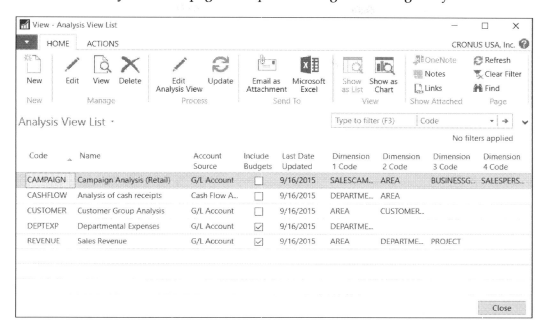

3.   Click on the **New** icon found on the ribbon bar. The **Analysis View Card** page will open.

4. Fill up the **Analysis View Card** page with the data shown in the following screenshot:

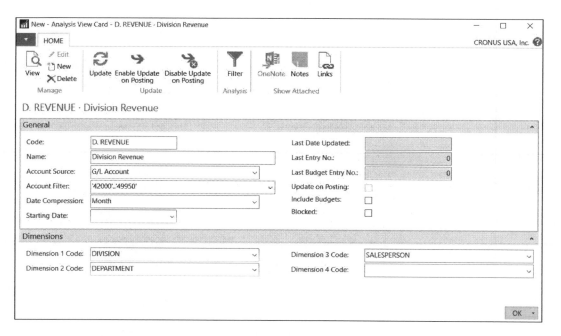

5. Click on the **Update** option found on the ribbon bar to create analysis view entries based on the criteria that you set up on the card.

   The system will create one summarized analysis view entry for each G/L account, period, and dimension combination.

   In the preceding example, we will get one entry for each G/L account from account numbers **42000** to **49950**, for each month, and also for each combination of dimension values of the **Division**, **Salesperson**, and **Department** dimensions.

6. Open the **Analysis View Entries** page to see the entries created by the system. You can find it by navigating to **Departments/Financial Management/General Ledger/History/Analysis View Entries**.

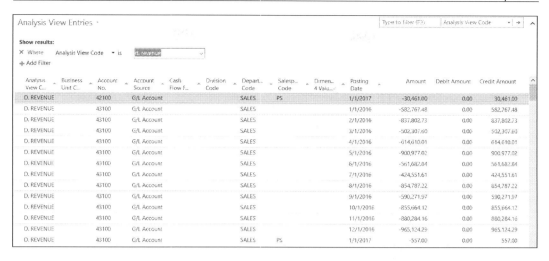

Updating analysis views

An analysis view is a fixed photo of the posted G/L entries grouped with specific criteria.

If you change any of the fields found on the **Analysis View Card** page, for instance if you change the **Starting Date** field, you will get the following message:

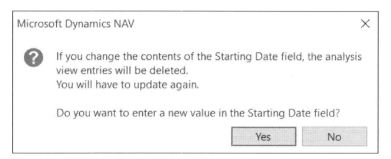

If you select **Yes**, all entries will be deleted and you will have to click on the **Update** option again to create analysis view entries according to the new criteria.

You will also have to use the **Update** action to include the new general ledger entries posted after you last updated the analysis view. You can also let the system update it automatically when new G/L entries are posted by checking the **Update** on **Posting** field found on the **Analysis View Card** page.

It is not recommended to use the **Update on Posting** option because it penalizes performance when posting.

Using analysis views

Analysis views can be used in different scenarios:

- In the **Analysis by Dimensions** functionality
- As source for account schedules

In this section, we are going to see an example of using analysis views on each of the scenarios detailed.

Analysis by dimensions

The analysis by dimensions functionality is used to display and analyze the amount derived from the existing analysis views.

Follow the steps to see an example of how **Analysis by Dimensions** works:

1. Open the **Analysis View List** page by navigating to **Departments/ Financial Management/General Ledger/Analysis & Reporting/Analysis by Dimensions**.
2. Locate the **D. REVENUE** analysis view that we created earlier in this chapter. Then click on the **Edit Analysis View** option found on the ribbon bar.
3. A new page opens. In the **Division Filter** field, select the value **RENT**.
4. Click on the **Show Matrix** icon found on the ribbon bar. The **Analysis by Dimensions Matrix** page now shows the amounts posted on the general ledger under the **RENT** value of the **Division** dimension.

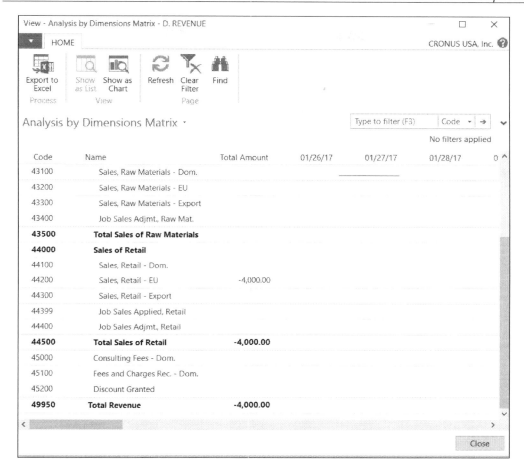

5. Close the current page and go back to the **Analysis by Dimensions** page.

6. Select different values for the following fields, and click on **Show Matrix** to see the results. The main fields you can change to analyze data are **Show as Lines**, **Show as Columns**, **Dimension Filters**, **Show**, **Show Amount Field**, **View by**, and **View as**.

Analysis views as a source for account schedules

If analysis views are selected as a source for account schedules, the amounts in the account schedules are calculated based on the analysis views entries. Since analysis views entries are based on general ledger entries, the result should be the same.

The difference is that, when analyzing account schedules, you can only filter the amounts based on global dimensions. If you use analysis views as a source for account schedules, then you can filter on any of the four dimensions selected on the **Analysis View Card** page. These dimensions can be global dimensions, shortcut dimensions, or any other dimensions.

To use analysis views as a source for account schedules, follow the given steps:

1. Open **Account Schedules Names** by navigating to **Departments | Financial Management | General Ledger | Analysis & Reporting | Account Schedules**.

2. Locate the **REVENUE** account schedule. Note that an analysis view is selected in the **Analysis View Name** field. This is what makes it possible to use the analysis view as a source for the account schedule.

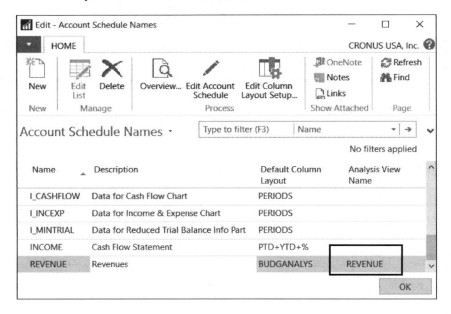

3. Click on the **Overview** option found on the ribbon bar.

4. The **Acc. Schedule Overview** page opens. Note that you can now filter on any of the three dimensions that were set up on the analysis view. Select different values on these fields to see the results.

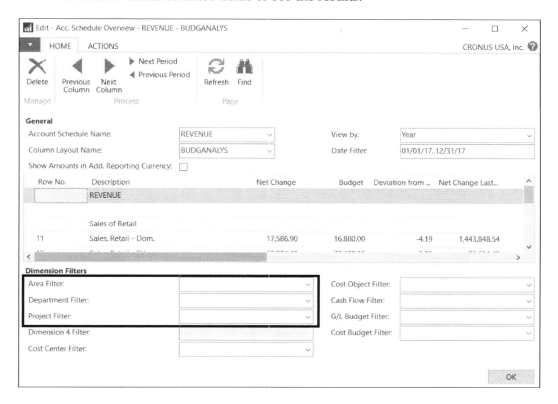

Extracting data

Dynamics NAV offers several ways of analyzing and reporting data inside the application. If that is not enough, you can also extract data from the application and use external tools to report and analyze your data.

In this section, we will see the different ways you can extract your data from Dynamics NAV. Once it is outside the application, you can use the most convenient tool for you.

Data in Dynamics NAV can be extracted in multiple ways. The various ways include:

- Copying and pasting to Excel
- Extracting data through SQL Server
- Any external data/reporting tools that can connect to SQL Server
- Web services
- EDI

The list goes on and on…

In this section, we'll focus only on two ways of exporting the data:

- Sending data to Microsoft Office applications
- Using web services

Sending data to Microsoft Office applications

Dynamics NAV data can be sent to either Microsoft Word or Microsoft Excel by the users.

Whenever that is possible, which is on all the pages in Dynamics NAV, except on the **Role Center** page and on the menu pages under the **Department** area, the export option will be available on the application menu.

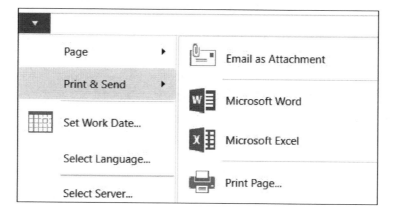

The data exported will be the one that the user is seeing at the moment, including filters and columns shown/hidden on a list. Imagine you are looking at the customer list. In that list you have only chosen the columns **No.**, **Name**, and **Contact**, and you have applied a filter to only see the blocked customers. When you export that to either Word or Excel, you will export only those three fields and only the customers within the filter.

Sending data to Microsoft Word

The following screenshot shows how data exported to Microsoft Word looks:

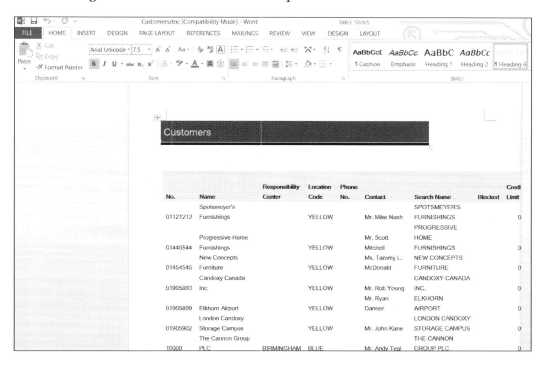

When data changes in Dynamics NAV, it has to be sent to Microsoft Word again if you want your data in Word to be updated with the most recent changes.

Sending data to Microsoft Excel

The following screenshot shows how data exported to Microsoft Excel looks:

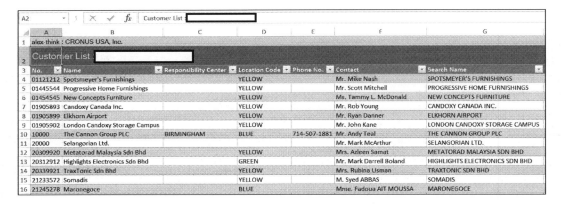

Note the **Dynamics NAV** tab on the Microsoft Excel ribbon and the **Refresh** button in that tab. When data changes in Dynamics NAV, there is no need to send it again to Excel. You can click on the **Refresh** button and the data in Excel will be updated with the most recent data from Dynamics NAV.

The Dynamics NAV add-in for Excel gets installed when you install the Dynamics NAV Windows client.

Extracting data through web services

Any Dynamics NAV codeunit, page, or query can be published as a web service. Codeunits are published as SOAP web services. Pages are published as both SOAP web services and OData web services. Queries are published as OData web services.

> Refer to the *OData web services* section in *Chapter 2, What's New in NAV 2016?* to get a detailed step-by-step explanation on how to publish a web service.

Any application that can consume SOAP web services or OData web services will be able to extract the Dynamics NAV data.

In *Chapter 12, The Query Object*, we have included an example of consuming a query OData web service using Excel.

Other ways to extract Dynamics NAV data

Dynamics NAV data is actually stored in a Microsoft SQL database, and thus, all available tools for SQL to extract data can be used for the Dynamics NAV database.

Understanding report development

Report development is completely different from what it used to be. The report development experience changed in Dynamics NAV 2009 with the introduction of the **Report Definition Language Client-side (RDLC)** report, but it changes again with the actual release of the application.

With Dynamics NAV 2009, RDLC-based reports were introduced, but reports were still compatible with the classic definition of reports in Dynamics NAV. RDLC reports were actually based on the classic definition of the report.

From Dynamics NAV 2013, the reports classic definition has disappeared and only RLDC-based reports are available. This is why the report development experience has changed again. It now resembles the development experience of pages, queries, or XMLPorts.

Reports anatomy

Creating reports includes designing both the business logic that covers the kind of information the report will contain, and the layout that deals with how the report will look when it is printed.

In Microsoft Dynamics NAV 2016, to design a client report definition (RDLC), you design the data model with **Report Dataset Designer** and the layout with **Visual Studio Report Designer**. To do this, Visual Studio 2010 Professional or above is required.

Visual Studio Report Designer offers several new options and features. Furthermore, due to its thorough integration with Microsoft SQL Server, it is possible to take advantage of the reporting capabilities of Microsoft Report Viewer, including the following:

- Richer formatting
- Interactive sorting
- Graphics and charts
- Export possibilities (PDF, Microsoft Office Excel, and Microsoft Office Word)

A report object is composed of a report dataset and a visual layout. You design a report by first defining the dataset and then designing the visual layout. The report objects also contain properties, triggers, code, and an optional request page.

The following diagram shows components of a report and how they are related in Microsoft Dynamics NAV:

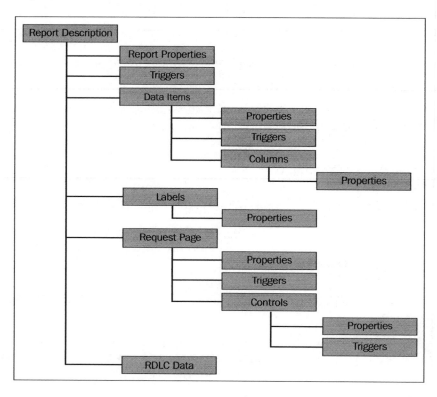

Reports in Dynamics NAV 2016 are executed in two steps, which reflect the two steps in the report design. The first is the data set design in C/SIDE followed by report layout design in Visual Studio.

The C/AL runtime retrieves the data from the involved source tables, performs the necessary calculations, and combines the data in a single flattened dataset. This is performed by the NAV server. The produced dataset is transferred to the report viewer's runtime hosted on the NAV client, which, in turn, renders the dataset data according to the report layout definition.

Defining the dataset

The dataset is defined on the Report Dataset Designer in the Microsoft Dynamics NAV Development Environment. The report dataset is built from data items and columns. A data item is a table. A column can be one of the following:

- Field in a table
- Variable
- Expression
- Text constant

Typically, the data items correspond to the fields in a table. When the report is run, each data item is iterated for all records in the underlying table with an appropriate filter defined.

When a report is based on more than one table, you must set relations between the data items so you can retrieve and organize the data. In Report Dataset Designer, you indent the data items to establish a hierarchy of data items and control how the information is gathered.

For example, to create a report that displays a list of customers and lists the sales orders that were placed by each customer, you must define the following data items:

- A data item that corresponds to the `Customer` table
- A data item that corresponds to the `Sales Line` table

You indent the second data item, which is the `Sales Line` table. As the report works through the records in the `Customer` table, it finds each customer's sales orders by examining the records in the `Sales Line` table that's related to the customer number.

The following screenshot shows the dataset definition of **Report 108 Customer – Order Detail**:

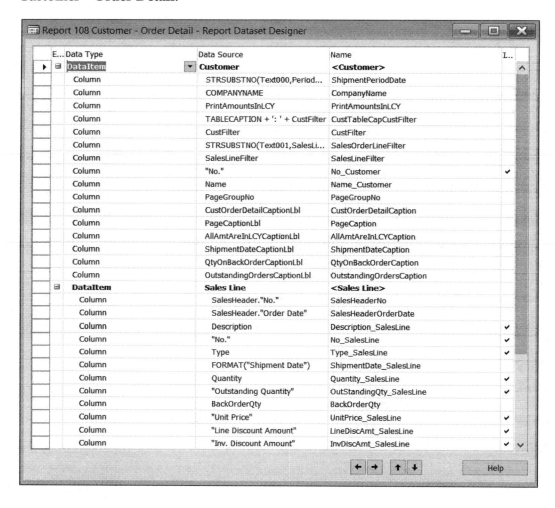

And this is how the dataset looks on Visual Studio:

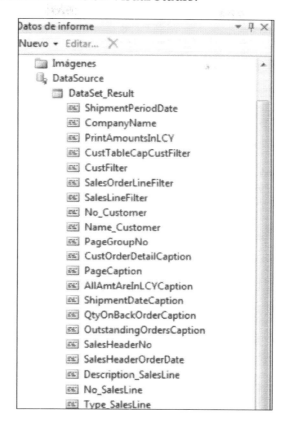

Designing the visual layout

You build the visual layout of a report by arranging the data items. A report that is displayed or printed must have a client report definition (RDLC) layout. You use Visual Studio Report Designer to design the RDLC layout. You generally display most data in the body of a report, and you use the header to display information before any data item record is displayed. For example, you can display a report title, company, and user information in the header of a report.

With Visual Studio Report Designer, you can add useful features to your report layouts, such as:

- Providing links from a field on a report to either a page or another report
- Inclusion of images and graphs
- The ability to toggle columns so you can hide or display data
- The ability for the users to interactively change the column on which the data in the report is sorted
- The ability to display RTF text

A report in Visual Studio always has exactly one body, and it is not possible to add more than one. Optionally, it can have one page header and one page footer. Extra headers or footers cannot be added. However, you can dynamically change the visibility property of objects on the report layout to control how the report will look.

When the report runs, it first runs the page header, then the page body, and then the page footer. It will not run the page body for each record. Looping through records is done by using a data region in the body section.

Reports use a variety of report items to organize data on a report page. The design surface is not *what you see is what you get*. The report items have an initial layout position that can change when the report is processed. The following list describes typical uses for different report items:

- **Textbox**: It is used on titles, date stamps, and report names.
- **Table, Matrix**: It is used to display tabular data from a report dataset. Table and matrix are templates of a Tablix data region and provide a starting grid layout for data from a report dataset.
- **Chart**: It is used to graphically display data from a report dataset.
- **Gauge**: It is used to present a visual image for a single value within a range of values.
- **List**: It is used to create free-form layout, such as the forms on a web page.
- **Image**: It is used to add existing images to a report.
- **Line**: It uses lines as graphical elements.
- **Rectangle**: It can be used as a container for other report items. Rectangles are often used to help control how the report items appear on a report page when the report is rendered.

The following screenshot shows the layout definition of the **108, Customer – Order Detail** report:

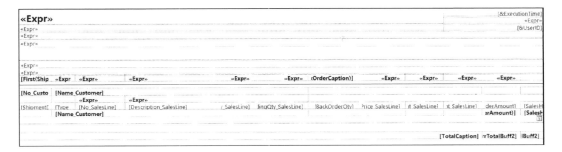

 Detailed report writing using Visual Studio is beyond the scope of this book. For more in-depth detail on writing your own reports in Dynamics NAV, check out *Microsoft Dynamics NAV 2015 Professional Reporting* that's also published by Packt Publishing.

Summary

In this chapter, we learned that there are several ways of analyzing and reporting data inside Dynamics NAV. We can use filters and FlowFilters, create views, take a look at the statistics pages of Dynamics NAV, define charts and use them in multiple pages, use all the available reports, use analysis views to analyze our data based on dimensions, and use account schedules to analyze our accounting information.

If that is not enough, we also learned that there are several ways to extract data from Dynamics NAV and do the analysis and reporting outside the application by using external tools.

In the next chapter, we will cover how you can debug error messages while the users work through the system.

11
Debugging

Microsoft introduced a new debugger from version Dynamics NAV 2013. The purpose of the revamped debugger is to allow the IT persons to easily pinpoint the problem any specific user is facing while using the software. For example, conditional breakpoints, debugging other user sessions, and debugging C/AL code in the Windows client instead of incomprehensible C# code. All these new features will convert the debugging experience to a happy experience.

The following topics are covered in this chapter:

- The art of debugging
- Starting the debugger
- Placing breakpoints
- Line-by-line execution

The art of debugging

By definition, debugging is a methodical process of finding and reducing the number of bugs in an application. Normally, the first step in debugging is to attempt to reproduce the problem. On some occasions, the input of the program may need to be simplified to make it easier to debug. Then, the debugger tool is used to examine the program stats (values of variables, call stacks, and so on) to track down the origin of the problem(s), and, finally, fix it.

Debugging, however, can do so much more than just solving issues. It is a fantastic way to understand how an application works. You could just open the involved object, read the written code, and follow it up. However, it will be hard.

First of all, Dynamics NAV code is run after an event occurs. If you take a look at an object, you will see code in the events, but it will be hard to know when an event occurs or which event is the one that first causes the code to be executed.

It will also be hard to just read the code because you don't know which values a variable is taking. If you turn the debugger on, you read the code with a specific example that makes variables take specific values. This is really helpful!

Of course, this means that, depending on specific variable values, some lines of the code won't be executed and you won't be able to follow them. Therefore, you will have to create significant and varied examples in order to cover all (or almost all) code in a given object.

Debugging in Dynamics NAV 2016

The debugger starts from the Dynamics NAV Development Environment. The user with which you are logged in must be assigned as a user in SQL Server. Go to **Tools | Debugger | Debug Session**.

The **Session List** page will open, as shown in the following screenshot:

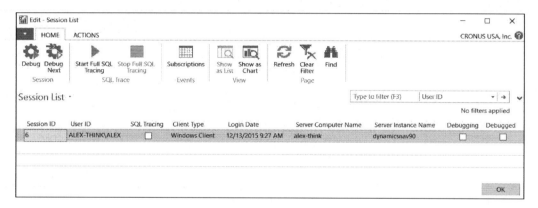

 Note that the page shows all sessions on the current database from all companies.

The session you select can be any of the following:

- A **Windows Client** session
- A **Web Client** session
- A **Tablet** or **Phone Client** session
- An **OData Web Services** session
- An **SOAP Web Services** session
- An **NAS Services** session

Place the cursor on the line corresponding to the session you want to debug and then click on the **Debug** button from the ribbon bar. You can select your own session or any other session from any other user. You can also click on the **Debug Next** option to debug a session that is not on the session list. The next session can be a session of any client mentioned previously.

The user won't be able to work with his/her session while you are debugging; therefore, whenever possible, open your own session and debug your session. If you cannot reproduce the bug because of user setup conditions, debug the session of the user that is encountering the problem, but remember to warn him/her.

The **Debugger** page will now open, as shown in the following screenshot:

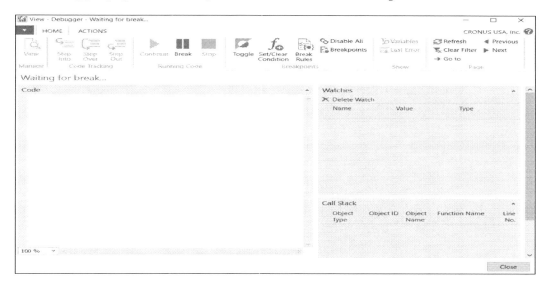

Note that the **Code** area is blank. You can still work with the session you have selected, but no code appears on the debugger. There are three options to start to debug code:

- Place a breakpoint on an object and wait until the session reaches the breakpoint. The *Placing breakpoints* section of this chapter explains how to do this.

- Click on the **Break** icon on the ribbon bar. The debugger will stop on the next line of code that the session executes.

- When the user you're targeting the debugger on runs into an error message using Dynamics NAV.

You will notice that on the **Debugger** page, you can only see the **Code** area, but you are missing two important parts that you will need to debug. The **Call Stack FactBox** is a list that shows the functions and triggers that are currently active. The **Watches FactBox** will allow you to select variables to see their current value.

Break Rules

This can be considered as the debugger setup. From the **Debugger** page, click on the **Break Rules** icon found on the ribbon bar. The **Debugger Break Rules** page opens, as shown in the following screenshot:

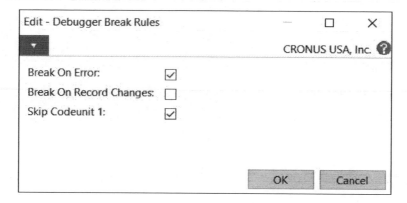

In Dynamics NAV 2016, you can find three basic options on the debugger feature:

- **Break On Error**: If the debugger is set to **Break On Error**, it breaks execution both on errors that are handled in code and on unhandled errors. By default, the debugger is set to **Break On Error**.

- **Break On Record Changes**: If the debugger is set to **Break On Record Changes**, it breaks before creating, modifying, or deleting a record. Therefore, the debugger stops on any of the following statements: INSERT, MODIFY, MODIFYALL, DELETE, and DELETEALL. By default, the debugger is not set to **Break On Record Changes**.

- **Skip Codeunit 1**: Many of the triggers in codeunit 1 Application Management are not important for debugging a business scenario. This is due to the fact that they are seldom important for debugging and because the codeunit 1 triggers are called frequently in the application. So you can specify that the debugger skips all code in codeunit 1. If you skip codeunit 1, the debugger does not break on code when you break on the next statement in codeunit 1. It continues until the first line of code after codeunit 1. In addition, when you step through the lines of code, the debugger does not step into code in codeunit 1. If you skip codeunit 1, you also implicitly skip all code that is called from codeunit 1.

If you explicitly set a breakpoint in codeunit 1 or in code that is called from codeunit 1, the debugger breaks execution when it hits the specific breakpoint, regardless of whether you have selected the setting to **Skip Codeunit 1**.

By default, the debugger is set to **Skip Codeunit 1**.

If the debugger is set up to **Break On Error,** the best way to determine the cause of a runtime error is to disable all breakpoints and click on **Continue**. The debugger will automatically stop the execution of the code when it encounters an error.

Placing breakpoints

A **breakpoint** is an intentional stop or pause placed in an object. It is a mark that you can set on a statement. When the program flow reaches the statement, the debugger intervenes and suspends execution until you instruct it to continue. During the interruption, you can inspect the environment or start a line-by-line code execution.

There are several ways of placing and removing breakpoints. This section will show you all the different ways so that you can choose the one that best suits your debugging needs.

From the Object Designer

From the Microsoft Dynamics NAV Development Environment, select **Table 270 Bank Account** and click on the **Design** button to open the **Table Designer** window. Then press *F9* or click on **View, C/AL Code** to open the C/AL Editor.

Place the cursor on one statement, a line of code, and press *F9*. A red bullet will appear on the left-hand side of the statement, as seen in the following screenshot. Press *F9* again; the bullet is now a white bullet. Press *F9* again and the bullet disappears; you have removed the breakpoint.

```
Table 270 Bank Account - C/AL Editor
 1  Documentation()
 2
 3  OnInsert()
 4  IF "No." = '' THEN BEGIN
 5    GLSetup.GET;
 6    GLSetup.TESTFIELD("Bank Account Nos.");
 7    NoSeriesMgt.InitSeries(GLSetup."Bank Account Nos.",xRec."No. Series",0D,"No.","No. Series");
 8  END;
 9
10  IF NOT InsertFromContact THEN
11    UpdateContFromBank.OnInsert(Rec);
12
13  DimMgt.UpdateDefaultDim(
14    DATABASE::"Bank Account","No.",
15    "Global Dimension 1 Code","Global Dimension 2 Code");
16
17  OnModify()
18  "Last Date Modified" := TODAY;
19
20  IF (Name <> xRec.Name) OR
21    ("Search Name" <> xRec."Search Name") OR
22    ("Name 2" <> xRec."Name 2") OR
23    (Address <> xRec.Address) OR
24    ("Address 2" <> xRec."Address 2") OR
25    (City <> xRec.City) OR
26    ("Phone No." <> xRec."Phone No.") OR
27    ("Telex No." <> xRec."Telex No.") OR
28    ("Territory Code" <> xRec."Territory Code") OR
100 %
```

The red bullet indicates that a breakpoint is enabled for that statement. The debugger will stop when the program flow reaches that statement.

The white bullet indicates that a breakpoint was placed before, but it is now disabled. This means that the debugger will not stop on that statement.

In the current statement of the debugger

With the debugger on, place the cursor on a line of code and press *F9*. A red bullet will appear on the left-hand side of the statement. Press *F9* again; the bullet is now a white bullet. Press *F9* again and the bullet disappears. You have now removed the breakpoint.

Instead of pressing *F9*, you can also use the **Toggle** icon found on the ribbon bar, as shown in the following screenshot:

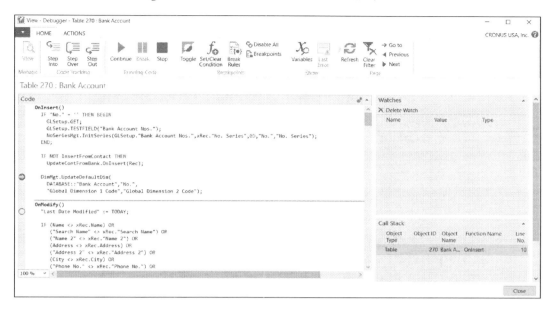

Red and white bullets indicate the same breakpoints as explained in the last section. This means that you can place breakpoints from the **Object Designer** window or from the debugger with the same effect.

The only difference is that breakpoints placed from the **Object Designer** window are seen from the debugger, but breakpoints placed from the debugger cannot be seen from the **Object Designer** window.

The end of each function contains a blank statement where you can also place a breakpoint. If you do so, the execution flow will stop right after all the code on the function has been executed and right before returning to the calling function. This is something we could not do in the previous versions of Dynamics NAV.

Conditional breakpoint

You can place a conditional breakpoint in Dynamics NAV. The debugger will only stop the execution if the program flow reaches the breakpoint and the condition is true. Otherwise, the execution continues.

The condition can include any variables or fields that are currently in scope of the following types: BigInteger, Boolean, Code, Decimal, Integer, Option, Text, and WideText.

Place the cursor on the statement where you want to place the conditional breakpoint and then click on the **Set/Clear Condition** icon found on the ribbon bar. The following page will now open:

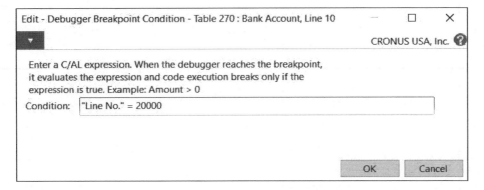

Write your condition using any of the supported operators: =, <>, <, >, <=, and >=. Then click on **OK** to go back to the debugger.

On the left-hand side of the statement, a red bullet with a white cross inside will appear. This indicates that the statement has a conditional breakpoint.

Debugger Breakpoint List

From the debugger breakpoint, you can view, set, enable, disable, or delete breakpoints. You can also set, modify, or delete conditions for the breakpoints.

From the **Debugger** page, click on the **Breakpoints** icon found on the ribbon bar to open the **Debugger Breakpoint List** window, as shown in the following screenshot:

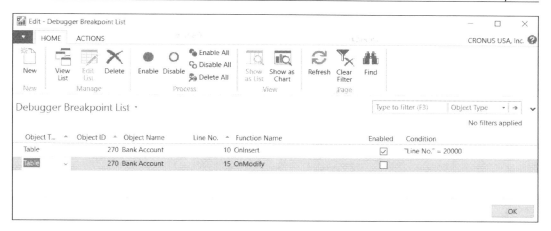

On the ribbon pane of the page, you will find options to create new breakpoints and to enable or disable the existing ones. You can also modify the **Condition** column of any existing breakpoint.

Line-by-line execution

When the debugger stops the execution of the program flow, you have four options to continue the execution. You can find those options on the ribbon pane of the **Debugger** page, as shown in the following screenshot:

The following is a description of each of the options available to continue execution:

- **Step Into**: Click on the **Step Into** icon or press *F11* to execute the current statement. If the statement contains a function call, execute the function and break at the first statement *inside* the function.

- **Step Over**: Click on the **Step Over** icon or press *F10* to execute the current statement. If the statement contains a function call, execute the function and break at the first statement *outside* the function.

- **Step Out**: Click on the **Step Out** icon or press *Shift + F11* to execute the remaining statements in the current function and break at the next statement in the calling function.

- **Continue**: Click on the **Continue** icon or press *F5* to continue until the next break.

Let's see an example of each execution mode: the insertion of a new record on the Bank Account table. We will use the same example for all the four options.

The Step Into option

The **Step Into** execution starts with the first statement of the OnInsert trigger of the Bank Account table. The yellow arrow (shown in the following screenshot) shows the line that is currently going to be executed:

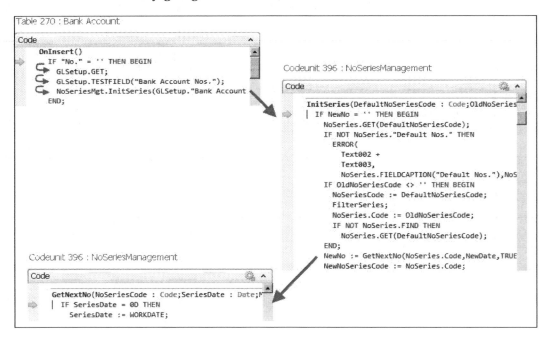

If you press *F11* (**Step Into**) repeatedly, you will see how each statement is executed. Four statements later we find a function call. The debugger then stops on the first statement of the InitSeries function. A few statements later, we find a new function call, and the debugger goes to the first statement of the GetNextNo function.

Using these options, the debugger stops on each and every single statement. If you keep on debugging this example, you will see that after pressing *F11* a few hundred times and visiting numerous functions and triggers, the new bank account will get inserted.

For a person who wishes to learn the ins and outs of how to develop in Dynamics NAV, going through this process will give you a good sense of what code is run at what time. Many developers learned how the application worked when they started out in NAV development.

Try to avoid this option unless you don't know what you are looking for and you have no other option than executing all the statements one by one, especially for long transactions.

The Step Over option

In the last section, we used the **Step Into** option until we reached the first statement of the GetNextNo function. We will continue debugging from that point, but using the **Step Over** option, as shown in the following screenshot:

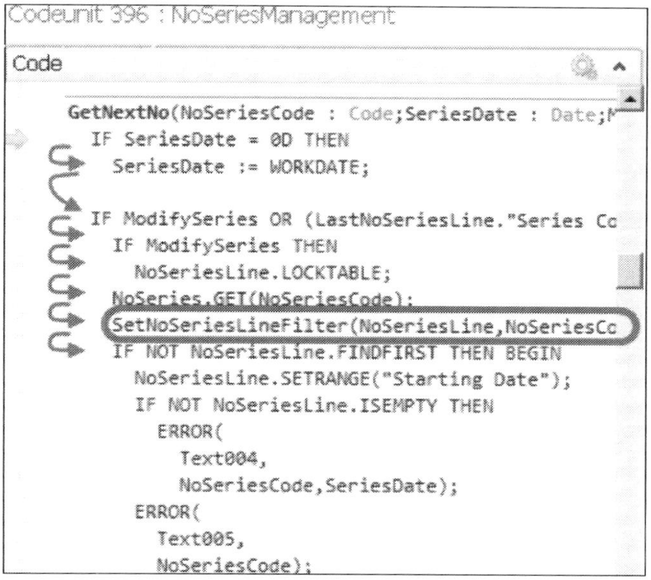

If you press *F10* a few times, you will see that the debugger stops on each statement, just as the **Step Into** option does.

The seventh statement of the function is a call to the `SetNoSeriesLineFilter` function. If you use the **Step Over** option on that statement, the debugger will execute all the code inside the function without stopping and will stop on the first statement after the function call, that is, the next statement in the current function.

Use this option when you already know the code that executes inside the function and you know that the function that is going to be called does not contain the bug you are looking for.

The Step Out option

In the last section, we used the **Step Over** option until we reached the first statement after the `SetNoSeriesLineFilter` function call, which is the `GetNextNo` function. We will continue debugging from that point, but using the **Step Out** option. Please refer to the following screenshot before proceeding:

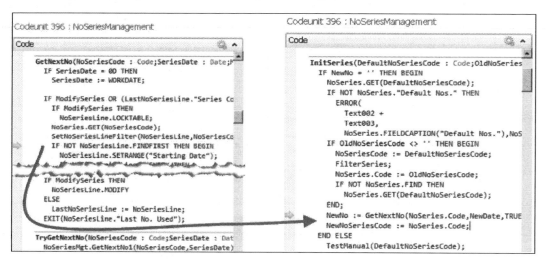

The **Step Out** option executes all the statements in the current function, and stops on the first statement of the calling function.

We are now on the `GetNextNo` function that was called from the `InitSeries` function, as we have seen in the *The Step Into option* section. If you click on the **Step Out** option, the debugger will execute all the remaining statements in the `GetNextNo` function, including the statements inside the new function call. After that, the debugger will stop on the next statement of the calling function, the `InitSeries` function.

Use this option if you have stepped inside a function to see its code and variables but, once inside the function, you have realized that the bug you are looking for is not there.

The Continue option

In the last section, we used the **Step Out** option until we reached the next statement after the call of the `GetNextNo` function. We will continue debugging the code from that point, but using the **Continue** option.

With the **Continue** option, the execution of the code continues until:

- A breakpoint is reached.
- We click on the **Break** option again.
- An error occurs.

Now, click on the **Continue** option in our example and see what happens.

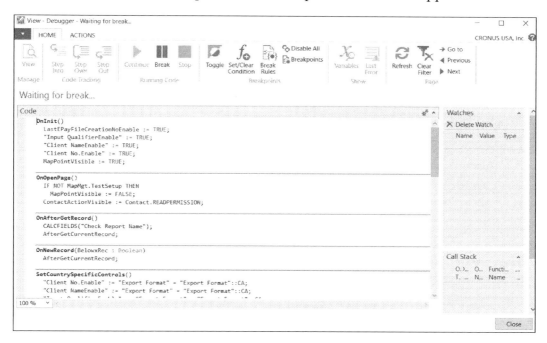

In the **Code** part of the debugger, we keep seeing the code we had before the **Continue** option was clicked. But the yellow arrow that showed us the current line is not there anymore. At the top of the preceding screenshot, we can read that the debugger is now waiting for a break.

The execution of the code has continued, a new bank account has been created, the user gets back the control of the execution, and the debugger is waiting for a new breakpoint.

You can use this option if you don't need to follow the code line by line and want to wait for a breakpoint instead. You also can use this option if an error occurs on a process and you want to know where the error has occurred. In this case, you can turn on the debugger, reproduce the process that is causing the problem, and use the **Continue** option to let the debugger find the line causing the error. Of course, you will need the **Break On Error** option enabled. You can read the *Break Rules* section for more information about this option.

The Call Stack FactBox

The **Call Stack** FactBox shows the active functions of the current execution. The **Call Stack** FactBox gives us information about the function that is currently on execution and also from where this function has been called.

Object Type	Object ID	Object Name	Function Name	Line No.
Codeunit	408	DimensionM...	GetGLSetup	139
Codeunit	408	DimensionM...	UpdateDefaultDim	406
Table	270	Bank Account	OnInsert	10

In the preceding screenshot, we can see the call stack corresponding to the code execution we were analyzing in the **Step Into** option.

We started debugging on the OnInsert trigger of the Bank Account table. We used the **Step Into** option until we reached a call to the InitSeries function. With this, we kept using the **Step Into** option until we reached the GetNextNo function. The *The Step Into option* section stopped there.

This is exactly what we see on the **Call Stack** FactBox.

The top line shows us the current function, while the bottom line shows the first function from where we started debugging. It also gives us valuable information such as the object that contains the functions that are executed.

You can select any of the lines of the **Call Stack** FactBox. We have selected the bottom line. Now, in the following screenshot, you can see that the **Code** area of the debugger changes, showing the code of the line selected on the **Call Stack** FactBox.

```
Code
    OnInsert()
      IF "No." = '' THEN BEGIN
        GLSetup.GET;
        GLSetup.TESTFIELD("Bank Account Nos.");
        NoSeriesMgt.InitSeries(GLSetup."Bank Account Nos.",xRec."No. Series",0D,"No.","No. Series");
      END;

      IF NOT InsertFromContact THEN
        UpdateContFromBank.OnInsert(Rec);

      DimMgt.UpdateDefaultDim(
        DATABASE::"Bank Account","No.",
        "Global Dimension 1 Code","Global Dimension 2 Code");

    OnModify()
      "Last Date Modified" := TODAY;

      IF (Name <> xRec.Name) OR
        ("Search Name" <> xRec."Search Name") OR
        ("Name 2" <> xRec."Name 2") OR
        (Address <> xRec.Address) OR
        ("Address 2" <> xRec."Address 2") OR
        (City <> xRec.City) OR
        ("Phone No." <> xRec."Phone No.") OR
```

The arrow points to where the code is reading

 Note that an arrow shows us the last statement executed before the execution flow jumped to a new function.

We can now place a new breakpoint on the function, as can be seen a couple of statements after the green arrow.

The Watches FactBox

The **Watches** FactBox is used to view the values of variables. You can select some variables from the **Debugger Variables List** window and add them to the **Watches** FactBox. Those variables will be shown until you delete them, even if they run out of scope. If this happens, the **<Out of Scope>** text will be displayed in the **Value** column of the **Watches** FactBox. All the variables added to the **Watches** FactBox persist between debugging sessions.

There are two ways to add a variable to the **Watches** FactBox:

- From the **Debugger Variable List** window
- From the **Code** viewer

Adding variables from the Debugger Variables List window

To add variables from the **Debugger Variables List** window, follow these steps:

1. On the **Debugger** page, click on the **Variables** option found on the **Actions** pane. The **Debugger Variable List** page will open, as shown in the following screenshot:

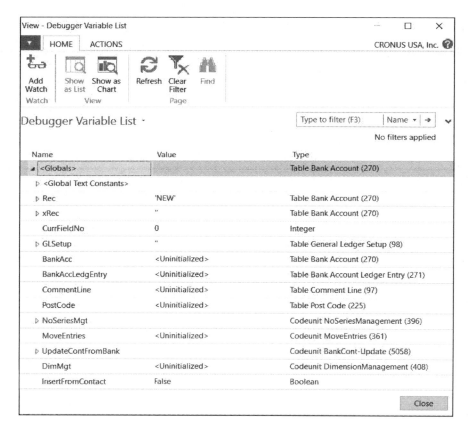

2. Select a variable from the list and click on the **Add Watch** icon. Then click on the **Close** button.

3. Back on the **Debugger** page, you will see the selected variable on the **Watches** FactBox. You can view the name of the variable, its value, and its type, as shown in the following screenshot:

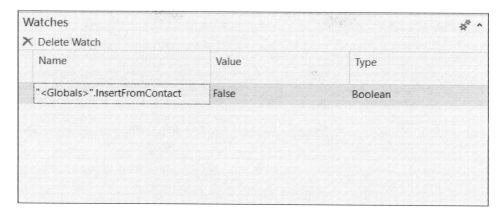

Adding variables from the code viewer

To add variables from the code viewer, follow these steps:

1. In the code viewer, hover the mouse pointer over the variable that you want to watch or select it, as shown in the following screenshot:

```
Codeunit 396 : NoSeriesManagement

Code
    IF NOT NoSeries."Default Nos." THEN
      ERROR(
        Text002 +
        Text003,
        NoSeries.FIELDCAPTION("Default Nos."),NoSeries.TABLECAPTION,NoSeries.Code);
    IF OldNoSeriesCode <> '' THEN BEGIN
      NoSeriesCode := DefaultNoSeriesCode;
      FilterSeries;
      NoSeries.Code := OldNoSeriesCode;
      IF NOT No  Globals
        NoSerie       NoSeries.Fields.Code (Code[10]) = 'BANK'
      END;
    NewNo := GetNextNo(NoSeries.Code,NewDate,TRUE);
    NewNoSeriesCode := NoSeries.Code;
    END ELSE
      TestManual(DefaultNoSeriesCode);
```

2. A data tip appears, as you can see in the preceding screenshot. Click on the Watch icon found on the left-hand side of the data tip (the glasses with a green plus symbol).

3. The variable will now be shown on the **Watches** FactBox, as shown in the following screenshot:

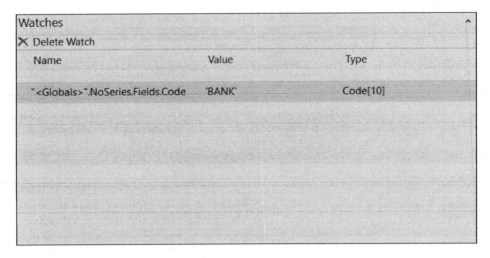

Summary

In this chapter, you saw that debugging is kind of an art that is used to examine program stats, find bugs, and be able to fix them. In addition, you saw that debugging can also be used to understand how an application works.

You also learned how to use the Dynamics NAV Debugger: how to start it, select a session to debug, place breakpoints, and do a line-by-line execution. We have also explained the **Call Stack** FactBox and the **Watches** FactBox.

In the next chapter, we will talk about the Query object, an object type included in Dynamics NAV that will quickly summarize data for charts and reporting.

12
Popular Reporting Options with Microsoft Dynamics NAV

Without messing with the standard out-of-the-box reports, which requires a very seasoned VB developer to create and customize, you can utilize external reporting and spreadsheet tools with live data from Dynamics NAV.

It's no secret that Microsoft is trying to make printing reports obsolete in favor of real-time analysis that can be consumed with any of your electronic devices. Printed reports, in essence, are obsolete the moment you print them out. Imagine if you can look at the important metrics of your company with real-time data at any given moment and make impactful decisions right away. Think about how much of an impact that will have on your business. This is the future we're looking at.

With every release of Microsoft Dynamics NAV, there are more and more companies that are designing their applications around Dynamics NAV. In addition, with Microsoft's introduction of Office 365, there is now a native integration to Power BI.

You can also utilize web services to publish queries data to be consumed by any external applications such as Excel. Third-party reporting developers such as Jet Reports Express offer a free version of their Excel-based reporting that integrates with Microsoft Dynamics NAV.

This chapter will explain some of these popular reporting options and how they can be used with your existing Dynamics implementation. In this chapter, we will cover the following topics:

- Defining queries and charts
- Defining web services for external applications
- How to configure and use PowerPivot in Excel
- How to configure and use Power BI with Office 365
- Downloading and installing Jet Reports Express

What is a query?

Query is the name of a Dynamics NAV application object that was first introduced in Microsoft Dynamics NAV 2013. This application object is only meant to retrieve data from the database. It is a read-only object. It cannot modify, delete, or insert new data into the database.

There are many things about queries in Dynamics NAV that point to the future of our *reporting* world:

- They allow us to retrieve data from multiple tables at the same time
- They allow us to retrieve only specific fields in a table
- They allow us to group the retrieved data according to certain fields without the need of any explicit key for them
- They allow us to total the retrieved data using different totaling methods (sum, count, average, min, and max)

If you are a Dynamics NAV programmer and you have worked with the previous versions of Dynamics NAV, you will see the advantages and the possibilities of this new object right away. The Query object makes the summarizing of data much easier without complicated coding in reports. It makes data retrieval a lot faster.

In this chapter, we will show you how to define a query using the query editor and where and how to use queries on your developments. Once we know how to write and execute queries, we will compare them both in time and effort of development and in speed, against the old ways of retrieving the exact same data out of the application.

Query Designer

Queries, just as any other objects in Dynamics NAV, have their own designer or editor.

To open **Query Designer**, perform the following steps:

1. Open the Microsoft Dynamics NAV Development Environment.
2. The **Object Designer** window will open.
3. On the left pane of the **Object Designer** window, click on **Query** to see the list of existing queries, as shown in the following screenshot:

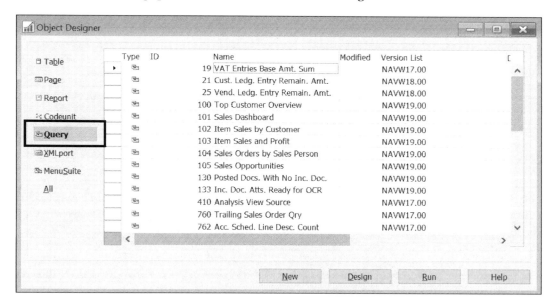

4. Select the query **9150 My Customers** (or any other existing query) and click on **Design**.

5. The **Query Designer** window will open, as shown in the following screenshot:

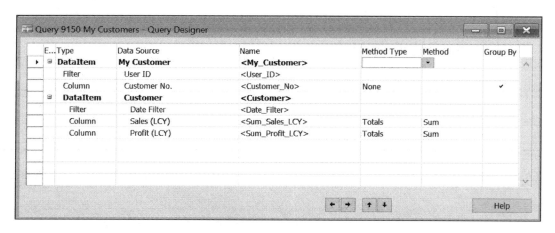

The **Query Designer** window looks a lot like **Page Designer** or the new **Report Dataset Designer**. This will make it easier to get used to developing queries.

In the **Query Designer** window, we can select one or more **DataItem** values to define the database table from which we want to retrieve data for the query. Through properties, we can define the relationship between different **DataItem** values. We can also select the columns or fields that will be included in the query and specify the totaling methods and groupings for the fields. Finally, using properties, we will be able to define filters and to modify the behavior of certain columns, such as reversing their sign.

We will see the fields and properties of the **Query Designer** window by creating our first query.

Defining our first query

In our first query, we will try to retrieve the items that our customers buy per month. To do so, we will use the `Item Ledger Entry` table as our main data source, but we will also use the `Customer` and the `Item` tables to get additional information from customers and items, such as their name or description.

First let's define the main data source and the fields that will be retrieved:

1. Open the **Object Designer** window in the Microsoft Dynamics NAV Development Environment and select the **Query** object type on the left pane of the **Object Designer** window.

2. Click on **New** to create a new query.

3. An empty **Query Designer** window will open.

4. On the first line, in the **Type** column, choose **DataItem** from the drop-down list.

The first line in the **Query Designer** window must be a **DataItem** field and not a **Column** field.

5. Select **Item Ledger Entry** in the **Data Source** column.

You can choose the up arrow that will appear on the right-hand side of the **Data Source** column when you select it to see a table list and select the desired table. You can also type in the name or the number ID of the table (if you know the name or the number ID of the table) you want to use on your query.

6. The **Name** column will be automatically populated once a **Data Source** value has been selected. Default names are usually fine, but you can change them if you want to.

7. Display the **Properties** window for the data item. To do so, select the **DataItem** row and click on **View | Properties** (or press *Shift + F4*).

Names in queries must be **Common Language Specification (CLS)** compliant. The first character must be a letter. Subsequent characters can be any combination of letters, integers, and underscores.

8. Select the `DataItemTableFilter` property and click on the **Assist Edit** button. The **Table Filter** window will open. Set **Field** to **Entry Type**, **Type** to **CONST**, and **Value** to **Sale**. Click on **OK**.

9. Back at the **Properties** window, the value for the `DataItemTableFilter` property should be what is shown in the following screenshot:

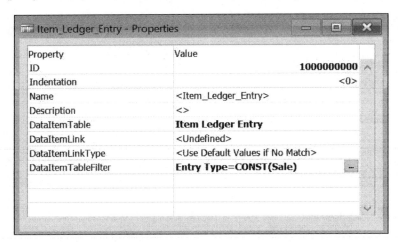

Using the `DataItemTableFilter` property, we have applied a filter so that only entries of type **Sale** are retrieved on this query. We are analyzing sales; we do not want other types of entries to be shown in our query.

10. Close the **Properties** window.

11. For the **Item Ledger Entry** data item, select fields **Item No.**, **Posting Date**, **Quantity**, and **Source No.** as **Column** in the rows below **DataItem**.

12. Once you have selected all those fields, the **Query Designer** window should look like the following screenshot:

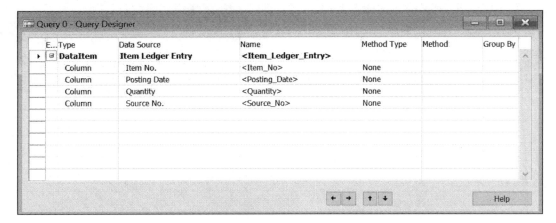

13. For the row **Posting Date**, select **Date** as **Method Type** and **Month** as **Method**.

14. For the row **Quantity**, select **Totals** as **Method Type** and **Sum** as **Method**.

    Notice that, in the following screenshot, right after a **Totals** method type is selected, the **Group By** field is automatically selected for all the other columns in the query that are not of type **Totals**. This defines how the results of the query will be grouped.

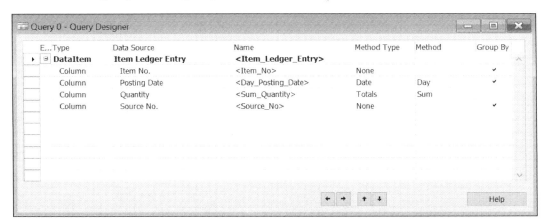

 Group By is a read-only field that is automatically calculated. The value of this column cannot be modified

15. In the **Properties** window of the **Quantity** field, select **Yes** for the **ReverseSign** property.

    We are analyzing sales. Sales represent a decrease in the item's inventory. Being a decrease, the **Quantity** field for entries of type **Sale** is a negative value. We want to reverse this sign because we want to see quantities sold as positive values.

16. Save and compile the query. To do so, click on **File | Save** (or press *Ctrl + S*).

17. We will be asked for an ID and a name for the query. We will set the **ID** attribute to 50000 and the **Name** attribute to My First Query.

18. The **Query Designer** window will be closed and we will be taken back to the **Object Designer** window. We will now run the query and take a look at the results. To do so, select **Query 50000 My First Query** and click on the **Run** button.

19. The Windows client will open and the result of the query will be shown as follows:

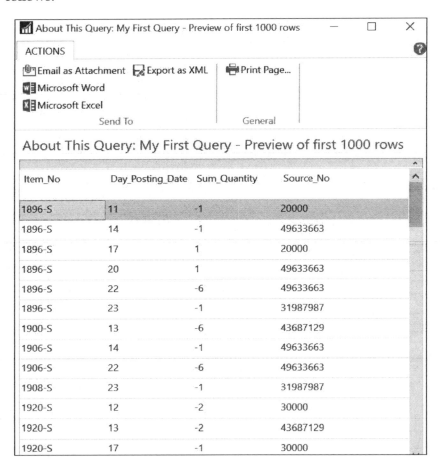

So far so good! We have defined a pretty simple query with a single data item, but we have already seen how to filter the results and the different method types, and how the results are grouped.

Adding additional data to the query

We will go further into the example by adding a couple of extra data items to the query.

1. In the **Object Designer** window, select **Query 50000 My First Query** and click on the **Design** button. The **Query Designer** window will open with the query we were creating.

2. On the first empty row, enter a **DataItem** value for the table **Item**.

3. Open the **Properties** window for the **Item** data item.

4. Click on the **Assist Edit** button for the **DataItemLink** property. Select **No.** as the *field*, the **Item_Ledger_Entry** data item as *reference DataItem*, and **Item No.** as the *reference field*. Click on **OK**.

5. Back at the **Properties** window, the value for the **DataItemLink** property should be what is shown in the following screenshot:

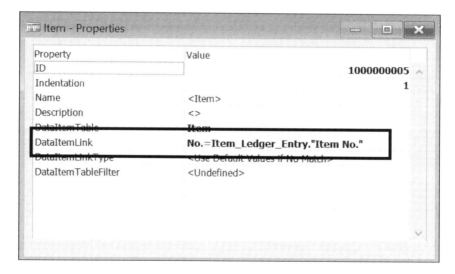

6. Close the **Properties** window.

7. For the **Item** data item, select the field **Description** as the **Column** type in the rows below the **DataItem** field.

8. On the first empty row, enter a new data item and select **Customer** as the **Data Source**.

9. Open the **Properties** window for the **Customer** data item.

10. Click on the **Assist Edit** button. For the **DataItemLink** property, select **No.** as the field, the **Item_Ledger_Entry** data item as the reference data item, and **Source No.** as the reference field. Click on **OK**.

11. Close the **Properties** window.

12. For the **Customer** data item, select the fields **Name** and **Customer Posting Group** as the **Column** type in the rows below the **DataItem** field.

13. Set the **DataItemLink** property to `No.=Item_Ledger_Entry."Source No.".`

The final query should look like the following screenshot:

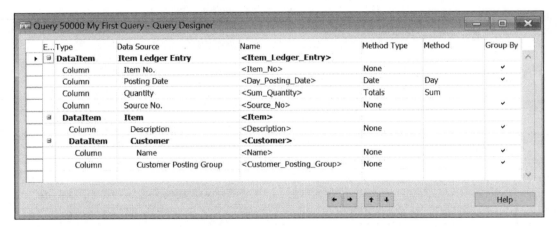

14. Save and compile the query.

15. Run the query to see the results, as shown in the following screenshot:

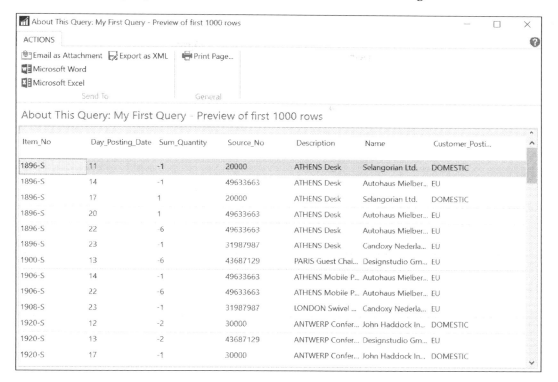

Charts

The Windows client can display a set of predefined charts that use Dynamics NAV data. With Microsoft Dynamics NAV, queries can be used as data sources for those charts.

We will use the query defined earlier on in this chapter as the data source of a chart and we will display it on the home page of the Dynamics NAV Windows client.

To define a query as the data source of a chart, perform the following steps:

1. Open the Windows client for Microsoft Dynamics NAV.

2. Navigate to **Departments | Administration | Application Setup | RoleTailored Client**.

3. Select **Generic Charts**.

4. Click on **New** on the ribbon bar to add a new chart.

5. The **New-Generic Chart** setup page will open as shown in the following screenshot:

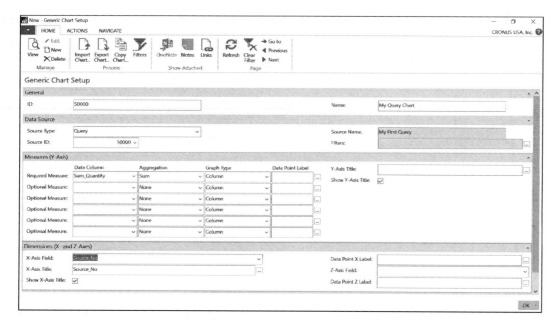

6. Give the new chart an **ID** value and a **Name** value. For example, set **ID** to 50000 and **Name** to My Query Chart.

7. On the **Data Source** tab, select **Query** as **Source Type** and **50000** as **Source ID**.

8. On the **Measures (Y-Axis)** tab, select **Sum_Quantity** as **Data Column** on the **Required Measure** row.

9. On the **Dimensions (X- and Z-Axes)** tab, select **Source_No** as **X-Axis Field**.

10. Click on **OK** to close the **New-Generic Chart** setup page.

To display the chart on the home page of the Windows client, perform the following steps:

1. Go back to the home page of the Windows client for Dynamics NAV.
2. Click on the Dynamics NAV icon found on the upper left corner of the page and select **Customize** and then **Customize This Page**.
3. Select **Chart Part** from **Available parts**.
4. Click on **Add**.
5. A blank chart will appear on the **Role Center layout** section. Select the blank chart and click on **Customize Part**.
6. Select chart **50000 My Query Chart** and click on **OK**.
7. Click on **OK** to close the **Customize the Role Center** page.
8. Back at the home page of the Windows client, the chart should be displayed as shown in the following screenshot:

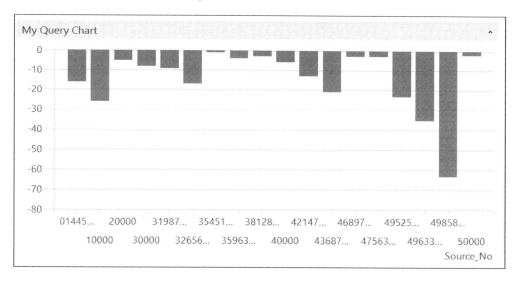

Web services

Starting from Microsoft Dynamics NAV 2009, it was possible to publish page and codeunit objects as web services to allow external applications to access Dynamics NAV data and business logic. In the later releases of Microsoft Dynamics NAV, it is also possible to publish Query objects as web services.

Page and codeunit objects can be accessed through **SOAP (Simple Object Access Protocol)** web services. Queries can only be accessed through the OData web services protocol.

You will need to first enable the SOAP and OData services from the Dynamics NAV Administrator.

1. Start the **Dynamics NAV 2016 Administrator** from the start menu.
2. Click on the service that's running Dynamics NAV. If you did the full installation, the default service should be **DynamicsNAV90**.
3. Select the **service** and click on **Edit**.
4. Place a checkbox on the **Enable SOAP Service** and **Enable OData Service**.
5. Click on **Save** after you're done:

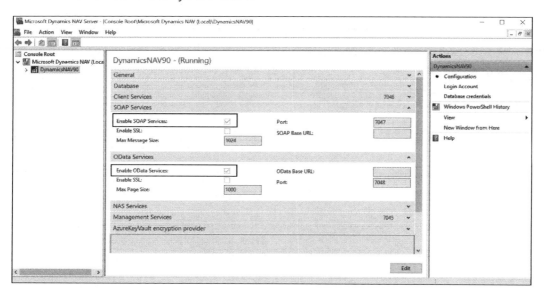

To publish a query as a web service from Dynamics NAV, perform the following steps:

1. Open the Windows client for Microsoft Dynamics NAV.
2. Navigate to **Departments | Administration | IT Administration | General**.
3. Select **Web Services**.
4. Select **New** on the ribbon bar to publish a new web service.
5. The **New-Web Services** page will open.
6. Select **Query** as **Object Type**.

7. Enter `50000` in the **Object ID** field.

8. Enter a name in the **Service Name** field. For example, let's use **MyQueryWS** as **Service Name**.

9. Check the **Published** field, as shown in the following screenshot:

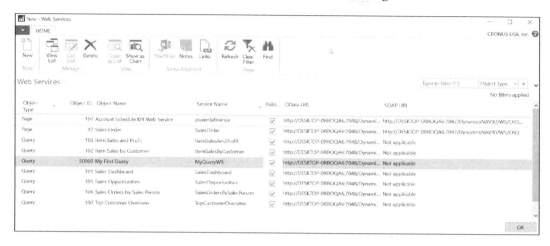

At this point, the query is already published as a web service. You can check to see if it is accessible using your browser by clicking on OData URL, and then clicking on the hyperlink symbol or copying and pasting the URL to your web browser.

Note that if you're using the Windows Edge browser from Windows 10, the web service will not display. You will only be able to run using Internet Explorer, Google Chrome, or other full browsers.

External applications

Because Dynamics NAV queries can be published as web services, they can be accessed by absolutely any application that can consume OData web services. It can be an external application developed by you for the only purpose of reading Dynamics NAV data or it can be a commonly used application that supports OData web services.

If you are integrating NAV with an external app via web services, it's always recommended not to expose directly the NAV web services but use a custom WS that talks with NAV (via standard web services exposed as described) and the external system.

In this section we will see how to use Dynamics NAV queries in Microsoft Office Excel.

Excel and PowerPivot

Among all the applications that are out there, an extensively used one is probably Microsoft Office Excel. There is a free add-in for Excel called **PowerPivot** that can consume OData web services.

We can do that as follows:

1. If you're using Excel 2013, you can enable the **PowerPivot 2013** by going to the **Add-in** page from the **Options** menu. Or you can download PowerPivot by performing a quick search on the Internet, which will lead you to the download page.

2. The installation of PowerPivot will create a new tab in the ribbon bar of Microsoft Office Excel.

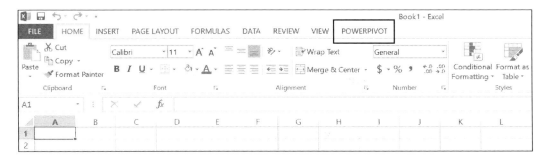

3. Open Microsoft Excel 2013.

4. On the **POWERPIVOT** tab, select **Manage**.

5. Select **Get External Data | From Data Service | From OData Data Feed**.

6. You will be asked to enter a friendly connection name and a data feed URL. Enter NAVMyQueryWS as **Friendly connection name** and copy and paste the OData URL from the Dynamics NAV web service screen, or you can type in the following path as the value for **Data Feed URL**:

   ```
   http://localhost:7048/DynamicsNAV90/OData/Company('CRONUS%20
   USA%2C%20Inc.')/MyQueryWS
   ```

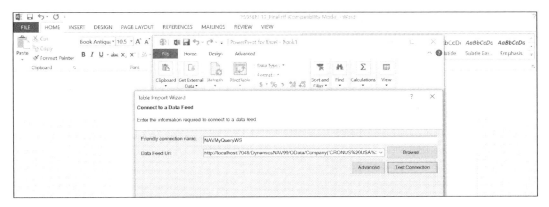

7. Click on **Test Connection** to check if PowerPivot can access the published web service.

8. Click on **Next** and then click on **Finish**.

9. An import process will start. Once it is finished, click on **Close**.

10. The imported data will be displayed on the **PowerPivot for Excel** window.

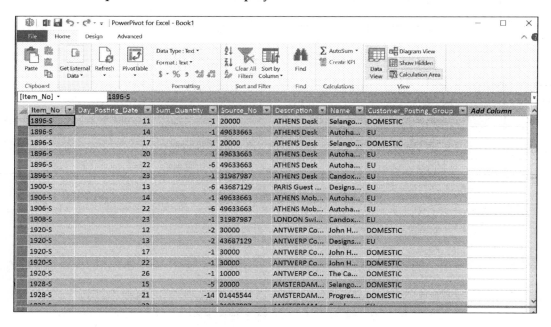

11. Select **PivotTable**, and a PivotTable that uses data from Microsoft Dynamics NAV will be created. Select the fields that you want to see on the PivotTable.

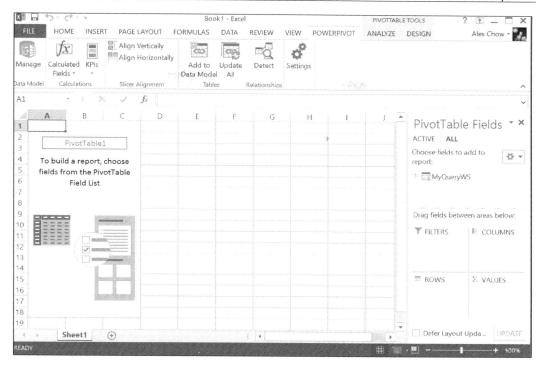

Power BI

Power BI is a tool that is part of the Microsoft Office 365 offering. It provides web-based analytical tool for your data that can be set up to gather real-time data. The aim of Power BI is to provide business intelligence to companies at a fraction of the cost of buying a regular business intelligence solution.

There is also a content pack that's specifically designed for Dynamics NAV within Power BI in Office 365. Within the content pack, it provides some of the graphs and charts Microsoft believes most company will want to see.

You will need an Office 365 account in order to use Power BI. To access the content pack, proceed to `https://app.powerbi.com/getdata/services/microsoft-dynamics-nav`.

Once you sign on using your Office 365 account, find the Microsoft Dynamics NAV content pack and click on **Connect**.

You'll be prompted to put in the OData web service. If you're using the default setting, it should be displaying the following screenshot:

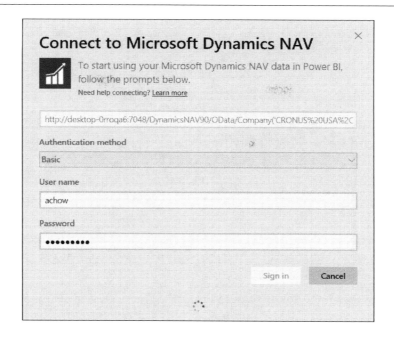

Use the basic authentication and type in the username and password that you've set up on your machine.

It will then prompt you that the system is importing the data from the web services. After the information is loaded, you will see the dashboard.

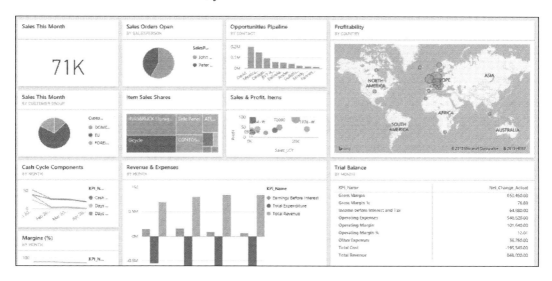

For more information on connecting with Power BI, visit `https://powerbi.microsoft.com/en-us/documentation/powerbi-content-pack-microsoft-dynamics-nav/`.

Jet Reports Express

Jet Reports Express for Microsoft Dynamics NAV is a business-reporting tool meant to let users create high-impact reports in a familiar environment such as Microsoft Excel. With Jet Reports Express, you can use all Excel capabilities such as formatting, slicers, charting, and pivot tables.

Note that this is a free version of Jet Reports. There's also a paid version that Jet Reports wants you to buy, so a lot of the functionalities have been stripped out of the free version.

Visit the Jet Reports website for updated information of this application. On the website, you will also find a few demo videos that show you how to start using it.

Downloading Jet Reports Express

There are two components of Jet Reports Express to download as follows:

- The installation files of Jet Reports Express
- A Microsoft Dynamics NAV business object file (or the file with a `.fob` extension)

The installation files and the business object file of Jet Reports Express can be downloaded from `http://jetexpress.jetreports.com/`.

You will need to provide your information to download the installation files. The installation file should be called `Jet Express Setup.exe`.

The Microsoft Dynamics NAV business object file can be downloaded from the same page under the heading **Jet Reports Business Objects for Microsoft Dynamics NAV**. If the business object file is compressed in a ZIP file, then extract the file and place the file somewhere on your computer.

The name of this the business object file is `Jet Reports Objects.fob`.

Installing Jet Reports Express

The step-by-step guides on how to install and enable Jet Reports Express is detailed on the preceding website listed under **Jet Express for Microsoft Dynamics NAV Configuration**.

Make sure you use the guide that's appropriate for your version. Basically, there's a version prior to NAV 2013 and a version that's for NAV 2013 and above.

Report pack for Jet Reports Express

On the Jet Reports Express website, there is also a report pack available for download that you can utilize right away for your business. The link to the prebuilt reports can be accessed from the Jet Reports Express main page or from `http://jetexpress.jetreports.com/resource-center/reports-library.php`.

After going through the installation process that's detailed from the website, you will be able to connect the data sources to your NAV database and start using the prebuilt reports with your data. The following screenshot is an example of the report from Jet Reports Express from the prebuilt reports:

At last count, there are 47 prebuilt reports from Jet Reports. You can also submit the reports that you utilize most often and get them incorporated into future releases.

Summary

In this chapter, you saw a couple of reporting and analysis options that are included in Dynamics NAV that extend its functionality and are very useful to users and companies. Utilizing web services, the options for analyzing your data are endless!

Index

A

Access Control service (ACS) 57
accounting 132, 133
account schedules, Analysis & Reporting
    section 383
Agile approach 147
Agile project type, Sure Step 153, 154
analysis by dimensions
    functionality 398, 399
analysis views
  about 386
  creating 394-396
  dimensions 387
  updating 397, 398
  using 398
  using, as source for account
    schedules 400, 401
analyst 158
application changes
  about 63
  automatic payment and bank
    reconciliation 69
  Bank Data Conversion Service,
    signing up for 69, 70
  bank statements, reconciling
    automatically 71
  deferrals 79
  document exchange service
    (OCR Services) 77
  documents, e-mailing 76, 77
  exchange rates update 78
  improvements, for application users 64
  native Integration, with Dynamics CRM 78
  new application, features 69
  payments, reconciling automatically 71
  Posting Preview function 79
  Power Business Intelligence 72
  RapidStart services 72-74
  schedule reports 74-76
  Social Listening 72
  tablet client 67, 68
  universal app 78
  workflow management 78
approvals area
  about 26
  planning 26, 27
  pricing 26
  request limits 26
ask for help feature 294
aspects, for project
  acceptance of developments 144
  billing 142
  communication between team 144
  communication with customer 144
  development and testing 144
  documentation 145
  planning 143
  purchases 144
  reporting and control 145
  time and cost, estimating 142, 143
Azure Active Directory (Azure AD) 57

B

bank entries 231
basic object types, data model principles
  about 296, 297
  object elements 299-302
batch jobs 329, 330

bill of materials (BOM) 30
breakpoints
    conditional breakpoint 420
    debugger breakpoint list 420, 421
    placing 417
    placing, from Object Designer 417, 418
    placing, in current statement of
        debugger 418, 419
Break Rules 416, 417
business consultant 156, 157

C

calendars
    machine center's availability 36
    resource capacities 36
    shop calendar 36
    work center calendar 36
Call Stack FactBox 416, 426, 427
capacities
    calendars, creating 36
card pages 313-317
CardParts 323
change management 185, 186
charts
    about 368, 441-443
    adding, to role center page 369-371
    building 368, 369
    configuring 371, 372
    creating 371, 372
    Show as Chart option 368
Codeunit 223
Codeunit Web Services 60
code viewer
    variables, adding from 429, 430
code, XMLport
    data, changing 221, 222
    data not included in XML file,
        filling 219, 220
    document structure 217, 218
    writing 217
Common Language Specification (CLS) 435
conditional breakpoint 420
configuration questionnaire
    about 210
    completing 212
    creating 211

configuration templates
    about 208
    creating 208, 209
    using 209
configuration worksheet
    about 200
    migration structure, creating 201-203
    related tables, copying 203-205
ConfirmationDialog pages 313, 324
consolidation 18
Continue option 425, 426
Copy Data from Company function 205
Cost of Goods Sold (COGS) account 110
customer entries 226-231
CustomerSource
    URL 274
customer's team
    key users 160
    project manager 160
    users 160
customized code, Dynamics NAV
    batch jobs 329, 330
    fields, validating 328

D

data
    converting, from old system to Dynamics
        NAV's needs 223, 224
data analysis and reporting
    account schedules 383-385
    analysis views 386
    charts 368
    Customer Statistics, viewing 366, 367
    data, extracting 401, 402
    filters and FlowFilters, using 362-364
    report development 405
    View, creating 364, 365
data conversion package
    configuration package, applying 199, 200
    configuration package, creating 196-198
    creating 195
Data Exchange Framework 69
data extraction
    alternative ways 405
    data, sending to Microsoft Excel 404

data, sending to Microsoft Office
 applications 402
data, sending to Microsoft Word 403
through web services 404
Data Feed URL
 URL 447
data migration tools
 about 189
 custom tools, writing 223
 RapidStart Services 190, 191
 XMLports 213
data model
 about 98
 documents 99-102
 entries 108-110
 journals 104-108
 master data 98, 99
data model principles
 about 295
 basic objects 296, 297
 page structure 313
 table structure 302
data navigation
 about 123
 data browsing, ways 125-127
 data, filtration 127-129
 list pages, sorting on 127
 navigate functionality 123-125
 views, saving for filters 129, 130
dataports 213
debugger, options
 Break On Error 416
 Break On Record Changes 416
 Skip Codeunit 1 417
 variables, adding from variables list
  window 428, 429
debugging
 about 413, 414
 breakpoint list 420, 421
 Break Rules 416, 417
 in Dynamics NAV 2016 414-416
Department 387
deployment phase
 about 169
 configuration 170
 data migration 170
 end users' training 171

go-live 171
hardware installation 169
software installation 169
user-acceptance test 171
developer 159
development changes
 .NET interoperability 90
 about 79
 changed data types 86
 changed functions 87-89
 changed objects 90
 changed properties 85
 changed triggers 86
 document reporting 80-82
 encryption enhancement 84
 RoleTailored client control add-ins 90
 security enhancement 84
 upgrade automation 83
development considerations
 about 293
 customized code, formatting 330
 customized code location 328
 data model principles 295
 posting process 326
 setup, versus customization 293-295
development environment 9
development phase 168
dimensions
 about 184, 387
 global 387
 rest 387
 shortcut 387
dimensions, analysis views
 accessing 391-393
 categorizing 389, 390
 setting up 388, 389
document pages 313, 322, 323
document tables 306-309
Dynamics NAV. *See* **Microsoft Dynamics
  NAV**
Dynamics NAV 2013
 prior upgrades 245
 upgrades 245, 246
Dynamics NAV 2016
 debugging 414-416
Dynamics NAV database
 about 133

data rules, coded 136, 137
TableRelation property 134-136
Dynamics NAV user group
  URL 295

E

end user
  about 159
  involving 187
Enterprise project type 151
Enterprise Resource Planning (ERP) 1
entries
  Customer Entries 121
  General Ledger Entries 121
  Item Entries 121
  ledger entries, creating 111-116
  VAT (Tax) Entries 121
entry tables 310
European Union (EU) 15
Excel templates
  using 205, 206

F

financial management area
  about 10
  account schedules 12, 13
  cash management 14
  fixed assets 14
  general ledger 11
  G/L budgets 11, 12
fixed asset entries 233, 234
Fixed Assets 333
FlowFilters
  using 362
functional areas, Microsoft Dynamics NAV
  approvals 26
  financial management 3, 10
  human resources 4, 52
  intrastat 15
  job 3, 39
  manufacturing 3, 33
  purchase 3, 25
  resource planning 3, 44
  sales and marketing 3, 19
  service 4, 46

Value Added Tax (VAT) 15
vertical and horizontal solutions 54, 55
warehouse 3, 28
functional change, Dynamics NAV
  about 331, 332
  customized functionality, extending 334
  Fixed Asset functionality 333
  general guidelines 331, 332
  Item Tracking 333
  Requisition Worksheet 332
functional change, implementing
  about 343
  customized functionality,
    extending 348, 349
  Fixed Assets implementation 345, 346
  Item Tracking implementation 347, 348
  Requisition Worksheet
    implementation 343, 344
functional change, planning
  about 351
  Requisition Worksheet 352, 353
functional change, right time selecting
  about 349
  customized functionality,
    extending 351, 357-359
  Fixed Assets 350, 354-356
  Item Tracking 350, 356, 357
  Requisition Worksheet 350

G

General Ledger
  about 11
  balances 235
**generally accepted accounting principle
  (GAAP) 11**
goals
  defining 176
  measuring 177, 178
  SMART 177
go-live date
  beginning of fiscal year 239
  cons 240
  middle of fiscal year 240
  selecting 239

H

historical data 235, 236
human resources area
  about 52
  absence registration 54
  country localizations 54
  employees 53, 54

I

implementation process 140, 141
implementer 159
improvements, for application users
  about 64
  cues, with color indicator 64
  mandatory fields 65
  simplified user interface, for small
    businesses 65-67
interactions, with functionalities
  about 334
  customized functionality,
    extending 342, 343
  Fixed Assets, with Financial
    Management 335, 336
  Item Tracking, with functional
    areas 336-338
  Requisition Worksheet, with Purchase
    functionality 334, 335
intercompany transactions 17
internal processes
  defining 179
  FAQs 179-181
Inventory 31
IT changes
  about 91
  Dynamics NAV Server administration 91
  Windows PowerShell cmdlets 91-94
item entries 231, 232
Item Journal 110
**Item Tracking, interacting with functional
  areas**
  item, creating 338
  Item Tracking, enabling 341, 342
  purchase order, creating 339, 340
  purchase order, posting 339, 340
  sales order, creating 341
  sales order, posting 341

J

Jet Reports Express
  about 452
  downloading 452
  installing 453
  report pack for 453
  URL 452, 453
job area
  about 39
  invoice jobs 43
  Job card 40
  phases and tasks 40, 41
  planning 41, 42
  time sheet 43
  work in process (WIP) 43
Job Queue 74
journal tables 311

K

key users 157

L

line-by-line execution
  about 421, 422
  Continue option 425, 426
  Step Into option 422, 423
  Step Out option 424, 425
  Step Over option 423, 424
line types
  contract 42
  schedule 42
  schedule and contract 42
list pages 313, 317-322
ListPart pages 313, 323
list report 380
Lot Specific Tracking 336

M

manufacturing area
  about 33
  capacities 36
  costing 38
  execution 38
  planning 37

product design 34, 35
subcontracting 39
master data 225
Master Planning Schedule (MPS) 37
master tables 304
MergeTool
about 259, 281
downloading 281
installing 281
URL 281
using 282
MergeTool, using
all versions, merging 287-291
new base version, importing 284, 285
new custom version, exporting 292
new custom version, importing to
Dynamics NAV 2013 database 292
old base and new base versions,
comparing 285-287
old base version, importing 282, 283
old custom version, importing 283, 284
methodology
about 142
Agile approach 147, 148
both approaches, using 148
Microsoft Dynamics Sure Step 148
Waterfall approach 145, 146
Microsoft Dynamics Community
URL 294
Microsoft Dynamics NAV
about 2
development considerations 293
goals, defining 176
goals, measuring 177
functional areas 3, 4, 9
history 5-9
three-tier architecture 5
Microsoft Dynamics NAV 2009
URL 275
Microsoft Dynamics NAV 2016
application changes 63
development changes 79
features 63
IT changes 91
Microsoft Dynamics NAV, accessing
about 55
development environment 60, 61

SharePoint client 59
tablet client 58
Web client 57, 58
Web Services 59
Windows client 55, 56
Microsoft Dynamics Sure Step
about 148
Agile project type 153
On Premise deployment 148
On the Cloud deployment 148
project types, based on Waterfall
approach 149
MSDN
URL 245, 278, 294, 330
multicurrency 18

N

NavigatePage pages 314, 325
Navision A/S 5
NAV Service Tier (NST) 134
No Save button
about 117
advantages 118, 119
data, verification 119
main drawback 120

O

Object Designer 213
OData Web Services 60
open documents 236,-238
open entries
about 226
accounting balances 226
bank entries 226, 231
customer entries 226-231
fixed asset entries 226, 233, 234
item entries 226, 231, 232
vendor entries 226, 231

P

page structure, data model principles
about 313
card pages 313-317
ConfirmationDialog pages 313, 324
document pages 313, 322, 323

list pages 313-322
ListPart pages 313, 323
NavigatePage pages 314, 325
role center pages 314
worksheet pages 313, 323
Page Web Services 60
PartnerSource
   URL 274
partner's team
   analyst 160
   business consultant 160
   developer 160
   implementer 160
   project manager 160
phases
   about 161
   deployment 169
   development 168
   post implementation support 172
   presales 161, 162
   project requirements 162
   solution design 165
philosophy
   upgrading 244
post implementation support phase
   about 172
   issues, handling 172
posting process
   Codeunit structure, for sales
       posting 326, 327
   Codeunit structure, for general
       journal posting 327, 328
posting report 380
posting routines
   about 120, 121
   posted data, modifications 121, 122
Power BI (Power Business Intelligence)
   about 72, 449-451
   URL 450, 452
PowerPivot 446
presales phase 161, 162
process
   automation, improving 183
   requisites, getting 183-185
process checklist, upgrading
   about 246
   from 3.60 or 3.70 266

from 4.0, 4.0 SP1, 4.0 SP2, or 4.0 SP3 263
from 5.0 or 5.0 SP1 261
from 2009, 2009 SP1, or 2009 R2 259
from 2013, 2013 R2, or 2015 247
project manager 156
Project Requirements Document (PRD) 156
project requirements phase 162-165
project types, based on Waterfall approach
   about 149
   Enterprise project type 151
   Rapid project type 149
   Standard project type 150, 151
   Upgrade project type 152
purchase area
   about 25
   order processing 25
   vendors 25

Q

query
   about 432
   additional data, adding 439, 440
   defining 434-438
   features 432
   publishing, as web services 443-446
   using, in Microsoft Office Excel 446-448
   using, in PowerPivot 446-448
Query Designer 433, 434
Query Web Services 60

R

Rapid project type 149
RapidStart Services
   about 190, 191
   configuration questionnaire 210
   configuration templates 208
   configuration wizard, using 194
   configuration worksheet 200
   data conversion package, creating 195
   Excel templates, using 205-207
   new company, creating within
       PowerShell 191, 192
   profile, changing to RapidStart Service
       Implementer 193, 194
   summarizing 212

read feature 294
referential integrity 133
report anatomy, report development 405
Report Dataset Designer 405
report development
 about 405
 dataset, defining 407-409
 reports anatomy 405, 406
 visual layout, defining 409-411
Reporting Definition Language Client-side
  (RDLC) 80, 278
reports
 about 373
 document report 381
 examples 382
 list reports 380
 posting report 380
 running 376-378
 searching 374-376
 selecting 381, 382
 test report 380
 transaction report 381
 types 379
reports, request pages
 about 377
 Buttons section 378
 Filter sections 378
 Options section 377
report transformation
 about 278
 classic reports, upgrading 280
 hybrid reports, upgrading 279
Requisition Worksheet 332
research feature 294
resource planning area
 about 44
 pricing 46
 resource card 44, 45
role center pages 313, 314
roles
 about 155
 analyst 158
 business consultant 156, 157
 developer 159
 end users 159
 implementer 159
 key users 157

project manager 156
 salesperson 156
 summarizing 160, 161
Role Tailored Client (RTC) 5
Role Tailored ERP 2

S

sales and marketing area
 about 19
 approval 23
 customers 20
 marketing 24
 order processing 21, 22
 pricing 24
salesperson 156
sales tax
 about 15
 tax area 16
 tax details 16
 tax groups 16
 tax jurisdiction 16
scripts
 URL 258
secondary or subsidiary tables 304, 305
service 184
service area
 about 46
 contracts 49
 fault reporting 52
 price management 49, 50
 service item 47, 48
 service orders 51
 service tasks 51
service orders
 about 51
 service header 51
 service item lines 51
 service lines 51
service tier
 URL 251
setup tables 195, 305
setup versus customization 293-295
SharePoint client 59
SMART 177, 178
SN Specific Tracking 336
SOAP Web Services 60

Social Listening tool 72
solution design phase
  about 165
  configurations 165-167
  data migration 168
  new functionalities 168
  standard Dynamics NAV functionality,
    modifying 168
Standard project type 150
standard software 141
Standard Solution 141
Statistics 366, 367
Step Into option 422, 423
Step Out option 424, 425
Step Over option 423, 424
stockkeeping units 344
subcontract work
  managing 39
  subcontracting worksheet 39
  subcontract work center 39
  work center cost based on units or time 39
Sum Index Field Technology (SIFT) 131
system
  testing 186

T

TableRelation property 134-136
table structure, data model principles
  about 302
  document tables 303-309
  entry tables 303, 310, 311
  final picture 312
  journal tables 304, 311
  master tables 303, 304
  register tables 303
  secondary or subsidiary tables 303-305
  setup tables 303-305
tablet client 58
test report 380
tools
  upgrading 275

U

upgradation, application code
  about 271

customizations, performing 273
forms, transforming to pages 273
objects, converting to Dynamics
  NAV 2013 format 272
object versions, getting 271
reports, transforming 274
upgradation, Dynamics NAV 2013
  about 269
  application code, upgrading 271
  database, testing 270
  data, upgrading 274
  preparing 269
  SQL Server, migrating to 270
upgradation, from 3.60 or 3.70
  3.60 or 3.70 application code,
    upgrading 267
  3.60 or 3.70 data upgrading 268, 269
  about 266
upgradation, from 4.0, 4.0 SP1, 4.0 SP2,
  or 4.0 SP3
  4.0 application code, upgrading 264
  4.0 data, upgrading 265, 266
upgradation, from 5.0 or 5.0 SP1
  5.0 application code, upgrading 261, 262
  5.0 data, upgrading 262, 263
  about 261
upgradation, from 2009, 2009 SP1, or 2009 R2
  2009 application code, upgrading 259
  2009 data, upgrading 260
  about 259
upgradation, from 2013, 2013 R2, or 2015
  about 247
  application code upgrade 253-255
  application data, upgrading 257, 258
  automating, PowerShell used 258
  code, merging 255, 256
  Dynamics NAV Server, connecting 250-253
  merged code, importing 257
  technical upgrade 247-250
upgradation, tools
  about 275
  form transformation 278
  report transformation 278
  text format, upgrading 276, 277
  text tools, comparing 280
  toolkit, upgrading 275

upgrade automation
  about 83
  application code 83
  data 83
Upgrade project type 152

V

Value Added Tax (VAT) 15
VAT reporting and intrastat area
  about 15
  consolidation 18
  intercompany transactions 17
  multicurrency 18
  sales tax 15
vendor entries 231
View
  creating 364, 365
Visual Studio Report Designer 405

W

warehouse area
  about 28
  assembly 30
  inventory 31-33
  items 28-30
  locations 30
  pick and put-away 31
  transfer orders 30
Watch FactBox
  about 416, 427, 428
  variables, adding from code
      viewer 429, 430
  variables, adding from Debugger
      Variables List window 428
Waterfall model 146, 147
Web client 57, 58
Web Services
  about 59, 443, 444
  Codeunit Web Services 60
  external applications 446
  OData Web Services 60
  Page Web Services 60
  Query Web Services 60
  SOAP (Simple Object Access Protocol)
      Web Services 60, 444

Windows client
  about 55, 56
  AccessControlService 57
  NavUserPassword 57
  username 56
  Windows credentials 56

WIP methods
  about 43
  completed contract 44
  cost of sales 44
  cost value 43
  percentage of completion 44
  sales value 44
Work In Process (WIP) account 43
worksheet pages 313, 323

X

XMLports
  about 213
  code, writing 217
  elements 215
  for data migration 213
  running 216
  structure 214

Made in the USA
San Bernardino, CA
17 May 2016